STELLA!

STELLA!
Mother of Modern Acting

Sheana Ochoa

APPLAUSE
THEATRE & CINEMA BOOKS

An Imprint of Hal Leonard Corporation

Published in 2014 by Applause Theatre & Cinema Books
An Imprint of Hal Leonard Corporation
7777 West Bluemound Road
Milwaukee, WI 53213

Trade Book Division Editorial Offices
33 Plymouth St., Montclair, NJ 07042

Printed in the United States of America
Book design by Kristina Rolander

Library of Congress Cataloging-in-Publication Data
Ochoa, Sheana.
 Stella! : mother of modern acting / Sheana Ochoa.
    pages cm
 Includes bibliographical references and index.
 ISBN 978-1-4803-5553-8 (hardcover)
 1. Adler, Stella. 2. Acting teachers--United States--Biography. 3. Method acting.
 I. Title.
 PN2287.A433O34 2014
 792.02'8092--dc23
                            2014003395

ISBN 978-1-4803-5553-8

www.applausebooks.com

*To Irene Gilbert, whose contagious commitment
to Stella Adler's legacy inspired this book*

CONTENTS

FOREWORD

I was eighteen years old when I first encountered Stella Adler. I had decided to become an actor and took the train daily from San Diego, where I lived with my parents, to the Stella Adler Conservatory of Acting in Los Angeles. I didn't have the money to pay for school, so I was put in a work-study program. One of my many jobs was to assist Stella from her car to her dressing room, where she would prepare for her classes.

I had read her book *The Technique of Acting* and carried it around with me in a backpack that contained virtually everything I owned at the time. I took the liberty of asking her to sign it for me. In it she inscribed, "The young actor wants to give back to the world some of the greatness he finds in himself."

Stella Adler wanted us to find some of that greatness and make us capable of imparting it to the world. One always had the sense that when she looked at you she was scanning you for the depth of your greatness and would accept nothing less. She would not stand for the diminishing of one's self in any way. Nor would she accept any excuses that barred one from being exemplary. She refused to allow race, class, religion, intelligence, or anything else one might use as a crutch or excuse for being anything other than better than what one was.

I can still remember Stella's voice cutting through the dark theater where we all sat in attendance straight-backed and wide-eyed, half out of deference and half out of fear: "You must be better then what you are! You must build yourselves, your bodies, your voices, your minds, because you are part of a two-thousand-year-old tradition! You are an actor and therefore you are an artist, and because you are an artist you have an obligation and responsibility to make yourself better! You are American aristocracy!" Stella's demand that one better oneself was really at the root of what she and her teaching were about. In that vein she went to the Soviet Union in 1934 to study the Moscow Art Theater; that same year she became the only American teacher to work with Stanislavski to gain a deeper and more articulated understanding of his "method."

Although ultimately what she was after was an honest, naturalistic style of acting, her love of the big ideas of the playwrights and her keen sense of social justice drove that naturalism toward nobility. She was always worried that the naturalistic style would lead an actor to believe that he or she could drag the material down to the humdrum personalities of "stars" while missing the greater and deeper ideas of the plays. She would often quote George Bernard Shaw: "You should have to pay to go to church and the theater should be free." For her, the theater was where we really learned about mankind and how we were supposed to be in the world.

An actor is as significant a part of the culture or society as any priest or spiritual teacher, and therefore the actor is of service to something much greater than him- or herself. Stella Adler understood how transformational theater and film could be and held acting in the highest regard as a vehicle for the transcendent power of the written word. The actor's job is to ensure that the words of the great writers echo out into the ethos of our time.

Her high ideals and devotion to the greatest and most noble assertion of her acting technique made Stella Adler one of the most influential acting teachers and theater personalities of modern times.

It's been a long day's journey from the day Ms. Adler signed my copy of her acting book. I still look for that greatness within myself. I still see where I can improve. I still believe that my chosen profession is a significant art form and that the artist must be an agent of change in the evolution of humanity. I hope that this book illuminates her journey and reveals her purely original life and devotion to her craft to another generation of actors.

Mark Ruffalo
New York, 2013

ACKNOWLEDGMENTS

I want to thank the first teacher who imparted the inestimable art of storytelling to her students, Gwyn Erwin, with whom I began working on this book many years ago. Biographies are a difficult genre in that it may take weeks, months, even years to obtain or discover materials. I want to acknowledge all the librarians who helped me to find and gather materials. In particular I want to thank Jeremy Megraw of the New York Public Library of the Performing Arts, Billy Rose Theatre Division, not only for his expertise, but also for his ongoing support in the form of sending speedy replies to inquiries, finding materials I needed to unearth again, helping with rights and permissions, and being an all-around pleasant person. Helen Baer at the University of Texas in Austin, which holds the bulk of Stella's papers, has also been an invaluable and reliable resource; she facilitated my efforts with licensing and permissions from both written materials and photographs. I have to give special thanks to Robert Ellerman for challenging any assumptions I may have made and lending me the invaluable materials listed in my notes on the sources.

It has been a long journey, and along the way I was wise enough to seek professional consultants for the book's proposal, which helped the book's structure and encouraged me to keep working. I thank Dorothy Wall and Marcela Landres for their expertise. There were those uncompensated readers—writers and friends—who helped shape the book. I am grateful to the critical feedback—not always what I wanted to hear, but what I needed to hear—from Deborah Martinson, Patrick Scott, Leo Braudy, Charles Waxberg, and Cyntia Taylor. Then there were my sisters-in-arms who may have read the book or given me that much more valuable gift that every artist who finds herself stumbling in the dark from time to time needs in order to make it back out into the light. These were my cheerleaders who nurtured me spiritually. From the bottom of my heart, thank you, Mary Gulivindala, Beth Philips, Lara Anderson and Rue Drew, for your radiant beauty and encouragement. I would also like to give thanks to Stella's grandniece Allison Adler and her granddaughter, Sara Oppenheim, who seemed to understand that I did not have any particular agenda besides telling the story of Stella's life for posterity. It was invaluable to have their support throughout the years. I want to thank my family—my beloved son, Noah, and especially my husband, Jordan Elgrably, who entered my life during the book's home stretch and who has been supportive, patient, and compassionate through the peaks and valleys of bringing it to publication. Speaking of publication, thank you, John Cerullo and the "family" at Applause, for guiding me through to publishing *Stella!* with professionalism, open-mindedness, and support. Lastly, I could but perhaps would not have written this book without my parents' unflagging support of me. They fostered my belief that I could be and do whatever I set my mind to—the greatest gift a child can be given.

PROLOGUE

On a Wednesday in February of 1982 the telephone rang in Stella Adler's Fifth Avenue apartment in New York. With a view of the Metropolitan Museum of Art, her home displayed her love of architecture and art history and her flair for the dramatic. Flamboyant yet elegant, the apartment's Italian color scheme of gold and Venetian green theatricalized its French Provincial décor. The front rooms' floor-to-ceiling mirrored walls reflected yet more giltwood cased mirrors, putti, and ornamentally framed portraits of her family. Baroque crystal chandeliers and sconces glimmered in the low light.

Where there were no mirrors, inlaid pilasters bookended mahogany walls sloping up to the crown molding. A silk brocade couch in the living room, where she may have gone to answer the phone that winter day, sat in front of a piano adorned with antique statues and fresh flowers. Across the room stood a writing desk, stenciled with gold trim and supported by cabriole legs. A Buddha statue atop a shelf somehow harmonized without being gauche under a filigree-framed painting behind the desk. Stella's home, like the woman herself, was excessive yet tasteful.

It would have been early, and as Stella was accustomed to staying up until two or three in the morning, she probably hadn't yet had her morning coffee. Perhaps dressed in a blue floor-length satin nightgown, which would favor her sea-colored eyes that changed from blue-gray to emerald, Stella answered the call. The voice on the other end was her old friend Jack Garfein.

Garfein was the only person Stella would not allow to sit in on her classes. "Anyone but you, Jack," Garfein remembered her telling him.[1] A talented director and acting teacher in his own right, Garfein had been shuffled through thirteen German concentration camps before he was finally liberated and brought to the United States. A lover of acting as a boy, Garfein finished high school and landed a role in a play that Erwin Piscator, the director of the Dramatic Workshop at the New School for Social Research, came to see.[2]

Piscator invited Garfein to the New School, and it was most likely there that Garfein met Stella, who had been teaching acting at the school since 1940. Piscator told Garfein that he saw in him a director, not an actor. Disappointed, the young man sought out another teacher. He found Lee Strasberg, who was also teaching at the Dramatic Workshop. Strasberg also told Garfein he had a director's eye.[3] By then only twenty-two years old, Garfein continued developing relationships with theater's most notables, including Elia Kazan and Harold Clurman, with whom he would become close friends. So it was Garfein who, throughout the years, made the round of telephone calls to the people of concern when a major event struck.

On that day in 1982, Garfein was calling Stella to let her know that Lee Strasberg had passed away. Strasberg had suffered a heart attack and been taken to Roosevelt Hospital, where he was pronounced dead a little before eight o'clock in the morning.[4] "There was a kind of silence," Garfein recalled. Then Stella finally said, "I'm sorry to hear that."[5] There was more silence. Perhaps she glanced at the portraits of her parents: Jacob Adler in a black-and white-photo from his role as Shylock in *The Merchant of Venice*, Sara Adler in a sepia-toned portrait from Tolstoy's *Resurrection*.

Stella's parents loomed large in her life, a reminder of both the joy and loneliness of growing up in the theater. She once said that as a child she was often "left in dressing rooms. Later when I tried to create a home, it was completely an illusion of theater—a stage set."[6] Her apartment, like most everything else in her life, harked back to the era of her parents. Jacob was the first person in Stella's life that she had loved and lost. Ever since his passing Stella had recoiled from death. It seemed unthinkable to go on with life in the face of such loss. But Stella would have thanked Garfein for giving her the news. She wouldn't have to learn about it in the paper. Over the past fifty-five years, the man who had been at different times her friend, her colleague, her director, and her nemesis was gone.

Stella would have dressed in black for her class that afternoon at New York University. While putting on her makeup, she may have thought it strange that she should continue teaching while Strasberg would not. Before leaving the house Stella would have accessorized her outfit with gold jewelry, perhaps a chunky chain necklace with an elaborate medallion and a heavy gold pin on her lapel.

Although the temperature was in the high thirties, the snow along the sidewalk began to thaw as Stella's cab waited outside her building. Just one week past her eighty-first birthday, Stella slipped into the car, agile and youthful, her only physical complaint the Adler family curse of high blood pressure. Sitting in the warm cab, driving south toward downtown, Stella would have watched the scenery outside the window. The snow-slung branches throughout Central Park marked the ebb of another season. At Fifty-ninth Street, the city's steel-and-concrete landscape came into view, measuring out memories. Fifth Avenue was replete with hotels, restaurants, and old haunts where Stella had stayed, dined, mingled, and even prayed.

At Sixty-sixth Street she would have noticed Temple Emanu-El, the largest synagogue in the world, perhaps catching a glimpse of its wheel-shaped window, another reminder of the circle of life. At Sixtieth, the Sherry Netherlander Hotel would have reminded her of a day in 1942 when, relieved to be home after a long train ride back from Hollywood, Stella settled for a maid's room on the thirty-first floor because her subletters were staying at her apartment.

Going back farther in time, Stella may have recalled first meeting the diminutive, reticent Strasberg at the American Laboratory Theatre in 1927. Two original members of Constantin Stanislavski's Moscow Art Theater had stayed in the United States to found the Lab after the Moscow Art Theater returned to the Soviet Union from their world tour. It was the first place in the United States where one could learn the teachings of Stanislavski, the Russian director who had developed a comprehensive system on acting. Stella had already been studying at the Lab on and off for two years by the time Strasberg enrolled in his first directing class in 1927.

In 1926, during her time at the Lab, Stella's father, the legendary Yiddish actor Jacob Adler, died. The loss shattered Stella's world. At the time the Yiddish theater itself was expiring, and Stella was now without her first acting mentor and undoubtedly, up until then, the love of her life. It may have been something of a comfort that she had at least been enrolled at the Lab when she lost her father. The founders were Russian, like Jacob, and they focused on the actor's service to his art, which Jacob had taught her when she was a child actor on the Yiddish stage.

Stella's cab drove further south, reaching the main branch of the New York Public Library, where as a teenager Stella had spent many afternoons studying anything she could find on acting. Impervious to the cold, the stone lions, "Patience" and "Fortitude," that lay guarding the steps to the library's entrance embodied both Strasberg's and Stella's lifelong careers in acting. The fact that the two most influential acting teachers of the twentieth century met while studying Stanislavski's system at the Lab is no coincidence. Both were innately driven to deeply explore the craft of acting.

Within four years after he began attending the Lab, Strasberg became the director of productions for a new theater company, the Group Theatre, which he cofounded with the idealistic Harold Clurman and the pragmatic Cheryl Crawford. Urged on by Clurman, who would become Stella's second husband, Stella joined the company that would revolutionize American theater.

As the cab passed Madison Square Park, approaching Stella's destination on Broadway, Stella may have recalled the first summer the Group spent at an acting retreat in Brookfield, Connecticut. That year of 1931, the Great Depression had infiltrated the nation's psyche and set the tone for a theater group dedicated to socially relevant plays. Although Stella was not one to be part of a collective, she and twenty-seven other members were inspired by the Group's aim of achieving truthful acting. Strasberg's direction, which he based on the understanding of Stanislavski's system he had gained from studying at the Lab, opened up a new sense of creativity and focus on the actor's craft.

That summer Stella added her entry to the Brookfield Diary—a journal the company was keeping for posterity that set aside two days for each member to make an entry: "For the first time in many years," Stella wrote, "I would not want to be somewhere I'm not, or be doing something I'm not doing." Stella hadn't felt so connected to the theater since before her father's death. "I think the feeling that's most completely satisfying is the fact that I don't know where the work finishes and life begins. It's all related, linked, tied. The problems I have are the problems the play has. The things that are truest for the play can be so for me, perhaps for everyone." Stella felt most comfortable when life and theater were indistinguishable, although she continued to have doubts when it came to communal living, writing optimistically, "Is it possible that I'm a perfect specimen for the group? Lee said 'no' a few years ago."[7] And Strasberg was right. At her core Stella knew she was not a "group" person, but she was willing to sacrifice her comfort zone for the sake of the work.

Arriving at New York University, where Stella taught Tisch's students in affiliation with her Studio, Stella may have thought about the summer of 1961, when she ran into the Strasberg family at the Piazza San Marco in Venice. It was the last time she saw the family while Lee and his wife, Paula, who had also been an original member of the Group Theatre, were still married. Wanting to catch up, Stella invited the couple to lunch. Always the hostess, she chartered a boat to bring the Strasbergs to the Hotel Cipriani, where she was staying.[8] Over lunch Strasberg and Stella's ongoing debate over Stanislavski's system resurfaced. That argument lives on to this day. The question is, to what extent does an actor use his or her personal past to elicit emotion during a performance? Stella reached her class, perhaps still in Venice remembering that lunch with Strasberg, perhaps reflecting upon her own mortality.

When she entered the room, the students could see something was wrong. Stella usually whisked in late expecting applause. Not this day. Solemnly, Stella asked the class to rise for a moment of silence. "A man of the theater has died," she said, presiding over the moment as it was ceremoniously observed. Once the students had respectfully retaken their seats, with the same piety, as if it were an afterthought, Stella remarked: "It will take a hundred years before the harm that man has done to the art of acting can be corrected."[9]

CHAPTER ONE

To say that theater was in Stella's blood would be an
understatement—the theater was her blood.

—Peter Bogdanovich

S TELLA DESCRIBED HERSELF AS A "JEWISH BROAD FROM ODESSA,"[1]
even though she was born and raised in New York City. She held
a sentimental view of her father's hometown, which he had had to
flee in order to avoid persecution. Between 1880 and 1910 both of Stella's
parents, before they met, joined tens of thousands of Jewish refugees who
sailed across the Atlantic, took in the beacon of hope held by the strong-
armed Lady of Liberty, and landed among the most densely populated
pocket of penury the world had ever known: Manhattan's Lower East Side.
Jewish refugees faced crowded, unsanitary living conditions and long
workdays, but they were free to meet and organize, publish materials, and,
at least in the case of Jacob and Sara, pursue a life of acting in the Yiddish
theater, which had been banned in Russia.

Although they went through some rough times at first, by the time Jacob
and Sara met and married they had helped pioneer the Yiddish theater
in the New World, allowing them to build an upper-class life in a home
significantly north of the Bowery. By 1903, two years after Stella was born,
Jacob had leased his own venue, the Grand Theatre. Located on the corner
of Grand and Chrystie Streets, in a site at the northern end of the area that
is now Chinatown, it was the first venue in the city built specifically for
a non-English-speaking audience. The building had a Beaux Arts façade
and was split into two halves: the Grand took up the side facing the street
corner and had a gallery at its entrance, framed by simple pillars and a large
marquee running vertically along the building's edge featuring its name.

A comparably sized sign reading "Jacob P. Adler" formed an arch over the entrance of the two-thousand-seat theater.

WHEN STELLA WAS BORN AT HOME AT 85 EAST TENTH STREET ON FEBRUARY 10, 1901, she entered a world in which her role was assigned: the fourth and last daughter to be inducted into Jacob's troupe, the Acting Adlers. Named Ester, the appellation never stuck. She was always called Stella—as if the celestial legions had already appointed her their namesake.

The Adler children born ahead of Stella had each been initiated into the stage as soon as they could walk. When the eldest, Nunia—nine years older than Stella—enrolled in school, her teacher insisted the girl appear well groomed, her chestnut hair plaited with ribbons. Wanting to oblige, yet having no ribbons, Jacob took it upon himself to braid the child's hair, using swaths ripped from a bedsheet as ties.[2] Once, while traveling to tour abroad, Nunia became seasick. Accustomed to Jacob's renown, she asked her father to instruct the captain to turn the ship back. It was the "first shock in her life," her daughter later wrote, when she realized the ship wasn't heading back to shore.[3]

The legend surrounding Jacob's prominence nevertheless persisted. Nunia's two daughters, Lulla and Pearl, noticed how others deferred to their grandfather. Lulla remembered playing with her sister on a wide avenue in midtown Manhattan one afternoon. Pearl grabbed some apples from an outside vendor's bin and threw them across the street. When a policeman came along to ask her what she thought she was doing, Pearl replied that her grandfather owned the store.[4] The girls were under the impression that the great Adler owned everything in New York City.

After Nunia, Sara and Jacob had a son, Jay, whose outgoing personality charmed audiences. Like many naturals, he took his talent for granted, spending his time in the streets rather than at rehearsals, mingling with boys who knew nothing of stage life, hoodlums who spent their days swindling for change, playing stickball, and, when all the mischief was spent, loitering outside storefronts to make fun of the passersby. Jay was "neglected by the family," Stella remembered, "but he had the heart."[5] When Jacob discovered Jay had pilfered money from a savings account set aside for each of the children, he whipped the boy with a belt. No matter how hard Jacob was on Jay, his wayward nature always landed him back in trouble. It wasn't surprising that his future would involve petty crime and, in the manner of many of the Adler men, womanizing.

A year after Jay was born Sara and Jacob were performing at the Chestnut Street Opera House in Philadelphia. According to the *New York Herald Tribune*, "It was in between the matinee and evening performance that Julia (six pounds of her) first saw, as they say, the light of day."[6] Julia was the singer in the family, which pleased Jacob, who wished he had musical talent himself.

Two years later, a fair-haired girl arrived. With her gentile looks and willingness to please, Stella became Jacob's favorite. Luther came last in line. As the youngest, he was given more leeway and less attention than the elder siblings, but he was as aware as they that the theater came before everything else in the household. Once during Christmas, while the Acting Adlers were on tour, an adult gave Luther a peppermint pinwheel candy in honor of the season. When he returned to the hotel, Luther sat on the rim of the bathtub and studied the treat.[7] It held all the connotations of family and Christmas that he had never experienced—not because the Adlers were Jewish, but because there was no sense of family tradition during events like holidays or birthdays. Whether it was the Sabbath or somebody's wedding day, there was always a play to put on.

In 1903, when Stella was two years old, a pogrom in Kishinev, Russia, resulted in the deaths of forty-nine Jews and left an estimated two thousand families homeless. In response, Jacob taught Stella a four-line Yiddish verse. Together they embarked on a tour of lodges (the modern equivalent would be community centers) throughout the Lower East Side to collect money for the survivors. Jacob would carry Stella up to the stage, her wavy golden locks and sea-colored eyes already an attention grabber. On her father's cue, Stella would stand on a table, throw her arms out to the audience, and cry "in a voice that carried to the farthest gallery":

Jews, for the love of mercy
Give of your charity
For the dead, burial—
For the living, bread!

As soon as she spoke the last two lines, Jacob would begin to "go through the audience, stovepipe [hat] in hand, repeating, 'For the dead, burial. For the living, bread!' Men wept and emptied their pockets. Women with no money to give threw their wedding rings into his hat."[8] Jacob would lift Stella into the air and present her to the overcome spectators.

Eight decades later, at a tribute to honor Stella's career, she recalled a memory similar to the Kishinev tour, attributing to how common it was for Stella to accompany Jacob on his theatrical and political endeavors. Stella remembered being three years old, standing atop a table. She described how the actors would tell Jacob he couldn't "coach her [Stella] and give her lines and expect her to wait and get her cue,"[9] but Jacob insisted Stella could do it. Retelling the story eighty-four years later, Stella still remembered the rhyming Yiddish verse, the way adults remember nursery rhymes they were taught as children: "God is just in his judgment / One must never say that God is bad. / For God knows what he does / and he never punishes anyone without reason. / For God is just in his judgment." A teary Stella then explained how her father lifted her up and showed her to the audience, "and they screamed because they knew I couldn't talk . . . that I was a baby; that I was being trained, and I was being loved."[10]

Stella's childhood association of being trained with being loved informed her developing sense of self: love was earned through performing. When she recalled this moment in her life, Stella reveled in the memory of being held by her father and adored by the audience, a feeling of wholeness she would try to recapture throughout her life. There, in the theater, she was supported both physically by the arms of her father and emotionally by the crowd. It could never get better than that.

Small wonder Stella spent the rest of her life, as most people described it, "always onstage." Some thought it was an actress's conceit. For Stella, it had started out as a purposeful affectation, impersonating her parents, but like the British cadence of her speech (none of which her siblings possessed, as they too were all native New Yorkers), her larger-than-life presence became as natural a part of Stella as her unfettered laughter and alabaster skin.

Sources vary as to Stella's age during her stage debut in the play *Broken Hearts*, giving it as anywhere from three to six years old. But the play first opened in September of 1903 at Jacob's Grand Theatre, so Stella would have been two and a half years old. The play could have been revived when Stella was older, but given the play's scenario—that of a woman exiled for having a baby out of wedlock—it is more than probable that Stella played the heroine's baby.[11] In the introduction to her father's memoirs, Stella wrote, "My first feeling of self, my first true consciousness was not in a home . . . but in a dressing room."[12] Stella would spend the next twenty-six years performing in Yiddish in the Yiddish theater.

4

DURING THE FIRST DECADE OF THE TWENTIETH CENTURY, WHEN STELLA WAS working as a child actress, the Lower East Side was the most overpopulated area in the world. The immigrants resided in tenements that had been originally built as one-story row houses.[13] During the 1840s, when an influx of mostly German and Irish immigrants arrived, these houses were built up to five and six stories high, each flat typically consisting of three areas measuring only 325 square feet. The front "room" had access to open air, but the other two—a cooking area and a sleeping area—were unlit, airless cavities. Within such confines, the greatest danger came from the infectious diseases that spread through the tenements block by block—cholera, typhoid, diphtheria, and tuberculosis—killing and crippling the residents of the ghetto.

Stella probably never set foot in a tenement, but she did witness the conditions in which its residents lived. They had no room for indoor activity outside of eating and sleeping (and such sweatshoplike work as sewing). Their daily transactions, whether in work or at play, were conducted on the streets. Here, on her way to the theater—with her father, an older sibling, or an actor from Jacob's company—Stella observed the people and activity. The ghetto teemed with throngs in typical Edwardian dress. Unlike the early days, when Stella's parents struggled to earn a living in the Yiddish theater, by the time Stella was a toddler Jacob's Grand Theatre was generating a lucrative profit. There was no need to slit bedsheets for hair ribbons. Stella would have worn a lace-trimmed blouse and knee-length skirt with an ornately trimmed hem, woolen stockings, and black patent-leather shoes. Her hair would have been curled in ringlets, like that of most girls of the day, tied with ribbons to match her skirt.

Stella saw the squalor, smelled the sewage, heard the clamor of children and adults scrambling to earn a living. A shopkeeper would stand outside his door to welcome passersby in order to attract customers, offering a smile to Stella. In turn, Stella would have noticed his clothes were well maintained and clean, even if they were worn out. As an adult, Stella was known to use a safety pin to stand in for a missing button or broken zipper and for buying secondhand clothes even when money was not an issue—her immigrant mentality immune to symbols of social status.

Working-class women could be distinguished from society ladies by the quality of the fabric of their dresses, but most conspicuously by their hats. Everyone wore them, men, women, and children alike—a tradition Stella would have a difficult time relinquishing even after formal headwear went out of style. Upper-class women donned broad, top-heavy affairs adorned with everything from stuffed birds to floral bouquets, while a working-class girl might have a straw number, still broad, but not as ornate. It was the belle epoque—even shopgirls dressed in the fashion of the day: bodices with sleeves that puffed at the shoulders and slimmed at the elbows, a belted waist, and ankle-length skirts with narrow-toed shoes.

Stella would sometimes ask to stop and get a bite to eat before beginning her day's work at the theater, her mouth watering from the smell of blintzes filled with cheese, potatoes, or prunes. On any corner, she could have a snack and hear the merriment of familiar religious or folk melodies sung by street peddlers. Culturally, she came from the same stock as the ghetto dwellers. These people were her brothers and sisters, and her audience— although, unlike them, she could not fathom sacrificing a meal in order to buy a ticket to the theater.

Unlike most other immigrant populations, Jews had fled their homelands not simply because they wanted a more prosperous life but in order to escape persecution. The circumstance of their emigration engendered a deep personal interest in social issues. The Yiddish theater reflected and reinforced this social philosophy at the same time it provided a safe haven for world-weary Jews. The theater literally embodied its etymological definition as "the seeing place," where neighbors and family could catch up on the week's news, be entertained, and, most important, feel a deep identification with the Yiddish-themed performances that confirmed their humanity against the abrasive backdrop of their existence.

Providing a place of spiritual and cultural communion was lucrative for the Adlers. They mounted an average of seven performances a week in the two-thousand-seat theater. With those numbers, even at twenty-five cents a ticket and taking into account overhead (theater rental, actors' salaries, costumes, and so on), Jacob and Sara could easily afford a life of privilege. Yet while the neighborhood in which her family lived removed Stella from the daily lives of her fellow Jews in the slums, she was not removed from them psychologically. Their struggle for survival may have been with more immediate necessities such as food and shelter, but survival depends as much upon emotional as physical sustenance. Stella's parents enjoyed a better standard of living than most other immigrants, but it came at the cost of providing a sense of home for their children.

Just like the child laborers sewing buttons, hauling coal, and sweeping storefronts, Stella was put to work. She rehearsed for hours on end in cold, damp theaters. The plays' scenarios were based on folk tales or a Shakespearean classic whose elements were substituted with Jewish characters and themes. Being among her fellow Jewish immigrants, with whom she shared a language, history, and the simple ritual of drinking tea with a sugar cube between the teeth, made Stella feel as if she were part of something larger than herself, an inheritance from the Old World that told her where she came from and therefore who she was. This Jewish cultural identification instilled in Stella a reverence for tradition and an allegiance to family.

And yet, throughout her life, Stella would feel equal parts pride in and dread of the memory of her childhood, being put upon the "platform," the word she used for the stage, to perform night after night. It gave her an identity, but it also denied her a secure, nurturing childhood.

IN THE FIRST DECADE OF THE TWENTIETH CENTURY, JACOB'S VERSION OF *The Merchant of Venice* became one of the ghetto's most popular plays. The Acting Adlers presented Shakespeare's comedy starring Jacob as Shylock, with his children cast around him: Nunia played his Portia, Stella his Nerissa, and Julia his Jessica, while Luther played Lancelot Gobbo.[14] At a time before strict child labor laws were enacted, children were permitted to perform alongside adults. Jacob's granddaughter Lulla Rosenfeld retold the apocryphal story of how, when activists began advocating for children's rights, Jacob visited President Howard Taft to plead his case. As the story goes, the president asked Jacob, "Why do you put your children on the stage?" To which Jacob responded: "How else will I know where they are?"[15] Not that politicos were beyond the hubbub of the Lower East Side. New York City's mayor, George Brinton McClellan, was the guest of honor when the Grand Theatre opened. The following year Jacob's theater hosted the Democratic presidential candidate, Alton B. Parker, who lost to the incumbent, Theodore Roosevelt. On election day the theaters served as polling places.

A child could easily go unnoticed among the personalities and activities of theatrical life. Early on, Stella struggled to stand out; her job of entertaining the audience came second to that of gaining Jacob's approval. In one production of *The Merchant of Venice*, when Stella was four or five years old, Jacob spurred Stella onstage during the confrontation between the Jews and the gentiles, indicating that she do something to heighten the action. Instinctively, Stella threw herself from the stairs on the set and tumbled down into the chaos of the action, adding to the mayhem. Though her efforts earned applause, she did not receive any praise from her father. Jacob rarely acknowledged his children for their acting; they were expected to perform well. Still, Stella diligently pursued the path to her father's heart, an inaccessible recess from which the story of her life is drawn.

CHAPTER TWO

You always felt as if you were in a sordid family of gypsies.

—Allison Adler

After devoting his life to the Yiddish theater, Jacob spent the last few years of retirement writing his memoirs, which were translated by Nunia's daughter, Lulla Rosenfeld, as *Jacob Adler: A Life on the Stage*. Much of what we know of Jacob's early life comes from his own, perhaps at times inaccurate, but always utterly sincere recollections.

Jacob P. Adler was born in 1855 to a wheat merchant named Feivel Abramovitch Adler and his wife, Hessye. As a boy in the Jewish quarter of his hometown in Odessa, Jacob was drawn to the world of performance and art, frequenting cafés where Russian gypsies entertained. If lucky, he might scrounge a ticket to the Russian theater. Jewish theater was prohibited, but with the succession of Alexander II the same year Jacob was born, many anti-Semitic laws were being rescinded, giving Jews a semblance of religious and cultural freedom.

At the close of the nineteenth century a new phenomenon arose in Odessa: Jewish folk singers. These troubadours gathered in dank, fetid wine cellars where they sang ballads about Jewish daily life. News spread of the Yiddish poet Abraham Goldfaden, who had recently assembled a group of actors in Romania to perform the first Yiddish plays. As Jacob relates in his memoirs, he could hardly wait for the Yiddish theater to come to Russia. In the meantime, he kept devoted attendance at the only other theatrical venue available: the Russian theater.

One day Jacob received word that his childhood friend Israel Rosenberg would be coming to Odessa to perform Goldfaden's plays. When the company finally arrived, Jacob was thrilled to discover that he was already acquainted with another of the members, although it is unclear how Jacob had met the woman who would become his first wife. Born into a distinguished upper-class Russian family, Sonya Oberlander had been formally educated by tutors. She was passionate about acting and committed to the establishment of a Yiddish theater. In his memoirs Jacob admits that his lack of education made him feel inadequate by comparison, but that did not keep him from courting Sonya. He quit his job as an official at the Department of Weights and Measures and joined Rosenberg's troupe.

Upon receiving his first bad notice, Jacob wanted to quit the whole enterprise. Instead, he sought out the disparaging theater critic to ask how he might improve his acting. This was unheard-of. Actors were still emoting onstage through exaggerated gestures and vocal histrionics. Scripts were often pulled together from disjointed scenes; plots were nonlinear, entertainment was prioritized above art, and song-and-dance numbers were thrown in arbitrarily. Still, there were certain actors who had both stage presence and star quality, and Jacob wanted to be one of them. As if to seal his chosen path, he married Sonya, in a theater, before an audience—which would become a common tradition among Yiddish actors.

Yiddish players were notorious for their entangled personal and professional lives, and it was no different in Rosenberg's troupe. On the road, relationships formed with fervor and often disassembled just as feverishly. From some of these ties marriages were consummated and a generation of young players born in tow. Audiences knew about the real-life relationships between the actors by following the news of their favorite actors in the press. Jacob and Sonya were a popular item. When they played a romantic scene together, the spectators savored both reality and fantasy—not so different from today's celebrity-driven tabloids, only on a more intimate level.

In Rosenberg's troupe Jacob soon became a favorite among audiences. Girls flocked to meet him whenever he arrived at a new town. Some wrote him love letters; others trailed him through the streets waiting for him to notice them. If they were attractive, he did more than notice. Local brothels knew him by name; at times he would become possessive if one of the girls he was fond of paid too much attention to another client. Finally, in 1882, not three years into their marriage, Jacob confessed his sexual insatiability to his wife. Sonya pretended not to care, but Jacob's infidelities and penchant for young girls were unraveling their marriage. To make matters worse, Sonya was now carrying his child.

Sonya threatened to leave. The prospect gave Jacob pause. He was not getting any younger, and his lifestyle was sordid, his livelihood unstable. He decided to return to Odessa with Sonya, settle down, and find a steady, respectable way to earn a living. This did not last long. The irresistible lure of applause and approval called him back to the stage. Jacob rededicated himself to Sonya, and they formed their own troupe consisting of a couple of friends, their new baby daughter, and a wet nurse.

The timing could not have been worse. In 1881 Czar Alexander II, known for his sympathy with Jews, was assassinated. He was succeeded by a son who was as intolerant of Jews as his grandfather, Nicholas I, had been. In 1882 the newly crowned Czar Alexander III issued the May Laws, driving Jews out of their professions. The horror mounted with a series of brutal pogroms. The following year Yiddish theater was banned. Jacob followed the lead of hundreds of thousands of Jews fleeing the Russian Pale and decided to head for England.

Several months passed before Jacob was able to secure passage on a cattle boat sailing for London. Passengers crammed into small areas between decks, sleeping on soiled blankets or rags. Jacob kept the morale of his small troupe alive with the hope that in England they would be free to establish their own company. Upon arrival, these newest expatriates of the Russian Yiddish theater settled where thousands of persecuted Jews had wound up: London's East End. They had never seen such poverty. Entire families wandered the streets begging for food. Those lucky enough to have shelter crowded into crumbling warehouses, disused sheds, and the back rooms of private homes. Pestilence and disease spread through workhouses, sweatshops, and streets, where open sewers ran with the innards of animals slaughtered in public. Mortality rates were so high there were not enough places to house corpses; even children's bodies were piled in sheds.

Determined not to be numbered among the slum's casualties, Jacob took stock of the company's assets. While they had no money and did not speak English fluently, at least they were not alone. Expatriates from Russia, Poland, and Romania had already formed amateur Yiddish theatrical groups. They performed in small rooms where admission was taken under the table to avoid trouble from the authorities, but even rent for these venues was out of reach for the most recently arrived players.

In Russia, when his troupe fell into financial trouble, Jacob did not consider it beneath him to ask the local rabbi for assistance. With a letter his father had written in Hebrew, Jacob approached the Orthodox Chief Rabbi of Britain, Hillel Nissim Adler, a distant relative. The rabbi received him graciously, read over the letter, and inquired after the health of Jacob's family; but as soon as Jacob mentioned he had a Yiddish acting troupe, the rabbi grew grim. "The very way he had pronounced the word Yiddish," Jacob later wrote in his memoirs, "with such a twist of the mouth told me our beloved language held no honored place in his heart. And I had come to spread this 'jargon' further? To popularize it? Worse, to do so in public where, God forbid, strangers might come to jeer and make a mockery of our people?"[1] Rabbi Adler dismissed Jacob empty-handed.

Next Jacob went to the wealthy West End Jews, but with little success; he finally found support in the slums of Whitechapel itself. An ex-actor who owned a restaurant invited Jacob and his troupe to stay in the cramped rooms above his restaurant. A young journalist wrote about the new group in the local press. Jacob made friends with a man who turned out to be a relative of Sonya's who wrote music and provided them with plays. Eventually the group became financially solvent enough to put on their first show.

Within a year Jacob acquired a small theater and *patriotn* (Yiddish for "fans"). But just as life seemed to be going his way, his three-year-old daughter fell ill with croup, a respiratory infection common in children but no doubt worsened by the unsanitary conditions of the neighborhood. The couple spent several sleepless nights tending to their child, but the little girl died. Jacob blamed himself for traveling with a child through the cold and filthy streets of London. Sonya suffered her loss quietly and ministered to Jacob's grief.

Soon Sonya found herself pregnant again, but Jacob's wandering eye undermined any happiness she might have expected from the child's birth. This time it was more than mere sexual appetite. He had fallen in love with a seventeen-year-old named Jennya Kaiser. As Jacob recounted in his memoir, he was torn between his desire for Jennya and his admiration for Sonya. When Sonya bore their son, Abram, in 1885, Jacob thought he and his wife were being given another chance after the death of their daughter. But Sonya, weakened after her pregnancy, developed an infection. Jacob admitted her to a Christian hospital in Whitechapel, where he sat day and night by her bedside.

Sonya knew she was dying before Jacob would admit it to himself. As he wept, she took his hand and told him not to cry. "And still it was she," Jacob wrote in his memoirs, "who had come into my life together with the new Yiddish theater. The same Sonya who lifted me out of the empty worthless existence I had known until then . . . and she knew she was leaving in the stormy seas of life two children—one barely a month old, the other, for all his thirty-one years, also a helpless child."[2] Within a few weeks Sonya Adler died at the age of twenty-seven. Jacob cried out her name as he was dragged away from her body. She was the one who had ushered him into his life as an actor, stood by him through uncertain political, financial, and emotional circumstances, forgiven his disloyalty, and still believed in him. Without Sonya, there seemed no point in living. Even newborn Abe could not assuage Jacob's loss.

During the weeks that followed, Jacob withdrew from the world. His grief and remorse settled into a slow, saddening numbness. If it had not been for the biting shame that snapped at his consciousness, he may have submitted to his melancholy, for he could not see a way out, until one day his "longing for solitude and silence gave way to a raging need to be up and about, to do something, anything but not to be still. To be still," he wrote, "meant I accepted what had happened, accepted Sonya's death. And this thought drove me out like a storm into the boiling tumult of the London streets."[3] Yet to live meant Jacob would have to go on without Sonya. He returned to the stage and into the comforting but noncommittal arms of Jennya Kaiser, who was now pregnant with his child.

By the time Charles Adler, his son by Jennya, was born in 1886, Jacob had met a starstruck chorus girl who promised him love. But thirty-one-year-old Jacob had two children from two different women, and sixteen-year-old Dinah Shtettin came from a strict Orthodox family. His affair with Dinah became an instant scandal. Jacob realized he would have to marry the girl, which was not so unattractive an option. He had a motherless son, Abe, to care for, and he saw no satisfying remedy to his fiery relationship with Jennya, who would not marry him. Through marriage to Dinah he could start over again.

Jacob assembled a new acting troupe and began putting on his repertory from his days with Sonya. He triumphed in the title role of *Uriel Acosta*, about the intellectual whose Orthodox family fled the Spanish Inquisition. In the play Acosta ends his life when he cannot reconcile the conflict between his scientific and religious beliefs, a tragedy that Jacob performed with operatic melodrama. Audiences began to associate Jacob with his mawkish acting, counting on his performances to be tearjerkers.

He went on tour with *Uriel Acosta* and N. M. Sheikevitch's *The Penitent*, and later he tried out a new play titled *The Odessa Beggar*, an adaptation of Felix Payt's *Ragpicker of Paris*, with the ragpicker a Jew and the scenario moved from the streets of Paris onto those of Odessa. Jacob's public hailed his performances, giving him the title of the "great eagle" (*Adler* means "eagle" in German). News of Jacob's fame reached the United States, where an actor by the name of Morris Heine was looking for new talent for his company. Heine was married to an imperious woman with a luxuriant fall of onyx-colored hair named Sara, one day to become Madame Adler and Stella's mother.

CHAPTER THREE

*I did what everyone else did to learn how to act. I went to
the Lower East Side to watch the Yiddish theater.*

—John Barrymore

I N 1904 THREE-YEAR-OLD STELLA PLAYED ONE OF THE CHILDREN IN
Henrik Ibsen's *A Doll's House*. Stella suffered from stage fright her entire
life, and her stomach was likely tossing as she heard the theater filling up,
the din of greetings, and the finding of seats. Neighbors would meet mid-
aisle to catch up on the week's news. Mothers would remove newspaper-
wrapped herring and knishes for dinner. Small children sat on the laps of
older siblings to save money on their ticket. When the house was full, the
entrance doors closed, muting the sounds of the vendors and carriages
outside. The audience's whispers would hush in anticipation of the night's
performance. Their beloved Jacob and Sara Adler were starring in the play.

Stella had rehearsed her role over and over. She had to bring her one-
year-old brother, Luther, onstage, where they would sit under a table and
wait for the leading actress to play with them. That same actress made her
entrance wearing a red Victorian dress; her coal-black hair and dark eyes
were nothing like the girl's fair features. Something about the woman was
familiar, but then Stella had rehearsed the play numerous times and knew
her cues.

Looking out at the audience, Stella would not have been able to see past
the footlights. Beyond the edge of the stage a gulf of darkness encircled her.
There were people out there, and the gaze of hundreds of eyes was like one
large creature lying in wait. It was another world on the platform. Every
movement mattered because it was being witnessed. The creature's attention
on the dark-haired woman redirected to Stella and Luther as the woman
crossed over to play with them. That was when it sank in. Stella nudged

her brother: "Luther, I think that's my mother."[1] Ironically, Sara's character, Nora, embodied the dilemma of modern motherhood: to what extent does a woman sacrifice her own happiness and ambition to care for her children?

As a leading star of the Yiddish stage, Sara Adler was not a typical mother. Stella would have seen more of her in the theater than she would have at home. Her earliest memory of recognizing her mother for the first time, therefore, was not at home reading her a bedtime story or cooking dinner, but on the stage.

SARA AND HER FIRST HUSBAND, MORRIS HEINE, HAD ARRIVED IN THE United States in 1884. Fresh from a tour through Europe, they were members of the Karp-Silberman Yiddish Acting Troupe, but Morris soon broke out with his own company: Heine's Opera Company. The players were trained in the Russian theater. Sara Heine had been reared in a half-Russian home, and although she could memorize the lines, her Yiddish was inferior to her Russian. Sara brought a natural quality to the stage long before realism was introduced into the theater, and though audiences were not sure how to interpret Sara's acting style, they admired her sincerity and singing voice.

Realism took hold in art and literature by the mid-1900s. It arose with the scientific theories of Charles Darwin and Karl Marx, wherein social thought—and by extension artistic expression—turned from a Romantic worldview toward science, reason, and social reform. Though Sara and her husband were still performing the plays of Goldfaden, she recognized the realist aim that the purpose of art was to educate and enrich society. By the time Sara began performing Ibsen and other modern playwrights, she understood that acting had to evolve in order to meet realism's artistic goals. Characters in modern plays were ordinary people struggling with contemporary questions of poverty, disease, social status, and family relations. Employing the acting style used by spectacle operettas, vaudeville, and melodrama could not illuminate these issues.

When the Heines arrived in New York, near the end of the nineteenth century, the Yiddish theater was nonexistent except for one amateur company of factory workers created by the teenage upstart Boris Thomashefsky. The baby-faced youth with close-set eyes and thick, wavy hair would become a great comedian in the Yiddish theater, and by the first decade of the twentieth century, Thomashefsky's comedies would compete with Jacob's soul-piercing tragedies.

The Heines opened on May 23, 1884, at Turn Hall at 66 East Fourth Street on the Lower East Side. They were an instant success, playing twice weekly to a full house. One patron wrote an anonymous letter to a Yiddish paper asking that the "orchestra play more softly so as not to drown out the electrifying voice and speech of Madame Heine."[2] Unable to compete with professionals, Thomashefsky and his troupe of factory workers-turned-actors left for Philadelphia and then went on to other East Coast cities where no one had ever encountered theater performed in Yiddish. Morris and Sara Heine were glad to be rid of the competition. But Thomashefsky would return after having spread the Yiddish theater to the New World.

Within two years the Heines had to contend with new arrivals: the Jewish Opera Company of Romania. But box-office returns were the least of Sara's concerns. Accustomed to the opulent theaters of Europe, she found the Oriental Theatre at Grand Street and the Bowery, where they were currently performing, noxious and depressing: the dressing rooms were not even heated, and the theater resembled an assembly hall more than an auditorium. A reporter for the *New York Sun* described the space as "long and narrow, the stage is deep and wide . . . and ordinary chairs bound in line by strips of pine are substitutes for the upholstered seats."[3] Adding insult to injury, Heine controlled the money even though Sara was the star audiences came to see. Heine knew that if he did not make changes, he would lose his company and his wife. Jacob Adler, the acclaimed "great eagle" from London's East End, seemed a promising option to revitalize his troupe. Heine wrote to Jacob asking him to join his ensemble.

Although he was well-known throughout Europe, Jacob saw the New World as a prospector stumbling upon an unmined quarry. He seized on the chance to go to New York, arranging passage for himself and his son, Abe, with his wife, Dinah, to follow shortly after. Jacob arrived to a fanfare he had not anticipated: "If my chariot was not hung with flags and trophies of my triumphs in Europe," Jacob later wrote, "it was greeted on every side by posters screaming in huge letters that the 'new Salvini,' the 'great eagle' of the Yiddish stage, had flown to the shores of America."[4] Heine cast Jacob in *The Odessa Beggar*, a tragicomedy in which Jacob had shone in London, but New York audiences responded coldly to his performance. Jacob was famed as a tragedian, and they expected a heartrending melodrama. Feeling himself to be a failure, Jacob sat alone in his dressing room. But

Sara Heine, who was also in the cast, saw talent in Jacob. She was the only one to go and console him with praise.

Jacob's next role, as Uriel Acosta, won the audiences back. In the Yiddish theater, the star of the company was also its manager. Jacob considered it only a matter of time before he would be popular enough to form his own acting group. In the interim he would bide his time in Heine's troupe. There was another good reason to stay with the company: Sara Heine. Jacob was drawn to Sara's acting style. Though she strove for naturalism on the stage, off the platform Sara wore a mask of congeniality, engaging in surface chatter that was charming but hardly authentic. When Sara met Jacob, a man uninhibited about expressing his feelings, she was lovestruck.

Inconveniently, Jacob's new wife, Dinah, who had borne him a daughter named Celia, arrived in the midst of this affair. One evening the lovers were out together when Jacob told Sara he had to get home to his wife and child. Sara followed Jacob to his rooms, entreating him to stay the evening with her. Jacob refused, leaving Sara waiting for him outside his door. When Dinah found Sara still there in the morning, the wife insisted that the mistress go home.[5] Sara would never forget the humiliation of being shooed away by Dinah. She took revenge years later by prohibiting her children to associate with Dinah's daughter, their half-sister.

At work Heine and Jacob had their own problems. One night a dispute over Jacob's contract erupted backstage. When the curtain rose the two men were still arguing. Another actor went on in Jacob's place. Slighted, Jacob left Heine's company for good. His last resort was Boris Thomashefsky, still on the road introducing audiences outside of New York to the Yiddish theater.

Upon receiving word from Jacob, Thomashefsky was thrilled at the prospect of combining efforts with the "great eagle." He took the next train to Manhattan and headed directly for the Occidental Hotel, where Jacob and Dinah were living with their baby daughter. "It made my heart ache," Boris wrote in his memoirs, "to see the great Adler with his beautiful, clear eyes staying in the rundown hotel. He sat and joked, his majestic form in a torn silk jacket, his feet thrust into out-of-shape slippers."[6] They decided to join forces and take *Uriel Acosta* to Philadelphia. Jacob had one condition: he wanted Thomashefsky to cast Sara Heine in the play. Sara agreed, deciding to divorce her husband and go on tour with Jacob.

Thomashefsky rented the Standard Theatre on South Street for the troupe's Philadelphia debut. The run of the play was interrupted, however, by Dinah's unexpected arrival, and rather than face his spurned wife, Jacob fled town.[7] He went to Chicago, where he immediately wrote Thomashefsky to bring Sara so they could start performing in the Windy City. With a recalcitrant husband who had now abandoned her twice, Dinah resolved to divorce Jacob, leaving him free to propose to Sara.

TOGETHER, JACOB AND SARA ESTABLISHED THE THIRD YIDDISH COMPANY on the Lower East Side, along with Heine's troupe and the Rumanian Opera House. These three theatrical companies competed for the multitudes of homesick Yiddish-speaking Jews living on the Lower East Side during the early 1880s.[8]

The ghetto of the Lower East Side—consisting of the square mile below Fourteenth Street between the East and Hudson Rivers—comprised seven smaller ghettos. The Italians grouped along the blocks of the East River and the Irish bordered the Hudson River, leaving the Jewish population landlocked in between.

At the theater the Jewish immigrants commiserated with one another through laughter and tears. For many it replaced the synagogue, providing a communal bond. Audience members socialized between scenes. If restless, they did not hesitate to heckle the players. If moved, they would wait for the actor after the performance and carry him through the streets.[9] For thousands of expatriates living hand-to-mouth in New York's Jewish ghetto, the theater was not simply entertainment. It was soul medicine.

Inspired by Sara, Jacob came to see theater as a reflection of life. The comedic antics and *shtick* of *shund* ("trashy" art) theater, with its burlesque plays and farcical operettas, no longer served his evolving theatrical vision. In her memoirs, Sara Adler wrote: "Everyone caught the spirit. And if anyone clung to the old bad way, striving for cheap laughter, cheap effects, it only reminded us all the more how great was the change taking place before our eyes."[10] But they needed plays. One night a new Russian playwright, Jacob Gordin, went to see Jacob perform. After the show Gordin, who had previously disparaged Yiddish as inferior to Russian, admitted to the vast nuances and rich emotion of the Yiddish language. Gordin and Jacob soon collaborated, aiming to reform the Yiddish theater.

Audiences had to get used to Gordin's plays. The actors did not appear to be acting; rather, they sounded like someone one might encounter on the street. It was 1891, and audiences were confused as to whether they were viewing a performance or reality. On opening night of the play

Siberia, Jacob had to march downstage after the second act to admonish the restless audience for not supporting the "famous Russian writer Yakov Mikhailovitsh Gordin," inducing guilt in them by expressing his "embarrassment." At the play's climax, the audience "burst into tears."[11] However, there were even fewer in attendance at Gordin's next play, and Jacob wondered if he expected too much with his attempts at naturalism. Yet it was this third play that won audiences over.

Gordin set Shakespeare's *King Lear* in nineteenth-century Russia. He turned the king into a respected and wealthy Jewish merchant. On opening night, October 21, 1892, Jacob pulled the curtain aside to find the house full to capacity with the Russian-Yiddish intelligentsia. In the opening scene Jacob, as King Lear, presided over a Purim feast surrounded by forty family members, friends, and servants. "I have in my life witnessed ovations," Sara Adler later wrote. "Adler's Russian-Yiddish 'king,' discovered onstage as the curtain rose, created just such a moment. From the orchestra to the gallery, the theater crashed! His character had taken before he had spoken a word. And this was nothing compared to the scenes that came later."[12] Soon after *The Jewish King Lear* opened, Jacob had to move to a larger theater to accommodate his growing throngs of fans.

Audiences outside of New York were still not used to naturalism in the theater. On tour with *King Lear* in Montreal, a fan mistook the drama for real life. In the play, when Lear's favorite daughter disrespects him, a man came running up the aisle to the stage, reassuring Jacob (Yankl in Yiddish) he had a place to go: "To hell with your stingy daughter, Yankl! Spit on her, Yankl, and come with me. My wife will feed you. Come, may she choke, that rotten daughter of yours!"[13] The play even inspired moral sensibilities. After a weekend during which Jacob played Lear, one bank employee said the "bank was filled with young people sending money to their parents back in Europe."[14]

Jacob's *King Lear* received such laudatory reviews that he was asked to bring the show to Broadway. Although honored to be sought after by American audiences, Jacob did not feel confident enough with his English and declined the invitation until a friend convinced him, explaining, "You owe it to the gentiles."[15] Jacob performed in Yiddish surrounded by an all English-speaking cast. Every review, from the *New York Times* to *Theatre Magazine*, praised Jacob's performance. He returned to the Yiddish stage, his home, knowing he had succeeded as an actor of the world. Still, he found his greatest comfort in being the king of the Yiddish theater.

Jacob and Gordin's partnership ushered in a new era in theater by exploring the social issues unique to the ghetto. Reflecting the substandard living and working conditions and the cultural clash between the Old World of the *shtetl* and the brutal city streets of the Lower East Side, a brave new theater emerged. The emphasis on the higher art of the classics took some getting used to, but even the sweatshop worker developed an appreciation for Shakespeare when his characters were painted in with Jewish mannerisms and gestures.

In 1901 Jacob tackled the controversial role of Shylock in an adaptation of Shakespeare's *The Merchant of Venice*. *Theatre Magazine* reviewed the play:

> Adler's Shylock is a highly impressive creation, not only from the artistic but also from the racial viewpoint. The Jew of Venice, as he represents him, is indeed avaricious and vindictive, but above all, he is the passionate, proud and scornful vindicator of Israel against the despiteful usage of the Christian merchant and his son. His rich, sonorous voice can scarcely be matched on the stage today unless we hark back to the elder Salvini. Romantic tragedy is undoubtedly his forte, though his range is as wide as Irving's or Coquelin's.[16]

During the Yiddish theater's heyday, while Broadway was still showcasing farcical operettas and Victorian melodrama, the plays downtown highlighted current events, such as the Triangle Shirtwaist Factory fire and the Mendel Beilis trial, and political matters, dramatizing the issue of birth control in *The Great Question* while women's rights were debated in Gordin's play *Sappho*. Yiddish translations of the classics— Zola, Ibsen, Strindberg, Molière, Goethe, Shaw, and Shakespeare—gained immense popularity. The talent and enthusiasm surging out of the ghetto did not go unnoticed by mainstream theater folk and critics. Asked how he learned to act, John Barrymore responded that, like everyone else, he went to the Lower East Side to watch the Yiddish theater. In this vibrant atmosphere, Stella Adler was, as she put it, "born into a kingdom."

CHAPTER FOUR

*All of his children were in love with [Jacob], incestuously
in love with him.*

—Harold Clurman

"Look at her. Look at the way she walks. Look at him. Watch
the way he uses his hands. Imitate his voice."[1] On their way to the
Grand Theatre, Jacob prodded Stella to take note and examine
people. The Lower East Side was an ideal place to study character. Stella
would watch the hordes teeming through the crowded streets. A tavern
owner might step out into the sun wearing a silk vest and fancy cuffs. Stella
would notice how his clothes contrasted with the sidewalk peddler in a
secondhand bowler who advertised his goods in one drawn-out exhale of
crashing syllables.

By 1910 the Jewish ghetto had reached its peak at over half a million
people, making it one of the most densely populated areas on earth.[2] The
masses negotiated their way through sidewalks where goods spilled out
from storefronts, children clamored underfoot, and peddlers planted
themselves in the middle of pathways and at every corner. Everyone
scurried to get somewhere, sell something, and haggle for a good price. No
one flinched at the occasional horse-drawn carriage kicking up dirt from
the unpaved roads or the raw sewage afloat in the gutters. Every few feet
another pushcart brimmed with fruits, vegetables, and wares, while the
aromas of sour pickles and roasted chestnuts filled the streets. Tenements
lined each city block, stacked side by side and back to back. Sun-bleached
laundry hung between buildings like ghosts of the ghetto's inhabitants.

Near the Bowery Stella would notice placards announcing Yiddish plays
as well as shops that catered to the Yiddish stage and fueled the district's

economy. Photographers set up stands for everything from playbills to star portraits. Period costumes for historical spectacles and biblical operettas were in demand each season. Music stores began opening up shop in theater lobbies. Private teachers launched studios to teach dancing and music. Even a Yiddish acting school opened, although, as one Yiddish newspaper reported, "precisely what they taught remains a mystery."[3] Acting was a vocation handed down like blacksmithing or tailoring, not a craft or profession taught in school. Certainly actors were not considered artists. To the immigrants on the Lower East Side, however, the Yiddish actors were akin to royalty and as integral a part of their lives as family.

The theatrical season ran for thirty-six weeks, after which the headlines went on tour. The Acting Adlers traveled to Philadelphia, Cleveland, Chicago, and up to the Canadian border. Stella anticipated these tours the way she anticipated a new season at the Grand Theatre. It was an annual routine requiring much preparation. There were costumes to be made, trunks to be packed, a repertory to brush up on. Some seasons the family traveled overseas to South America and Europe, making the circuit from one city to the next. Although touring was hectic, it was Stella's introduction to what would be a lifelong love of travel. She would come to depend on travel for her artistic and spiritual sustenance.

Stella absorbed each new city with her evolving powers of observation, often tuning out the practicalities of life. The children had to avoid straying too far from the mayhem of travel—buying tickets, confirming schedules, monitoring luggage. Once, Stella was left behind. She looked around the station for her parents or one of her siblings, but they were already on their way to their lodgings. Someone would eventually realize she was missing and return for her, but in the interim Stella had to sit with the fear of being lost and alone.

Routinely cast when a child's role was required, Stella found her antidote to loneliness in the stage. However, one summer while on tour in California, she fell ill with a cold. It was difficult enough to have access to Jacob while you were in the production with him. If you were not even playing, it was almost impossible. With Stella out sick, her sister served as her stand-in. Although more inclined toward singing than acting, Julia knew a big break when she saw one. After rehearsing feverishly the whole day, Julia pulled off the evening's performance, forgetting only a few lines.[4] Stella would have been eager to resume her part as soon as she recovered.

Stella would steal time with Jacob by watching him prepare for a role. She would enter the narrow door to his dressing room at the Grand Theatre and quietly settle on the large couch that took up most of the room. The space had an aura of solitude, with costumes hanging on the walls, boxes of makeup stacked in the corner, and Jacob's mustaches and beards arranged delicately so as not to become soiled or misshapen.[5] Jacob's dressing table was the most fascinating: a surfeit of cosmetics in countless colors. She watched her father before a large mirror as he transformed into a madman, a Victorian doctor, an old rabbi. Whatever his character, he made the application of his makeup a ceremony as elaborate as that of a royal heir preparing for his coronation.

While Jacob admitted Stella into his dressing room, Sara's was off-limits. Stella didn't question the restriction, the unavailability of her mother, but this came at a cost to which a fellow Yiddish actor later alluded in his memoirs: "No one would have dared to speak to Jacob Adler's wife or to address her, even at rehearsals, without giving her the proper title of 'Madame.'"[6] As a result, "the Adler children were brought up like those of a royal family, always kept aware of the prestige attached to their parents' name. . . . Stella and Luther were younger than I was, but they seemed to me much older, self-controlled, mature. I had never met children like them before."[7]

When Stella turned five she enrolled at PS 170 Lexington School. There she encountered a whole new world. There were monotonous daily schedules, assignments, and the inevitable recesses, which placed Stella in the company of other children—with whom she had nothing in common. These children had families with homemakers for mothers. The family ate dinner together. Parents asked questions about teachers and marks. They wanted to know that their children were doing well and not misbehaving.

One day while walking home from school with her classmates, Stella saw her mother promenading along the same street. Sara wore a wide-brimmed hat and furs around her shoulders, looking so elegant Stella was embarrassed to introduce her schoolmates because, as she remembered, "they had just mothers, and here was this queen walking down the street."[8] Stella concocted an ordinary account of her life, telling the other children that she lived in a walk-up flat where her mother baked cookies. She promised to invite them over. If she could not identify with her schoolmates, she could at least create the illusion that they could identify with her. It was not so different from performing.

During the first decade of the twentieth century the Yiddish theater entered its golden age, coinciding with the rise of the rapidly changing metropolis. Where before slow-going wagons and horse-drawn carriages roamed the streets, sections of the city now bustled with streetcars, elevated trains, electric trolleys, and tangles of electric wires hovering over intersections. The main theaters on the Lower East Side—the Thalia, Windsor, People's, and Grand—were presenting eleven hundred performances annually for an estimated two million patrons."[9] The increasingly prosperous Adlers moved from their apartment on St. Mark's Place to 31 East Seventy-second Street, an area celebrated for its affluence. Across the street Central Park had been transformed from swampy wetlands into an idyllic getaway with meadows, lakes, and breezy pedestrian walkways. The mansions of James Duke, founder of Duke University, and of the robber baron Ian Fletcher were only a few streets north, on Fifth Avenue. The Carnegie and Vanderbilt mansions stood further north, on Ninety-first and Eighty-sixth Streets respectively.

Extremely modest compared to the millionaires' mansions, which took up entire blocks, the Adlers' four-story brownstone still boasted an elevator, a fountain, and a garden. The Adlers resided among the elite but would hardly have had the opportunity or commonalities to interact with America's upper crust. Nor would they have associated with the German Jewish population a few blocks northeast in Yorkville—not because of the social tension between earlier immigrants who had carved out middle-class lives in the New World and wanted to distinguish themselves from the new immigrant, but because, very simply, the Adlers were Yiddish actors. Their lives were lived on the stages of the Lower East Side.

In addition to Jacob's three children from previous marriages, Sara's two sons from her first marriage, and the five children of the immediate family, the house on Seventy-second Street swarmed with grandchildren, actors, intellectuals, and artists. Jacob added dogs, cats, and canaries to the mix. Sara required her children to study languages and take music and dance lessons. She traveled to Paris every spring for the latest Worth gowns. Her house was decorated in the style of Louis XIV with satin wallpaper and antiques. For Stella, a privileged lifestyle and lavish trappings signified home and family.

At times Jacob brought the cast home after a performance. He would rouse Stella from bed to come out to the party and entertain the guests. She had a knack for imitating her schoolteacher, among other people she knew. When there were no guests to entertain, she would be called on to perform in other ways. "Stella," Jacob would gently stir the girl from her slumber, "tell me about four people you saw today."[10] While the other children were sleeping, Stella reveled in the limelight.

The only constant in the house was Rouchel, the housekeeper brought over from Russia with Sara's parents. Rouchel could be counted on to observe the Sabbath with roast goose and braided challah. She kept strict kosher laws for a family that could not have been less traditional. Culturally, the Adlers embraced their Jewish roots, through their language, their livelihood, and their socialist politics. But neither Stella nor anyone else in the family observed Jewish religious customs with any consistency. Rouchel "was an *agunah*, a deserted wife, and as such could never marry again. At thirty she looked fifty. But there was something radiant, something of holiday about her immaculate person."[11] Rouchel brought up Jacob and Sara's children as well as their grandchildren.

In addition to school, Stella had a German and a French governess, but her real education took place at the theater. When she was eight years old Jacob cast her in the role of the young Baruch Spinoza, instructing her to go to the library and look up the philosopher. From home, Stella would have walked north on Park Avenue until she arrived at Seventy-ninth Street, also known as Hungarian Boulevard. The street was inundated with Austro-Hungarian culture, from butchers to restaurants. The closest public library was just past Third Avenue in Yorkville, a turn-of-the-century Palladian-influenced building.

Inside Stella would have asked the librarian how to use the library's system. She would have found pictures to get ideas for her costume as Jacob instructed. But pictures would not be enough. She would have to know something about her character. No doubt Spinoza's philosophy would have been incomprehensible to an eight-year-old, but Stella would have discovered that he lived in Amsterdam. She would have learned that as a boy he was a gifted student who studied the Torah at a Talmud school. Stella later recalled this early lesson by referring to Jacob, who "believed that an actor is responsible whatever age he may be."[12] Speaking to her class, she reflected on what that meant: "He was talking to a young actress. He was not talking to his child. He didn't have any children. He had actors."[13] Stella's personal reflection is not self-pitying. She meant to convey the actor's responsibility to his craft.

By age eight Stella was a seasoned professional. She knew her lines, she knew her part, she arrived promptly at rehearsals, and she took the stage on cue. Interviewed by the *New York Herald Tribune*, Stella remembered that "while other little girls she knew played with their dolls," she spent "hours of rehearsing in cold theaters, patiently going over lines until a scene was perfectly done."[14] Unable to fit in with other children, Stella felt she did not belong in the world outside the theater. She would feel this way for most of her life.

Onstage, however, Stella received the attention she needed to assuage her sense of alienation. Audiences loved her. On any given night she might have two engagements. She would play a peasant girl in the first act at one theater before changing costume to portray an ailing son in the final act at another playhouse across town. The theater was a bustling and chaotic playground in a tumultuous city—hardly a place for a girl to feel secure. But when feelings of loneliness came to a head, Stella could always find an empty room backstage to cry her eyes out, even if she didn't know exactly why.

AN INCIDENT INVOLVING THE GRAND THEATRE MARKED A TURNING POINT for the family. Ever since he first leased the Grand Theatre in 1903, Jacob had had trouble with his landlord; it seemed the rental contract was always in dispute. In the spring of 1909 Jacob rented the theater out on weekdays to an A. H. Woods. Jacob claimed that Woods was neglecting the theater and increasing the cost of his fire insurance. The argument culminated one evening when Jacob brought his family to squat in the theater before the night's performance. The family even schlepped a bed onto the stage for Sara to sleep on. An hour before curtain, Woods arrived with a sheriff to find the doors bolted.[15] The ticket holders gathered as the doors were forced open, then poured in behind Woods, who was armed with his walking cane. He headed straight for Jacob and struck him in the head. Jacob's "scalp was laid open" and bleeding.[16] Afterward Jacob found himself in court trying to hold on to the theater. The owners had their own agenda: they wanted to convert the Grand Theatre into a dime museum—the kind of place that showcased animal and human deformities. Jacob soon lost his lease on the Grand.

The Yiddish theater and its businesses had been revitalizing the Bowery since the 1880s, but by the first decade of the new century, crime, bars, vaudeville shows, and dime museums were gradually overtaking the ghetto. Where there were once one or two bars per block there were now six. Nickelodeons and movie houses replaced neighborhood bakeries and butcher shops. Tracks on Third Avenue were laid through the heart of the ghetto, blocking light and adding noise to the already dark and clamorous streets. The immigrants grew weary of the neighborhood's deterioration and began moving uptown. The golden age of the Yiddish theater was on the wane, and Stella could sense the loss.

Once the lease on his Grand Theatre expired, Jacob had to find temporary venues. He moved into a theater on Eighth Street, where he invited Alexander Orleneff and his wife, Alla Nazimova, to play in the Sunday performances of Chekhov's *The Cherry Orchard*. After leaving the Eighth Street Theatre, Jacob took up residency at the People's Theatre on the Bowery. One night Jacob called Stella and Luther into his dressing room to meet a tall woman dressed in a Greek tunic: Isadora Duncan, the world-renowned dancer whose troupe gave Sunday-night concerts at Jacob's new theater. After her performance, Duncan would throw roses to Jacob's box. Stella became enamored of the beautiful dancer and wanted Jacob to marry her. The childish wish reveals Stella's view of marriage— something so insubstantial that one could simply engage in it on a whim.

During this time the family found themselves part of a public scandal. Because nothing was more degrading than having one's personal life written about in the press, the family seldom granted interviews. One day Jacob opened the paper to read the headline "Love Making Scene Causes $20,000 Suit." The article described how Jacob Cone, an actor in Jacob's company, performed with Sara in various dramas: "It was while he was starring in one of these romantic plays," the article read, "that Jacob is said to have objected to the realism with which the star and Mrs. Adler enacted the love success."[17] Sara was known for her naturalism, but Jacob obviously preferred his wife to play love scenes less realistically.

Jacob took the children and moved out of the brownstone. Owing most likely to financial strain from the separation, he chose a home in a more economically reasonable neighborhood at 68 Lenox Avenue, several blocks south of the heart of Harlem. Sara didn't know which was worse, Jacob's adultery or his jealousy. Jacob once saw Sara's silhouette next to a man in a window. He darted up the stairs carrying a loaded gun, prepared to shoot, only to find the "other man" was his son.

When Stella was nine, Sara fell ill with tuberculosis. Although they were separated, marriage to Jacob continued to be a source of emotional strain for Sara. In order to live with his philandering she had to bury her feelings. Stella noticed the downcast mood of a woman who, at least in public, was outgoing and affable.

Sara went to stay at the Trudeau Institute in Lake Saranac. Lying in the confines of her bed day after day, she became depressed. She obsessed about Jacob's extramarital affairs. Sara's doctor noted her deterioration. Believing a healthy spirit to be as necessary for recovery as a healthy body, he confronted her: "Madame Adler, do you want to live or die?" Sara opted for life, so the doctor prescribed that she "tear Jacob from her heart."[18] After six months at the institute, Sara spent another three months in Lausanne and finally recovered in Berlin before returning home. She could no more rid her heart of Jacob than she could rid it of the theater, but she resolved to lead a different life.

When Sara returned, she leased her own theater away from the Bowery in Brooklyn. Sara opened the Novelty Theatre with Tolstoy's *The Kreutzer Sonata*, in which she cast Stella. Stella was surely relieved to have her mother back after almost over a year without her. Sara's new self-governing approach to life offered young Stella an example of an independent woman. In a rare intimate mother-daughter exchange, Sara related her secret to sustaining life with a man like Jacob by telling Stella it was "all right to love a man, but that [she] shouldn't allow the love to go too deep. Beyond a certain point there was danger."[19] Stella knew her mother was referring to her love for Jacob, but she didn't entirely understand the difference between Sara's romantic love and Stella's own feelings for her father. Love seemed to have nothing to do with loyalty, a distorted foundation from which to view relationships. "He wasn't just the father to his children," Stella's second husband noted. "He was a king; he was God. He was a very imposing and handsome man and all his children were in love with him, incestuously in love with him."[20] Stella herself once claimed, "He had three daughters . . . and none of them fell in love until after he died. Including me."[21]

At the Novelty Theatre Sara assembled a troupe of renowned actors and produced the plays of Ibsen, Shaw, and the Yiddish theater's own Jacob Gordin. It was her theater, and she chose the plays and directed them. If she had an idea for a specific costume, she would design and sew it herself, and she was not above polishing apples to sell during intermission.[22] She established herself as an independent star, away from Jacob's company. Meanwhile Nunia, her oldest daughter, took over as Jacob's leading lady, for which Sara never forgave her.[23] It added yet another grudge to a quarrelsome family.

At times Jacob couldn't resist joking around with his audience in onstage asides. Nunia had been raised by Jacob to disdain such antics and scolded her father, "Papa! Onstage they are laughing with you. Backstage they are laughing at you!"[24] Nunia went on to tell Jacob that her mother's theater was a big success. Sara had brought Rudolph Schildkraut from Berlin, where he had been a member of Max Reinhardt's company. Sara and Jacob revered Reinhardt, visiting his theater whenever they were abroad. From as far back as Stella could remember, Jacob had told her that she would study with the great Reinhardt. And now Sara had a member from Reinhardt's company as one of her own.

Unable to resist, Jacob went to the Novelty Theatre to see Sara's troupe for himself. Schildkraut was magnificent, reminding Jacob about the artistic responsibility of theater. With renewed dedication to the theater, Jacob gathered a troupe of twenty actors at the Thalia Theatre in the Bowery near Canal Street. He then asked Sara to join them. Never one to turn down what might be a successful engagement, Sara agreed and became vice president of the company. She returned to Jacob—a pattern of separation and reconciliation established long ago, but Sara admitted later that she "never loved him the old way again."[25]

With the family reunited it was easier for ten-year-old Stella to process the changes her world had undergone. The Grand Theatre no longer provided a stable home base, and in fact the Lower East Side was languishing before her eyes. The family no longer lived in the lavish brownstone, but in more modest housing in Harlem. Yet even with these changes and theaterhopping throughout the week, as long as Jacob was king of the Yiddish theater, everything was in its right place.

CHAPTER FIVE

Out of nowhere, she had won me over.

—Sergei Prokofiev

I N THE 1910S STELLA REACHED ADOLESCENCE WITH A PRECOCIOUS intellectual maturity, but she remained emotionally impeded. The Yiddish theater insulated her; she had nothing in common with her peers at school. In the theater the actors her age were not friends in the conventional sense of the word. They knew each other as colleagues, but not through confiding in one another, playing games, or spending time together outside the theater. Unlike typical children, who build an identity through their relationships with friends and parents, Stella's lack of intimacy with others made it difficult for her to establish her place in the world. As an actress Stella knew what was expected of her and how to accomplish it, but as a girl she felt as if she were scrambling in the dark looking for the stage door to return her to safety.

Compounding Stella's angst, the dynamics of the Adler family were changing, the most pronounced evolution being the departure of Nunia from the household. Nunia was playing a bride of another actor in Jacob's ensemble when the stage marriage turned into a real-life engagement. "Contrary, however, to the plot of the piece, in which Papa Adler is the officiating Rabbi," *Vanity Fair* reported, "he was enraged when the young couple sought his permission to marry."[1] Jacob and Sara wanted Nunia to marry someone of greater means and status. Facing their elopement, however, Jacob acquiesced. Nunia and Joseph Schoengold were married at the home of Justice of the Peace Henry Williams. In lieu of a honeymoon, the newlyweds prepared for the Tuesday-night performance. After the play, the family celebrated the nuptials with a late-night dinner at Young's Hotel.[2]

FOR STELLA, THE SECURITY OF THE STAGE CAME AT THE PRICE OF A CERTAIN amount of self-sacrifice: the audience had to be pleased. This lesson became clear when Stella was twelve years old. She was performing in *The Mendel Beilis Epidemic*, a play based on the murder of a boy in Kiev in 1911. The boy was found dead in a cave with forty-seven puncture wounds. Unable to solve the grisly crime, the Russian authorities accused a Jewish foreman at a nearby brickyard named Mendel Beilis. When Beilis was acquitted two years later in November of 1913, his story, like other drama-worthy current events, was presented on the Yiddish stage.

After one performance of *The Mendel Beilis Epidemic*, Stella did not want to take her bow. Perhaps she felt she had failed in her performance, or maybe the relentless stirrings of stage fright paralyzed her. Angered when Stella did not appear at curtain call, she remembered, Jacob stormed up to her and "took a glass vase and lifted it to kill me."[3] Someone standing nearby had to hold back Jacob's hand. Interestingly, Stella's point in retelling this memory is not to incriminate Jacob's behavior. Quite the opposite: she emphasizes that being an actor required discipline (which Jacob was justified in executing, it would seem). Behavior of any kind, even violent, was excusable if carried out in the name of art. One of Stella's oft-quoted mottos reflected her sentiment that theater was for the world, and therefore, "Nothing in the theater is personal." This belief created a ruthless attitude toward her profession that proved to be simultaneously a blessing and a curse.

Once, while lecturing on Eugene O'Neill, Stella said that every Irish family has a black sheep. Then, thinking of her brother Jay, she said, "It was in my family, too. Because of the strength of the father, Jacob Adler, there was a black sheep. Nothing could help him. My father tied him to a bedpost and whipped him, but nothing he did could stop him from being overpowered by the sense of being useless in that clan. Still, the boy worshipped my father more than anybody. But in my whole family, there was always this sense that nobody could ever really break away from that powerful father."[4]

In 1914 Stella enrolled at Wadleigh High School, the first public high school for girls in New York City. Stella could walk to school from 68 Lenox Avenue by taking 114th Street a quarter of a mile west. Wadleigh was built in 1902 as an example of an architectural innovation in the public school system wherein a new type of H-shaped building replaced the traditional corner locale for schools. Architectural renovations in Harlem at the turn of the century were part of the district's evolution into a neighborhood for middle- and upper-class families.

Julia had begun attending Wadleigh in September of 1913, a year prior to Stella's entrance, but she left after only four months. Julia's school record indicates that she had studied French, but it does not disclose why she dropped out; she would not have transferred to another school, since Wadleigh was the only school in the vicinity that was open to girls. While Stella remained enrolled at Wadleigh, one wonders why Julia would have abruptly stopped attending school in the middle of the academic year.

One answer may be buried in the sleeping arrangements of the Adler household. Stella confided in Stanley Moss, the on-again, off-again lover whom she met in 1948, that Jacob regularly "slept in her bed until she was eighteen years old."[5] Stella denied that she and her father had sexual contact, but she did convey that such expectations were part of Jacob's relationship with Julia.[6] Whether sexual intimacy was also part of Jacob and Stella's relations may forever be locked in the hearts of father and daughter, but clearly Stella's formative years were fraught with confusing filial boundaries. Without guidelines for sexual behavior and relationships, Stella's perception of sexuality was infused with a laissez-faire attitude in which it was normal for her father to sleep beside her at night. It was also acceptable that he enforced a patriarchal structure in his theater. This paradigm mirrored the world at large during an era in which girls were expected to comport themselves like proper young ladies, while men had sexual appetites that could be satiated with impunity.

Recalling her girlhood, Stella emphasized that "in that theatrical family, we never had boy business and girl business, no friends. People come [sic] to the theater and acted. No friends at all."[7] However, she did relate one incident when she was fifteen or sixteen years old in which a young man called on her at home. It was a warm evening, and this suitor suggested they go up to the roof for some air. Stella remembered: "I came home about eleven-thirty or twelve and my older sister gave me a slap and said, 'Where have you been?' And I said, 'I was upstairs.' In the meantime she had phoned the police, telling them, 'We have a sister and she's gone and she was wearing a brown coat and she left at eight-thirty and she's not home.' And the police said to her, 'She left at eight-thirty and now it's eleven o'clock? Well, give her a chance to get lost!'"[8]

The "gentleman caller" from Stella's anecdote would hardly have been the only boy seeking her attention during her high school years. She had matured into a striking young lady, known for her tall, slender figure and porcelain skin. During her last two years of high school, Stella's confidence grew. She seemed to have finally stopped trying to fit in at school and decided to just be herself. She was not always a model student. She refused to take gymnastics because she did not want to wear the required clothing,[9] and she was written up as "not punctual and had been given three censure cards for talking and general disorder in class."[10] The theater remained at the forefront of her life, while school was simply endured. In January of 1919 Stella, not yet eighteen years old, received her diploma. On the back of her record a secretary noted that Stella had been "commended by eleven teachers [and] since graduation, played in America and England as 'Lola Adler.'"[11]

Stella must have felt relieved to be through with the daily drudgery and structure of school. She could now spend her personal time doing more of the things she enjoyed. At the age of fifteen she had begun frequenting the opera house. More often than not, she had her own seat. The ushers knew her. Even when she didn't have tickets, she would wait in line for last-minute seating. One wintry evening soon after graduating from high school, Stella attended a performance by a new composer. Sergei Prokofiev had been in the United States over a year, starting out in San Francisco and debuting in New York with a solo concert. Audiences felt uncertain about his experimental style. But Stella connected to what she heard, deciding she should meet the virtuoso who would later pen such favorites as *Peter and the Wolf* and *Romeo and Juliet*.

The twenty-eight-year-old musician was a gangly figure, with a receding hairline slicked back and parted on the side. As he would later chronicle in his diary, Prokofiev took an immediate interest in the tall, attractive girl who knew enough about music, Russia, and coquetry to carry the conversation. They talked for three hours on their first meeting. When it was time to say goodbye, Prokofiev invited Stella to have breakfast with him later that week. This was not the first time Stella had charmed someone of the opposite sex, but Prokofiev was an artist, and he wanted to see more of her.

At breakfast Prokofiev presented Stella with a single rose to commemorate their new friendship, a romantic flourish Stella would have appreciated. She decided to accompany him back to his rooms, a rather bold move considering the social mores of the time. But this was New York City, and the concierge wouldn't have batted an eye at a respectable-looking young woman joining a hotel guest in the early afternoon.

Once they were alone Prokofiev proceeded to arrange pillows on a rug in front of the fireplace, preparing to woo his young admirer. Stella remained attentive but physically distant. Prokofiev turned to his piano and began playing Rachmaninoff. Apparently frustrated, he continued playing even after Stella announced that she was leaving. As she departed, Stella pouted and said that if he did not say goodbye she would "cry herself to sleep."[12] Still at his piano, Prokofiev began a waltz, ignoring Stella but thinking, as he later wrote in his diary: "If she leaves now, [my] meeting with her will remain a dream."[13] By the time he finished the waltz Stella was gone. She left the flower he had given her lying on the floor.

The following day Prokofiev sent her two dozen white roses. Standing her ground and not giving in to carnal impulses had paid off. The roses were irresistible to a romantic like Stella. She sent Prokofiev a letter of gratitude, to which he immediately replied. A week went by, and then another, without her hearing from him. Maddened by the uncertainty, Stella hatched a plan. From talking with him, she knew his schedule. One afternoon, just as Prokofiev was leaving his hotel to go to rehearsal, he "ran into" Stella on the street.

Prokofiev did not immediately recognize the young actress. She had undoubtedly dressed to the nines for the ambush. Seeing that he didn't realize who she was, Stella remarked playfully, "Well, there you go, you already forgot about me."[14] Prokofiev's diary entries reflect how wrong Stella was. Far from forgetting her, he had been awaiting her letters and dreaming of her sitting by the fireplace: "Out of nowhere, she had won me over."[15]

Prokofiev invited her to his next performance, instructing her: "Don't come up to me. You stay in the corner and wait till everybody talks to me. When they go, I will take you to supper." Years later Stella remembered, "Imagine how young I was that I would stay in the back and wait."[16] The affair proceeded in the manner in which it had begun, a tragicomedy of two artistic temperaments: Prokofiev's advances, Stella's retreats, music, flowers, and tears.

Despite the excitement of a budding romance, Stella remained devoted to the theater, regularly auditioning for new roles. Around this time, when she was beginning rehearsals for the role of a siren, Jacob happened by the theater and began laughing at her. Embarrassed, Stella dropped the part,[17] a testimony to the weight of her father's judgment. Jacob's derision may be interpreted on different levels. He may have wanted Stella to take on a more challenging role than that of a siren, or perhaps he was jealous that she would be playing such a provocative character.

That June Jacob booked a tour for the family in Canada. Prokofiev didn't take the news well. He broached the possibility of going with Stella. But she was a professional actress; the idea was absurd. The tables had been turned. Now it was her work that came first, and he who would have to wait on the sidelines. She told Prokofiev that he "wanted more from [her] than she could possibly give."[18]

The tour culminated in Philadelphia the following month when Jacob received news that the London Pavilion Theatre wanted to contract his company for the fall. Prokofiev must have been disappointed, but Stella knew her place was with her father and the company. The romance with Prokofiev had been impetuous, heady, and volatile; the theater, on the other hand, was something that could be trusted.

Departing from New York Harbor on September 18, 1919, Stella felt the nostalgia of ending one journey and embarking on a new one. She watched the sun set as the ship set sail and thought of Prokofiev, who had refused to see her off.[19] His absence, however, was hardly enough to dampen the prospect of debuting on the London stage.

It was a good time to be in London. World War I had ended, and the victors were celebrating. Stella debuted as Noumi in Jacob Gordin's *Elisa Ben Aviva*, in which she performed nine times a week. During the run of the play Stella met an English girl of Russian Jewish descent who was residing at the same hotel as the Adlers. A few days later Stella ran into the girl in the hotel elevator, where she was introduced to her new acquaintance's brother. Horace Eliascheff later said that he was immediately "stung" by Stella's beauty. He thought of her as a "retiring, hyper-sensitive girl" who was "wall-flowerish, shy, closed in her shell."[20] Eliascheff's description contrasts with the vital, provocative quality of which Prokofiev writes and is more in line with Stella's self-portrait, however apocryphal, of being meek as a young lady around the opposite sex. In any case, her reserve won Eliascheff over, and their affections grew. Unlike her liaison with Prokofiev, this relationship had a sober quality that made her think it might endure.

Over time it became clear that Eliascheff's intentions were serious, and Stella, never having been proposed to, was as eager to say yes to Horace as she would have been to agree to taking on a promising new acting opportunity. Eliascheff was a good match. He was handsome, with an aristocratic bearing—of Russian ancestry, but a born Englishman: his father owned a jewelry business that supplied jewels to the queen. Stella also had music in common with her new love interest: Eliascheff was a violinist who would later play with the Philadelphia Orchestra under Eugene Ormandy.[21] By the time Stella's stage engagement had finished, another, very different sort of engagement was on the horizon.

When the fall season closed at the London Pavilion Theatre, Stella returned to New York. She contacted Prokofiev weeks after her arrival, perhaps feeling lonely—the day was Valentine's Day, four days after her birthday. Prokofiev later wrote that the feelings between him and Stella had not changed but were still a mixture of "happiness and distrust," a feeling he realized was warranted when he saw upon Stella's hand a "thin platinum ring."[22] It was a bittersweet ending, but at least it was finally a clear indication that they had no future together. Stella was promised to another. Still, as with most of her lovers, she and Prokofiev would "remain friends till the day he died."[23]

Stella later admitted she did not think deeply about the decision to marry; she simply followed the expected social norms. "Anybody that marries at the age that I married," Stella said in answer to a question about the men in her life, "must know that they don't understand what marriage is. I have never really understood what marriage is."[24] Horace Eliascheff and his sister moved to the United States, and he and Stella were married less than two years later, in September of 1922, according to the passport application she filed in 1938. After losing this passport and filing for a new one in 1946, Stella stated that she had married Eliascheff on October 20, 1924. The dates of the marriage may be in question, but her decision to marry testifies to Stella's longing to follow the status quo by living as conventional a life as possible within an unconventional lifestyle. Stella and Eliascheff moved to the suburbs, but other than moving away from the family home, Stella's life did not change. Jacob and Stella remained at each other's side in the theater.

Like the girl who impersonated her teacher for her father's approval, Stella made a habit of waiting in her dressing room for Jacob after opening night. "All my efforts would have been amply rewarded," she later wrote, "by a single pat on the hand, a word of praise. But I never got it."[25] After a premiere, Stella's expectations were only answered with Jacob's admonition to "work harder."[26] There was one time, however, when Stella and her father were performing a play without having rehearsed in that particular theater. Stella noticed that the set was arranged haphazardly and took the liberty of changing the scene around to make it easier for the actors to work. The next day the newspapers mentioned the staging. Jacob immediately recognized this as Stella's doing and told her that he appreciated her presence of mind. "His rare smile of commendation meant more to me that any flowery address from another. This is the only time I ever recall him praising the work of any of us."[27]

Stella had little time for her new union with Eliascheff. Rather, it was work as usual. Stella's acting engagements required her to perform five to seven days a week in such plays as *Martinique* and *The Man of the Mountains*. She did a season of vaudeville, appearing from coast to coast on the Orpheum circuit. The imperative to deliver satisfying performances for her audience propelled Stella's purpose in life, which fueled an inherent narcissism. The personality emerging from her success as an actress emulated those of her parents: imperious, unequaled, someone to be reckoned with—not terribly conducive to a marriage.

While Stella and her siblings depended upon the Yiddish theater for their livelihood, they were acculturated as Americans. The natural progression for an ambitious actor was the English-speaking stage. Nunia, being the oldest, had been the first to test the waters with Jacob back in 1915. She had been offered a role in *The Yellow Ticket* at the Davidson Theatre in Milwaukee but first had to get Jacob's approval. The event spawned publicity in the *Evening Wisconsin*: "Frances [Nunia was now known by her stage name] Adler long ago confided to her father that she would like to broaden the field that was lying before her; sometimes she begged him to consent, but more often entreated."[28] In the end Jacob relented, setting a precedent for his remaining children.

The old guard of Yiddish stars was aging and being replaced by the next generation. Stella didn't concern herself much with the idea of Jacob's reign ending. To her, he was invincible, a giant—all the more reason the summer of 1920 jarred her to reality. She noticed her father moving more slowly, not quite himself. Then he announced that he wanted the family to join him at their summerhouse in Pine Hill. Everyone came: Abe, the child from Jacob's first marriage; Nunia and her two girls, Lulla and Pearl; and Jay, Julia, Stella, and Luther. Guests from New York flowed in and out of the house. It was an election year, and political opinions filled the air. Harding was a favorite because he looked like Jacob: a good-looking president went a long way in a family whose aesthetic principles preceded their political prowess. Meanwhile, Jacob rested; everyone knew he needed it. Still, he spoke about putting *The Merchant of Venice* on again; he appeared excited. Stella felt relieved.

One afternoon Jacob's physician, Isadore Held, paid a social call. He and Jacob soaked up the sun in the garden where Jacob's grandchildren were at play. Held sat in the grass while Jacob lay in his hammock. Stella looked through a window from the house at the moment Jacob stood up unsteadily and fell to the ground. She ran out to the garden. The children stopped playing as sounds of hysteria were heard from the house.[29] Nunia tried to collect her children but was overcome with crying. Stella gathered the two girls and led them away from the chaos. Alone in an enclosed pantry, Stella told the girls to pray for their *zayde*.[30] Comforting her nieces temporarily allayed her own fears. Her role at that moment was to be an aunt, a strong figure for the frightened girls.

Jacob had had a stroke; he never fully recovered. His final home, at 567 West 149th Street, still teemed with children, actors, and fans who came to visit, but at sixty-six years old, Jacob spent most of his time convalescing in his room, with its view of the Hudson River. This confrontation with mortality inspired Jacob to begin writing his memoirs. Installations appeared for the next three years in *Die Varheit*, predecessor to *The Daily Forward*, and were later translated by his granddaughter Lulla, the family historian.

IF SHE WAS GOING TO LIVE UP TO THE ADLER NAME, STELLA WOULD HAVE to become an international star of the "legitimate" stage. In 1922 she made the leap to Broadway. The play, by the Czech authors Karel Čapek and his brother Josef, was an allegory titled *The World We Live In*, also known as *The Insect Comedy*, where insects symbolize the darker side of human nature. Stella, under the stage name Lola Adler, played a Viennese butterfly named Apatura Clythia. *The World We Live In* opened on Halloween of 1922 at Jolson's Fifty-ninth Street Theatre. After a three-month run, the play closed in time for Jolson's to strike the set and prepare to welcome a new company, the Moscow Art Theater.

Realism in drama coalesced as a movement with the plays of Anton Chekhov as interpreted through the Moscow Art Theater's director,

Stanislavski. New Yorkers were eager to see the master's work firsthand. Opening night at Jolson's was "crowded literally to the doors, and there was an overflow in the lobby—or rather, a press of those who could not even get standing room."[31] The Russian's intense psychological realism thrilled New York audiences, who experienced a sense of entering the world of the characters' inner lives. Stella, who had gone on tour with the Yiddish theater, missed the entire event.

Though he was still recuperating, Jacob insisted on paying his respects to Stanislavski. Luther and Julia drove Jacob to the Russian master's hotel. When they arrived, Jacob was too weak to make it out of the vehicle. Instead he sent a message up to Stanislavski to apologize and explain that he had wanted to welcome him to New York. Stanislavski proceeded to "hurry out of the hotel in his bathrobe and slippers" to greet Jacob.[32]

While on tour Stella became quite ill. One night she began coughing up blood in the middle of a performance and had to be escorted out of the theater.[33] Later she observed, "Tuberculosis is a psychological sickness. It's a sickness of not belonging."[34] Her becoming ill happened to coincide with her struggle to gain leverage over her career. If she could not be at home in the world, she needed to ensure that she would always have a place in the theater, which meant that her life depended upon theatrical success. However, the hard work she did and the pressure she experienced in attempting to fulfill her aims only served to make her sick. This wouldn't be the last time her insecurities would affect her health.

Prior to the advent of antibiotics, a regimen of fresh air, rest, and a healthy diet were prescribed to tubercular patients. Sanatoriums had been built in the Swiss Alps where consumptives would "take the cure." When Sara was sick with tuberculosis she visited the European retreats, but she also spent time near home at a sanatorium in Lake Saranac, which is where Stella went.

The balsam-scented Adirondacks provided an ideal locale for a sanatorium, its grounds speckled with quaint individual cottages. The municipality itself fell in sync with the schedule of the sanatorium, becoming as quiet as a ghost town at midday during "rest" hour. Stella's treatment followed the sanatorium routine of rising at six-thirty in the morning to a glass of milk, followed by a hearty breakfast of "eggs, mutton chops or steak, bacon, poultry, bread and a quantity of fruits."[35] It was believed that a bountiful diet would keep consumptives healthy. The crux of the cure lay in wrapping patients in blankets outside on the cottage porches. Even during the winter, when temperatures fell below zero, patients would "cure" in the open air. Stella regained her health after several months of convalescing and was released to return home.

She found the city in the throes of the 1920s, an era known for its dizzying negotiation between socioeconomic contradictions and technological advances. Into this atmosphere of false security and revelry, Stella was eager to return to the stage and fulfill her aspirations of international stardom.

CHAPTER SIX

Upon Jacob Adler's death, Stella had turned from the happiest to "the saddest girl in the world."

—Lulla Rosenfeld

D URING THE ROARING TWENTIES, WHILE STILL MARRIED TO Eliascheff, Stella met a gangster who allegedly "stole her heart."[1] His name was Jules Endler, and he was a bootlegger. Stella was known as a raconteur, and the quintessential gangster-starlet affair was based as much in myth as in reality—another good story to tell at dinner parties, which captured the era as well as any Hollywood mob movie. It was the Jazz Age, the time of Prohibition and speakeasies, gangsters, flappers, and the twelve-inch-long cigarette holder. Stella communicated with Endler through a contact at a liquor store on Madison Avenue. The only catch was that Endler was also married. Stanley Moss, in whom Stella confided this affair, recalled how Stella "described that when she saw his wife she fainted, which was the least she could do, and that's where it ended."[2] No one seems to know much more about the romance.

A more enduring concern at this time in Stella's life was the future of her acting career. The golden age of the Yiddish theater, when an actor was regarded as royalty, receded into the past, but her association of the actor as aristocrat remained a seminal part of Stella's inheritance.

Almost seventy years later, still imparting the actor's inheritance of nobility, Stella articulated what as a young lady in the 1920s she could only feel: a life-and-death purpose of being. Fast-forward to the late 1980s: Stella leads her class in applauding two actors playing a scene from *The Dresser*. She is eighty-eight years old and has been applauding, playing, and interrupting scenes her entire life. She sits behind a foldout table the width of her arms. A purple metallic fabric dating from the 1980s covers the table, falling to the floor where the students had laid a handful of flower arrangements.

When the applause fades, Stella addresses the class—her self-dyed hair an unfortunate clownlike orange, her turquoise blouse clashing with the purple tablecloth like an out-of-tune chord. Although the table is inadequate and the colors are gauche, Stella's words have the ring of gospel. "The actor who has acted Macbeth [or] Othello," Stella begins in a soft voice. She is referring initially to the actor in general, but as she continues we see her begin to imagine a specific actor: "he is seventy and all the plays are in him." Stella tugs at her hair, as if trying to pull out the right word, but she is actually connecting to this Shakespearean actor conjured from her imagination: "All is in him and he has made a choice. It's either life or theater."[3]

Stella's voice takes on an urgent tone as she proceeds. "It's either life or being killed every night. Murdered. Slain. Devoured. Miserable. Dedicated, dedicated! And that's the life of the actor." There is a brief, almost imperceptible pause before Stella raises her voice like a mother scolding an insolent child. "It is not glamour! It is not money! It is serving the play and the public and giving everything to art!" No one moves in the complete, cowering silence. Stella must bring closure to her outburst, a bow of sorts. She finds equilibrium with a redundant yet effective coda: "That is the theater."

And that was the theater she was looking for as a young woman heading into the modern age of the twentieth century. The only entity resembling it was the Moscow Art Theater, though Stella had yet to see the company for herself. She learned that its director, Stanislavski, had developed a system for acting. The idea of an actual acting technique fascinated the scholar in Stella. She had been reared to study her characters, observe people, and challenge herself. She was keen to learn more about the current acting theory. Certainly, there was little to glean from the parlor-room melodramas still popular on Broadway. Therein lay Stella's dilemma. Broadway was her springboard to success, yet it was less concerned with the actor's growth and the audience's enlightenment than with box-office returns. With the exception of actually going to the Soviet Union to study, Broadway offered the only avenue she had to advance her career.

Broadway and Stella had in fact come of age together. New York theater had originated as far downtown as the Bowery, where subsequent incoming theater movements, including the Yiddish theater, had their origins.

During the first decade of the twentieth century a migration uptown began with an estimated sixteen theaters assembled along Broadway, with several more on side streets and other avenues.[4] The theater district ran from Thirteenth Street to Forty-fifth Street, ending in Longacre Square. When the Times Building replaced Hotel Pabst in 1904, the square was renamed Times Square.

The theater district around Times Square grew rapidly throughout the first two decades of the new century, selling entertainment with contrived and frivolous plots, spectacle-driven musicals, vaudeville, and burlesque. Seats sold from $1.50 to $2.00.[5] While the Yiddish theater had been presenting serious drama for over a quarter of a century, it took a world war to spawn a more serious intellectual growth on Broadway. In 1916 a small group of artists created the Provincetown Players, and it was they who were responsible for cultivating the work of a new playwright, Eugene O'Neill. Another group in Greenwich Village, the Washington Square Players, began to produce the modern realist plays of Ibsen, Shaw, and Chekhov. These early efforts were far and few between, hardly capable of competing with commercial-driven melodramas, especially when everyone wanted to forget the reality of war. It was much more agreeable to submerge oneself in the diversion of the zeitgeist.

Electric marquees appeared on more and more theater fronts beaming the names of stars and shows in bright white lights. By the time Stella was a well-known player on the Yiddish stage, Broadway had been named the Great White Way. Vaudeville houses began running "flickers," also called "moving pictures," in between shows. This new novelty would be responsible for luring Broadway's biggest stars to Hollywood, where silent pictures were being produced with such Broadway actors as John and Ethel Barrymore, Sarah Bernhardt, the Gish sisters, Douglas Fairbanks, Mary Pickford, Alla Nazimova, and Marion Davies.[6] Stella's distant cousin Francine Larrimore was already a noted star on Broadway. Coming from the marginalized immigrant theater, even with the glory that the Yiddish theater encapsulated, the Great White Way roused Stella's ambition, but not her soul.

There was one other option. The Yiddish theater had made its own exodus out of the ghetto and uptown. As the Lower East Side decayed, the Yiddish players moved their theaters north to Second Avenue between Houston and Fourteenth Streets. In the 1920s Second Avenue was in its heyday, marking the second golden age of the Yiddish theater. The season averaged thirty-six weeks a year, presenting five plays: the hit show to make money during the week and a benefit show to highlight individual talent during the weekend. Soon uptowners came to Second Avenue, which was appropriately coined the Yiddish Broadway.[7]

A typical night on Second Avenue consisted of a production at Maurice Schwartz's Yiddish Art Theater followed by dinner at Moscoitza and Lupositz's Rumanian Restaurant. Another popular establishment for meeting, dining, and advertising oneself was the Café Royal on the corner of Second Avenue and Twelfth Street. For the Adler family, the Royal served as an extended living room where they could go after a show or in the afternoons to discuss the theater.

Located directly across from the Yiddish Art Theater, the Royal was not a particularly fancy establishment. Its unkempt interior recalled Old World European décor with black-and-white terrazzo tile floors and wainscoted wooden walls.[8] Square and round tables were scattered about the place. During the summertime, when even the ceiling fans weren't enough to cool the place down, the café's mainstay, Herman, and some of the other waiters removed the two front revolving doors to allow patrons to sit outdoors.

As part of the famous Adler family, Stella received special treatment at the Royal. A seating hierarchy took effect, with the stars sitting on the right side of the restaurant, while "regular actors, writers, and the general public" sat on the left.[9] On any given day or night, an electrical current of excitement filled the air as "theatrical and financial negotiations left the Royal's white tablecloths a mass of figures."[10] Writers and theater managers discussed their next production; composers met to collaborate on their newest musical pieces. Stella and her family collected, raucously telling jokes and laughing into the morning hours.

Jacob's last role was in *The Stranger*, a play by his old friend Jacob Gordin. What started out as a benefit to raise money (since Jacob never saved any) ended up being a tour. His character, a sick and dying man, had very little to do in the play, which made it easier for Jacob to perform. The audiences knew of Jacob's failing health. Reports of audience reactions, shouting out Jacob's name and crying, became a part of the show itself. Several newspapers covered his final performance in 1924 at Kessler's Second Avenue Theatre. The *New York Morning World* reported that when Jacob made his entrance, the audience "wept unashamedly."[11] Afterward,

Jacob felt disappointed in his performance; he told Sara that they weren't weeping for his art, but out of pity.

According to the family historian, Lulla Rosenfeld, "People of sensitivity were shocked to see the sick man paraded in this way before the public. . . . Several years later a blind Bertha Kalich would be led around the stage in the tragic 'last performances' that were her only livelihood."[12] Eerily, although Stella would live a long, healthy life, she followed her Yiddish predecessors, continuing to give "performances" in her classroom through lecturing, assessing scenes, and directing. As in the case of Bertha Kalich and Jacob Adler, Stella kept working because she had financial concerns, namely providing for family members. Still, some people would have rather seen her retire, most notably her grandson Tom Oppenheim, who had the impression Stella was being "propped up and made to perform."[13] Oppenheim admitted he never saw Stella teach in Los Angeles toward the end of her life, but he perceived Stella's classes as a spectacle where "people would go see her rip [her students] apart."[14]

From videotaped classes of her last season teaching in 1989, a recorded "bon voyage" party, and audiotapes that her friend of thirty years, Irene Gilbert, recorded of her conversations with Stella, it is clear that although Stella might at times confuse the names of characters and playwrights, she still knew how to instruct the actors to seek the truth of their characters. It was also apparent to this author that Stella continued teaching until she decided unilaterally to retire at the age of ninety. Posthumously published transcripts of Stella's last years teaching include some of the richest material of Stella's career.

ALTHOUGH THE YIDDISH THEATER WAS EXPERIENCING A RENAISSANCE ON Second Avenue, Stella knew that a marginalized theater such as the Yiddish stage would not thrive in the United States. But the idea of leaving the artistic integrity and grandness—not to mention the familiarity—of the Yiddish theater was frightening. Where would she ever find the security of the kingdom she grew up in? How would she start all over in her own profession? Without a clear direction, Stella felt lost.

One fateful autumn day in 1925, "out of desperation,"[15] Stella went to the New York Public Library and looked up "techniques of acting" in the card catalog. Among other titles, she came across Stanislavski's *My Life in*

Art, which had been translated into English the previous year. Stella carried her findings to a nearby table. Across the way a young man took notice of her books, spurring him to inquire: "Have you seen the performance of *The Sea Woman's Cloak* by Emile Troubetskoy?"[16]

Stella was intrigued. The man directed Stella downtown to a walk-in apartment that was being used as a theater. She entered a room of seats for about twenty people. In the back Stella noticed a slight woman in black wearing a monocle. Stella took a seat. The room darkened, and Stella was instantly transported into another place, mesmerized by the action, the nuances of gesture, the subtlety of inflection.[17] Afterward she learned that the director of the production, Richard Boleslavski, had studied under Stanislavski in the Moscow Art Theater.

Boleslavski had been in the United States since 1922, when he began lecturing on the approach to the actor's training according to Stanislavski's system. When asked to found an American theater based on this philosophy, he paired with Maria Ouspenskaya—the monocled woman in black—and established the American Laboratory Theatre, commonly referred to as the Lab. All of the actors in the play that night were studying at the Lab. By a fate as irreversible as that of the falling leaves in the Manhattan autumn, Stella had found what she was looking for.

Stella rushed home to tell everybody what had happened. She remembered the family gathered around the dinner table, laughing and joking. This day Stella became the brunt of their jokes. An Adler going to acting school? Despite her family's mockery, Stella enrolled at the Lab.

The school was initially set up on Fifth Avenue at Sixtieth Street, more a large workroom with an adjoining office than an actual theater.[18] A majority of the enrollees, who had discovered the Lab through word of mouth since it was not advertised, worked during the day and attended classes at night. New students first encountered Mr. Martin, the Lab's secretary, who explained that members had a six-week trial, and that it "was up to [them] to make good."[19] The candidates paid ten dollars a week for tuition, which included "six hours a week with Miss Brundy, who teaches tone and voice production; Koiransky, two hours a week, who holds exhibitions in the most famous art galleries in New York; Scott, a pupil of Fokine's, twice a week for ballet; and Miss Findley, twice a week for Dalcroze eurhythmics."[20] On Monday nights students attended lectures by Aleksander Koiransky on the history of fashion, Luigi Pirandello on Italian art, and Norman Bel Geddes on stage architecture.

At first glance the curriculum seemed to follow basic actor training, which focused on the external talents of diction, fencing, dance, and singing. The more skills an actor had, the more talented he or she was considered to be. But traditional training fell short of developing the actor's inner resources. Stanislavski's system addressed the importance of the internal element by emphasizing the actor's artistic imagination and emotional canvas. His approach, which coincided with the era in which Sigmund Freud's theories of psychoanalysis took hold, examined the psychological and emotional life of the actor.

Students at the Lab typically studied with Boleslavski for two hours a day. With his gentle demeanor, Boley, as he was affectionately called, lectured on his vision of what an American theater could be: a theater served by the actors, not one that served the actors. It was the play that mattered, not the actors or the size of the parts they played. Boley emphasized that the entire history of the theater—and all art, for that matter—was the actor's heritage. Stella had been brought up on the star system of the Yiddish theater, where the actor was paramount, but she had also been instilled with reverence for the playwright. It made sense to Stella that the play had priority over the actor, and she felt a visceral impulse to serve the larger ideas and themes of the work. Still, she was conflicted by her desire to be a star like her parents.

Boley asked Stella to take part in a production of *The Scarlet Letter*. She was thrilled until she discovered the part had no lines. Testing Stella, Boley wanted to know if she would put the play before the part. Stella refused the offer. After that, Stella felt that Boley never trusted her again. Still, he was aware of her experience and recognized her talent, so that even when she spent time away from the Lab to perform, he always took her back. Stella's own success and her family's renown on the Yiddish stage afforded her special treatment at the Lab. Unlike most of the students, Stella took the classes she wanted to and dismissed the others.[21] Later she remarked that she should have taken what was suggested, admitting that her acting leaned toward the theatricality of the Yiddish stage. She had inherited her father's melodrama rather than her mother's naturalism.

At times Boley stopped lecturing to allow his students to perform scenes. During one of these performances, Boley queried as to what accent was being used. "The class laughed and came back at him with: 'English, Canadian, American—good American!'"[22] Many of the students were mistaken for being English, and this was true of Stella. While Stella's older sister Nunia had a thick Yiddish accent and her younger brother, Luther, had a distinctly American accent, Stella had adopted a rather aristocratic British manner of speaking. She once pondered the origin of her affectation: "Nobody spoke English. Where I picked it up I don't know. . . . I guess their [Jacob and Sara's] English was pretty good. It was not Yiddish English. . . . Their English was affected in London and it took all that Yiddishkayt away. So they spoke, maybe hesitantly, but not with an accent. Maybe that's where I picked it up and spoke as a child this way in school."[23] Whatever the source, Stella's desired effect of sounding lofty was achieved.

ON MARCH 31, 1926, JACOB COLLAPSED. A STREAM OF BLOOD SURGED FROM his mouth, and within seconds he was gone. Stella had only just discovered her own artistic path beyond the "great eagle's" wingspan when the breath of spring turned stale in his shadow. Without Jacob, the necessity and futility of her career ran circles around Stella's grieving heart.

The day after Jacob's death, the family sat with the body, where it lay in state for twenty-four hours at the Hebrew Actors' Union. Stella would have noticed the portraits of Abraham Goldfaden and Jacob Gordin, the fathers of the Yiddish theater. Was she able to stare into the face of her own father lying there? Perhaps she concentrated on the endless lines of mourners, as her father would have instructed her to do; their tears overflowing or bridled, their visages of sorrow or fear, grappling with their own mortality, some choosing to touch Jacob's hand, others incapable of such a gesture. By eleven o'clock the crowds waiting to pay their respects had grown so large that the doors had to be closed to the public. Perhaps then Stella took a moment alone with Jacob, restraining her own tears or freeing them; she would not be able to tell her father goodbye—something she seemed incapable of doing her entire life.

The following morning, more *patriotn* came to their king to accompany his journey to the grave. The number of mourners was estimated at somewhere from 50,000 to 100,000 people, warranting the deployment of twenty-four mounted police and one hundred patrolmen installed in stations along the avenues following the path of the procession. The pallbearers began their trek at Kessler's Second Avenue Theatre for funeral services. Jay Adler, incarcerated for his latest shenanigans, appeared at the funeral in handcuffs. Celia Adler, Jacob's daughter with Dinah, was the only one of Jacob's children not present: now a leading actress on Second Avenue, she was on tour with the Yiddish Art Theater.

Stella listened to the speeches at the Second Avenue Theatre. When she emerged into the daylight, the multitudes followed Jacob's cortège to its final destination—Stella one mourner among thousands. Along the Williamsburg Bridge men hung from the girders above the traveling hearse. More people were waiting at the burial grounds of Mount Carmel, where Jacob was laid to rest—the first of what would be a long line of Adlers to be buried there. Above the tombstone stands a large sculpture of an eagle with outstretched wings, a figure that has watched over each of Jacob's kin as they have followed him into this hallowed ground.

CHAPTER SEVEN

In Stella's eyes service to the great ideas of a play or film were the actor's greatest responsibility.

—Mark Ruffalo

A T TWENTY-SIX, STELLA HAD THE VIGOR AND EXPERIENCE TO pursue her dream of being an international star of the stage, but which stage? Jacob's passing intensified the loss of the first golden age of the Yiddish theater, when she knew who she was and where she was going. To make life more uncertain, only a month after Jacob's death, she and Horace conceived a child.

As with her mother before her, being pregnant did not interfere with Stella's work.

That autumn Boleslavski offered Stella a role with the Lab. When *Straw Hat* opened on October 14, 1926, Stella was more than six months pregnant. The play ended after fifty-seven performances just as Stella prepared to give birth. She had wanted a boy. In general she preferred the male gender. On January 31, 1927, a girl with dark brown eyes was born. Stella named the child Ellen, a euphonious echo of her own name.

Stella's resilient spirit tempered the grief of losing her father. It was clear to her how tragic and unjust life could be; it was not clear that she did not have a say in the matter. During the early years of her marriage, the life to which Stella was accustomed was still intact. Her tuberculosis put a halt to her career for numerous months, but by the time Stella gave birth to Ellen she was as robust and healthy as a teenager. Her acting engagements came one after another, keeping her from the marital hearth while fanning the flames of her real home: the theater.

Grandmothers and relatives came to see the baby soon after Ellen's birth. A nurse removed the child from the bedroom before the relations arrived. Within a half hour, Stella was in the heat of conversation. Had they heard that Paris was calling for either the release or execution of Sacco and Vanzetti? Had anyone gone to see the Russian artists' exhibit at the Corona Mundi Art Center? When the nurse returned to check whether Stella wanted to see the baby, Stella was jarred: "Oh my God. There's a baby!"[1] It seemed an omen for her budding motherhood, of which she would say, "Actresses are not famous for being great mothers."

One night the baby fell ill with a fever. With no prior experience at her disposal, Stella lay on top of the child in an "animal-like instinct" to keep her warm.[2] Stella was an affectionate person; she sat close to you in a conversation, took your hand and held it for a while. It was natural for her to avail herself physically to her ailing child, but she was not aware of the practical ministrations of checking a temperature, administering liquids, and applying compresses.

Stella recalled only one instance in which her own mother exhibited maternal behavior. Sara and Stella were riding to Boston to perform in the midst of winter. When Sara noticed Stella shivering, she collected newspaper, crumpled it up, and stuffed it into Stella's coat to keep her warm.[3] Stella deduced that her mother must have learned the trick growing up in Russia and observing the poor on the streets. At home Rouchel saw to the day-to-day tasks of cooking and cleaning and caring for the children. At the theater the job went to the least busy person in the production. Following this precedent, Ellen's welfare was left in the hands of whoever was nearby to help, since Stella did not have the means for a live-in nanny. In an interview with the author, Ellen explained, "My mother was an actress and I stayed where she could find me a place to stay, so it was different every time . . . the kindness of strangers, you could say."[4] Stella never considered forfeiting her life in the theater for domestic life. Family was simply incorporated into theatrical life, a fact that was no less painful for her daughter than it had been for the girl too embarrassed to introduce her schoolmates to her mother.

A couple of months after Ellen's birth, Stella returned to the Lab. Their next production, *Big Lake*, opened on Broadway on April 11, 1927. The following fall Stella was lured back to the Yiddish theater for an opportunity of a lifetime: Maurice Schwartz's Irving Place Theatre was putting on *Midway*, a drama in four acts starring Bertha Kalich, a Yiddish actress who had become a Broadway celebrity. Stella auditioned, excited at the prospect of working with the legendary director and the famed star, and landed the minor role of Gitel. *Midway* opened on October 3, 1927. The *Telegraph* mentioned that Stella Adler was "especially able in the star's support."[5]

To the extent that there was always someone from the Adler clan performing on Second Avenue, rumors circulated that Jacob had had numerous illegitimate children. The family loved to recount how in Jacob's role as King Lear—after the character is abandoned by his offspring—Lear mourns: "Where are my children?" As the story goes, audience members would answer, "Here I am, Papa!"[6] But the only acknowledged illegitimate child was the product of Jacob's tempestuous love affair with Jennya Kaiser. Their son, Charles Adler, also came to Second Avenue, where he ran a dance studio.

The longest-running theater on Second Avenue had begun as Maurice Schwartz's Irving Place Theatre, later renamed the Yiddish Art Theater. Schwartz was known for his commitment to literary theater. Among others, Celia Adler—Jacob's only child from his second marriage—founded the group with Schwartz. Besides producing works of literary merit, the Yiddish Art Theater was a repertory theater, with a revolving opportunity of roles to accompany the theater's revolving stage. The actors played different characters in different plays most nights of the week. It was a thrilling engagement for the ambitious actress looking for a new theater home, but Stella was not even a member of the Actors' Union.

The Hebrew Actors' Union was the first theatrical union in the United States, predating Actors' Equity by fourteen years. Housed on East Seventh Street, the union formed the central hub of Jewish life on Second Avenue. Its president, Reuben Guskin, was among the most important leaders of the worker's movement in the country. He also ran the Hebrew Actors' Union with an iron fist. The union decided actors' pay, where they performed, how their names appeared on the marquee, and, most important, whether they were accepted into the union. In a split-second decision, Guskin could exile would-be actors for years. Acceptance was based on "making rehearsal" before a group of peers with whom the actor was competing. "Imagine you're auditioning before your peers," a Yiddish actor who had grown up during the heyday of Second Avenue remarked, "and you know that they hate your guts. They sat there like gangsters."[7] Guskin presided, scrutinizing every nuance of the actor's audition.

Stella failed her first rehearsal. Yet, in order to perform on Second Avenue, she had no choice but to try again. The afternoon of her second audition was nerve-racking. Most of the members deciding her fate were younger and less experienced than she. They didn't come from the Adler dynasty, and she was certain Guskin had something against her or he wouldn't have rejected her the first time. Celia Adler, who had gone through the union's audition herself, remembered that when she made rehearsal she had felt "pierced by 150 pair of eyes who looked at her with contempt, irony, sympathy, and guilt."[8] Empathetically, Celia witnessed Stella's performance, later writing about it in her memoirs: "My sister Stella for her audition played the mad scene from Shakespeare's *Hamlet*. Her slender figure, so graceful in a white dress, demolished the audience. But apparently the whole procedure had a negative effect on her. At the end of the audition she really fainted. So it's hard even today to know with certainty what had had the most effect—that she was accepted almost unanimously as a member . . . or her fainting."[9] Someone jumped on the stage to pick her up. Another brought water. As she was recovering, Stella heard Guskin's announcement that she had been accepted into the union.[10]

Although she had a prior obligation to play in the Lab's production of *Much Ado about Nothing*, Stella auditioned for the 1929–30 season at the Yiddish Art Theater. When she got the part, she relinquished Shakespeare for a role in the hit play *Jew Süss*. Schwartz revived it with a new cast. A few weeks after opening, a special Monday-night performance was scheduled so the legendary playwright Sholem Asch could attend a performance of his own work. Surrounded by a cast of Yiddish actors with the author in the audience, Stella found herself back in her element.

The second production of the season at the Yiddish Art Theater began in December. Stella continued playing in *Jew Süss* on the weekends, while *Angels on Earth* played Monday through Thursday evenings. The latter, a satire, begins when the Archangel Gabriel embarks on a mission to New York to "cleanse" the city of sin. His fellow angels settle into domestic life, marrying, becoming fathers and millionaires, and succumbing to a life of sin themselves. Stella played the minor comedic role of Annie, the wife of one of these angels; a character actress, Stella could play both tragedy and comedy. By January of 1930 the third production of the season opened: *Roaming Stars*, a romantic comedy Schwartz adapted from a novel by Sholem Asch depicting the struggles of the Yiddish actors, from their bohemian beginnings in Russia to their success on New York's Yiddish Broadway. This was a story close to Stella's heart. A fellow player described her performance as so ethereal as to seem "no more than a perfume on the stage."[11]

Of all the actresses at the Yiddish Art Theater, Stella's half sister Celia Adler was legendary. Aware of Celia's star status on Second Avenue, Stella may not have known about the animosity between Sara and Jacob's previous wife, Dinah. Sara never forgot the humiliation of being turned out by Dinah when the latter discovered Sara on her doorstep waiting for Jacob. Once Dinah and Jacob were divorced, Sara retaliated by forbidding Jacob and their children to have any relationship with Dinah and Jacob's daughter, Celia.

In the early days of the Yiddish theater, when Jacob was in full force as the king of the Yiddish stage, Celia went one winter night to see her father's play, but she was wearing a shabby coat and felt too embarrassed to go to the box office and tell them she was Jacob's daughter. Standing outside the theater, chilled by the wind, Celia saw a grand car drive up. Her half sisters Julia and Stella, dressed in lovely coats with white fur collars, alighted and ran into the theater without noticing her.[12]

As a young actress Celia married a fellow Yiddish actor, Lazaar Freed, and had a son, Selwyn. The marriage failed a few years after their child's birth, but both actors remained contracted with the Yiddish Art Theater. Not having spoken directly to one another since their divorce, Celia and Lazaar communicated with each other through Selwyn. "Tell your father such and such," was the usual manner of communication. The former husband and wife maintained their silent treatment even through productions in which they had to portray lovers. Once Celia told Selwyn, "I noticed your father is turning gray; tell him to touch up his hair."[13]

In the afternoons when his school day was over, Selwyn explored Second Avenue—a huge, exciting playground. From time to time he went into a theater to watch the actors play and to get out of the weather. One fall day he went to see his father in the Yiddish Art Theater's production of *The Witch of Castile*. Backstage he entered a dressing room that Stella was sharing with three other actors. "I was in the dressing room," Selwyn remembered, "and Stella was an unusually attractive woman in a state of undress. And of course nobody bothered just because a young boy came in. . . . I have no guilt about this being my own aunt I was ogling."[14] Selwyn introduced himself to Stella, whereupon she embraced him, crying out his Yiddish name, "Zelig!" Unbeknownst to either aunt or nephew, the production in rehearsal was at risk of being taken to Philadelphia, where Schwartz hoped it would fare better without having to compete with the half dozen theaters along Second Avenue. However, Schwartz managed to keep his company in New York and stage his version of Sholom Asch's historical novel.

The Witch of Castile is set during the persecution of the Jews in Rome under Pope Paul IV. A rumor has circulated that amongst the Roman

Jewesses is the Virgin Mary. As the Jews are sentenced to drowning, a local painter recognizes the girl in question amid the condemned. The pope has the girl brought before the Inquisition, where she is sentenced to burn at the stake with the stipulation that if she is the Holy Mother, God will spare her. Stella played the Jewish Madonna. The *New York Times* observed that Stella "makes more use of silence than words, as the natural in an object of veneration; and she does so with considerable finesse. She is particularly fine in the scene where the painter pays coourt [*sic*] to her and she doesn't utter a single word."[15]

When her season with the Yiddish Art Theater ended, Stella did not know if she would be invited back. She longed for the comfortable, familiar way of life she grew up with. She wanted a theater that she belonged to, where the people worked in concert. She wanted both the familiarity of the Yiddish theater and the legitimacy of Broadway. She wanted a home. However, outside forces kept her from finding such a place on Second Avenue. Only five years previously the *New York Times* had predicted, "[Theater operators] rest assured in their knowledge that the Yiddish theater has been thoroughly Americanized . . . it is now a stable American institution."[16] In reality, by 1930 immigration restrictions had depleted the flow of Yiddish-speaking émigrés; competition with Broadway and the new phenomenon of movie houses threatened ticket sales; and, most drastically, the onset of the Depression ensured the steady and final disappearance of the Yiddish theater.

Second Avenue today no longer resembles its heyday as the Yiddish Broadway. Most of the old theaters have been razed. The cafés and restaurants have a different ethnic flavor: Pakistani, Thai fusion, Polish. The Hebrew Actors' Union declared itself obsolete in October of 2005. Its offices held a sparse array of deteriorating signs of its former self: dirty ashtrays, fading portraits of old Yiddish stars, and dusty file cabinets full of scripts and musical scores. The trove was eventually given to the YIVO Institute for Jewish Research.

Still, traces of the old days can be found. Built in 1926, the Yiddish Art Theater still stands. Its Romanesque Revival architecture harks back to a time of glamour that defined the Yiddish Broadway. And though the Café Royal is long gone, a corner deli near St. Mark's Place serves up soups and blintzes, while St. Mark's church bells clang through the neighborhood, declaiming the hour just as they used to when they spurred Stella on to her next engagement.

With neither a domestic or artistic home, Stella returned to the Lab. There she would meet Harold Clurman, the man who would offer her what appeared to be the best of both worlds: the family-oriented quality of the Yiddish theater and the legitimacy of Broadway.

CHAPTER EIGHT

Here was the very flesh of my secret yearning.

—Harold Clurman

Harold Clurman and Stella Adler were born the same year with a common raison d'être: the theater, which was waiting like a listless child to be reigned in, cultivated, and fostered into maturity. Harold's family had emigrated from Ukraine and settled on the Lower East Side, where his father started a medical practice. The Clurmans lived in one of the rare private homes in the ghetto, across from Harold's elementary school, near a pool hall where every kind of riffraff leaked into the doctor's office.

Harold was exposed to hoodlums seeking care for their brawling wounds, victims of street accidents, and near-dead children who had fallen from windows. The ghetto's criminal element, the long days of toil and business, the bustle of bodies teeming through the congested streets served as a constant drama that mesmerized Harold. To him his surroundings resembled an elaborate theatrical set. At night peddlers worked by the light of kerosene lamps while electric lights filtered through bottles of colorful liquids standing in drugstore windows. The varying shades of luminosity and shadow seemed to be staged to light up the ghetto, while the melodies of peddlers' cries and cantors' praise served as the drama's musical accompaniment. The sights and sounds of the Lower East Side culminated in its most thrilling element: the Yiddish theater.

When Harold was six years old his father took him to see Jacob Adler in *Uriel Acosta*. Jacob instantly became Harold's boyhood hero. Though he did not understand Yiddish, Harold gleaned the plot from the action and emotion onstage. With an imagination as brimming as the streets of his neighborhood, Harold believed he had found somewhere to channel his creativity. For an extra twenty-five cents, Harold shared an orchestra seat with his father. When his father was too busy, Harold convinced his older brother to take him to the theater.

With the degeneration of the ghetto, the Clurmans followed the exodus of upwardly mobile Jews out of the Lower East Side. In 1913 they moved to the Bronx. Harold found himself living in what was then a verdant countryside, separated from the action of the ghetto. To stave off boredom he began writing, acting, and directing his own plays in his new neighborhood, but he could not wait to return to the city. The following year Harold enrolled in high school on West Fifty-ninth Street, gaining access to the theater world again, but this time it was Broadway. Clurman later wrote that going to the theater had become an addiction during his adolescence, and he endured school only in order to explore the theater district when classes let out. As it turned out, he performed well enough academically to be accepted into Columbia University upon graduation, but Harold wanted an education outside the institution. He wanted to be at the center of cultural arts. He decided to go to Paris to study theater at the Sorbonne.

Harold's brother's wife had a cousin who was also going to study in Paris. His name was Aaron Copland. The young men arranged to meet at Brentano's Bookstore on Fifth Avenue. They struck up a friendship, and Harold accompanied Copland down to the Battery to get his passport. They decided to room together in Paris. Two months later, aboard the SS *Paris* en route for Europe, Harold received a telegram from Copland informing him that he had rented an apartment for the two of them.

In Paris the kid from the Lower East Side found himself at the epicenter of a cultural renaissance. Artists, musicians, and writers gathered in the city of wide boulevards and fragrant gardens, inevitably merging at the city's literary center: Sylvia Beach's English lending library, where one was bound to run into such luminaries as James Joyce, Ernest Hemingway, and Ezra Pound. Before finding his apartment, Clurman walked the city to gain his bearings and discovered a poster announcing a recital by Copland, who was studying at the Fontainebleau school. He finally found his flat, but Copland did not appear until the following morning, bursting into the apartment announcing that he had sold a short piano piece called "The Cat and the Mouse." The future seemed limitless.

Clurman plunged into the city's theatrical world. He began attending the productions of the influential dramatist and director Jacques Copeau. He was first in line to get a ticket for the Moscow Art Theater when the troupe came to Paris. He determined that his thesis at the Sorbonne would be on French drama from 1890 to 1914. Yet, in the midst of his Parisian immersion, Clurman felt a nagging dissatisfaction. Copland had defined his artistic aim as the "express[ion of] the present day" in his music.[1] Clurman wanted to form the theatrical equivalent of this idea, to find the relevance of theater to contemporary society.

In June of 1924 Clurman returned from his studies in Paris to find New Yorkers exuberantly plunged in the Roaring Twenties. After a brief recession the United States' postwar economy stabilized, creating a national perception of plenty and wealth. President Calvin Coolidge announced that business was "one of the greatest contributing forces to the moral and spiritual advancement of the race."[2] Materialistic goals dominated the American psyche with images of dishwashers and automobiles. Not even Prohibition could deter an American spirit epitomized by the simultaneously lyrical and violent dynamics of jazz, which Clurman called a "Coney Island" of music.[3] Underneath it all, a vulnerable economy teetered on the national tendency toward indulgence.

Clurman was unemployed. Worse, he had no idea what avenue of employment to take. Acting or playwriting? A set designer or producer? He began making contacts in the theater world, debuting as an extra in *The Saint* for the Provincetown Players; an experience that confirmed his role was not as an actor. He hadn't the looks, and his expectations went beyond performing. Clurman turned a critical eye upon the current plays on Broadway. Even the plays running at the Theatre Guild, known for supporting literary productions, lacked an American vision and purpose.

Clurman went to see his friend Sanford Meisner at the Theatre Guild, where Pirandello's *Right You Are If You Think You Are* was playing, with a young man by the name of Lee Strasberg in the lead role. Upon meeting, Clurman and Strasberg discovered they shared a common dissatisfaction with American theater. Stella, performing on Second Avenue, still floundering between a declining Yiddish theater and the semicontemptible Broadway, would have found solace in the existence of two other like-minded people. It was only a matter of time before they would all meet.

LEE STRASBERG'S FAMILY HAD IMMIGRATED TO THE UNITED STATES FROM Poland when he was seven years old. He spent his adolescence on the Lower East Side, where he was exposed to the Yiddish theater, but he had no particular interest in being part of it. Rather, the world of books was his constant companion, and even while eating he always had a book in hand. During his last year of high school his closest sibling died. Desolate, Strasberg neglected to make up the work he missed during his brother's illness and funeral to receive his diploma. Instead, he became a delivery boy in a wig factory, quickly moving up the rungs to become company manager.

In his early twenties Strasberg joined the Drama Club at the Chrystie Street Settlement House. Several settlement houses, or community centers, had sprung up on the Lower East Side to provide activities for neighborhood youngsters. Strasberg became devoted to his work in the drama club and found a fondness for acting. After work at the wig factory he would take the subway to Chrystie Street and work into the morning hours before returning to the factory by seven o'clock in the morning.

In 1922, when the Moscow Art Theater came to New York, Strasberg went to every performance, fascinated by the ensemble quality of the troupe. He knew of individual talent—Barrymore, Duse—but had never witnessed a production in which every single actor was as great as the next. A walk-on actor performed with the same conviction as the lead, and all of them worked in concert toward a unified purpose. Strasberg wanted to understand the method behind the company's work.

Like Stella, Strasberg found his way to the American Laboratory Theatre by word of mouth. After six months he decided he understood acting, and because in his view there was no more the Lab could offer him, he chose not to become part of their acting group.[4] Strasberg later explained: "What I had gotten was extraordinary. It changed my entire perspective. I had read Freud and already knew the things that go on in a human being without consciousness, but they showed me what it meant. They gave me the key to things I'd seen, heard, and known but had no means of understanding. So, from that point of view it was cataclysmic, but, in an odd way, I didn't feel their theater as such would work anymore. It didn't have a sufficiently American base."[5]

While Strasberg and Clurman continued to meet and discuss the theater, they discovered it was not so much that the American theater fell short, but that it did not exist. They began defining their vision of a national theater in conversations that continued for months. The Theatre Guild hired Clurman as a stage manager for the *Garrick Gaieties*, and during the production Clurman and Strasberg would meet backstage to resume their colloquium. The exchange was so boisterous they soon gained the attention of the Guild's assistant stage manager, Cheryl Crawford. A Smith College graduate from Ohio, Crawford had aspirations of becoming a director. Crawford's practical business sense, Strasberg's dogged ambition, and Clurman's artistic idealism created a perfect triumvirate to build an American theater.

In 1927 Jacques Copeau, Clurman's first theatrical mentor, whom he had met in Paris, came to the United States to direct *The Brothers Karamazov*. While in rehearsals Clurman invited Copeau to the theater on Chrystie Street to see Strasberg's staging of Copeau's *The House into Which We Are Born*. After the play Copeau went backstage to commend Strasberg, but the novice director refused to speak to him. Strasberg's biographer Cindy Adams wrote that Strasberg's upbringing never taught him the social graces, postulating that Strasberg "was too pathologically shy to speak first. Then, when too many embarrassing minutes passed . . . he absolutely did not know how to begin."[6] The encounter would have been equally embarrassing for Clurman but subordinate to the more important matter of creating an American theater.

Clurman watched Copeau during rehearsals of *The Brothers Karamazov*, later realizing that "a first-rate director, who is also the author of the play, working with such incomparable actors as Lunt and Fontanne, does not inevitably produce a satisfying theater event. . . . This is not from any lack of mutual respect or from temperamental conflicts between the American actors and the foreign director; it is just that the company and the director do not speak the same artistic language."[7] It was becoming clear to Clurman that the United States, being a new country, had yet to develop its own defining theatrical language.

In 1927 Strasberg and Clurman enrolled in a directing class at the Lab, where they met Stella Adler. Deeply optimistic about building an American theater, both young men would have been instantly impressed by a professional actress who literally embodied the theater. Clurman was attracted to Stella, while Strasberg's interests were purely intellectual. When Strasberg discovered the Italian theater on the Lower East Side, he was so taken by the realistic acting of Giovanni Grasso that he invited Stella and Morris Carnovsky, a fellow Yiddish theater actor who was also working at the Guild, to see Grasso perform. Of the love scene, Strasberg later recalled, "He wasn't acting . . . He *really* was *loving*."[8]

One evening Clurman went to Second Avenue, where Stella was playing in Shakespeare's *Much Ado about Nothing* at the Irving Place Theatre. For Clurman, everything seemed to come together in this one woman:

I had, to my surprise and almost against my will, fallen in love. . . . [Stella] was somehow fragile, vulnerable, gay with mother wit and stage fragrance, eager to add knowledge to instinct, spiritually vibrant, as if forever awaiting the redemption of a faith as realistically substantial as it was emotionally exalting. Here was the very flesh of my secret yearning. Here was the personification of something I wanted to integrate with my whole sense of life, someone who was indeed a living symbol of so much I treasured in life.[9]

In addition to personifying the Old World European theatrical ideal and the modern American spirit, Stella was also married with a baby and entirely unavailable. And yet, Stella later confessed, she automatically endeared herself to men, insinuated herself to them, and gave them her full attention. "I was not a conscious flirt," Stella once said; "I didn't know that I was flirting all the time."[10] Stella's coquettish proclivity and beauty rarely left her without an admirer, which gave her a sense of security. However, she had simultaneously cultivated a capable, exacting exterior; she did not show vulnerability. Love interests were insurance that she would not be left alone, but Stella was not one to bide her time. She would not invest in someone who did not stimulate her intellectually and artistically.

When Stella realized, however, that Harold had fallen in love with her, she had to navigate the ardor of his feelings while figuring out the nature of her own. She was intrigued with Clurman's zealous ideas about the theater and respected his intellect and ambition, but he was far from the man she envisioned for herself. Stella's standard of comparison dwelled in her father, with his regal visage, tall stature, and athletic, graceful physique, a man who had not only built his own theater, but also pioneered the golden age of the Yiddish theater. About the same height as Stella, with unexceptional looks, Harold "could not compete with a dead man,"[11] as he later remarked.

In the meantime Clurman worked on assembling a company of actors. He, Strasberg, Crawford, and a few others met regularly to discuss the theater they wanted to build. They would gather backstage at the Guild, one another's apartments, or a smoky establishment on West Forty-fourth Street called the Double R Restaurant. Soon Clurman went to work for the Guild as a play reader, which augmented his dissatisfaction with the Guild, as he realized it had "no blood relationship with the plays they dealt in. . . . They didn't want to say anything through plays, and plays said nothing to them."[12] The idea of art for art's sake was not good enough, and the

Guild's members were becoming restless. They were displeased with the disparity in theater where directors, actors, and writers worked separately. In response, the Guild created a subsidiary for experimental Sunday performances. In charge of casting the play, Clurman chose a Soviet work called *Red Rust*. Clurman invited Stella to join the production, but she declined, choosing to watch from the sidelines to see how events would unfold. Her brother Luther, who was also fluctuating between the Yiddish theater and Broadway, took a role in the production. It marked Clurman's first managerial-type theatrical endeavor, and it gave him the confidence to proceed with his plans of having his own theater.

Clurman began gathering actors he worked with or admired from the Guild, the Lab, and the Civic Repertory Theatre to meet on a weekly basis. A natural orator, he spewed forth his ideas with electrifying ardor. He would stand in front of a small gathering at eleven-thirty (after Friday evening performances) and begin his speech: "We have on the American stage, all the separate elements for a Theater, but no Theater. We have playwrights without their theater groups, directors without their actors, actors without plays or directors. . . . Our theater is an anarchy of individual talents."[13] What began with fewer than a dozen attendees grew to as many as two hundred people some nights.

The actor-refugees continued to meet and Clurman continued to preach, but he remained plagued by Stella's ambivalence to his romantic overtures. One night he showed up backstage at one of her shows, urging her to come hear him speak. She agreed. Afterward, though she was still equivocal toward their romantic prospects, Stella admitted she had been sold on Clurman's vision: "There was something about Clurman's persuasiveness," she later said, "which was what people were looking for in their dreams and there he was saying it and being extremely magnificent in his statement and you believed the dream. And we did."[14] By May of 1930 Clurman had literally talked his theater into existence. He, Strasberg, and Crawford held auditions for their new company. Calling themselves the directors, the trio settled on twenty-seven members and began planning their first rehearsals.

Stella remained reluctant to join. She was employed for the 1929–30 season with the Yiddish Art Theater, but as the summer approached she worried about her future. The Yiddish Art Theater could not guarantee her a contract for the next season, and the uncertainty of her immediate career was magnified by her personal life. Stella's marriage to Eliascheff could hardly endure. He was a quiet man, uncomfortable with the booming personalities and lifestyle of the theater. The girl whose beauty had "stung" him that London winter when they first met had grown up to be a vibrant woman, full of idealistic dreams and a relentless gluttony for life's offerings. He decided to return to England.

On a larger scale, the Yiddish theater could not compete with Broadway and the movies. That fall Fox Film Corporation announced that "talkies" had made silent films obsolete. The Yiddish theater struggled to keep an audience growing up American and doing its best to assimilate.

In the autumn of 1929 there were more serious problems than art and the theater. In October the stock market crashed, setting in motion the longest and most severe economic depression in the nation's history. Stella's floundering sense of security sank as unemployment rose from 1.5 million before the crash to 3.2 million by the spring of 1930. Despite the signs around her—the opening of the Chrysler Building, the installation of the city's first traffic lights, and President Herbert Hoover's insistence that "any lack of confidence in the economic future or the basic strength of business in the United States is foolish"[15]—the evidence in the streets told a different story.

On Manhattan's corners unemployed professionals were reduced to selling apples for a nickel apiece. The drought in Arkansas that began in the summer of 1930 spread across the Great Plains, threatening the livelihood of thousands of farmers, with no relief in sight. The president may have believed otherwise, but the fact was, the country was in crisis. Clurman's fervor for building a new American theater offered a beacon to guide Stella into the unsteady modern world. She had given him enough hope to declare his love and allowed him to court her. Harold took what he could get although they both knew her heart was not entirely in it, just as they knew that Harold was there to stay.

Like an unexpected but sorely missed visitor, Stella's mother provided the most immediate solution to Stella's sense of a foreboding future. Sara organized the Adler children together to pay tribute to their late father. Nunia's husband, Joseph Schoengold, directed the troupe in one of Jacob's favorite plays, *The Wild Man*, a quintessential Yiddish melodrama about an older man who brings home a young wife to a suspicious and unwelcoming family. Luther took on the role that had been immortalized by Jacob, while Stella played the daughter, Lisa, who ridicules the young bride. A tragic ending caps the play when the idiot son kills his stepmother.

The show premiered in Boston on May 4, 1930, at the Franklin Park Theatre, where the production was so well received it was brought back by popular demand the following week. The cast included Abe, Jacob's son from his first marriage; Charles, from his affair with Jennya Kaiser; and his children with Sara: Frances, Jay, Julia, Stella, and Luther. It marked the first time that all of Jacob's children, with the exception of Celia, were assembled on one stage at one time. From Boston the company traveled to New York for five performances at the Second Avenue Theatre and then up to Montreal, where "the rare hereditary acting ability revealed itself in every instance, transcending the moodiness of Gordin's depressing piece."[16]

In Toronto a large audience awaited the Adlers, with the *Toronto Daily* headlining their performance as "striking." On their return they stopped in Detroit at Littman's People's Theatre, where the actors performed "according to the best, or worst, traditions of its [Yiddish theater's] era, without any attempt to reform, subdue, modify, or modernize."[17] Another review from Detroit noted that "'The Wild Man" hardly deserved its programmatic label of melodrama . . . superb acting accentuated the tragedy's almost grim realism."[18] Sara, not to be left out of the limelight, yet without a part in *The Wild Man*, chose to play a scene from Gordin's *The Homeless* about an insane woman returning to her home. It was her first time onstage after a fifteen-year hiatus.

In transit on this tour, the family did not always travel together. On one occasion Luther was on a train heading to the smoking car to join his brother Jay when he caught a glimpse of an attractive woman seated in one of the cars he passed. He told his older brother, "There's a wonderful blonde back in coach." Jay, a reputable ladies' man, bumbled down the aisle to see the flaxen-haired beauty, got a look at her, and returned to Luther in the smoking car: "Son of a bitch, it's Stella!"[19] Stories like this became the comic relief of many a dinner gathering throughout the years, where the family would assemble, as Clurman described them, like a "litter of cats":

Despite the family's extreme individualism and even more extreme disputes, they seemed to dwell in a cozy nook, all heaped upon one another. They wriggled, twisted, parried, shoved, scratched, and flayed, which only testified to their consanguinity and their indissoluble unity. They kept warm together and exuded a most captivating heat. They were a race unto themselves; nothing in the world could separate them. They all loved the theater passionately, down to its minute details, and were "idealistic" about it withal. They would talk all through the night, reminiscing, telling tall tales, and, above all, laughing. "We shall laugh our lives away," Stella would say.[20]

By summer the family troupe had disbanded to return to their paying gigs around the world, but Sara was determined to keep this new company together. In September she sent for everyone to return from his or her respective engagements. Frances and Joseph Schoengold came from Buenos Aires, where they had established their own theater. Their daughter, Pearl, did not have to travel so far; she lived in Boston. Luther was summoned from Johannesburg, South Africa. Charles took the next ship from London back to New York. From Philadelphia, even Celia was beckoned to join the company.

Stella, however, was engaged with the Yiddish Art Theater, with which she was on tour in Buenos Aires. Fearful of the stability of her future employment with the company, she did not feel at liberty to join the family effort. Unfortunately for three-year-old Ellen, the entire family was working, and Stella could not take care of her in South America. Stella found a woman from the Yiddish theater who ran a boarding school in the Bronx for kindergarten-age children. Ellen would have been socially and emotionally challenged among five- and six-year-olds.

From Argentina Stella sent Harold a telegram that encapsulates the cat-and-mouse nature of their relationship: "If you're forgetting me I'll come back; if you aren't I'll stay in S.A. [South America]."[21] In Clurman's memoir about his life in the theater during the 1930s he delivers an honest, if self-deprecating, portrait of the dynamic between himself and Stella:

I was probably peculiar, but very persistent. We saw each other a good deal; I "rushed" her. I belonged to another world; that is, I was of the theater, but more bookish. I had very little worldliness, masculine savoir-faire, form, or elegance—all qualities that she rightly prized. We got on fitfully. I supplied the storm and she the surprise. She ran away and I ran after. I ran away and she called me back. She was unkind and I was foolish. She warned me of difficulty and I wouldn't heed. I promised some magnificent release for her that I hardly understood myself; and she wondered. I was going to have a theater some day; and she believed. We ran round and round till it was difficult to know who was chasing or following whom.[22]

Stella returned from South America in time to see her family open with *Millions* at the New Yorker Theatre on October 2, 1930, a comedy about the Rothschilds. Celia Adler stood out as "giving the outstanding characterization of the evening."[23]

Years later Ellen remembered the day Stella returned to pick her up from boarding school. Stella hid from her in an attempt to engage the girl in play.[24] Hiding from a daughter she had left with strangers may seem an odd choice to most mothers, who would likely embrace a child upon first sight, not only to alleviate the mother's feelings of separation but also those of the child. Stella's choosing to play hide-and-seek at what should have been an emotional moment of reunion indicates her lack of maternal instinct. Then again, perhaps it was an unconscious act of guilt. Even in the twenty-first century, the onus upon a mother to selflessly care for her child at the expense of having a career remains a dilemma for women. This would be the first of many boarding schools for young Ellen.

While on tour Stella had done a lot of thinking about the limited options of the Yiddish theater. One day while walking with Harold they stopped to rest outside a church on University Place. Stella noticed how pensive he was, dreaming about his theater. Clurman remembered that Stella "suddenly smiled . . . [and] grabbed Harold's hand, announcing, 'I'm with you!' meaning she would leave the Yiddish theater and join" his endeavor.[25] With the Yiddish theater in decline, it was the best ticket in town. Stella moved to the next logical topic of importance: "Will I get a good part in the first play?"

"Oh, yes," Harold replied, serious-faced, "a maid—a walk-on."

"I'll die! Harold, don't do that to me."[26]

They both knew Harold was joking; he was not about to jeopardize their tentative relationship with anything less than fervor for Stella's acting career.

CHAPTER NINE

Stella was fun and she was elegant and she was classy and she was smart and she was sympathetic and she was understanding and she was spoiled rotten.

—Elaine Stritch

FULFILLING HER ROLE AS COMPANY MANAGER, CHERYL CRAWFORD procured lodgings in Brookfield, Connecticut, for the company's first retreat, where they would study and rehearse for the upcoming season. On June 8, 1931, twenty-eight actors and the company's three directors rendezvoused in a downpour in front of the Guild Theater. The caravan set off for Brookfield, more than an hour's drive from the city, where they would spend the next ten weeks.

Stella and Harold drove with Dorothy Patten, an actress from Tennessee who had had some success on Broadway. Unshaven and disheveled, Harold had not been able to sleep the previous night, which he spent ruminating over the theater he had been formulating in his mind over the last six years. Now here he was, with Stella beside him, and the entire company en route—like a traveling band of old to realize his dream of an American theater.

Just back from a three-month tour with Maurice Schwartz's Yiddish Art Theater, Stella's vision of the summer couldn't have been further from Harold's. Her palpable ambivalence rankled him. Stella flashed a letter from Schwartz with a proposal to tour with the Yiddish Art Theater that summer. Flaunting the letter in front of Patten insulted Clurman and undermined his role as codirector of the company. He snatched the letter from Stella and ripped it up,[1] which seemed to be what they both needed to loosen up and enjoy the rest of the drive.

Arriving at Brookfield Center, the actors unloaded their cars and divvied up the five bungalows they were to share for the summer. The main house served as a communal space for dining, with four bedrooms for additional accommodations. The Christ-in-the-manger barn offered a large rehearsal space; country hills rounded out the picturesque paradise of the company's first enterprise. After everyone got settled, some of the men started up a baseball game; others explored the surrounding areas. Stella took in the environs, still wondering whether it had been a mistake to come. Had she really agreed to camp out in the country with virtual strangers for the entire summer?

Her doubts were assuaged that evening when the company assembled in the barn. United under the rafters of the creaky Victorian stables, the actors felt the camaraderie of a common purpose. Overcome with emotion, the triad of directors spoke about the exceptional nature of their company's endeavor. This was not just the beginning of a new theatrical group; its reach went as far as reshaping the landscape of the American theater.

While Crawford took charge of logistics, scheduling, and the overall operations of business, Strasberg assumed the role of acting director and interpreter of Stanislavski's system. Strasberg experimented with sense memory exercises to hone the actors' concentration. The actor would use an object—say, a bar of soap—concentrating on it until he had memorized its texture, smell, taste, even its sound in his hand or as it fell onto a surface. Once the soap was removed, the actor would recreate the object in his imagination. Strasberg later explained that "concentration on an object implies believing in it, seeing it so precisely that you really do become convinced, so that the senses come alive as they do in real life when you see a real object."[2] The goal is to hone the actor's concentration so that even if the object is not present onstage, he can still experience it, as opposed to acting *as if* he were experiencing it.

Strasberg's most controversial exercise, also borrowed from Stanislavski, stems from sense memory and is referred to as "affective memory," a phrase that is synonymous with "emotional memory." The term originates from the French psychologist Theodule Ribot, who noticed that his patients could feel a specific event in the past by "reliving the event in the imagination."[3] The emotion that arises when hearing a love song with which one has a nostalgic association is an example of how the sense of sound elicits an emotional response from the past and sets it in motion in the present. Strasberg stressed that an actor should not remember the event itself. Rather, the actor should call on his faculties of sense memory: "The important thing in using affective memory is to maintain one's concentration, not on the emotion, but on the sensory objects or elements from the past of the memory before [the actor] attempts to work in emotional memory."[4]

Say an actor has to recall making the decision to take his grandmother off life support. An affective memory exercise would have the actor remember the room, its temperature, the color of the walls, whether there were windows or paintings; the actor would remember the bed and how his grandmother was positioned in it, whether her nails were painted, the color of her hair. The actor would recall the sounds in the room: the rhythmic beeping of the heart monitor, the respirator's oscillation, the background voices on the television. The actor would not recall how he or she felt. According to Stanislavski's theory, the senses would trigger the emotion.

Naturally the question arises: what if an actor has never experienced an emotion that his character is experiencing? In this case, Strasberg would use a substitution. While working on their first production for the season at Brookfield, Paul Green's *House of Connelly*, Strasberg directed the actress Margaret Barker in a lovemaking scene. Barker later recalled that Strasberg "didn't think my type of gentle lovemaking on stage was strong enough (which God knows in terms of my lack of life experience must have been rather gentle). So he would have me do an exercise of anger recall. And the anger would get something that was as passionate as he wanted Patsy to be in the play. It was a total substitution of what the real emotion was, put into the mold of the scene."[5] That summer Strasberg instructed the actors to probe personal, sometimes painful memories. While the work was often disturbing, it delivered results. New doors were being opened to the acting craft.

Years later, while teaching at the Actors Studio, Strasberg would stress: "We never use real, that is, literal emotion in art, only affective memory emotion, only remembered emotion. Only remembered emotion could be controlled."[6] Yet Strasberg could not always guarantee that an actor used remembered emotion as he would have it done: methodically, through concentration and sense memory exercises. From a scientific perspective, we know very little about the operation of the brain, or exactly how thoughts affect our emotional states, let alone how those emotional states are managed. The demarcation between real and remembered emotion is amorphous.

Throughout the years, many students who studied with Strasberg criticized his application of affective memory, but none as vehemently as Stella. That first summer she was open to exploring whatever Strasberg decreed. Certainly she had already been exposed to affective memory at the Lab, something Stella spoke about in an unpublished interview with the Group Theatre scholar Jerry Roberts. Roberts asked Stella, "Before 1934, had you had any disagreement with the way the work was being done at the Group Theatre on the basis of your prior experience at the Lab?" Stella responded: "Yes. Boleslavski was very, very graphic—external in his emphasis as a director. I don't think the Group Theatre was; it was very internal. It tried very much to work emotionally first and left the outside bare. Boleslavski didn't do that."[7]

One of Boleslavski's students, Blanch Tancock, who began studying at the Lab in 1924, provides a description of Boleslavski's teaching style that may explain why Stella would not have felt troubled by his use of affective memory: "He [Boleslavski] had a wonderful capacity for releasing the creative resources in those he worked with. He never dictated. He threw out suggestions and led the actor to find his own conclusions and solutions."[8] Having grown up on the stage, Stella could not tolerate someone (with a few exceptions) mandating how to approach a role; she would have appreciated being able to come up with her own ideas, to which Boleslavski seemed amenable. In comparison, Strasberg's directing in the Group Theatre commanded the actors' full cooperation without allowing for their input—a significantly different education no matter what Stella's opinion of Strasberg's emphasis on affective memory.

A clear difference between how Stella experienced affective memory at the Lab, as opposed to how Strasberg taught it, appears in Stella's copies of Boleslavski's lectures. In particular, Boleslavski believed some actors may need to use affective memory, while others may not. He demonstrated an example by comparing the great actresses Eleonora Duse and Sarah Bernhardt:

> To some people it [affective memory] comes with difficulty, and they use it in their own way, by themselves in dressing rooms and they concentrate and some of them use it quite easy and naturally. Eleanore [sic] Duse had so much of it that she used it always in life. Her simple sincerity and simplicity in grief in dramatic situations, in sadness, was so close to her own life that she could not differentiate whether she was acting and whether it was life. . . . That was an overdone memory of feelings [Boleslavski's synonym for affective memory]. Now, some actors underdo it, using technique only. Sarah Bernhardt did not use memory of feelings most of all. She used it

only as a preparation, as a feeder to her imagination while preparing a part, but not using it while acting. She preferred to use technique. A person who is strong enough and has a good memory of feeling prefers to use that, but a person who is not strong in memory of feeling prefers to use technique. If you would ask Duse, "How will you act this part today?" She would say, "I don't know." But some people will tell you exactly to the point of how they are going to act.[9]

Like Bernhardt, Stella did not need the extra prodding of an affective memory exercise. It makes sense that because of her emotionalism, Stella preferred to rely on external technique, which she would stress as she developed her own approach to acting through the actor's external actions rather than his emotions. The anatomy of a character's actions was also a tenet of Stanislavski's, one that both she and Strasberg had been taught at the Lab.

The argument over whether an actor should use real emotion or acquire an external technique to play a character is an age-old debate. Prior to Stanislavski, little had been written about how an actor develops a role. The director Jack Garfein points out in his book *Life and Acting: Techniques for the Actor*:

Up until the time of Stanislavski's published work and V. I. Pudovkin's *Film Acting and Technique*, there existed only two well-known books on the subject—one by Francois Delsarte filled with illustrative clichés ("Put your hand on your heart to show love") and a philosophical one by Diderot, *The Paradox of Acting*. In his book, Diderot is trying to comprehend the nature of the actor's emotions on stage and the ones he experiences in actuality. He is unable to differentiate.[10]

Garfein saw affective memory as a potentially dangerous way to work, since personal emotions can unleash unpredictable results. In conversation with the author, Garfein explained why he agreed with Stella's reliance upon the actor's physical actions to access emotion:

The reason for the action is that through the action the latent content of life is revealed. Whereas without that, it's simply emotions, which by the way in life are the consequence of actions. But in Strasberg's teaching, particularly towards the end of his life . . . he would lead the actor emotionally to a certain point. The actor would go into his life and then he [Strasberg] would leave him hanging because unlike an analyst or a psychiatrist who would keep going with it, who takes care of the patient, in Strasberg's case, they would be left hanging.[11]

The first summer at Brookfield, however, Stella was years away from developing her own technique. Like her fellow actors, she tried her best to follow Strasberg's direction, but she was finding affective memory more and more troublesome. She had grown up researching her character, his or her historical period and every detail therein down to the selection of costume and makeup, which was all carefully thought out so that when she was onstage she was free to inhabit the character. It was distracting to simultaneously experience the character and also focus on a personal memory that in her mind had no relevance to her character. Later she observed, "You couldn't be on stage thinking of your own personal life. It was just schizophrenic."[12]

Stella had a point, which Strasberg himself brought home in class years later by explaining how the actor must

face the problem of bringing it [affective memory] into the scene he is playing. He must fuse his personal emotion with the character and event he is portraying. For example, when the actor's partner is speaking, he listens and answers naturally, but *at the same time* [author's italics] he tries to concentrate on the objects of his own event and thus to fuse his material with the author's. . . . In the Group Theatre, where we worked with affective memory in production, we would set a definite amount of time. We would allow the actor a minute before the emotion was needed to carry out the affective memory.[13]

In an interview in 1966, Stella succinctly stated why she did not use affective memory with her students: "A student is encouraged to respect his creative, imaginative life as a source for his acting craft. To go back to a feeling or emotion of one's own experience I believe to be unhealthy. It tends to separate you from the play, from the action of the play, from the circumstances of the play, and from the author's intention. All this has to be embodied in the action."[14] Equally important, Stella stressed, was knowing the cultural and political circumstances of the characters and their setting.

While teaching *The Glass Menagerie*, Stella would tell the actors in the scene to "create the room." She would say, "Are the drapes torn? Whose picture is on the wall? Washington? Put something there that's very American. What kind of view does she have? A fire escape. What's on the other fire escapes? The key is 'drab'—not just the room, the life. It's lower-middle-class life. The Gentleman Caller is not of exactly that same class. Know the difference in their larger circumstances."[15] Then with Stella's finesse of mixing pedagogy and humor, she would prod: "C'mon, get going! You can't be stupid if you're a modern actor. You have to be sharp. You don't have to be so intelligent in Shakespeare. He's a giant, so he carries you—if you speak ever so precisely and have lots of good teeth."[16]

For someone as "emotionally fluent" as Stella,[17] using psychological exercises to create emotion was akin to a typist concentrating on each keystroke even after having memorized the keyboard. The natural flow of typing would be hindered, just as thinking about emotion tripped Stella up. She would rather experience the emotion by doing. A correlative conjecture could be applied to Strasberg, who was notoriously aloof and unapproachable. Delving inward to unleash what is sublimated may be useful for such a personality.

Strasberg was a perfectionist. He worked tirelessly to make every movement in a scene matter. No one questioned his authority. Egos could not be tolerated; actors unwilling to listen were unacceptable. "Lee was a God to us," Phoebe Brand remembered. "We truly admired him. We wanted to do what he wanted even if we didn't always understand."[18] By the middle of the summer the actors began calling him Dr. Strasberg. He kept strict rules where he worked; the barn was deemed a sacred place. Anyone caught smoking or reading a magazine during rehearsal was subject to Strasberg's explosive temper. During one rehearsal, Strasberg directed Morris Carnovsky in a scene in which he had to climb atop a table and raise a glass. Frustrated with repeatedly climbing up onto the table, Carnovsky finally retaliated by throwing his glass down. The room stilled to silence, and Strasberg exploded. "You! You are committing a central crime against the whole spirit of the group. We are aiming to form a collective theater here. For anyone to transgress is a crime."[19]

Between Crawford's pragmatism and Strasberg's despotism, Clurman remained the voice of inspiration, with his fervent theatrical ideology. The company had the responsibility of studying and working together on a theater that addressed the sociopolitical milieu of the Depression. Within this microcosm there would be no stars. Everyone would have equal billing and equal work on a project, which meant that if you were the lead in a play one season, you might serve as a stagehand the next. The democratic ideals were nice in theory for Stella, but she preferred playing lead roles. From the beginning, this sense of entitlement, coupled with her aristocratic temperament, aggravated her relationship with the company. As in her childhood, she struggled to integrate.

Throughout the sweltering summer, the idealism that accompanies youth and experimentation ambled through the grounds with the country breeze. When spirits grew restless, when affective memory exercises, listening to the Victrola, swimming, playing tennis, and loafing around in pajamas grew monotonous, some of the actors asked to return to the city for a night on the town. Wary of any desire for "a world outside the group,"[20] Clurman felt disheartened by these requests. He wanted the actors to cherish their limited time at Brookfield, knowing how quickly their summer would come to an end.[21]

Within this idyllic atmosphere romances abounded, some stable, others, like Harold and Stella's, stormy. Morris Carnovsky and Phoebe Brand roomed together and would later marry, as did Strasberg and Paula Miller. Others, such as the young recruit Clifford Odets, would mail daily love letters to Eunice Stoddard, whose bungalow was walking distance from his, but she never answered his missives. Luther Adler made the trip to the country to partake in the amorous possibilities.

Tall and fair, with chiseled facial features as opposed to Stella's soft ones, Luther had recently turned twenty-eight. He was as charming as Stella was charismatic, both having inherited Jacob's sex appeal. Luther felt as disturbed as Stella by the lack of artistic integrity on Broadway compared to the Yiddish theater. Clurman's collective seemed an attractive alternative.

Predictably, cliques formed among the twenty-eight actors. Bobby Lewis—the youngest thespian of the group—and Sanford Meisner gravitated toward Stella and Harold. In the evenings, while Odets repeatedly played an E-minor chord on the piano and Franchot Tone played chess, Stella would tell stories about the Yiddish theater. Finally giving up on Eunice Stoddard, Odets began setting his sights on a different girl every week, most of whom steered clear of him. One night, he proceeded to throw a billiard ball at Margaret Barker's door—behind which she was securely ensconced. The racket was numbing. Finally, Stella bellowed, "Clifford, if you don't turn out to be a genius, I'll never speak to you again."[22]

For the first play, *House of Connelly*, Strasberg cast Stella in the role of an aging southern belle. She resented playing an older woman when she was so fully in her prime and ready to flaunt her physical attributes. Adding insult to injury, the company's darling, the tall and handsome Franchot Tone, played Stella's *younger* brother. Ironically, the character in the play is dealing with the loss of southern tradition, just as Stella was grieving the Yiddish theater. Even though Stella could readily dip into her emotional palette, she followed Strasberg's direction of "taking an exercise," probing deeper into her senses to emote. The actors were emotionally raw, having peeled away layers of buried emotion. It rained on and off throughout the summer as if even the weather understood Strasberg's demand for a constant flood of scrutiny, washing away until there was nothing left but a pliable, exposed canvas on which to work.

As the summer approached its end and the thought of actually performing *Connelly* before an audience drew near, anxiety spread through the company. The directors managed to keep the focus on what they had come to Brookfield to create, which still had no official name. Already familiar with addressing themselves as a "group" and fortified with the camaraderie of having gone to battle together all summer, it was a natural choice to call their operation the Group Theatre.

Returning to the city and to reality was a difficult adjustment. Unemployment continued to increase, despite President Hoover's assurance that "no one is going hungry and no one need go hungry or cold."[23] Apparently he did not notice the millions in line for bread or the women and children in queue at soup kitchens. Homelessness was pandemic. Families resorted to building ramshackle structures out of wood scraps, cardboard boxes, and fenceposts in sprawls on the outskirts of cities and towns. These makeshift spreads were referred to as Hoovervilles. By the end of 1931 unemployment had reached eight million; a few months later it approached twelve million.[24] The Group's relevance became more evident than ever. Just as the Yiddish theater uplifted and enriched the immigrants of the Lower East Side, the Group Theatre endeavored to serve as the social and artistic barometer for a nation in crisis.

During the rehearsal of *Connelly*, Stella had informed Harold: "If it's a success I'll leave; if it's a failure I'll stay."[25] The play opened on September 28, 1931, at the Martin Beck Theatre. The anxious cast knew the future of the

Group depended on the night's performance. No one could be paid until the box-office returns came in. Clurman and Strasberg sat together in the orchestra section, cringing every time an actor spoke too softly. It appeared to them that the players were exhausted, their usual energy depleted. Crawford sat in the mezzanine with the playwright, Paul Green, also on pins and needles, while the audience remained quiet. It was impossible to tell whether they loved it or hated it.

The directors' prayers were answered at the final curtain with an eruptive cheer from the audience demanding repeated curtain calls. By the sixteenth curtain call, the audience beckoned the playwright. Crawford grabbed Green and hastened him to the stage. The *New York Times* critic Brooks Atkinson, the dean of critics, lauded the Group's performance as "tremulous and pellucid, the expression of an ideal."[26] Atkinson struck a chord with the Group's ensemble mission, describing the performance as "too beautifully imagined and modulated to concentrate on personal achievement . . . they play like a band of musicians."[27] Stella would not live up to her ultimatum to Harold. After twenty-two curtain calls, she was there to stay.

The next Group production of the season, *1931*, told the story of a warehouse worker who loses his job during a mass unemployment epidemic. Following Group policy, the actors who had leading roles in *Connelly* were given small parts in *1931*. Stella was cast as a tourist. The play received poor reviews, prompting it to close after only twelve performances. During those twelve performances, the Group noticed a distinct change in its audience. The typical upper-crust theatergoers, obviously put off by the play's reviews, left the orchestra empty most nights, while the balcony was filled with the Group's ideal audience: middle-class workers. Ticket prices were lowered from the usual dollar to fifty cents for these balcony seats. When the play had to close, the Group received letters pleading to keep it running.

Brooks Atkinson was not as turned off by the socialist slant of the play's plot as were other critics. He recognized that although the writing was "bad," the purpose was successful: "By visualizing the tragic tale of unemployment '1931' shows how terrifying a bad play can be when it discusses a public calamity and reminds us of homely facts that we dare not believe."[28] But recognition of the Group's mission did not pay the bills. Clurman feared his theater would never be stable if it continued to operate on a play-by-play basis. Meanwhile, the actors' idealistic mentality, a holdover from their summer at Brookfield, fell away as the reality of business on Broadway became clear. The winter of 1931 hit the Group with an outlook as ugly as the muddy slush covering New York City's sidewalks.

In an effort to revive the actors' enthusiasm after the disappointment of *1931*, the directors planned a tour for *Connelly* to important eastern cities. By the time they reached Washington, their next play, written especially for the Group by Maxwell Anderson, was ready. They began rehearsing for *Night over Taos*, a play about a Spanish landowner who struggles to maintain the feudalistic society of the past.

At this juncture Luther came on board. His presence comforted Stella. The actors admired Luther's acclaimed acting career. He had forfeited a better role on Broadway to take the bit part of Don Fernando in *Night over Taos*. Stella's part as Doña Josefa wasn't the lead, but she felt relieved to be working again with her brother. Joe Bromberg, who had become the audience's favorite for his character roles in the Group's two previous productions, played the lead role of Pablo Montoya.

Night over Taos opened at the Forty-Eighth Street Theatre on March 9, 1932. The notices were lukewarm: critics were impressed with the set but displeased with the actors' diction. The actors received their paychecks at the end of the week. The pay scale varied; Luther and Harold earned $25; Stella received $70; and Franchot Tone, who played a lead role, made $150.[29] The following week the play did not generate enough income to pay the actors at all, and despite the actors' agreement to have their salaries cut, the play had to close.

Used to Old World decorum and garnering a certain reverential attention from Yiddish audiences, Stella continued to wonder if she had made the wrong decision by joining Harold's theater. Clurman later wrote about Stella's quandary: "The old was flattering, pleasant, homelike, but without very much creative future. The new struck her as raw, cold, indifferent to her as an individual."[30] Clurman was determined to marry the old with the new, if only to keep Stella by his side.

Stella took her dissatisfaction out on Harold. Both believed he was responsible for making her happy. Didn't he promise her the Group would be everything she could hope for professionally? Didn't she give up a fulfilling engagement with the Yiddish Art Theater in order to join his theater? She was trapped in the age-old artist's dilemma, one with which the Group itself struggled: how to be artistically authentic in a commercially driven field. Compounding the problem, the tension between Stella and Harold inevitably affected the other Group members. They especially resented how Clurman's focus steered away from the Group whenever there was trouble with Stella. This became a point of contention for many members throughout the years.

At the end of the first season, Stella could not ignore what was at once gratifying and terrifying about the Group. She did not fit into communal life, but in the end the work remained her priority. The Group Theatre, like the Yiddish theater before it, pursued the ideal of enriching and enlightening society. Stella knew she could not obtain such devotion and reverence for the work in any other company on Broadway. Meanwhile, the country headed toward a dark period that the escapist machinations of the 1920s no longer served. For Stella, the safest place was with the Group.

The first season of the Group Theatre closed with one success and two failures, but they had created a mystique. Their acting differed from that on Broadway, and critics and audiences alike were trying to figure out just what the actors were doing. Clurman didn't like the emphasis on the technique of acting; he believed the focus should be upon the social significance of the play, not how the actors performed. In reality, both the thematic choices and the acting were what created the intrigue. Broadway had never seen this particular type of theater. It was modeled after the Moscow Art Theater, but built upon the Yiddish theater, with purely American themes. American theater had witnessed a revolution.

CHAPTER TEN

The greatest performance she ever gave was in Success Story.

—Lee Strasberg

B Y THE END OF THEIR FIRST THEATRICAL SEASON THE GROUP'S funds were depleted. They lost their office at the Forty-Eighth Street Theatre. They had no plays to rehearse for the next season. To earn money some of the actors, including Stella, put on an improvisation show at the MacDowell Club on East Seventy-third Street. At least Crawford had secured a summer retreat: Sterling Farms, a camp in Dover Furnace, New York. A couple of Group members were released and new ones hired to take their place. Two inexperienced drama students came on board as apprentices. One of these was Elia Kazan.

A twenty-two-year-old student at Yale, Kazan wanted to be a director and told Clurman and Strasberg as much when he met with them. Kazan introduced himself to Clurman, but Strasberg characteristically kept himself occupied with the sports page. Strasberg finally tore his eyes away from the box scores and said, "Tell us what you want."[1] Kazan replied that he wanted Strasberg's job. Strasberg didn't appreciate the joke. Kazan then backpedaled, explaining that he wanted to direct. Despite the shaky introduction, Kazan received a letter inviting him to the Group's summer retreat as an apprentice.

The campgrounds at Sterling Farms, enveloped by hills and orchards, created a much-needed calming environment for the Group members after they had struggled through fall and winter in the city. The facilities included a cluster of cottages, a main building, a barn for rehearsing, and an array of recreational accommodations, including tennis courts and a swimming pool. What with playwrights, apprentices, spouses, and hangers-on, there were almost twice as many residents as there had been that first summer at Brookfield.

Strasberg remained sequestered from the Group out of preference, but also to reinforce his authority as the Group's director. The actors weren't as impressionable and blindly eager as they had been the previous summer. They wanted to develop their craft beyond Strasberg's emphasis on affective memory, which translated into experiments with improvisation and physical movement that left the actors exhausted and sore, yet happy to be stretching other creative muscles.

Politics remained part and parcel of contemporary life. The leftist members of the Group were endemic of a larger American idealization of Communism. The Communist Party, which surfaced after the Russian Revolution of 1917, saw the crash of 1929 as further evidence of the downfall of capitalism. Radical liberal groups and idealists held on to the hope of the Soviet Union's alternative economic system, which symbolized just the type of reform the United States needed to repair itself. Vehement political arguments were served up with dinner every night.

The next play, *Success Story*, by John Howard Lawson, reflected the nation's larger social issues through the relationship of Sarah Glassman, played by Stella, and Sol Ginsberg, played by Luther. Sol is a goal-oriented man with a radical leftist viewpoint in favor of the worker. His powerful ambition propels him to the top, but during his ascent he abandons his leftist politics. By the end of the play, rich yet unfulfilled, Sol searches for happiness in Sarah Glassman, who has loved him throughout but will not condone the betrayal of his former principles. At the end, Sarah shoots Sol in a struggle.

Sarah's character created controversy within the Group. The directors wanted Sarah to be vindicated by having the character explicitly tell Sol why she has turned against him, essentially asking the playwright to rewrite the scene. Lawson argued that he wrote Sarah as a character just as caught up in escaping her life as Sol, only her political idealism appears to be a more acceptable escape than Sol's blind ambition. The debate over the play dovetailed with a strikingly similar development in the Group. One of the Group's leading men, Franchot Tone, announced that he was leaving for a career in the movies. It was a tremendous blow to morale. The very fabric of the Group was built upon service to the work and not oneself. Stella felt disillusioned, although Tone's departure magnified Stella's own conflict with wanting international stardom. Yet Stella's growing animosity toward Strasberg's direction still proved to be her most immediate challenge.

From her point of view, Strasberg didn't have any serious theatrical experience besides a couple of years with an amateur group of students and a few months at the Lab. She begrudged Strasberg's position as the director of the Group, which gave him unlimited authority. In the Yiddish theater, the actors were paramount. There were no directors. The actors directed and played their parts, participating in both the interpretation and the execution of the play. Strasberg stifled Stella's creativity. Meanwhile, Stella's entitled attitude and flamboyance irritated Strasberg. He found her tendency toward emotionalism artificial. At one point during rehearsals, he told her, "If you cry, I'll kill you."[2] Strasberg later explained, "I wanted it all pent up. If she cried she'd be Stella again. Stella cries the contents of several buckets. . . . Her problem's defining and containing the emotion. If I'd let Stella act like flamboyant Stella then she'd play only one part over and over."[3]

The company returned to the city destitute. Worse, a new policy had to be enacted, one that betrayed the previous Group practice of keeping all its members on the payroll. Now it could afford to subsidize only those actors in the current production. Once again, everything depended upon the upcoming season.

Success Story opened on September 16, 1932, at the Maxine Elliott Theatre. It bothered neither Stella nor Luther that they were cast opposite one another as romantic leads; in the Yiddish theater siblings were often cast as lovers. Still, the question of how Stella's character would be vindicated after murdering Sol remained to be seen. Bobby Lewis, assistant manager of the production, remembered how Stella solved the problem:

Luther and Stella are in the office in the middle of the night, and although she has tried to wipe him out of her heart, he pleads once more for her to save him from himself. In the ensuing struggle, with Stella trying to free herself from his grasp, she grabs the gun he has brought along and fires it into his side. Holding his body in her arms, all the while paraphrasing the biblical Song of Solomon (make me a wilderness, etc.) Stella set up a kind of keening that was shattering to her and to the audience. She had taken as her emotional reference the legend that, during World War I, young British soldiers, under the unbearable pressure of relentless shelling, had been heard to speak Chaucerian English. It was found that when agonized by overpowering, relentless stress you can suffer a regression not only to your own earlier age, but to a period long before your time. Anyone who witnessed that acting feat of Stella's might well wonder when he would see the like again.[4]

Initially, the play was both praised and rebuked. A week into the performance, the review in the *New York Times* read, "As Sol Ginsberg, Luther Adler makes the play his. He acts with brimstone passion. . . . Stella Adler gives a splendid performance, profound, emotional, true."[5] Stella's performance in the final scene became legendary overnight. Noel Coward was one of several actors who showed up during the last act just to see the finale.[6]

As the production carried on, Stella held up in energy while Luther seemed to be growing weary. Exasperated by her brother, Stella instigated arguments, perhaps to rouse him to action. Some nights he seemed to just go through the motions. The arguments became so frequent that the quarrelling siblings couldn't even keep it backstage, proceeding to take stabs at each other between curtain calls.

Meanwhile the Group came up with creative new ways to promote the play. "The directors took out ads stressing the Adlers' highly praised performances."[7] A month after *Success Story* opened, the Group organized a Sunday symposium. Everyone was invited: the playwright, the scene designer, the lead actors, even the electrician. The front lights of the Maxine Elliot Theatre beckoned while the rest of Broadway's theaters were dark, as was the custom on Sunday evenings. The idea behind the gathering came from Clurman's often-voiced opinion that his communal Group Theatre should not be restricted to the people putting on the play; rather, there should also be a "Group" audience. The attendance that night consisted of a "comfortable-sized" crowd, according to the *New York Times*, with a "warmth and excitement about things theatrical such as one rarely encounters even at the congregation of first-nighters."[8]

The evening consisted of questions and answers, with the audience suggesting some of the answers. Ironically, one attendee complained to the playwright that the ending, the very scene between Sol and Sarah that had been problematic during rehearsals, was not logical. Lawson defended himself by relying on his position as author and authority, explaining that in drama, emotional logic is different from intellectual logic. The passionate interest of these theatergoers inspired the Group while demonstrating the impact it was making on the modern theatrical scene.

That fall Stella rented out her living room to Harold's best friend, Aaron Copland, attesting to her increasing financial difficulties with maintaining a certain standard of living. Though times were difficult, Stella scraped by on poetry and scene readings. She did whatever it took to maintain an outer presentation of affluence. That November Dawn Powell, the author of the next Group play, attended a concert by the harpsichordist Sylvia Marlowe. She spotted Stella at the concert in an extravagant ensemble of evening gown, hat, and gloves. Powell wrote about her impression of Stella that night in her diary: "Stella looking lovely and vain as she should. Portrait of her in bedroom in rococo, luscious (almost lush, almost blowzy) style, and I said 'Very good of you.' 'Why is it good?' she angrily demanded. 'Because it looks lush and arrogant.' She almost stamped her foot. 'I am not arrogant. I'm only a little Jewish girl in a big hat!'"[9]

Stella's defensiveness no doubt came from feeling judged by Powell. At a time when over ten million Americans were unemployed, Stella's opulence could easily be dismissed as frivolousness; it also flew in the face of the Group Theatre's socialist ideology. In truth, Stella's expense account did not allow for frivolity. Her ensembles were costumes she put together: bought at discount, handed down, borrowed, and arranged creatively with pins to look tailored to fit. The majority of Stella's clothing and accessories were given to her. Sought after for her celebrity and grandeur, people, men in particular, had a propensity for giving Stella presents, from articles of clothing to dinners. When gifts were not forthcoming Stella would "borrow" what she wanted. Bobby Lewis used to tell how Stella would repeatedly order pianos she could not afford. The piano would be delivered, Steinway would call, and Stella would tell them she was sending in a payment. When they called again, she would tell them the check was on the way. Finally, when she moved out of the apartment, she called the store to inform them that they needed to pick up the instrument, never having made a single payment.[10]

Stella's expectations conformed to those of her parents' era in terms of her extravagance of dress and home. However anachronistically, Stella resented accounting for the way in which she so conspicuously differed from her contemporaries—another reminder of not fitting in. Her queenly flare was less an attempt to stand out than her way of upholding the majesty of her upbringing.

By contrast, Stella's comrades in the Group shared a railroad flat at 440 West Fifty-seventh Street that they called Groupstroy, after the Dnieperstroy Dam, a hydroelectric plant erected in Ukraine and a symbol of Russian achievement.[11] The digs at Groupstroy could have come straight from the set of a Gorky play: a bleak, unheated, cramped top-floor apartment with ten rooms. The actors amassed their resources to pay the rent of fifty dollars and buy groceries for meals, which they took turns cooking. Odets started writing a play in the kitchen closet, which he aptly titled *I Got the Blues* but would one day become *Awake and Sing!* Strasberg cloistered himself with his books in the room he shared with Paula Miller. Kazan introduced his comrades to his native Anatolian dish: bulgur flavored with tomatoes, onions, and lamb-kidney bits.[12] Even Harold moved in after he lost his small apartment on Fifty-eighth Street. Stella didn't want to take him in, for various reasons—a wise choice with a five-year-old and Madame Adler in the house. Neither of them was good at toning down the volume of their arguments.

Success Story was still running in November, and though tickets were selling, the theater owner insisted on money up front from the box office. None of the actors received an increase in salary. Not knowing how long the play would run, the Group began where they left off on rehearsals for their next play: *Big Night*. It would be Crawford's directing debut. Stella's small role allowed her to simultaneously play in *Success Story*, which closed in early January, and rehearse for *Big Night*, which opened mid-January. The play was not the usual Group material, but rather a light comedy. The actors, used to preparing for their performances through rigorous exercises, wanted to imbue their characters with a depth the play did not have. *Big Night* closed four days after it opened. Its failure was not as disappointing as the fact that the Group had no other plays to work on.

The directors decided to close the season, destroying Stella's dream of having a permanent theater. She blamed Harold. An already troubled relationship resulted in a more serious fissure between the two. Kazan later wrote about his impression of the quarrelsome couple at the time: "Harold was holding the actress rather against her will that he believed he had to be constantly flattering. . . . The anxious devotion he showed her gave him the aspect of a cuckold. . . . In Stella's court, Harold was the clown and like the clown didn't seem embarrassed by his behavior."[13] Throughout the years, many people would have this same impression of Harold, but he seemed to be neither self-conscious nor hindered in his attempts to make Stella happy.

Desperate and broke, the idea arose of relocating the Group to Boston or Chicago, in the hopes that productions would fare better outside New York. The directors couldn't agree on the move. Crawford wanted to go, Strasberg didn't. Clurman was indecisive—New York seemed to be the place to make the most profound impact. He calculated that the Group needed $60,000 to begin a repertory season in New York. Little did he know that a sum close to his calculations had been offered to Strasberg.

A socialite with a love for the theater wanted to invest $50,000 in the Group. She tried contacting Strasberg, but he neglected to return her calls. Finally she tracked him down at Groupstroy. The benefactress patiently waited for Strasberg in the dreary apartment when he finally appeared in his usual tight-lipped way, not even introducing himself, but waiting for her to explain her reason for visiting. She conveyed how much she admired the Group and its ideals and wanted to invest with a check she had brought. Strasberg did not respond and remained silent until the woman finally left with the money. Years later Strasberg ruefully explained that he didn't know what the Group would have done with the money at the time.[14] Perhaps feeling indebted to some entity was merely too compromising for a man who liked to retain creative control. There were plenty of ways the Group could have used the money, not the least of which would have been to follow Clurman's idea of creating a season of repertory and choosing their own plays.

Instead, the members of the Group fended for themselves during the remainder of that long winter of 1932. Just as the snow was melting the following March, the nation witnessed an unprecedented fatality to its economic system. In early February Michigan was the first state to put into effect a weeklong bank holiday. By March 1 several more states had shut their banks' doors. On March 4 Chicago and New York, the two financial nerve centers of the country, closed their banks. Just as the national banking system collapsed and widespread panic rippled through the country, a voice came over the radio to reassure the people. Franklin Delano Roosevelt delivered his presidential inauguration speech: "This is pre-eminently the time to speak the truth, frankly and boldly. Nor need we shrink from honestly facing conditions in our country today. This great nation will endure and has endured, will revive and will prosper. So, first of all, let me assert my firm belief that the only thing we have to fear is fear itself—nameless, unreasoning, unjustified terror which paralyzes needed efforts to convert retreat into advance."[15]

In the same spirit, the Group did not crumble under a precipitous closing season. By summer, ready to revive itself, the Group arranged their retreat in Green Mansions, a place Kazan described as a "camp for adults who like to pig out on kosher food, then chase each other into bed."[16] That summer Kazan became an official member of the Group, assigned the job of stage manager. In his effort to be indispensable to the Group, he earned the nickname Gadget (or Gadge, as most called him), presenting himself with every opportunity to be on hand to fix a broken prop or deliver a timely message.

In exchange for room and board, the Group had to entertain the camp guests three times a week. Clurman arrived early with ten actors to put on a Memorial Day show; he expected Stella to come with the rest of the company on June 19, but she did not show up. Nor did she bother to tell Harold when she might arrive; rather, she told Odets to inform Harold that she would be coming a few days late. From Stella's point of view there wasn't much reason to report on time. She knew she would have little to do after having been cast as the lead in two plays the previous season. She was disappointed that Harold had still not asserted himself in the Group beyond the role of spiritual guru. She and many of the other actors wondered if Clurman would ever practice what he preached and actually direct a production.

Strasberg directed the play that summer, *Crisis*, later renamed *Men in White*, with an intense regimen of improvisation and sense memory. He arranged to have the actors visit a hospital to study doctors and nurses in the workplace. The first five weeks he had the actors work on improvisations based on situations that would heighten their sense of being doctors. For the operation scene he rehearsed the actors' tempo by having them run through the scene to Beethoven's Seventh Symphony and then again to the farcical quick-paced rhythm of Jacques Offenbach's *Gaîté Parisienne*.[17] They rehearsed the choreography more than a hundred times over three months. As for individual characterizations, Strasberg continued to emphasize the actors' internal emotions, asking the actor what would motivate him to behave a certain way. Stella observed rehearsals, more interested in getting at what the character felt than what the actor felt.

The newer members of the Group invested themselves in Strasberg's methods, but by the third season most of the original players had begun questioning his demands. Phoebe Brand, who played the love intrigue of one the doctors in the play, felt Strasberg's direction made her acting more difficult. Deeply involved in an affective memory exercise, by the time she had to act, she "was so full of . . . conflicting emotions" she couldn't "play the scene."[18] Another actress in the Group, Margaret Barker, had to play a love scene in which she was supposed to be sitting in her lover's lap while thinking about a personal memory that took place in Italy. "Well, that was mad! It took me out of the reality of the play."[19]

The actors were actually relieved by the effortless responsibility of playing for their meals. They forgot about affective memory and offered the retreat's guests everything from melodrama and improvisation to musical revues. On the Fourth of July, Stella and the other actresses danced in a chorus line, scantily dressed in patriotic colors. Odets continued working on *I Got the Blues*, with Clurman trying out scenes with Luther and Stella.

Men in White opened on September 26, 1933, and was an instant box-office success. The play's sentimental plot about the lives of doctors and nurses dedicated to healing others seemed hackneyed to the Group. They were more interested in the socialist ideals of plays like *Success Story*. While only a few years earlier the nation reveled in their personal dramas and ignored political and social matters, by 1933 any astute citizen was prone to be a Communist sympathizer and brother-in-arms with the factory worker and sharecropper. Upper-crust debutantes were marching with garment workers or raising money for the defense of Haywood Patterson in the famous case of the Scottsboro Boys. Intellectuals all over the country were studying Marx and Lenin. Stella, who was not engaged in the current Group production, followed the trend and enrolled in a class on Marxism at the New York Workers School.

People from all walks of life joined the Communist Party and left it just as readily when they lost interest or their democratic principles pulled them away. It was a citizen's right, and one commonly exercised, to join any political party he or she wanted. Meanwhile, conservatives still benefiting from the capitalist system feared the Communist inclination toward rebellion.

In December Odets finished *I Got the Blues*. He had been setting his hopes on the Group performing the play, but with *Men in White* still in production and making money, Strasberg was not open to reading the play. Ironically, Odets ended up optioning the play to the management company that became the recipient of the $50,000 Strasberg had turned down. Meanwhile, for their second production of the season the Group decided to put on John Howard Lawson's *Gentlewoman*.

Stella was cast in the lead role as Gwyn Ballantine, much to the dismay of the other Group actresses, who hadn't had one lead role while Stella had had two. As in *Success Story*, when Strasberg threatened to kill Stella if she cried, her theatricality unnerved him. Indeed, having grown up in the Yiddish theater, with its gut-wrenching melodrama, Stella allowed her emotional nature to pour forth. Stella followed Strasberg's direction loyally, repeatedly practicing gestures and laboring over speech patterns for her character's personality and submerging herself in affective memory exercises, but she was desolate. Under Strasberg's direction, there was no joy in acting. Lawson "felt that not only was she [Stella] all wrong for Gwyn, but the method made her worse."[20]

Gentlewoman opened on March 22, 1934, at the Cort Theatre. "The critics," wrote Group Theatre scholar Wendy Smith, "divided about fifty-fifty on whether Stella Adler was miscast or not: quite a few praised her intelligence and attention to detail in the role, and even those who found her mannered and ill at ease went out of their way to mention how good her work had been in the past."[21] The play itself was criticized for being convoluted; it closed a little over a week later. Stella grew restless and ambivalent. The Group Theatre seemed the best place for her, but Strasberg's interpretation of Stanislavski's method eroded her spirit for the stage. It was time to go to the Soviet Union and see the Moscow Art Theater for herself.

The failure of the play did not bode well for the actors, not the least of reasons being the toll *Gentlewoman* had taken on the Group's purse. More injurious to morale, non-Group actors had been cast in the play. The company felt they no longer had a part in the decision-making process of the Group; furthermore, they resented the fact that some actors were favored over others, and that consequently salaries were allotted arbitrarily. Stella, being one of the "favored" actors, couldn't say much to that grievance, but she was bothered by the inconsistency of the Group's promise to provide financial and professional security for its members.

Before Stella's departure, the Group planned a meeting. Clurman prepared a forty-page paper analyzing the Group's problems. He timed his speech for the evening before Stella's trip to the Soviet Union. "This was no easy matter," Clurman later wrote, "because what had to be taken into consideration was the whole complex of facts that went into the making of the theater: the state of our audience, the question of backing, the actual availability of new play scripts."[22] Clurman stressed that the goal of the Group was to become not a political theater company, but an "American theater."[23] Stella sat and listened, but her mind was already on things Russian. She left the next day on a trip that would mark the end of her dependence upon others for artistic fulfillment. She and the profession of acting would never be the same.

CHAPTER ELEVEN

We had all been suffering and Stella saved us.

—Phoebe Brand

I N 1934 THE SS *ÎLE DE FRANCE* WAS CONSIDERED ONE OF THE MOST beautifully decorated ships, the forerunner of the Art Deco design that dominated future passenger ships, but it wasn't the largest or swiftest ocean liner. Stella's trip would be a leisurely spring passage to the Continent. Packing for transatlantic travel was an arduous task, but also a bit like wrapping presents: the excitement of opening the trove still lay ahead. Stella's itinerary included stops in several European cities before reaching the Soviet Union. Packing for the voyage necessitated deliberation: she needed day and evening outfits, bathing suits, recreational attire for shuffleboard and tennis, cocktail dresses for dinner, and an assortment of hats. The bulk of her wardrobe and that of her daughter would be delivered to the ship separately. A fashion-conscious woman like Stella could require as many as twenty trunks full of gowns, hats, and shoes. Stella had arranged for Ellen's father, now residing in England, to meet the ship. Seven-year-old Ellen would be staying with him in London for the remainder of the spring and through the summer.

After setting sail, Stella had ample time to ponder Harold's address to the Group the previous night, especially the part about its taking "ten years to build a theater." She had been at it for four years and already felt taxed. In his speech Harold had delineated the major complaints: a lack of Group morale, socially relevant plays, and secure salaries. But it was one thing to identify the problems and an entirely different thing to correct them. Interestingly, Strasberg was also traveling to the Soviet Union. Who knew what he would glean from seeing Stanislavski's system at work? Stella no doubt hoped Strasberg might grasp on to something beyond affective memory. As for Stella, she just wanted to rekindle her love of acting.

Stella and Ellen arrived in London, where Ellen became reacquainted with her father, whom she had no recollection of previously meeting but thought upon first impression as a "a nice man."[1] In Europe Stella encountered a continent imbued with an atmosphere particularly intolerant of Jews. Hitler had been the chancellor of Germany since 1932, and already Germans were indoctrinated with the Hitler salute. Only a year prior to Stella's visit, in 1933, the Sturmabteilung (SA), Germany's storm troopers, had attacked several Americans who had unknowingly failed to salute a passing parade. Years later, Stella recalled a story of how a society's training inheres in people's psyches. Six years after the war ended, Luther Adler was in Vienna playing Hitler in the film *The Magic Face*. Stella recalled, "He was out shooting a scene in an open car, and when people in the street saw him, they saluted! They couldn't get over their training."[2] Prior to the war, when these assaults on Americans increased to once or twice a month, the American ambassador to Germany, William E. Dodd, met with the German foreign minister to protest the episodes, even while making efforts to keep the incidents from the ears of the American press for fear of "exaggeration."[3]

That spring Heinrich Himmler appointed Reinhardt Heydrich chief of the Gestapo. The earlier brutality of Germany's secret police paled in comparison to the outright terror the new leadership would unleash. Germans were afraid to voice anything that might be construed as unpatriotic. Jews were removed from positions in various fields such as the press and the police. Jewish doctors and dentists were barred from treating patients under Germany's social insurance system. Boycotts were led against Jewish-owned shops and businesses. Earlier that year Jewish holidays had been removed from official German calendars. En route to Moscow, Stella may have come across the latest edition of Julius Streicher's magazine, *Der Stürmer*, which featured a story accusing Jews of murdering gentile children for ritual sacrifice. The resurfacing of the centuries-old blood-libel myth would have been especially poignant for Stella, returning to the Soviet Union, the land from which her father had had to flee only half a century before, and now the cultural hotbed of acting craft.

Stella spoke rudimentary Russian, but the emotional language of the stage was universal. Almost immediately she found acting in the Soviet Union to be as near to perfect as she could imagine. It was not so different from her Yiddish upbringing in that the theater was open year round, but unlike American actors, the Russians studied. All the important theaters were connected to a "technicum" or master, whose technique they studied for three years. "The courses they have!" Stella gushed in an interview published in *New Theater* the following year. "I've never seen anything like it: three or four forms of acting work, dancing, acrobatics, plastique, gymnastics. . . . In the Meyerhold classes I saw feats of diction performed by boys and girls eighteen and twenty, such as no actor I've heard could do. They actually stylize the voice production. They juggle with sounds. It is theatrically efficient speech."[4] There were classes on the history of theater and music; the leftist theaters studied Marxism and society. The acting companies lived together in collectives, dividing the work.

Most impressive was how the actors were appointed work. After studying, an actor either entered the company or was placed into another theater of the same tradition in the Soviet provinces. Stella marveled: "There's practically no unemployment!" Because the theaters were self-supporting and well attended, they could afford the best equipment. Stella was impressed by the costumes, which she thought "finer than anything I've seen by the best Paris couturiers. . . . But their equipment! In almost every theater, two revolving stages or three, and elevator stages."[5]

Stella lived on a menu of classes during the day and theater at night. One evening she saw *The Marvelous Metal* by V. Kirchon, which she thought a weak production. Not one to keep her opinions to herself, Stella asked the director why the audience cheered such a bad play. She saw how limited her perspective was when he assured her that the writer had talent, the designer had a "growing gift,"[6] and the actors were playing interesting roles. Audiences did not care about perfectly polished productions, he explained. They were interested in the development of the company and would keep attending until the production worked. Stella thought it was too good to be true. "The work isn't wasted," she realized, "it's seen. It's criticized seriously . . . it isn't kicked and annihilated the morning after. I tell you, I could weep. It's an actor's paradise."[7]

Stella inevitably ran into Strasberg at the theater. No doubt she wondered what his impression was. Strasberg was not impressed: "It was so bad I couldn't believe what I saw," he later told his biographer. Initially he had wanted to meet Stanislavski and express his gratitude, but after being so disenchanted with the productions he attended, Strasberg decided it was best not to. "What could I do? Tell him what I think of his theater? Say there is nothing more I can learn from him? How could a young shnook say to the Master, 'What do I see on your stage?'"[8]

Clurman arrived in Moscow in June. Later he wrote of how his experience there had been a turning point: "The effect of my Moscow trip was to release me. For four years I have lived, theatrically speaking, in Strasberg's shadow. . . . The variety of Soviet theater styles helped me find myself by showing me concretely how many possibilities there were."[9] One wonders whether he shared these thoughts with Stella during the ten days he spent in Moscow. Clearly, Clurman had turned a corner, or perhaps taken a short cut, toward the purpose that had long eluded him. He was meant for directing. After Moscow Clurman looked up his friend from his college days, the director Copeau, who informed Clurman that Stanislavski was presently in Paris convalescing from a heart attack. Clurman immediately sent a letter to Stanislavski and received a response with an invitation to meet. By then Stella had also left Moscow; she joined Harold in Paris.

There were few people whom Stella considered her equal, and even fewer who she thought were her superior. She had a childlike, almost starstruck fear of meeting people she admired, which was how she felt about the prospect of being introduced to Stanislavski. Clurman insisted they go, making his way to Stanislavski's hotel at the appointed hour with Stella in tow.

In the hotel elevator, Stella wrestled with her nerves as if it were opening night. She followed Harold to the entryway, where they could see Stanislavski in his room, as Harold later wrote, "ransacking his dictionary for the French equivalent of a Russian theatrical term."[10] Stanislavski's doctor was present, as well as Olga Chekhova, the widow of Anton Chekhov. Once Stella saw Stanislavski, she couldn't move.[11] Clurman proceeded into the apartment and greeted Stanislavski, while Stella remained at the door. Madame Chekhova turned to her: "You must go over and shake Mr. Stanislavski's hand."

"No." Stella responded. She couldn't find the ability to speak.

"You must," Madame Chekhova pressed.

"No, I musn't." Stella stood her ground, "unable to move forward or backward."[12]

Stanislavski's doctor had prescribed fresh air, and so it was the master's habit to venture out to the Bois de Boulogne every day. "I was touched and amused to see how shy he was," Clurman wrote, "as we all went down from his apartment in the lift, one of those tiny cubicles that could hold no more than three. . . . He was regally handsome, with beautiful white hair, and must have had a decided appeal for Stella: her father had also been majestically tall, with snow-white hair."[13] Harold was in the habit of seeing the world through Stella's eyes.

After promenading along the avenue, the coterie settled by a bench, everyone surrounding Stanislavski. After some time, as Stella wrote in an essay titled "How I Met Stanislavski," the master turned to her: "Young lady, everybody has spoken to me but you." Stella met his gaze and finally said, "Mr. Stanislavski, I loved the theater until you came along and now I hate it!"[14] "Perhaps," Stanislavski countered, "you don't understand the system. But if it really worries you, forget it."[15] Sharon Carnicke, a professor of theater and Stanislavski scholar, writes that Stanislavski "hated the dogmatic teacher who insists upon a single correct way."[16] Carnicke compares the system to a map for actors who could choose their own pathways to "reinvent and personalize the System."[17]

Strasberg and Stella held onto their own pathways, or interpretations, of Stanislavski's system. Strasberg delved into affective memory, which was a psychological approach, while Stella focused on what she gleaned from Stanislavski that fateful summer: the actor performs within the context or imaginary circumstances of the play through specific actions. "To play the simple truth of the play," Joanna Rotte, Stella's former student, writes, "from action to action, was, in Adler's memory, the single most important teaching given to her by Stanislavski."[18] When something works, it is natural to latch onto the "solution" as if it were the Holy Grail, especially if it is to be handed down to others. In the end, Stella and Strasberg had the same goal of truthful acting, but they each believed that their path to attaining that goal was the correct way.

With Stella in such a state of desperation, Stanislavski offered to help. The previous season she had grappled with Strasberg's direction of her as Gwyn Ballantine, her character in *Gentlewoman*, and so she chose a scene from that play to be translated into French, the language in which she and Stanislavski worked. For the next five weeks Stella and Stanislavski met to elucidate the system. Stella hired a secretary to facilitate communication and take notes.

Years later Stanislavski recalled meeting Stella. She had told him that her acting had been suffering since following his system. Stanislavski had wondered where his students Boleslavski and Ouspenskaya, who founded the Lab, had gone wrong. "They say my method is being introduced in America," Stanislavski said, "yet suddenly this talented actress who has studied my system 'withers away' before everyone's eyes. I had to take her on, if only to restore the reputation of my system. I wasted a whole month on it. It turned out that everything she had learnt was right. She had been shown and had studied everything in the school."[19]

Stanislavski asked Stella if she knew about the "through-line action and task." She asked for clarification, at which time they "broke up the part into pieces and made a chart of the main stages in the role." The chart illustrated forty categories for an actor to address. Stanislavski said that after explaining the chart, "she acted so brilliantly that we absolutely 'howled with delight.'" "Only an understanding of the through action and tasks," Stanislavski concluded, "can completely remake a person. Without this understanding everything is merely exercises on the system."[20]

In the scene from *Gentlewoman* Stanislavski pointed out that Gwyn's action was to end her friendship. Meanwhile, the action of her opposite character, Eliot, was to continue his offer of love.[21] Each gesture, response, vocal tone, and use of a prop should align with the overarching action of the character in the scene. The implications were groundbreaking for Stella. In every scene of a play, a character has an action or series of actions that lead to an overarching action, or what we might call the character's objective. The actor must know the character (and his physical surroundings, including props) so well that the choices he makes for his action are truthful.

The difference between Strasberg and Stella was simply the approach. Stella's grandson Tom Oppenheim summed it up when he wrote that for Stella, "the actor must first do, and the feelings will follow; for Strasberg the actor must first feel and doing will follow."[22] Stella would say you couldn't act feelings: the audience can't see what the actor is feeling, but they can see what he is doing.

In theory the difference was clear to Stella, but in practice it could get blurry. According to a transcription of one of Stella's classes, she said, "When I worked with Stanislavski in Paris he stressed the importance of the imagination. He explained in detail how important it was to use the circumstances. . . . All the emotion required of you can be found through your imagination and in the circumstances of the play."[23] But then she added: "If you need an action you can't find in a play then you can go back to your own life—but not for the emotion, rather for a similar action. In your own personal experience you had a similar action to which you had an emotional response. Go back to the action and the specific circumstances and remember what you did. If you recall the place, the feelings will come back to you."[24] Stella was not espousing the idea that a student take a moment to place himself in the memory of his past while also being in the play's circumstances. Rather, she emphasized remembering a "similar action," and "remember[ing] what you did," not what you felt—which, although it has been misinterpreted, is exactly what affective memory asks of the actor. The Stanislavski scholar Sharon Carnicke argues the same point when describing how Stanislavski told

> actors [that] analogous experiences help create characters, [but] he does not advise the use of personal memories in a direct way. He may write that every time you perform a role you must "experience feelings analogous to your own," . . . and that "thanks to the analogies between your sentiments and the character's, many places in the role will come to life easily and quickly in you," but he also reminds you that "analogies spring from recollections gleaned from your reading and from stories about other people" as readily as from your personal life.[25]

Just as Strasberg taught the character's overarching action and the importance of the imagination, Stella utilized affective memory in the way that Stanislavski intended it to be used. The Method, as David Krasner writes, is not "mutually exclusive; one facet of the Method does not cancel out another."[26]

At her last lesson with Stanislavski, Stella vowed that she would take her knowledge back to the United States and correct the "misinterpretations" of the master's system. She would lead acting back in the right direction, making it an artistic mode an actor could spend his lifetime practicing and honing, a mode based on action. A mode that would stand up performance after performance because it was discovered through rigorous examination of the play until the actor understood and could portray his character as a pianist would play a concerto, experiencing the music—or the character— in the raw presence of the performance. "As I walked away [from Stanislavski]," Stella recalled, "somewhere in me I said, 'I'll pay you back for this, Mr. Stanislavski, with all my heart. I'll pay you back.'"[27]

For the first time, Stella couldn't wait to get back to the Group Theatre.

In August Stella returned to New York carrying the building blocks that would diversify, enhance, and hone a model for the future of acting. Entering the harbor on that hot day—thirty-three years old, a seven-year-old daughter in tow—the most important thing on Stella's mind was going upstate to the Group's retreat in Ellensville.

Cheryl Crawford had procured a place in the Catskills featuring a rickety, damp Gothic hotel where the Group would rehearse for the next play season. The fog-enshrouded grounds were perennially wet. The company included an entourage of new apprentices, one of whom was the young Jules (John) Garfield, "8 dogs, 21 victrolas, 3 radios, 14 motor cars, a complete library of symphony records, a lot of books on the theater, 4 colored waiters, [and] Alexander Kirkland's dog who has lost all his fur."[28] The only solace to another summer with such a motley crew was Stella's excitement over sharing the news from Stanislavski.

The minute Stella arrived she assembled a meeting. "Lee sat strong-faced," writes Cindy Adams, "all tucked in, salvaging whatever he could of his plucked plumage. . . . Short on underplay and humility, Stella, looking glamorous in her fresh-from-Paris wardrobe, stood tall, towering over even those who were standing."[29] Stella displayed Stanislavski's chart, explaining that if the actor worked through the various points in the chart, the emotions needed for his performance would derive from the play itself, from the character's through-line action. The actors didn't need to drudge up personal memories.

That year several of the actors had enlisted in the Communist Party. "There were pamphlets and slogans everywhere," writes Cindy Adams. "There were commitments to join marches and sign petitions."[30] A rebellious air ran through the troops. Odets resented Strasberg for not supporting his plays. Many of the actors were tiring of Strasberg's tyrannical direction. Stella's news was received like a doctor's second opinion, which miraculously provides a cure.

That summer of 1934, Stella began giving her first classes.[31]

Stella acknowledged that an actor naturally draws upon himself to create a character, but only so far as to choose the actions that elicit a truthful emotion in himself for the character. This is what she meant when she told her fellow Group member Eunice Stoddard, in a class she taught in 1936, that "the choice of the things that you do is your talent."[32] That dictum—in your choice lies your talent—would become Stella's hallmark. The focus on choices lifts the actor to the status of coauthor—not simply an interpreter, but a craftsperson whose most valuable resource is his creative imagination.

Bobby Lewis, recalling the summer Stella returned, remembered that he "felt the fog lifting."[33] While Strasberg sat in silent embarrassment, the rest of the room was charged. Afterward Phoebe Brand summed up the actors' reaction in an interview with the author: "We had all been suffering and she saved us. . . . because she brought back the word from Stanislavski so we didn't have to do that [affective memory] kind of nonsense."[34] The next day Strasberg called his own meeting and outlined his experience in the Soviet Union over the summer: the Group did not use Stanislavski's system, he announced; it was "Strasberg's method" that they practice.[35] According to Clurman, Strasberg "decided to take advantage of the suggestions furnished by Stella's report, and to use what he could of the "innovations" in Stanislavski's method." However, Clurman said, "the 'improvements' of recent import tended to weaken Strasberg's grip on his own method."[36]

That summer marked the genesis of a lifelong argument between Stella and Strasberg and spawned the greatest polemic in twentieth-century acting.

The actors wanted to learn more. Stella explained that the actions performed on the stage must be figured out before going on in order to "find freedom on the stage."[37] Again, she reminded the actors that they didn't have to substitute their own personal memories, but could experience and portray the character's emotion when truly connected to the physical world of the play, right down to the props. Once the actor personalizes the character's inner and outer world, truthful acting will result. "In life," Stella explained, "we take the paper off the flowers and put them down. It is not a problem, but for the stage you must get acquainted—the look, smell, do you like them, how big a vase do they need, etc. Stanislavski says you must know these things as well as you know your aunt. You must be free of them when you act."[38]

Tension in the Group climaxed at rehearsals for *Golden Eagle Guy*. In one of the final rehearsals Margaret Barker, playing the character of a high-society hostess (a character not dissimilar to one from Barker's own upbringing), was pouring tea for a group of women gathered in her home. One of these, played by Ruth Nelson, fell to the floor in a faint. Barker made a slight move toward Nelson before realizing she was not supposed to respond as dictated by her part. Strasberg asked, "What did you do that for?," to which Barker responded, "I'm terribly sorry, Lee. I know I'm not supposed to react to that. I made a mistake. May we go on?" But Strasberg slowly repeated the question. Barker apologized again and asked if they could continue. Strasberg pressed, "What did you do that for?"[39] Strasberg would not let it go, although it was clear the actress understood her mistake. Clearly Strasberg needed to feel, in the midst of the Group's dissension, that he was in control.

Nelson could not stand by and let Barker be demoralized. Describing the scene, Odets's biographer writes, "Ruth said, in a way that you knew she meant, 'I'm going to kill him.' No drama in it, just very simply and quietly. . . . Lee saw her coming at him and saw genuine murder in her eye, and he turned around and ran out of the theater, and never came back to the rehearsals of the play, which was finished by Harold. And that was the first directing Harold did—Lee refused to come back to production."[40]

The summer dragged on miserably. Many of the animals died, and the wet weather spread ringworm from the dogs to the actors. The company was no longer united under Strasberg's guiding hand. Stella's relationship with Harold was as strained as ever; he simply wasn't living up to her or the rest of the Group's expectations of a leader. Clurman found his own validation through a playwriting class he began teaching that summer, analyzing "dramatic technique from the Greeks to Sean O'Casey."[41] This mood of inadequacy and frustration culminated in Odets's struggle to be taken seriously as a playwright. He wanted to express the decaying American society around him. Something needed to be done, and yet even the man Odets admired most, Harold Clurman, could not stand up to his girl: "Stella is tearing out Harold's heart: she takes a bite and spits the whole business away,"[42] Odets wrote in his diary.

Oblivious to Odets's resentment toward her, Stella was fond of Clifford. She remembered how removed he was that summer. When they spoke to each other "he was always so phony," she remembered, "but also so babyish, sweet, and crazy."[43] Odets continued to hammer out *Awake and Sing!* Clurman had gone through the edits of the play. He believed in the play and wanted to put it on, but he was the odd man out. When Odets offered up the play, Strasberg struck him down, saying, "You don't seem to understand, Cliff. We don't like your play."[44]

That summer Odets began a new play titled *Paradise Lost.* One evening he had such an exceptional bout of writing that he put away his script and went out to celebrate with some of the other actors. They ended up drunk and went shouting through a neighboring town, where "Kazan started throwing flower pots around."[45] The troublemakers had to spend the night in jail.

Stella looked upon Odets as a creative, impetuous child. He was only four years younger, but she was worldly and more experienced than he. Stella intuitively connected to the artistic potential in people. She did not know he would turn out to be one of the most important playwrights of the century, but she recognized his creative spirit and encouraged his art.

By early October the Group was ready to present the previous season's plays, taking them to Boston to see how they would fare. *Men in White*, now a recognized Broadway hit that had been adapted into a film, seemed a perfect candidate for a revival, but the production coincided with the play's movie release. Unable to compete with the big screen, *Success Story* was remounted, opening at the Majestic Theatre on October 29 with Stella revisiting her character, Sarah Glassman, opposite Luther. The reviews were superb. The *Boston Herald* highlighted Luther's journey to find the right costume for his character, Sol, which had to be balanced delicately between shabby and presentable. "He had scoured the second-hand mart, had looked over his own wardrobe, had tried on all his friends' clothes to no avail." Still without a costume on the day of dress rehearsal, Luther spotted the Group's scenic designer, Mordecai Gorelik.

> On Mr. Gorelik was a gray woolen suit. He was going innocently about his business when he found himself pleasantly distracted from his work by a torrent of enthusiastic remarks from Mr. Adler. The latter's interest in the setting and in the art of the scenic design in general was so deep that it required Mr. Gorelik's accompaniment in the dressing room of Mr. Alder for further discussion. . . . Ten minutes later one man came down the stairs arrayed in a gray woolen suit, well worn with precisely the awkward roominess of a suit that Sol Ginsberg would wear as a $25-a-week clerk who had not been around much. Mr. Adler was costumed![46]

Stella used the press's attention to voice her own beliefs. She told the *Boston Globe*, "The theater should be the actor's home. It should not be the place where he comes for a few hours a day to rehearse a play. Being an actor isn't just a job."[47] No doubt her recent trip to the Soviet Union had kindled her nostalgia for and belief in the theater as a lifestyle. There were other important causes that her time in Europe illuminated. As when she was three years old raising money for the Kishinev survivors, Stella found herself returning to Jewish assistance work. On November 2 Stella addressed the Associated Jewish Philanthropies headquarters: "Everywhere on the continent there is Jewish suffering and a fear of what the morrow might bring is in the heart of every Jew and Jewess. . . . This is the first Jewish gathering in many months where I've heard laughter and joy prevailing. That you have the opportunity to give should be even a greater joy after knowing what is going on throughout the world."[48] Stella's words were touching, but Americans in general, even Jewish Americans, were out of touch with the plight of their brethren across the ocean. It was 1934, and the United States was contending with an economic crisis.

To make matters worse, that spring a two-day dust storm destroyed land ready to be planted, blowing wind and debris clear to the East Coast.

The Dust Bowl would continue to ravage the American prairie throughout the 1930s, further buckling the economy. Though President Roosevelt had introduced his New Deal reforms to battle the economic catastrophe, ordinary Americans saw little improvement in their day-to-day lives. The Communist Party criticized the government's perceived impotence and continued to focus on fighting for civil rights and labor organization. The time was ripe for the ideals set forth by the Group Theatre, crystallized through the plays of Clifford Odets.

One day Odets read in the *New Masses* about a taxi strike and set out to write a one-act play about it. On October 31, 1934, Odets rounded up the actors in the basement of the Majestic Theatre and read his short play, titled *Waiting for Lefty*. Set at an assembly of cab drivers planning a strike, the play frames the audience to be included in this meeting. It was a perfect Group play, socially relevant and audience inclusive. The "workers" play energized and unified the actors. Referring to Odets, Luther Adler said to Clurman, "Harold, the Group has produced the finest revolutionary playwright in America."[49]

After six weeks in Boston the ensemble returned to New York to open *Gold Eagle Guy* on November 28 at the Morosco Theatre. The reviewers appreciated the play more than audiences, though in ambiguous remarks such as "the Group Theatre has found a salty script and given it an interesting production."[50] Stella had a small role, of which Brooks Atkinson wrote: "Although Stella Adler's portrait of Adah Menken, the 'divine Jewess,' is not precisely voluptuous, it has character."[51] Backstage Luther quipped, "Boys, I think we're working on a stiff."[52]

After eight floundering weeks in New York, the directors met. Clurman, always the optimist, wanted to figure out a way to save the production, but Strasberg decided to close the play. Ticket prices had already been discounted, and actors were getting job offers elsewhere. Cheryl Crawford, caught between Strasberg's resoluteness and Clurman's reluctance, voted in favor of shutting down the play. Again the odd man out, Clurman was charged with the unpleasant task of breaking the news to the company.

Clurman entered the basement of the Belasco Theatre, where the company of sour-faced, disgruntled actors had assembled. This wasn't the first time the directors had preemptively closed down a season. It wasn't the first time they had been at a loss with what to work on next. What good were leaders if they couldn't come through with their promise of steady employment?

Clurman announced the decision to close the season. Stella was livid and came armed with her own special threat to Harold: his heart. She "scornfully told [Clurman] that it was the most abject weakness for the directors to close our season in January."[53] She turned to the actors and, with the vehemence of a general's call to arms, said, "We'll find our own play!"[54] The company responded in keeping with the revolutionary spirit of the times, demanding to keep the theater running.

Several days later Odets gathered the actors to read the play he had started writing in a closet at Groupstroy, *Awake and Sing!* The directors were not invited. It was a cold January evening when the actors first listened to the turbulent true-to-life portrait of a Bronx family struggling through the Depression. By the third act, their faces glowed with delight. The directors entered the room toward the end of the reading; a palpable current of excitement charged the air. At the last word, Luther Adler stood up and said, "This is the play we are going to do."[55] Strasberg grimaced at such unilateral decision making. Stella chimed in: "Is it better to disband, and those who can get jobs will, and the rest go cold and hungry? What's the matter with this play, why shouldn't we do this play? Put it on!"[56] The Adlers had spoken with the weight of the Yiddish theater behind them. They knew a theater could employ its actors year around. Not only was it possible, it was the way theater worked; it was the actor's life. It had been decided. The next Group production would be *Awake and Sing!*

CHAPTER TWELVE

*Stella showed us how to plunge into life, not imitate it, and
then send it out, selected and purified, to the audience.*

—John Randolph

W HEN STELLA WAS A CHILD, TWO WORLD-RENOWNED ACTORS CAME
to play at Jacob's Grand Theatre. One of the visitors gave Stella
a hat with two rabbits on it that she was quite fond of and wore
to watch the production. Normally Stella was either backstage or onstage.
This night she sat in the audience. From her box seat Stella could feel
the excitement of the playgoers shuffling in, the intangible anticipation
of a night at the theater and the wonderful, although sometimes tragic,
world the entire house would enter. Yiddish audiences didn't adhere to
the concept of the fourth wall: they cried and laughed with each other
and the players onstage. Being at the theater was like being in one's living
room, absorbing one another and the characters in the play as a unit, a
family. Stella marveled at how life and theater mingled into one undeniable
happening night after night.

Being in the audience, however, was an exciting change for the girl.
Before the play began, she couldn't take her eyes off the red plush stage
curtain, which was embroidered in gold and green satin thread with a
tableau of colorful scenes.[1] Stella studied the two-dimensional work of art
spread out in front of her, promising to unveil a world that would spirit her
away.

Some two decades later, on January 6, 1935, Stella found herself again
sitting in an audience. Instead of her father's theater, she was at Eva Le
Gallienne's Civic Repertory Theatre watching Odets's *Waiting for Lefty*.
An announcement was tucked in on a throwaway leaflet of the program

without the playwright's name on it. It simply said that the cast of *Golden Eagle Guy*, the latest Group Theatre production, would present the play.

Stella's mother and elder brother Jay accompanied her. After sitting through a short play by Paul Green and a dance performance, the audience relaxed to wait through the final act of a typical benefit show. Stella knew better. She had heard Odets's play the previous October with the rest of the Group. The show about to begin was no ordinary play.

Waiting for Lefty opens with six or seven cab drivers sitting in a semicircle, working-class men dressed the part. Morris Carnovsky, playing Harry Fatt, says: "You're so wrong I ain't laughing. Any guy with eyes to read knows it. Look at the textile strike—out like lions in like lambs."

The audience immediately identified the sound and demeanor of the common New Yorker off the street, and as the other actors chimed in about the question of a strike, the viewers leaned forward as if to jump from their seats and join the debate. Clurman watched from the side: "The first scene of *Lefty* had not played two minutes when a shock of delighted recognition struck the audience like a tidal wave. Deep laughter, hot assent, a kind of joyous fervor seemed to sweep the audience toward the stage. The actors no longer performed; they were being carried along as if by an exultancy of communication such as I had never witnessed in the theater before. Audience and actors had become one."[2]

That winter was a particularly harsh one, the Atlantic Ocean packed with ice from Nantucket Island to the mainland, but the sincerity of Odets's characters warmed the spirits of an audience weather-worn and beleaguered by three long years of an economic depression. The previous year's passage of the National Recovery Act and its section giving employees the right to organize "and bargain collectively through representatives of their own choosing . . . free from the interference, restraint, or coercion of employers" prompted the formation of labor unions across the nation, demanding better work conditions and wages.[3] Odets's prescient play voiced the anger and promise of the new year, a year in which 1,834 work stoppages and strikes interrupted industry across the country.[4]

At the close of *Lefty*, the audience is directly addressed: "Well, what's the answer?" Odets and a couple other stagehands had rehearsed to reply, "Strike!" To the actors' astonishment, another cry of "Strike!" echoed across the auditorium, and then another, until an entire choir of "Strike! Strike!" erupted as hundreds of people rose from their seats, stomping their feet so relentlessly that Ruth Nelson later recalled her fear that "they're going to bring the balcony down!"[5] Applause and approval shook the house for forty-five minutes and a total of twenty-six curtain calls, at which point the audience stormed the stage. Cheryl Crawford later recalled how the audience "wouldn't leave. I was afraid they were going to tear the seats out and throw them on the stage."[6]

The playwright watched, astonished by the audience's reaction: "There was such an at-oneness with audience and actors that the actors didn't know whether they were acting, and the audience got up and shouted 'Bravo! Bravo!' and . . . I found myself up on my feet shouting, 'Bravo, Luther!' In fact, I was part of the audience. I forgot I wrote the play. . . . The proscenium arch disappeared . . . when that happens . . . not by technical innovation, but when that happens emotionally and humanly, then you will have great theater."[7]

Stella had experienced the disappearance of the proscenium all her life. She understood how adversity unites people who otherwise—during socioeconomic and cultural stability—tend to isolate from their fellow man. A theater that acknowledges the intimate undercurrent of the spectators' lives will stir that audience in ways even the greatest tragedies cannot. Once again the union of life and theater, a coupling that was the essence of her own existence, revealed itself to her.

With an audience reluctant to leave, the stage manager finally closed the curtain, clearing the audience out onto the street, where they remained discussing the play. Sara Adler was surprised that the playwright was the same man who, when visiting their home, scavenged the plentiful bread on the table. Odets had been used to eating "shredded wheat," recalling that, "when I saw all that Jewish bread on the table, I'd just die."[8] Sara congratulated Odets while Jay ingratiatingly asked the young playwright for his first autograph.

Adrenalin and triumph took the cast and crew out into the night, embracing and laughing, raucously reliving what only a few hours earlier had enlarged their perception of the potential of theater. It was a vessel to empower the people, just as Clurman had preached in his Friday-evening talks. Wandering deliriously through the streets, some of the cast ended up in cafés and bars, unwilling to surrender the night. Odets finally settled into a cafeteria with his codirector, Sanford Meisner, who watched "Clifford at one of those long tables, very, very pale, tense, and absolutely quiet. He seemed like a person in shock."[9] Twilight nudged everyone home. By the following year *Waiting for Lefty* would be more frequently produced and more frequently banned all over the world—from Union Square to Moscow, from Tokyo to Johannesburg—than any other play in theatrical history."[10]

When the intoxication of *Lefty*'s premiere wore off, Clurman, who would be officially directing his first play, began casting *Awake and Sing!*

Stella came unglued when he gave her the part of Bessie Berger, the middle-aged head of the household. She categorically refused the part, envisioning herself as playing parts that would brandish her beauty. In her early thirties, at five feet eight inches tall, broad-shouldered and thin-wasted, Stella met or surpassed the height of the average man or woman, while her alabaster complexion complemented her almond-shaped, sea-colored eyes. The audacity of asking her to play a woman of fifty!

The role, it seems, had been preordained for Stella when Odets began drafting it. "On old notes for *I Got the Blues*," Odets's biographer points out, "we see the name 'Stella' changed to 'Bella' to 'Bessie.'"[11] Odets's portrait of the character couldn't resemble Stella more: "She loves life, likes to laugh, has great resourcefulness and enjoys living from day to day. A high degree of energy accounts for her quick exasperation at ineptitude. She is a shrewd judge of realistic qualities in people in the sense of being able to gauge quickly their effectiveness. In her eyes all of the people in the house are equal. She is naïve and quick in emotional response. She is afraid of utter poverty."[12]

Harold knew Stella well. The only way to skirt her vanity was to play to her artistry. Perhaps, he ventured, Stella was not *able* to pull off the role. Stella hastily corrected him: she could play *any* part. And with that, Bessie Berger was born, a role that remains "one of the fabled performances of American theater."[13] Stella may have won out in the end, as Bobby Lewis noted: "As the play's run continued, I began to notice distinct signs of old Bessie Berger getting a subtle, but unmistakable, facelift. One age line per performance would disappear from the make-up. When she started forgetting pieces of body padding, I cautioned Stella one night if she didn't stop, she'd soon end up as young as a fetus."[14]

As stage manager, Kazan kept an eye on Clurman to learn the trade. He studied Clurman's notes and copied down everything he said to the actors after rehearsals. Kazan stuck to Clurman's side day and night, querying him on all subjects. Stella began to get irritated by all the attention Kazan was giving to Clurman. She asked offhandedly if perhaps Kazan were "queer."[15] She had little tolerance for the fledgling Gadget's industrious attentions toward Clurman, especially when such devoted homage was usually paid to her. What did please Stella was Harold's consequent advance in the world. During the past year he and Odets had shared a run-down apartment on Horatio Street. Now they were moving into a "large, modern apartment on the nineteenth floor at One University Place."[16] At $85 a month, the rent was four times as much as for the Horatio Street place; they were literally banking on Odets's mounting success.

Though Stella respected Harold's education and critical dramatic interpretation, she seemed to think that their relationship bought her the right to criticize him. Even after agreeing to play Bessie Berger, she continued to complain about the extra padding and gray wig and question Clurman throughout rehearsals. It seemed to be in the Adler blood. At one rehearsal Luther so inflamed him that Harold hurled a chair at him. Kazan observed how Clurman took the Adlers' fighting in stride, noting how afterward no one had any hard feelings. Perhaps it was their common Lower East Side mentality coupled with an inherent theatrical flamboyance, but Clurman behaved just like an Adler. Whether they were telling stories over dinner or working out a character's scene, interchanges between Harold and Stella reached full volume. And though Stella begrudged her character as a woman of a certain age, she was proud to finally see Harold directing the Group.

Clurman's "directorial style was essentially different from Lee's," Kazan observed. "He encouraged actors and admired them, instead of confronting them with their inadequacies. . . . He had the culture to know that if you attempt difficult tasks you're bound to fail as often as not. . . . Harold made me feel that artists are above all other humans, not only in our society but in all of history. I'm not impressed with any other elite, not of money, power, or fame. I got that from Harold."[17]

As *Lefty* was being translated into other languages and put on around the country, *Awake and Sing!* opened at the Belasco Theatre on February 19, 1935. The *New York Times* announced the curtain at eight forty-five, with tickets ranging from 55 cents to $2.75. Taking advantage of Stella's sex appeal, the Group ran a portrait of her in its advertisements, dolled up in an evening gown, her eyes shadowed with kohl, and holding Dizzy, the dog from the earlier Group production of *Big Night*. The same photograph had been used on the cover of *New York Amusements* in 1933.

Stella met Odets's mother for the first time at the opening. The keenly observant Stella noted, "Like a shadow with Clifford's frame over her, she made him seem overpowering."[18] Odets and his mother, Pearl, shared a loving but frayed relationship despite that he felt emotionally abandoned by her. Odets's father thrived on bullying and philandering, physically and verbally abusing his wife throughout their marriage. Pearl had emigrated from Galicia when she was a child, and she never adapted to life in the United States. Her early marriage to Odets's father and Clifford's premature birth began a lifelong depression, which Odets experienced as emotional withdrawal. Mother and son bonded in adversity. When he left home in his early twenties, Pearl set aside money from her household allowance to send to her son. She was the silent, long-suffering type.

Awake and Sing! revolves around the lives of a beleaguered Jewish family from the Bronx, with Bessie Berger as the domineering mother who tries to keep the family afloat by sheer will. Luther played Moe Axelrod, a heartsick boy in love with the Berger daughter. New York critics named Luther's performance one of the ten best performances of the season.[19]

Women's Wear observed that Stella, playing "double her age in real life, gives a moving and tragic performance."[20] The *Brooklyn College Beacon* gave Stella special mention as Bessie Berger: "[she] evoked much applause from the audience through her excellent characterization of a tyrannical Jewish mother, who at heart means all for the best."[21] Two months after the opening, *New Theater* offered an entirely different take on Stella's performance: "not busy enough, not enough driven, not broad enough. There was not enough of sink and baby carriage and furniture polish and grocery accounts implicit in her relationships, her compulsions, her emotional outburst. They seemed creations of the moment rather that out of realization of a complete person."[22]

By contrast, a syndicated article that ran from Syracuse to Atlantic City admired how "the gestures, the inflection of the voice, the shrugging of the shoulders and all the indefinable characteristics which are part of a second generation Jewess, asphyxiated in the close Jewishness of the Bronx, are handled so perfectly by Stella Adler as to remove completely any feeling of stage enactment. This is authentic, cruelly authentic."[23]

Alfred Kazin wrote an account closer to what applauding audiences felt:

Listening to Stella Adler as Mrs. Berger in *Awake and Sing!*, I thought that never in their lives would my mother and the other Brooklyn-Bronx mamas know that they were on stage, and that the force of so much truth could be gay. . . . Sitting in the Belasco, watching my mother and father and uncles and aunts occupying the stage in *Awake and Sing!* by as much right as if they were Hamlet and Lear, I understood at last. It was all one, as I had always known. Art and truth and hope could yet come together. . . . I had never seen actors on the stage and an audience in the theater come together with such a happy shock.[24]

Kazin had captured exactly what the Group Theatre aimed for: humanity mirrored by art. Mothers and families from the boroughs did witness themselves onstage, as was documented night after night by the laughter and applause resounding from their less expensive balcony seats. They identified with the characters. Their struggles and aspirations were the same: a better future for their children. When Stella dramatically stripped off her gray wig at curtain call to reveal her flaxen locks, the audience members delighted in the theatrical gesture familiar to them from the Yiddish theater. Stella knew the inextricability of life and art. She would spend the rest of her life in pursuit of that truth, teaching that truth, and painfully missing it when it could not be found, relying on nostalgia as its substitute.

THE COMMUNIST PARTY BOLSTERED THE MOBILIZATION OF UNIONS across the country. For many members of the Group Theatre, Communist philosophy aligned with the Group ideals, giving rise to a Communist cell consisting of a handful of company members including Odets, Kazan, and Paula Miller. The cell held meetings to reinforce their agenda and social perspective on American theater. Kazan later encapsulated what the Communist interest was, to the extent that it believed "theater is a weapon. A play must teach a lesson. The third-act climax must send the audience home with hope and courage born of a sweeping revolutionary insight."[25] This is exactly what Odets's plays had done, although he was writing not from a Communist agenda, but rather out of the spirit of the times.

The same literary currents punctuated the work of Thomas Wolfe, Pearl S. Buck, Margaret Mitchell, William Faulkner, and the poets Archibald MacLeish and Edna St. Vincent Millay. Carl Sandburg was writing, "Stocks are property, yes / Bonds are property, yes / Machines, land, buildings are property, yes / A job is property / no, nix, nah, nah."[26] Communism was a symptom of the tumultuous 1930s and of a system in collapse, not the force behind the decade—although the conservative powers in government preferred that the public believe otherwise.

The Communist cell in the Group Theatre, and many other Communist sympathizers such as Stella, would have to come to terms with the tragedy under Stalin of the Soviet Union, the country they looked to for sociopolitical and artistic inspiration. For now, the atrocities playing out in the Soviet Union were suppressed by the mainstream media and easily ignored by idealistic Americans wanting to believe in something.

Still, despite Roosevelt's reforms and labor union organization, left-wing politics did not agree with everyone, which the Group realized when *Waiting for Lefty* played uptown in the spring of 1935. The traditionally conservative Broadway audiences came to see the much-publicized "radical" play out of curiosity, but they did not identify with the play the way the downtown audiences did. When the novelty wore off, so did box-office sales. Though the immediate response to *Awake and Sing!* was appreciative, only time would allow critics and audiences to realize the full impact of this new kind of theater. Brooks Atkinson, who had initially written that Odets was awake but "[did] not sing with the ease and clarity of a man who has mastered his score," later apologized, agreeing with other critics who thought "Odets had outstripped O'Neill."[27]

On April 13 Clurman left for Moscow, where both he and Cheryl Crawford planned to study the Russian theater in more depth. The time away from Stella was as necessary as the work itself. "Stella's attachment to me and I to her," Clurman later wrote, "had to do with a feeling of being married to each other through the theater, which was our life, or mine at the time . . . we were . . . separated and at odds, murdering each other and it [the Group] and its members at the same time! Here was the paradox, the fusion and confusion of the intellectual and personal life."[28] Stella would have agreed that the theater was her life, but her intellectual or artistic life was one and the same with her personal life, a fact to which Harold could not reconcile himself. He didn't want his personal feelings for Stella to interfere with the work they were creating.

Stella had long been used to the fusion of personal life and the theater, having performed with and among the complicated relationships in her family. When working with intimates, an instinctual identification among the actors colored the play—a shorthand of communication. A similar sense of collaboration existed among the Group actors and was intensified by their personal relationships. Conflicts arose, but she stayed because, as she explained later, the advantages "outweighed the disadvantages."[29]

Meanwhile Odets's resentment toward Stella over her treatment of Clurman continued to go unnoticed by her. "He was a real theater man," she said of Clifford. "Where there was a need, he would always meet it. If you needed a part, a rewrite, a sketch, a monologue, you'd never be stranded."[30] Stella respected the artist unequivocally, to the extent that she could divorce her personal opinion of the individual (except when it came to Strasberg) in the interest of his or her artistic merit. More accurately, Stella was not always in touch with the individual apart from his or her artistic work. Her relations with others were primarily through art, hers if not theirs. She reconstituted the model in which she grew up, wherein her nourishment, her human connection sustained itself with art. This made for an inspirational life experience, but it was not conducive to creating intimacy with her fellows.

The play Strasberg didn't want to put on, the play in which Stella did not want to portray a middle-aged woman, became Odets's masterpiece. *Awake and Sing!* also turned Clurman from Group evangelist to a Broadway director.

The entire body politic of the Group changed hands, placing Odets under pressure to churn out another play. In need of another one-act to run as a double bill with *Lefty*, Odets wrote *Till the Day I Die*, one of the earliest anti-Nazi plays. The piece had its flaws, having been written in under a week, and did not receive as much acclaim as his previous plays. Nevertheless, in the span of a year Odets had become the hottest ticket on Broadway. Clurman's theater was beginning to look like the one he had envisioned.

Strasberg grasped at any chance to get reestablished in Group life, but much had changed since the early days of Strasberg's reign as Group guru. Most affronting to Strasberg were the democratic adjustments in the Group's hierarchy. The socialist ideals of the plays reflected the need for a change in the power structure of the Group itself. Unhappy with the shift, Strasberg announced his plans to take a leave of absence—which, he hinted, would most likely result in a permanent retirement—but the committee in charge while Clurman and Crawford were away in the Soviet Union convinced him to hold on at least until the two other directors returned.

IN THE MIDST OF HIS MOUNTING SUCCESS, ODETS'S MOTHER WAS DYING. She had been ill for some time, but his father failed to communicate exactly how ill she had become, which kept Odets from going to her. And so it came as a shock to the young writer when he learned that his mother had died. Stella was the only Group member to attend the funeral. She had an inherent respect for honoring life's seasons: marriages, successes, failures, births, and deaths were events to be observed with proper reverence. Stella experienced the reception at the Odetses' home in Philadelphia as spiritually and intellectually oppressive, recalling the house as "small and without distinction. I remember the suburban neighborhood and a sense of the lives of cigar-smoking salesman and merchants."[31] Later Odets remarked, "No matter how I resented Stella's treatment of Harold, I could never hate her after that."[32] Her presence at the funeral demonstrated Stella's paradoxes. She could be abrasive and inconsiderate to the people she cared about and simultaneously compassionate and giving of herself.

Clurman returned from Europe in June and called a meeting for the commencement of the fall season, which would include yet another play by Odets: *Paradise Lost*. Odets had two hit plays and was opening a third. He had gone from anonymity to celebrity over night. Times were turbulent, and although, as Stella noted, he could be counted on, writing did not come easily. He struggled with *Paradise Lost*, and even after submitting it he continued revising and handing the rewrites to the actors in rehearsal. By the end of July both *Lefty* and *Awake and Sing!* had closed. Stella had played Bessie Berger in a successful play for five months straight and earned a steady income. Taking a month off was a luxury by her standards, but she would have been relieved knowing the Group would be reopening the double bill in Philadelphia.

On October 30, 1935, Odets's plays opened at the Broad Street Theater. The *Philadelphia Record* ran a review that read, "The actors of the Group Theater have a conviction, a credo, to preach. They take the lines Odets has written and pour their souls into them. Actors don't prance around the stage of the Broad Street Theater. Not by a long shot. It is the young left wing of America voicing its religion."[33] While Clurman didn't like the idea of the Group's being pigeonholed as a left-wing theater collective, the actors were happy to be understood and to be fulfilling the Group's mission of producing socially relevant plays. The Group had accomplished the impossible: an ensemble theater producing artistic plays of social relevance on Broadway. Interviewed that year, Luther Adler remarked: "It is this spirit that was foreign to the American theater only a decade ago. Of course, the entire picture now appears to have changed, and for the better. But Yiddish theater was the pioneer in this mass conscious drama."[34] Luther's statement encapsulates what many have since forgotten: the roots of American theater, the seeds of American acting, owe their existence in part to the Yiddish theater.

For Stella, there was finally a sense of home in the theater. It fulfilled her requirements of being "open" all the time, providing the financial stability and artistic nourishment she had been seeking for almost a decade since her father's death. It was not exactly the familial dynamic of the

Yiddish stage, with the natural warmth of a common culture and outlook. Consequently, she still felt herself a stranger among the members of the company and disliked how they had developed a similar style of dress and even a common diction. She remained an individual within the Group, which naturally alienated her from the other members. Still, it was a kind of home, a place where she could unpack her bags and stay for a while.

CHAPTER THIRTEEN

I was a great admirer of Stella's mind.

—Arthur Miller

S TELLA AND THE GROUP CAME HOME FROM THEIR RUN AT THE
Broad Street Theater in Philadelphia to find themselves out of work.
Unemployed—at least until the fall season got under way—Stella
agreed to conduct a seminar for the New School for Social Research. "The
Actor in the Theater" came third in a series of lectures on acting. Stella
wasn't the only American out a job. During 1934 and 1935, although the
country wasn't sinking into greater economic malaise, there were still nine
to ten million people out of work.[1] The drought in the Dust Bowl continued
to displace farmers and their families as the world's political situation grew
grimmer by the day. Nazi Germany was armed and ready to invade the
Continent. Many underestimated Germany's power, and few realized the
world was on the brink of another war. The Soviet Union moved from the
model of revolution to an exponent of fascism, forcing those in the Group
to reexamine their inspiration, their beliefs, and their goals.

Stella's goals, however, remained the same. Her parents were known
around the world and treated like modern-day film idols. To follow in their
footsteps during the film era meant it was not enough to be an international
star of the stage. She needed to be a movie star. Yet, after working with
Stanislavski, Stella's dreams of stardom seemed less important—the
yearning for celebrity was replaced by the greater cause of refining the
craft of acting. Artistic truth for Stella was the truth in life: the human
longing to find meaning to existence. As an actor she was charged with
both interpreting and conveying that truth, unraveling human nature

and holding it up to the light for others to witness. Still, the recognition and glamour of the screen seduced her. Her next move would have to be Hollywood, which by her own and the Group's standards was nothing short of "selling out." She was caught, on many levels, between her ego and her art.

Everyone in the Group loved Odets's latest play, *Paradise Lost*. It was a condemnation of the middle class, whom the Group thought of as "lost" in the paradisal illusion of the American Dream. Whereas the upper class focused on maintaining the status quo and the lower class drudged through day-to-day survival, the middle remained caught up in making money and amassing material gains. The play magnified how this Sisyphean advance upward destroyed the spirit of middle-class Americans.

Clurman cast Stella in a lead role as Clara Gordon, another middle-aged character. Stella was furious. Clurman knew she had her sights on the big screen, which she felt would never materialize unless she could showcase her movie-star looks. For Stella, it was a form of betrayal from the man she trusted to expound her acting and her physical beauty. Harold rationalized that he did not want his actors to be pigeonholed by type. Yet, Stella had already demonstrated her versatility as Bessie Berger in *Awake and Sing!* Did Harold enjoy the power he had over the weapon Stella held over him—her beauty and sex appeal? Outside the theater Harold could not control Stella's flirtations and affairs with men, but inside his theater, he was in charge.

Clara Gordon was at least a little more sophisticated than Bessie Berger. Stella described her character as "a modern woman. She went shopping, went to Saks, smoked cigarettes."[2] As for home and family, "the home [was] of substance and everyone is more articulate. They are still Jewish, but not in the ghetto sense."[3] Stella appreciated playing characters of breeding.

On opening night, December 9, 1935, Stella stole a look from behind the curtain of the Belasco stage to find elite businessmen and bankers in the orchestra seats. These people were at the wrong show. They "had paid loads of money," she remembered thinking, "to see a play which said to them, 'Your lives are junk.'"[4] Critics were "disappointed" in Odets's new play, calling it unfocused and convoluted with strange characters. The Group took out an ad the following day in response: "We believe Clifford Odets' *Paradise Lost* is a great and important play. We are proud to present it." No one, most of all Stella, with her lead role, wanted to see the play flop.

One evening at University Place after the unfavorable reviews came out, Stella turned to a defeated-looking Harold and announced, "I feel I need to sin and you make me feel I have no right to."[5] While she was alluding to carnal sins, Odets chimed in, agreeing with Stella for a change. "She's right!" he exclaimed. His version of sin, however, was to take advantage of the Hollywood offers he had been receiving since the success of *Awake and Sing!* Hollywood was a cheap facsimile of theater, and yet in the middle of the Depression and a dark stage, it beckoned with a seductive golden horizon.

Odets was devastated by the poor reviews. He wrote to the major critics, informed them of his appreciation for their critique, that he was making "an effort to work several of [their] critical statements" into the play, and that they should "look in again" in a few weeks.[6] Invitations to attend the play were delivered to Albert Einstein, Eleanor Roosevelt, John Dewey, Irving Berlin, Sinclair Lewis, Mayor Fiorello LaGuardia, Ernest Hemingway, Dorothy Parker, and Harpo Marx, among others. Yet, despite the publicity efforts, ticket sales did not increase. The play was losing money, even though the actors once again agreed to cut their salaries. *Paradise Lost* closed two months after it opened.

Strasberg began directing the season's next production, *The Case of Clyde Griffiths*. Stella busied herself coaching some of the actors in the play, attesting to Strasberg's diminished authority. Her interference would never have been tolerated in the early days of the Group, but certainly Harold had to find something for Stella to do. *The Case of Clyde Griffiths* opened on March 13 and ran for only nineteen performances before closing because of the Group's depleted funds. Once again the Group was out of plays for the remainder of the season. Some relief came in the form of Odets's new play, written for radio about an incident in the life of Sarah Bernhardt. In April the ten-minute drama aired nationwide on *The Rudy Valle Show*, with Stella playing Bernhardt. Although she was unimpressed with the script, the paycheck at least assuaged Stella's immediate concern over paying bills.

Without a source of income and with nothing to do until the annual summer retreat, the Group decided to take *Awake and Sing!* and *Waiting for Lefty* on tour again. The tour commenced in Baltimore on April 27, then went on to Chicago for a month. Clurman went to Chicago to see how the production was doing and to see Stella. On opening night the audience was restless and outspoken. A group of pranksters had brought fruit to throw at the stage. Someone struck Phoebe Brand, who played the daughter, Hennie Berger, with a grapefruit. Just as Jacob had had to reprimand his audience in the past, Stella marched downstage to the footlights and spoke directly to the spectators: "It's up to you ladies and gentleman out there to protect these actors."[7] The mischief ceased, and the guilty party was arrested.

Arthur Miller, a young student at the University of Michigan, was in the audience that night. Seeing the Group Theatre perform made him want to become a playwright. Jacob Adler had been his own father's hero, and here he was witnessing the legacy of the Yiddish theater. He later recalled: "To this day I can replay in memory certain big scenes acted by Luther and Stella Adler . . . Elia Kazan, Bobby Lewis, Sanford Meisner, and the others, and I place each actor exactly where he was on the stage fifty years ago. This is less a feat of memory than a tribute to the capacity of these actors to concentrate, to be on the stage. When I recall them, time is stopped."[8]

Not needed in Chicago, Clurman headed on to Hollywood. Odets had given in to the offers from Hollywood and moved into a large house in Beverly Hills. He had to keep up appearances, as he was pursuing Luise Rainer, the German-born star who had caused such a flurry when she landed in Hollywood that year.[9] Clurman observed Odets and the Hollywood scene in general, writing his impression in a letter to Stella: "Actors are paid fabulous salaries, work all year in pictures specially written for them. . . . But in the Group! We have no money, our success is momentary. We have difficulty in finding plays . . . we quarrel, beat our heads against stone walls, shout, shiver, and shake. The Group is wonderful."[10] Clurman spent his time in Hollywood recruiting new playwrights and visiting old friends.

When summer arrived the Group reunited at the Pine Brook Club in New Jersey. The New York publication *Midweek Pictorial* featured the Group's summer retreat under the headline "Actors Take Their Hair Down." The layout highlights the actors at play, sunbathing, canoeing, and playing chess. The dominant photograph on the front page is deceiving. Strasberg, Clurman, Stella, and Kazan are reclining on a grassy hill, candidly interacting in animated mid-gesture. Stella's attention is on Strasberg, to whom she seems, smiling and gesticulating, to be telling a story. The image betrays nothing of the rancor between Strasberg and Stella. No longer is Strasberg the untenable master cloistered in his room; rather, he is one of the Group members keeping company with Clurman and "his girl." The actors seem unaware or unconcerned that the directors have no concrete projects for the fall season. They were all back from tour with Odets's hits and glad to be together, staving off the unknown of their immediate future.

Stella and Harold appear to be a serene couple in the front-page photograph, his grasp securely around her shoulder. While Odets's new romance with Luise Rainer and Franchot Tone's romance with and marriage to Joan Crawford were copiously covered by the press, Clurman and Stella's relationship was conspicuously missing from the headlines. The

acob Adler.

Jacob's Grand Theatre presents *The Broken Hearts*, ca. 1903.

Stella (*left*) with her sister Julia, ca. 1903.

Program from *The Jewish King Lear*.

Stella with her mother in *The Kreutzer Sonata*, ca. 1911. (FROM THE AUTHOR'S COLLECTION)

Sara Adler.
(PHOTO BY HERMAN MISHKIN, IRENE GILBERT ARCHIVAL COLLECTION, STELLA ADLER ACADEMY AND THEATRES LOS ANGELES)

Stella as an adolescent. (HARRY RANSOM CENTER, THE UNIVERSITY OF TEXAS AT AUSTIN)

From left: Luther, Stella, Julia, Jay, Frances, Abe, Jacob.

Stella in *The Beautiful Lady*, 1920–1921. (IRENE GILBERT ARCHIVAL COLLECTION, STELLA ADLER ACADEMY AND THEATRES LOS ANGELES)

Stella in rocking chair, the Group Theatre
at Brookfield Center, Connecticut 1931.
(COURTESY OF THE ESTATE OF RALPH STEINER)

Stella and Luther Adler, 1933.
(IRENE GILBERT ARCHIVAL COLLECTION, STELLA ADLER
ACADEMY AND THEATRES LOS ANGELES)

Stella in *Awake and Sing!*, 1935. (IRENE GILBERT ARCHIVAL COLLECTION, STELLA ADLER ACADEMY AND THEATRES LOS ANGELES)

Stella with John Payne in the film *Love on Toast*, 1937. (FROM THE AUTHOR'S COLLECTION)

Stella in *Love on Toast*. (FROM THE AUTHOR'S COLLECTION)

Publicity photo of Stella, 1937. (IRENE GILBERT ARCHIVAL COLLECTION, STELLA ADLER ACADEMY AND THEATRES LOS ANGELES)

lack of media attention could be attributed to Stella's revulsion—which was for the most part disingenuous—toward the press, a holdover from her parents' belief that being in the papers was vulgar and common.

The photograph is a rare glimpse into the camaraderie and unique bond between even the most contentious of Group members. Though they disagreed with and resented one another, they still admired each other and even enjoyed each other's company—the mark of the familial ties several years of starving, striving, climbing, and succeeding had created. But this idyllic summer retreat marked a turning point in the Group's history and in Stella's career. *Midweek Pictorial*'s article ends: "with sixteen members of the original company still active and playing, with new blood coming in from the apprentice school the Group maintains, this theater organization stands as a talented, inventive, vital combination of playwright, actor, director with a bright future still ahead."[11] Nothing could have been further from the truth. Things were unraveling quickly.

The actors wanted good plays that would feed them, both figuratively and literally. Clurman interpreted the actors' complaints as reflecting poor group morale and a lack of discipline. In his mind he was doing his best to keep them working while constantly pursuing new plays representative of their endeavor. In retaliation, he criticized individual members, including Stella, whom he accused of being too "subjective." He included himself in this critique, admitting that the last act of *Awake and Sing!* could use more precise direction. What the group needed, Clurman claimed, was steadier leadership, as opposed to the democratic control the Group had been moving toward. He proposed that he should be the Group's managing director and offered a paper he titled "Group Organization," laying out the role of the managing director as having the final say on Group policy. An Actors Committee consisting of four Group members would be in charge of communicating Group concerns to the director. If three-quarters of the Group agreed, Clurman's plan would go into effect.

The proposal was like putting a Band-Aid over a shotgun wound. The problems of the Group were unresolvable at this juncture. Throughout its career the directorate had financed the Group through the support of the commercial theatrical business. In order to remain independent, it relied upon its financial backing and, ultimately, critical approval. The idea of creating a Group Theatre audience had been the goal from the beginning, and indeed it had been what kept balcony seats filled, but the working class was not solvent enough to keep the Group afloat. The middle and upper classes remained lost to the Group's ideals, as they were pursuing the paradise of the American Dream. Without audience support, the Group struggled to earn a living and still be true to the Group agenda.

The personal dynamic between the Group members had also tainted the company. The actors had grown up and lost belief in their directorate. The zeitgeist of the 1930s dictated reform and equality. Stella was never very comfortable with the latter. That summer at Pine Brook, unwilling to participate any longer in communal living, Stella rented a house for herself and Ellen. Bobby Lewis later recalled that Ellen was often left alone during the summer retreats. He remembered that Stella would sleep in, leaving whoever was around to feed Ellen breakfast and keep an eye on her.[12] That summer Harold lived with Stella and Ellen, which would have at least provided a live-in caretaker for Ellen in Stella's absence.

Although Stella seemed to be missing the maternal instinct, she made an effort. Stella told her former student Elizabeth (Betsy to her friends) Parrish a story about having to go to Ellen's school for an important day. Perhaps recalling her embarrassment as a girl walking home from school and seeing Madame Adler dressed so ostentatiously that she had to steer her classmates in another direction for fear of their finding out her mother was "this queen," Stella took it upon herself to look "normal." Parrish said, "Stella thought, 'I know what I am. I know the role. I'm her mother. Okay, so I dressed in a lovely suit. Fine. I don't look too theatrical. I won't frighten anybody; and I went in to talk to her teacher.' And her teacher kept looking at her and she couldn't understand why she kept staring at her. Seems that a stocking was coming out of her blouse!"[13]

Ellen recalled the summers with the Group Theatre fondly.[14] Like the members themselves, a familial atmosphere resulted from the close quarters, work, and common aim. Being around the theatrical and artistic personalities seemed more of an education than a burden for young Ellen, who knew no other kind of life. Like Jacob, Stella loved having artists and actors in the house; she entertained throughout the summer in her rented house in Pine Brook. Among her guests were Kurt Weill, the exiled German composer, and his wife, Lotte Lenya. Weill was composing the score for *Johnny Johnson*, the as yet unfinished musical on the roster for the fall season. Odets also rented a place off the main campgrounds, where he was finishing *The Silent Partner*, which was the second play scheduled for the upcoming season. The third play had not been decided upon yet.

With little to do except perform once a week for the Pine Brook Club guests, the actors began studying. Since the Group was planning a musical, there were both vocal and choral classes. Stella participated even though she had no part to play in *Johnny Johnson*, of which she made Harold painfully aware. He kept her busy in the meantime by giving her her own classes to teach. Stella assigned scenes to her students and critiqued their performances. Kazan felt these classes "deepened the rift between" Clurman and Strasberg by reawakening the debate between Strasberg and Stella concerning Stanislavski's system.[15]

At the other end of the spectrum, around this time Sanford Meisner penned a letter to Luther Adler:

> The joylessness of Group productions to me comes from a false i.e. unnatural approach to acting. Actors are not guinea pigs, to be analyzed, manipulated, dissected, "let alone" in a purely negative way. . . . You all know what I'm talking about. My point is this. Stella Adler is eminently capable of working in the only way I would consider as being the right "common method" for the Group. She alone in the entire theatre understands and practices the Stanislavsky system. . . . My suggestion therefore is this. That Stella Adler be given an executive position with complete authority over the artistic problems of the theatre. . . . I maintain that only by working in her way which is humanly true and theatrically sound and desirable (and to make it completely kosher, really the system) can we revive the "spirit" in our work.[16]

From the moment Stella agreed to join the Group, she made Harold feel that she was taking a risk by leaving what was a sustaining, full-time livelihood in the Yiddish theater. In turn, Harold took on the responsibility of her career as if he thought that his success depended as much on Stella's artistic satisfaction as the Group's. He didn't seem to know how to reconcile the two, and the Group members were aware of it. Kazan was the most vocal with his dissatisfaction: "We all resented the lady, believed she'd scattered Harold's concentration and corrupted his good sense. We thought the problem that had been distracting him—what to do about her professional life—irrelevant."[17] Kazan's "we" appears to be as subjective as Strasberg's "we" (as in "We don't like your play, Cliff"). When the votes came in, the membership agreed to Clurman's plan of action, electing Roman Bohnen, Morris Carnovsky, Kazan, and Stella to the Actors Committee.

Perhaps it was this gesture of the Group's approval that gave Clurman the confidence to propose that Stella direct *Johnny Johnson*, with Kazan as her "assistant." "Stella was with Harold," Ellen recalled, "and they fought and they fought. She wanted Harold to be involved with her, and her development, and her career and if it wasn't going to be in acting, it would have to be in directing."[18] Kazan had always resented the sobriquet "Gadget," but when Clurman suggested that Kazan's "mechanical competence" would supplement Stella's direction, it was the last straw. Kazan aspired to be a director, and now Stella, of all people, was put forward to direct, despite having no experience.

Strasberg, knowing that neither Stella nor Kazan had the experience to direct a musical, refused to allow the idea to go any further. Clurman offered himself as director, but when Strasberg pointed out his doubts about Clurman's ability to deal with the play's mechanical demands, Clurman responded, "What difference does it make who directs it?"[19] Such a reckless declaration demonstrated the extent to which even Clurman felt defeated by the daunting problems the Group faced. Strasberg was angered by Clurman's apathetic comment, and the two directors were never more at odds.

When Odets finished *The Silent Partner*, he gave it to Clurman for feedback. It wasn't a good sign when Harold, known for his critical dramatic eye, remarked that a good part should be written in for Stella. The play was incomplete and needed revision, but Harold's suggestion was out of line. That October Stella publicly voiced her frustrations in an interview in which she "confessed" (Stella's word) to the writer that "unless she is given better opportunities in the future, she may have to kick over the traces and take matters into her own hands."[20] She no longer had any patience with the Group's blundering management and broken promises. The time was coming for her to break out on her own.

By December the Actors Committee, fed up with the mounting Group problems, submitted a twenty-nine-page typed litany of complaints, beginning with the play at hand: "The rehearsal period for *Johnny Johnson* was eleven weeks . . . nobody yet knows what the production is supposed to say. . . . The director of this production, or *someone*, should have been assigned early in the summer!" The document listed gripes over everything from the unavailability of costumes to the Group's defeated morale. It accused Strasberg of being uptight and Clurman of being impotent. It demanded that Clurman and Strasberg communicate and make peace: "If the theater is to go on, it must be built upon love, theater love, between equals who need each other and derive benefits from each other and through working with each other." The voice of Stella, one of the executors of the document, resounds through its accusation of Clurman and "his regime of managing director" as a failure: "[Harold] really works under the spell of inspiration, crumbling just before rising to heights." The document ends with "a call to action for the Organized Approach for Artistic Reorganization, for unsparing self-analysis. . . . Today thirty people are ready and waiting to Function. . . . What are we going to do?"[21]

The question remained unanswered by anyone at the moment. Too many caustic words had been exchanged, first by Clurman of the actors and now by them of the directors. To make matters worse, *Johnny Johnson* was floundering. They had only two weeks of rehearsal when they returned to New York. Clurman's new role as sole managing director of the Group had him so tied up that Strasberg took on directing a musical that was due to open without having had a dress rehearsal.

Clurman recalled having to "beg, borrow, and steal" the money to put the play on.[22] The first two previews were the "most distressing experiences [Clurman had] ever gone through in the theater. The large production—nineteen sets—and the orchestra had not had sufficient time for rehearsals. . . . The actors were lost. After five minutes of the first preview, half the audience left."[23] In the midst of the mayhem a midnight conference was held in which Strasberg declared, "I know more about acting than any of you!"[24] Everyone was trying to hold on to some stability, and yet it was unraveling—not merely the production, but all the years of Sturm und Drang. Seeing how distraught Harold had become, Stella approached him backstage, her heart full of love and sympathy for his suffering, and said the sweetest words he could have asked for: "Harold, would I help?"[25] By this she meant, would her personal commitment to their relationship help him better deal with the chaos of the present situation.

By the time this declaration was made, however, Stella had already made plans to move to the West Coast, where she was determined to take her career into her own hands. On December 21 the *New York Times* announced: "Since she is not acting in *Johnny Johnson* and because there is no role for her in *The Silent Partner*, the Group Theatre's Stella Adler is leaving today for Hollywood. She may do a film out there."[26] Her reservations about "selling out" to Hollywood seemed minuscule compared to the catastrophe of spending a season out of work. Franchot Tone and Odets had already made the move, and their careers were the better for it. It was time for Stella to embrace her dream of international stardom, and Hollywood was the most direct route. With the Group morally and financially depleted, *Johnny Johnson* closed on January 16; there were no concrete plans for another production. Clurman had finally reached a breaking point. It was only a matter of time before he would follow Stella out to Hollywood.

CHAPTER FOURTEEN

*Stella was one of the two most brilliant actor's directors I
ever worked with, Orson Welles being the other.*

—Peter Bogdanovich

I T WAS THE DEAD OF WINTER IN 1936 WHEN STELLA ARRIVED AT GRAND
Central Terminal, undoubtedly accompanied by a hired valet for her
notoriously ample luggage. The chill temperature of twenty-eight
degrees invites us to imagine Stella in a knee-length fur-trimmed coat over
her slim-fitting, mid-calf dress, the ensemble topped by a jaunty felt hat set
just right by her gloved hands.

Passing through the doors into Grand Central, Stella merged into the
pocket of warmth the throngs provided as they took their respective paths
along the marbled floor hall. The Beaux Arts interior, with its 125-foot-
high vaulted ceilings and arched windows at half that height, may have
called Stella's attention to the winter zodiac painted on the ceiling. Perhaps
the cerulean blue oil background attracted Stella, all 2,500 stars steering
their namesake forward. Months later, dispirited by the repetition of
California's sunny skies, Stella would long for the invigorating seasons back
home, perhaps recalling the astronomical mural if only in the hypnagogic
moments before sleep.

Stella was likely booked on board the *20th Century Limited* out of New
York to Chicago, the train of choice during the first half of the century.
Stewards would roll out a deluxe crimson carpet for passengers arriving
and disembarking, whence came the saying "getting the red carpet
treatment."[1] In Chicago she would have caught one of the new streamliners
directly to Los Angeles, a trip that could have taken as few as three nights.
Settled into her private Pullman, Stella undoubtedly felt excited about this

new chapter in her life. She saw such actresses as Greta Garbo, Marlene Dietrich, and more recently the Group Theatre's own Clifford Odets's future wife, Luise Rainer—whose role that year in *The Great Zeigfeld* would win her an Oscar—doing what she could do blindfolded, and she wanted the recognition. Never mind she was born and bred in a theatrical community where she had already been showered with approval and applause on three continents. She was now thirty-five years old, and time was running out.

Clurman spent New Year's of 1937 in New York but headed to California by mid-January. Even Strasberg showed up at the train station with some of the other Group members to see him off. No one knew what the future held for the company, least of all Clurman. He was exhausted and confused. "The truth is that I did not really know what was troubling me most," he later recalled, "except for the fact that I was tired—very tired. My erstwhile fellow directors assured me the seat of my confusion was my troubled relations with Stella Adler, who had gone to the coast thoroughly fed up with the Group."[2] Indeed, Stella's move west came from a conscious relinquishment of the Group. She remembered feeling "no longer interested . . . in the ensemble quality of the acting,"[3] and put all her energy toward becoming a movie star. But the Group wasn't that easy to get rid of. One by one, they came west after her.

Cheryl Crawford had gone ahead of Clurman to make a deal with the producer Walter Wagner, of Paramount Pictures. The plan was that Clurman and a handful of Group actors, including Luther Adler, Roman Bohnen, Morris Carnovsky, and Kazan, would work with Wagner while they figured out the Group Theatre's future. Wagner agreed to pay the actors $150 a week on "standby" and $750 when they were actually working on a film. It was the most money the actors had seen in a long time.

In April Stella signed with Paramount Studio's Major Pictures Corporation as the star of *Love on Toast*. Stella's debut screen role as a young, charismatic executive, Linda Craven, gave her something the Group never had: a shot at playing a smart, sexy, and attractive modern woman. To enhance the latter, Stella went in for rhinoplasty. In a letter back home to Strasberg, Kazan sardonically commented that the "new nose is a huge success, and she should photograph marvelously," continuing with the real point of the missive: "if she makes a big hit in movies, Harold will have to make the Inescapable Choice,"[4] referring to the choice between Stella and the Group.

When it was time to release the film, Stella did not want to change her last name, which countless other Jewish actors had had to do. When asked why, Stella explained that she didn't feel she could change her name because it didn't belong to her. As if in passing, she added, "It belonged to the world,"[5] revealing her continued reverence for her parents. The sentiment is not as hyperbolic as it seems: after all, Jacob Adler was known throughout the world at the height of his career. Even Franz Kafka, in a diary entry from 1910, mentions Adler's renown.

The columnist Sydney Skolsky finally convinced Stella that she really didn't have a choice if she wanted the film to be released. "I said yes," Stella recalled. "What do you want me to call myself, Beverly Wilshire? I was living there. . . . And I said that's not bad, and Luther's going to be Bullocks Wilshire."[6] Stella smiled and then, with her mind never far from the lives of her fellow Jews in Europe, realized it wasn't a laughing matter. She turned the conversation back to a level of gravity, "The whole thing became a comedy. And it took Auschwitz to change that."[7] Still, she finally agreed to change her name, settling on Stella Ardler.

Walter Wagner hired Clurman as his assistant, just the respite he needed from the demands of running the Group. Harold moved in with Stella at the Beverly Wilshire Hotel with her daughter and two servants. Stella made a point of having household help whenever she could afford it and even when she could not. It reminded her of her girlhood, with everything in its right place, her socialist politics subordinated to comfort and familiarity. In this cozy household under the temperate California skies, Clurman began to unwind. When Crawford started organizing Group meetings, Clurman wanted nothing to do with them. He actually became unresponsive.

Strasberg threatened to move forward without Clurman, but he didn't have the charisma to pull it off. Clurman had a way of rounding up the troops that Strasberg utterly lacked. The Group needed him. One day Kazan tracked Harold down and accused him of being in a "comatose state that he seemed to have lost his own appetite, desire and personal dynamics . . . that he seemed to be further embedded in his concern for Stella than he had ever been before."[8] Clurman agreed with all these accusations without offering up a defense. He just wanted to be left alone.

Not the only member of the directorate to be exhausted, Crawford responded by submitting a letter of resignation. Strasberg's came a few weeks later. Whereas Crawford's letter revealed a conscious struggle over the decision, Strasberg's directly addressed Clurman: "I wouldn't mind waiting ten years and ten summers. But to wait because fundamentally the people aren't up to action (that's what I feel) and so they can rest up etc. seems to me valueless. . . . For the people of the Group to have gone ahead and wrecked the Group organization without any immediate and definite plan and assumption of responsibility was a criminal act."[9] Clurman acknowledged their resignations, but he was still not ready to make any plans for the future.

Spring swept a clear canopy of blue skies, a difference hardly detectable to the restless East Coast transplants. Kazan returned to New York. Luther landed a role in a film but ached to return to his real acting life. The actors, including the ones who had stayed in New York, anxiously waited for Clurman. Stella felt conflicted regarding his indecision. She wanted the security of his presence, but she knew his heart was with the Group. One night she turned to him and said, with tears in her eyes, "You shouldn't be here. You should be back in New York where your real work is."[10] Finally Kazan wrote to Clurman, a letter that he later described as "a shrewd mix of flattery, subtle criticism of Harold's subservience to Stella, and a thinly veiled threat that the Group would go on without him if necessary."[11] It was just what the doctor ordered. "I answered," Clurman recalled, "as if there had never been any question of what I would do. There were no two choices. There was only one course: to begin work again next season with the Group."[12]

There are times when distance from a problem is the very thing needed to work it out. This was true in the case of the Group. If the same people with the same personal dynamics and resentments had trudged forward, the inherent problems of the Group would have persisted. Clurman identified these obstacles to Group success back in 1931, but little had changed by the tumult of 1936–37. Without a reserve of funds and without plays that resonated with the Group, a theatrical company of thirty permanent actors was impossible to sustain. Clurman had to change the entire body politic of the Group. Shifting the power structure by putting himself in charge had not worked; he could not take on by himself all the pressures a theatrical company engendered. The Group had to concede to the realities of Broadway if it wanted to remain there. The fact that it had survived for six years was a testament to the sheer will and commitment of its members. The United States had yet to found a national theater like the Old Vic in England, the Comédie-Française, or the Moscow Art Theater. Clurman still believed the Group would be America's equivalent.

On May 10 a press release announced that a board consisting of Clurman, Luther, Stella, Kazan, and Roman Bohnen would now be making all Group decisions. Only the actors presently in a production would remain on salary. The others were promised nothing and encouraged to find work elsewhere. Many of these actors, some of whom had been original members of the Group, never forgave Clurman for betraying the

Group's promise to support permanent members throughout the season. Lastly—and this was the stinger—the Group was now looking for new talent with star quality to attract audiences. Two immediate additions were Leif Erickson and his wife, Frances Farmer.

Odets immersed himself in a new play titled *Golden Boy*, about a man who betrays his dream of becoming a violinist in order to seek fame and fortune as a boxer. Thematically, Odets's play resonated with Stella's own dilemma. By taking the Hollywood route, she compromised her artistic ideals for fame. But the Group Theatre, she could easily justify, was as reliant upon popular success as her film career. Indeed, only a commercial success was going to allow the Group to make a comeback.

By the end of the summer Clurman had finished his work in California. It was time to get back to New York and move forward with producing *Golden Boy*. Stella remained in Hollywood. However well she understood his decision intellectually, she felt abandoned by what she perceived as Harold's allegiance to the Group over their relationship. Ellen described the conflict Harold faced, which had been the same since the beginning: "He couldn't give her up for the Group, and he couldn't give the Group up for her. He needed them both, and he drove everyone crazy with his efforts to bring them together, whether they liked it or not."[13] *Golden Boy* went into rehearsals on September 13 with Luther Adler as the protagonist and Frances Farmer as the female lead.

Meanwhile, Stella celebrated the completion of her first film with a trip to San Francisco. She stayed at the Sir Francis Drake hotel, where she granted press interviews. Stella was intrigued by the local political climate wherever she traveled, no less so in the City by the Bay. The cause célèbre of the moment was Harry Bridges, San Francisco's own "golden boy," who pioneered the resurgence of unionism on the waterfront through the International Longshore and Warehouse Union and inspired organizations in other industries across the country. A national icon at his height in the 1930s, the United States government did not condone Bridges's "subversive" ideas on labor. Bridges would spend over a decade fighting three presidents trying to deport him.

Stella liked the tall, lean, Australian-born "working stiff," as he referred to himself. Whether her affair with Bridges was what initially brought her to San Francisco is a matter for speculation, but it certainly would not have been the last time a romantic liaison landed her in the middle of a historically significant political moment. While learning about the local labor climate, Stella said in an interview: "I am not so much concerned with labor politics as I am with observing the American scene for myself. For that reason I am interested in San Francisco, where the labor situation is particularly engrossing and the union organization furnishes food for thoughtful study."[14] In between her investigations, a press photographer captured Stella having tea at her hotel. The photograph shows an elegant woman in her prime, sitting with a white napkin on her lap. She is holding her teacup daintily, looking up as if to greet someone approaching her table. Having starred in her first feature film and with a seasoned career on Broadway affirming her talent, anyone would say she had arrived.

Back in New York, *Golden Boy* opened at the Belasco Theatre on November 4, 1937. Both Cheryl Crawford and Lee Strasberg came to see the play. Strasberg remembered, "I came out with a very warming feeling kind of thing, because it seemed to me that it was worth it . . . the work I had done, that I had been part of, had not been wasted.[15] *Golden Boy* was an immediate commercial success, generating revenues that stabilized the Group financially. A week after the opening, Harold returned to Hollywood to reconnect with Stella, no doubt wondering where their relationship stood after his return to the Group. She may have felt left out, not being involved in the success of the current production.

Seeing Harold back at work, Stella became restless. After *Love on Toast* "we sat in a beautiful house and had two cars and you didn't know what to do with your life," Stella lamented. "You were waiting for the next movie to come along. That takes time in Hollywood . . . you did your film and then you were finished. Then you were part of the landscape. . . . I didn't like that. I didn't like the leisure."[16] *Love on Toast* was due to premiere in December, and though she was thoroughly bored with California's monotonous blue skies, Stella was still committed to a career in the movies. After three weeks Harold returned to New York, without Stella.

At this juncture Bobby Lewis and Elia Kazan initiated the idea of creating a Group school of acting. With the Group barely scraping by each season, an actual studio where actors could study their craft had been a pipe dream. Now, with the box-office success of *Golden Boy*, Bobby Lewis took over recruiting students for the Group Theatre school, selecting fifty out of 1,000 applicants. The first semester Lewis and Kazan taught the acting technique classes, but they quickly realized they could not run a school, teach, and pursue their careers in the Group. The studio was terminated after its first semester. A seed, however, had been planted for what would become the most famous acting school in the United States: the Actors Studio.

Love on Toast premiered in early December. *Variety*'s write-up criticized the film's slapstick antics but lauded Stella: "Miss Ardler, from legit stage, not only looks well despite faulty makeup but fits into the cinema acting scene whenever given opportunity. An outstandingly strong actress, she shines despite the grotesque hokum."[17] In late December Harold asked Stella to return to New York with the renewed temptation of directing a Group production. With Strasberg out of the picture, Kazan had jumped at the first of those opportunities and was directing the Group's second play of the season, *Casey Jones*. He ran into trouble directing the lead actress, giving Clurman an excuse to bring Stella back with the job of coaching this problematic actress.

Without a film offer in sight, she returned to New York; one of the first things she remembered doing was passing out antifascist leaflets at the public library. Fascism was winning out in Spain with the aid of Germany against the Spanish Republic. Many prominent figures, including Hemingway, Paul Robeson, and the poets Muriel Rukeyser and Langston Hughes, paid homage with their art and joined international brigades on the side of the Spanish Loyalists. The Group had been active in the cause since its beginning in 1936, garnering support through meetings and supporting committees and organizations that urged the United States to end relations with Spanish fascists. Stella endorsed a petition with the Artists' and Scientists' Division of the North American Committee to Aide Spanish Democracy—one of many petitions she signed that would be used against her during Senator Joseph McCarthy's Communist witch hunt.

Golden Boy was still drawing revenue in the fifth month of its run. Warner and Columbia began bidding wars to produce the film with offers to Odets of $100,000.[18] Upon the play's 150th performance, the Group gave a benefit show, with proceeds going to the Spanish Loyalists. Clurman took advantage of the play's popularity to negotiate a deal with Homer Curran to produce *Golden Boy* on the West Coast. Clurman assigned Stella to direct the play. It was just what she needed, and he would have been sufficiently rewarded. Stella returned to Los Angeles, energized and excited about her first directing assignment.

The *Los Angeles Examiner* knocked at Stella's door as soon as she arrived. They ran an article titled "Directing Offers New Careers for Women" in which Stella discussed a field rarely open to women at that time and still, eighty years later, dominated by men: "Act, star if you can, but be sure to direct a few players too, and round out your theatrical life," she advised. "Women have had to fight for a chance to direct . . . if you know what you are doing—and why, people will respect you for it, whether you are staging plays, writing them or acting in them."[19] Having begun her theatrical education at such an early age, Stella had little doubt about her ability to do anything onstage. Theater was her first language, and the fluency with which she navigated the theatrical world instilled in her an innate confidence. Directing was not as intimidating as it might have been for another woman of the era; it was familiar, and Stella took the reins with as much know-how as any director out there.

West Coast actors were thrilled at the prospect of a new play in their midst; it had been months since one had even been cast in Los Angeles. Stella held auditions at the Biltmore Theatre, with anxious thespians lined up outside to audition for the hottest play of the season. Stella had already cast the matinee idol Francis Lederer as the Italian prizefighter. When asked why she had not been cast as the lead female role, which was being performed by Frances Farmer, Stella explained:

> It meant playing opposite my own brother which we have done many times. But because there were so many love scenes in the play I decided to give Luther a "break." I thought it best that another actress play the part. After all, it was tougher for Luther and me to imagine ourselves as sweethearts. Then, too, the audience, recollecting our relationship, could never believe in the boy and girl romance. And so to sum it up, the whole thing had too morbid a touch to it. Which is why I bowed out. I would like to play it here for Mr. Curran but I can't do that and direct at the same time.[20]

Stella deftly masked dishonesty with modesty. She had never been offered the lead in the play. Nor was the argument that she and Luther were siblings a valid reason. Stella grew up with siblings and spouses playing romantic opposites. Yiddish audiences appreciated the feat of divorcing the true person from the character. As for "bowing out" of the original cast, Clurman had hired Farmer for her star appeal, and he had done something right. *Golden Boy* saved the Group.

Engaged to open in San Francisco, Stella's production of *Golden Boy* went on the road. En route—on April Fool's, of all days—the play gave its first performance before an audience in Santa Barbara. Sending telegrams to family members in the city where they were opening had been an Adler tradition begun by Jacob, who would wire an encouraging note to his children when they were performing out of town. Now, nine-year-old Ellen followed this tradition by dispatching a Western Union message to her mother: "Dear Mommy, I wish you all the luck in the world tonight . . . kisses from your pretzel."[21]

Stella had cast Joseph Greenwald, an actor she knew from his career on the Lower East Side, as the lead's father. On the evening of the premiere Greenwald came onstage and handed a violin to his son. During the exchange, Greenwald began his lines, "All my life," and subsequently collapsed onstage. The audience thought it was part of the play until the curtain was called and the theater evacuated. Greenwald died backstage, memorializing Stella's directorial debut with a dramatic note. Greenwald was replaced and the tour continued its course, opening at San Francisco's Curran Theatre as scheduled and returning to Los Angeles's Biltmore Theatre three weeks later before closing.

In the meantime Clurman had traveled to Cuba with Irwin Shaw to iron out the latter's script for *The Quiet City*, scheduled for the final production of the season. In his perennial effort to unite Stella and the Group, Clurman suggested that Stella codirect the play. By the time he returned to the United States, that suggestion had been printed in the *Los Angeles Morning News*, although it would never come to fruition. The day Clurman arrived in Hollywood, another headline ran, "Gotham Chief Here for Conference." The article stated: "Harold Clurman, director of the Group Theater, has just arrived from New York for a series of conferences with Miss Adler about two plays which the organization will shortly produce."[22] Despite her reputation to the contrary, Stella had a knack for self-publicity. With Harold out of town, Stella was free to depict the nature of their relationship to the press, making sure to keep her professional life in the forefront. Her work as an actress or director for the Group Theatre had nothing to do with her personal relationship with the "Gotham Chief," and she had no reason to publicize it.

Weeks later the *Morning News* interviewed Clurman as he prepared to return to New York: "[Clurman] sat down for a rest and a smoke amidst a clutter of suitcases and one or two trunks in his apartment."[23] He was eager to return to New York, even during its notoriously sweltering summer. "There's so much to do when I reach New York. I've got to plan the Group's new season." When asked about the various rumors about the Group, most of which had been circulating since its inception, Clurman added one of his own: "I love to listen to yarns about our supposed fancies. I'm just as fascinated as any ordinary listener to the fabrications. The latest one heard is that just before the curtain goes up we of the Group gather on the stage and pray."[24]

Once Clurman was in New York, a London producer contacted him to ask about bringing *Golden Boy* to England. Still without any screen offers, this time Stella would not remain far behind.

CHAPTER FIFTEEN

Stella is an actress: divide everything by ten.

—Alexandra di Lampedusa

O

N JUNE 8, 1938, THE *LOS ANGELES MORNING NEWS* ANNOUNCED Stella's departure by plane to New York en route to London, where she would "direct *Golden Boy* for the Group Theater." The article erroneously mentioned her as the director of *Golden Boy*'s New York production, which had in fact been directed by Clurman. After completing their 248th performance, the cast of *Golden Boy* packed to board the SS *President Harding* to London. Stella arrived home in time to board the swifter HMS *Queen Mary*, along with Ellen, Luther, Harold, and Odets.

The voyage began on a dramatic note. On her way home Stella had read in the afternoon paper that Luise Rainer was divorcing Odets. Ever the diplomat, Stella volunteered to break the news to Odets, but she needn't have bothered. Rainer telegraphed Odets herself, telling him how much she hoped he understood her decision. When Clurman took his turn comforting Odets, he found his friend removing his wedding ring, preparing to cast it into the ocean. On that same trip Luther announced his engagement to Sylvia Sydney, the popular film actress.[1] Compared to their shipmates, Stella, Harold, and Ellen appeared the model of a stable family unit. Harold had long since embraced Ellen as his own daughter, and he and Ellen remained close regardless of how things were going between him and Stella.

The passengers arrived safely, but they were leery of the kind of reception they might encounter in England. It remained to be seen if the ever-so-polite English would relate to Odets's uniquely American, at times vulgar dialect. On June 21 *Golden Boy* opened at the St. James Theatre in the West End. The crowd didn't make a peep, and the actors thought their fears had come true until the curtain came down, when a wave of applause told them otherwise. Audiences and critics hailed the play. The Group enjoyed the attention. They were invited to Parliament and dinners with London's elite. Stella had reserved rooms at the fashionable Dorchester Hotel, unavoidably mingling with full-uniformed Nazis and Franco supporters. Stella would have reveled in the thought—while discussing the weather with a Nazi soldier in the hotel lobby waiting for a cab—that she had been corresponding with an underground friend critical of Europe's acquiescence to fascism. This friend would soon enlist Stella to help German Jews escape Germany.

Had *Golden Boy* contained Jewish characters like *Awake and Sing!* it never would have been invited to London. In 1938 Hitler's encroachment into Central Europe marked the beginning of unfathomable consequences for European Jews. During the run of *Golden Boy* in London, Clurman remembered a general obliviousness: "Everyone I met seemed very nearly unconscious of the coming war. . . . At a grand party on some rich lady's terrace . . . I suddenly blew up at all the complacency around me. . . . The actress Ursula Jeans turned to me and said, 'You're just upset because Hitler is unkind to your people.'"[2] Stella saw the escalating anti-Semitism during the summer of 1934 on her first visit to Moscow, but she could not have imagined the events that would unfold that year while she lived in England, or the extent to which she would become involved in the fight for her people.

That summer presses across the globe printed remarkably little about Germany's treatment of its Jewish population. The reasons for the lack of attention and seeming apathy are complicated. They date back prior to 1935, when Hitler's Nuremberg Laws stripped Jewish Germans of their citizenship. Few saw then how vulnerable Jews had become, with no more rights than animals, and even less of a claim to the home where they were born.

London papers grasped on to any news that would distract the public from the grim world events. Luther Adler's plans to marry Sylvia Sydney were plastered across the tabloids. Sydney arrived in London in late July, while her fiancé was starring in *Golden Boy*. The couple married three weeks later at Caxton Hall Register Office, apparently not wanting a formal wedding. Stella wrote a letter to Ellen, who was staying with her father, telling her that Luther and Sylvia had been married: "Perhaps you could make them a picture for their wedding present."[3] At eleven, Ellen was a budding artist. The stage was not an avenue open to her; there was an understanding between herself and her mother that it was Stella who was the actress in the family, not Ellen.[4]

As Ellen grew older, their relationship became exponentially more complicated. Many years later Stella examined the life of the actress with children while lecturing on Chekhov's play *The Seagull*. The story centers on the lives of a theatrical family not unlike her own. Stella described Arkadina as the quintessential star actress, whose tensions with her son, Konstantin, reflect the problems she and Ellen faced as Ellen grew up, explaining how Arkadina "went to the big city, met a strong guy from the upper peasant class, got herself pregnant, and then finished with him— divorced,"[5] a trajectory similar to that of her first marriage, to Ellen's father. Horace may not have been a peasant, but he had not become a world-renowned violinist. In either case, Stella's life and career took center stage.

Lecturing on *The Seagull*, Stella elucidated: "I don't know any actress that does not have trouble with grown up sons and daughters. . . . You cannot have a Konstantin unless he is neglected as a child, kept in a corner. This hurt him terribly. Everyone around her was somebody. He was nobody."[6] Stella knew from her own childhood what it meant to stand in the shadow of a renowned actress, to be neglected and held at arm's length. Stella continued discussing Konstantin in her lecture: "You have to build up from when he was a kid and she [Arkadina] said, 'Don't be foolish, you are not a playwright. I love you and you are my baby, but now, shut up.' She babies him but then says, 'don't talk about theater, because you are an amateur.'"[7]

"Actresses never get older," Stella extemporized, "never get tired, never have rheumatism, never need glasses. An actress doesn't say, 'I don't feel well, I have a headache.' I learned this from my mother. 'My feet don't hurt. I don't sweat in the summer. I'm not cold in the winter.' It is very important that an actress doesn't age."[8] Stella had Ellen at twenty-six, and as Ellen blossomed into womanhood, Stella did of course grow older. From an actress's perspective, an aging child is threatening, a constant reminder of one's own fleeting youth.

Toward the end of August the time drew near for the company of *Golden Boy* to return to the United States. The producers urged the Group to launch a second cast of actors to perform the play in London. Stella zealously took on directing this second string of players. With Stella working and the Group enjoying a semblance of stability, Clurman had found a happy medium. He may have begun to feel he could rest on his laurels, but it so happened that Luther and Odets were unhappy with the state of the Group. They figured it was time to begin running the Group on a "repertory basis."⁹

Luther wired Clurman, Kazan, and Kermit Bloomgarden, the Group's business manager, asking them to attend an urgent meeting at their apartment. Luther and Odets were already aggravated before the discussion began. Luther accused Clurman of being lazy, claiming that he didn't respect his own talent. Luther and Odets questioned Clurman's original intentions of building a national theater, one that had a reserve of plays suited for repertory instead of producing one play at a time. On the defensive, Clurman explained that repertory was still his goal, but financial matters precluded the Group from realizing their potential. Luther and Odets charged Clurman directly with the task of firing the press representative and raising $100,000. At one point Odets vented his frustration, saying he was tired of Harold complaining about his relationship with Stella, "screaming all the critical and jealous things he could not, in the daytime, say to Stella."¹⁰ Though one issue seemed to have nothing to do with the other, the debate over the Group versus Stella cornered Harold once again.

This was Harold's mindset when Stella, looking forward to her London directorial debut, planned a family week in Paris with Ellen and Harold before he set sail for the United States. According to Clurman, on the train from London to Paris he and Stella "conducted a running battle over the Group for which she felt I had developed an exclusive, fanatical devotion."¹¹ Stella was doubly snubbed when she discovered that Harold had invited Odets, Bloomgarden, and Kazan to Paris. At the end of the week Stella was glad to see the boys board the SS *Chamberlain*, while she and Ellen headed for the Riviera before returning to London.

After her vacation Stella started rehearsals of *Golden Boy* in London, writing to Ellen, who had returned to her father's, explaining that she had just arrived from rehearsals, which were not going well. The two and a half weeks she had been allotted were not sufficient, "And if it's bad it's not going to be entirely my fault."¹² Stella was right. The show ran for less than a month, closing in October.

In the broader scheme of events, that November seventeen-year-old Herschel Grynzpan assassinated the third secretary of the German Embassy in Paris. He had acted in retaliation for the recent expulsion of fifteen thousand Polish Jews from German territory, including his parents. In response to the assassination, Hitler launched Kristallnacht, the Night of Broken Glass, in cities throughout Germany and parts of Austria. The SS and civilians who took sledgehammers to Jewish-owned buildings and shops left the streets strewn with shards of glass and metal, ravaging towns and villages. When it was over, 1,668 synagogues had been scoured, 267 burned down; more than 7,000 Jewish stores were plundered. Thirty thousand Jews were rounded up and sent to concentration camps. Kristallnacht made it starkly clear to European Jews the extent to which their lives were at risk, but even those with the means to emigrate could not leave. Some were simply not granted exit documents. Others were detained because they had no place to go, no country to accept them, and no means by which to travel away from danger.

Meanwhile the United States, adhering to its postwar isolationist policy and battling an economic depression, maintained a strict anti-immigration protocol. Following Hitler's accession to power, American groups such as the German American Bund, the Silver Shirts, and the White Shirts organized, spouting anti-Semitic propaganda and holding mass rallies that emulated those of the Nazis. Anti-Semitism would continue to escalate in the United States, becoming rife by the 1940s.

Kristallnacht was widely publicized, even in American newspapers, but the reaction of Americans and even American Jews left much to be desired. American Jews had acculturated in their new country. They considered themselves American and were fiercely loyal. Any public expression obligating the United States to help European Jews could call American Jews' patriotism into question. No one wanted to go to war, least of all for what was largely perceived as a Jewish problem. However, to say that American Jews were reticent even as the atrocities unfolded at an increasing rate is to oversimplify the case. The extent to which American Jews remained minimally responsive to the growing danger in Europe is best seen through the leading rabbi of the time, Stephen Wise, who would later become an adversary of Stella's efforts with the Jewish cause.

As president of the American Jewish Congress in the early 1920s, Wise was one of the most outspoken of Jewish leaders. Yet within his political arena, he remained cautious, especially regarding the plight of European Jews. After Hitler was elected chancellor of Germany, Wise called attention to anti-Semitism in Germany at a protest in Madison Square Garden, but, rather than specifying Nazism as a threat to Jews, he proclaimed that "Nazism threatens to destroy the fundamental values of Americanism. . . . We Jews are not the only victims of Hitlerism"; among the other sufferers were "the great Catholic Church and the Protestant churches."[13] By setting Judaism and Christianity under one flag, Wise hoped to avoid framing Hitler's threat as a Jewish issue.

Stella was an exception among her Jewish American counterparts. When she agreed to stay on in London to direct *Golden Boy*, Stella was already intimately involved with the man who would introduce her to a group helping smuggle Jews out of Germany.[14] It is unclear when and where Stella initially met Wilfred Macartney. His first extant letter to Stella is dated February 16, 1938, confirming that they knew one another prior to her arrival in London. Among other things, Macartney was a playwright. By the nature of their correspondence, it is reasonable to infer he and Stella had met in the theater in New York.

When Stella was interviewed in her eighties, her memory of Macartney and of the events that took place during her time in London in 1938 were sketchy at best: "In London during one season I met somebody called McCarthy. I forget his first name. And he wrote a book called *Walls Have Mouths* and he was put in jail. He was a very wealthy, very great gentleman. He was put in jail because he stole English secrets to give to the Soviet Union and he was a Communist."[15] Stella was notoriously bad at recalling names, even those of lovers. She focused so wholly upon the present moment that such incidentals as names and dates often escaped her.

Wilfred Macartney was a tall, wealthy Englishman with thick, wavy hair, a handsome face, and all the elements of comportment and dress that one would call dashing. A Communist, a Soviet spy, and an ex-con, Macartney wrote for the *Reynolds News*, a paper founded for the radical English working class and later a weekly voice for the Labor Party. Soon after she arrived in England, Stella and Macartney rekindled their ties. He educated her about the German threat to European Jewry. He took her to the House of Commons. He courted her. Stella recalled Macartney inviting her to a meeting, with five "extremely capable men, a good lawyer, a good financier."[16] Stella's recollections, however, seem to overlap with those of her freedom-fighting work immediately after the war, when she smuggled stolen visas and passports into Germany to transport Jewish displaced persons to Palestine. Macartney's group asked Stella to enlist the help of Alvin Johnson, the cofounder and president of the New School for Social Research, where she had presented the lecture titled "The Actor in the Theater" during the mid-1930s and where she had taken classes herself.

As early as 1933, when Hitler came to power, Johnson began sponsoring Jewish scholars by providing a safe haven for them at the New School in a department he created called the University of Exile. Johnson provided visas and jobs for scholars and their families. Given Johnson's resources, Stella's memory of his having helped her with Jews wanting to leave Germany correlates with her work with Macartney's group. What remains unclear is whether Stella delivered forged visas to Germany herself in 1938 or simply confused traveling to Germany with similar work she did after the war. The nature of the two activities—dispensing identification documents to Jews—is so similar that it is understandable why, four decades later, Stella might confuse the two. What is certain is that her career in freedom fighting and her heightened awareness of the troubles of her Jewish brethren began while she was in London in 1938.

If Stella did smuggle documents into Germany in 1938, Macartney's group would have chosen her for the same reason she was chosen after the war: no one suspected a glamorous blonde actress. One account related to the author was that Stella had the pilfered documents sewn into the lining of her fur coat. Even so, it would have been dangerous for a woman traveling alone in Germany in 1938, and a Jewish woman at that. As early as 1933 the German police had "begun close surveillance of highways, routinely stopping travelers and subjecting them, their cars, and the baggage to detailed search. It wasn't unheard of for all traffic to be temporarily halted while trains, trucks and cars were searched.[17] Stella apparently managed to covertly deliver the illegal documents without incident.

Once, on the way back to London, her train stopped in Berlin. With time to spare, Stella found a seat at a bar in the station and ordered coffee. Across from her, two men ordered beer. The frosted steins enticed Stella: she called the waiter to tell him she had changed her mind and would have a beer instead. The German, perturbed by the foreigner's fickleness, reminded Stella that she had ordered coffee. They went back and forth in German, Stella conceding that yes, she had initially ordered a coffee, but now she wanted a beer. The waiter remained adamant that Stella keep her first choice. Frustrated with what she, under the circumstances, perceived as a reflection of the inhumanity against Jews, Stella's request took on all of the import of the rights of man. Stella raised her voice with an authority few could defy and pounded her fist on the bar. The waiter finally brought the glass of beer. Stella would later retell this story comically, but there was nothing humorous about the political situation she was witnessing firsthand.

As the end of the year drew near, Stella felt the need to return to her life. Macartney offered to financially support her career in London, putting Stella in a quandary for the remainder of 1938. It was a difficult decision.

What exactly would she be going home to? Harold had never been much of an incentive when it came to making decisions. Ellen was staying in England with her father to finish the school year. Stella did not particularly want to go back to the Group, which was once again struggling financially. Finally, though, she decided to go home.

When she arrived, at the beginning of 1939, Bobby Lewis threw a homecoming party for her, lifting Stella's spirits temporarily. She found her fellow actors doing their part to fight Nazism, raising money to boycott German businesses. Macartney's letters did not cease, and he continually alluded to the years she had already given to the Group as an argument for her returning to London, where he would provide for her:

> I cannot bear the thought of your so sweet green-grey eyes being filled with tears. . . . You are so good and beautiful, you have been such a fine friend, such a loyal lover, such a grand daughter, such a wonderful mother, so good to brothers and sisters—and strangers that now you owe yourself to be only good to yourself, think of nobody else. . . . I'll save for you. I'll open here an account in your name so that you know that always here is a life for you. I love you, so help me. I love you to the very marrow of my bones. Remember you are no Royalty to anyone but yourself . . . you have given 8 years, I swear Stella if I had you for 8 years I would be willing to slave for you . . . and expect nothing at all in return. . . . Do you know what sort of a woman you are, only seldom in an age does one come down from the sun, know your value, your beauty. . . . Stella, if things don't work out come back, (if they work out come back). . . . I swear I'll protect and secure you, give you all I make, and push you, hold you, and comfort you. . . . You are so young, such a child, when I think of you sleeping with [your] golden head lying down and pale slender hands between your long legs I'm sick with longing for you.[18]

In another letter Macartney wrote to Stella foretelling the coming war: "There will be a big scare over here after April 6th after the French Presidential Election and another one in Sept.: war will come I think next year when the Germans and Italians can detach France from England and if that happens, a fairly remote but distinct possibility, then goodbye to the British Empire and god knows what else."[19] In this same letter he writes that Ellen "is gay, her cheeks are actually rosy and she is getting fat, but you must not tell her because she will stop eating."[20] He sends Stella an article on sleeplessness: "I guess you're not happy. I can see that you have been working for nothing again, grooming your sister into *Awake and Sing* and getting tired and not sleeping."[21] Although Stella's letters to Macartney have been lost, from his references to them it is clear that she confided in him. The content and tone of his letters reveal the intimate nature of their relationship and how deeply he was in love with her. It is likely that the feeling was mutual, for Stella was not one to enter into an intimate relationship—or any endeavor, for that matter—lightly. She once said she had felt "seriously" about all her lovers,[22] and no doubt that was a correct assessment, at least while she was in their presence.

It was a dark period. Several of Macartney's letters to Stella refer to her drinking as a way of self-medicating. He urges her to return to London. When the Group decided to tour again with *Awake and Sing!* in March, Stella was not interested in resuming her part as Bessie. She appears to have entered the first of several bouts of depression with which she would have to struggle during her life. Stella asked her sister Julia to take her place. No doubt Stella was tempted to return to the safety and assurance of Macartney, but the decision to remain in the United States was as likely to have been due to the imminent war as it was to any definitive choice.

IT WAS BUSINESS AS USUAL FOR CLURMAN AND HIS THEATER. HE FORGED ahead with producing Shaw's *Quiet City*, which was proving to be troublesome. Shaw's wife, Molly Thatcher, organized a Group playwriting contest to recruit fresh playwrights for the company. In this competition, a twenty-seven-year-old unknown named Tom Williams entered his plays under the name Tennessee Williams. The pen name was invented in order for the author to be eligible for the contest, which was limited to writers age twenty-five and under, but the name proved to be more important than the second place Williams won in the contest.

That summer, while the Group set out for their retreat, movie fans saw Robert Donat in *Goodbye, Mr. Chips* and Bette Davis in *Dark Victory*. The hourglass figure was declared en vogue. Indeed, the word "glamour" was on everyone's tongue; even *Life* magazine "was calling Thomas E. Dewey 'Republican Glamour Boy No. 1' and Attorney General Murphy 'New Deal Glamour Boy No. 1.'"[23] With such frivolities in the United States no one imagined, or wanted to believe, a world war loomed in Europe.

In the early summer of 1939 Ellen's school let out, and she was free to return home. Macartney wrote to Stella to let her know that he saw Ellen's school play: "She dances beautifully. Now she is to sail in a few days with Horace and you'll seem very far away."[24] Ellen arrived safely in New York less than two months before the outbreak of World War II.

IT SEEMED TO HAVE BECOME A CURSE: NO MATTER HOW MUCH ACCLAIM the Group Theatre amassed, nor how many publicity efforts they made—even forfeiting their democratic principles to hire movie stars—by the end of a theatrical season, they entered the summer broke and without plays to rehearse for the next season. Their lodgings in the summer of 1939 were ninety minutes from New York, near Smithtown, where they gathered on July 15. The retreat was luxurious by any standards, but especially in contrast to the ramshackle summers of old. They rented a Christian Science school that covered a hundred acres of ground, with two dormitories, a gym, tennis courts, and a nearby lake. But despite the idyllic scenery, a storm was brewing within the Group, and Stella, as usual, was at the epicenter.

While Stella was in Europe Harold had a brief affair with Frances Farmer, whose marriage to Leaf Erickson had ended. Surely Stella would have heard of this upon returning, but it seems her relations with Macartney's supplanted her interest in Clurman's affair. Macartney's latest letter alluded to the two of them reuniting for Christmas. At the moment Stella was apparently back to her old self. Stella's immediate preoccupation concerned reviving a classic, one from her Yiddish repertoire: Chekhov's *The Three Sisters*.

As for Clurman, it was difficult enough to keep the company together even with Crawford and Strasberg helping him. As the Group's sole anchor, Clurman grew weary. He was reluctant to stage the play Odets was currently revising on the grounds that it was not ready. Odets was insulted, reminding Clurman how important his plays had been to the Group. In one of the meetings that summer Clurman admitted that he wanted the company to cease just so he would be relieved of the burden of carrying it: "Then I will cry and pretend I am heartbroken, but I will really be happy because I won't have this thing hanging on my mind. I push on because that is what is expected of me, but I want it to fail. I have just as much need of its failing as for it to succeed."[25]

The summer waned without rehearsals commencing for the following season. Finally, by the end of August, with only a week left of the retreat, the Group began working on *The Three Sisters*. The company was conflicted, not merely because the actors were unprepared for the season, but because the Russian play seemed somehow to be connected with the Soviet Union's agreement to remain neutral with Germany if war broke out. Many of the members had long looked to the Soviet Union as an artistic and social model. Its nonaggression pact tasted particularly sour to Stella: her fatherland was now an ally of the Nazis.

Aggravating matters, the tension between Harold and Stella worsened, as one writer-in-residence later recalled: "I am able to recall the first day of those rehearsals because it confirmed the feeling of fragility one felt about Harold's relationship to Stella . . . he seemed ill at ease as a high school orator in his first debate. He kept looking in Stella's direction as if to make sure his words were meeting with her approval."[26] Stella seemed at times to be holding Harold hostage emotionally; his uppermost concern was pleasing her.

On the last day of rehearsals, Friday, September 1, Hitler marched into Poland. Stella must have recalled Macartney's words about the inevitability of war. She undoubtedly tried to get in touch with him.[27] It was a long Labor Day weekend, and the entire nation stayed glued to their radios, wondering how England and France would respond. On Sunday the Group returned to a city on pins and needles until Neville Chamberlain's voice came over the radio from London. He announced that England and France had declared war on Germany.

THE GROUP STRUGGLED TO FIND FINANCIAL BACKING TO REVIVE A classic but moved forward with rehearsals for *The Three Sisters*. Stella was cast as Masha, with Morris Carnovsky playing her lover, Vershinin. Carnovsky, known for his indiscriminate directness, and Stella, who was just as acerbic, were not getting along. The drama reached a climax when Carnovsky accused Stella of not being a "truthful actress."[28] It was the worst insult anyone could level at her. True, Stella was known for erupting into emotion, and she could be as weepy as a three-year-old; but that did not mean the emotion was not authentic. She spent her life in search of the truth in acting, the very impetus for studying with Stanislavski in 1934. She knew Strasberg's emotional archaeology was not the truth of an actor's craft, and she clarified that truth with Stanislavski. That foundation continued to hone and shape her talent. And now, Stella thought, this man, this *nobody*, was going to tell her, the daughter of Jacob Adler, her acting was not truthful? Her response was appropriately theatrical: "You should be killed!" she hissed at Carnovsky. Stella sought out Luther, explaining that he would have to "kill Morris and defend [her] honor."[29]

Carnovsky's attack was the last straw in a series of insults Stella felt she had had to endure during her years with the Group Theatre. The decision had been coming on since her return from England. It was time to quit the Group for good. *The Three Sisters* never went into production. If it hadn't been for the war, it seems likely Stella would have returned to Macartney. He was committed to Stella's career and Ellen. Before Ellen went home, he took her on a trip to Oxford, no doubt intimating she might go to college there. But war had come. Instead of making a career on the London stage, Stella's life began a new chapter, one that was destined to shape the course of twentieth-century acting.

The timing was fortuitous. Erwin Piscator, a renowned director of the contemporary theater and a refugee from Europe, came to the United States to organize what the *New York Times* called "one of the most ambitious projects for instruction for the dramatic and lyric stages ever attempted in this country."[30] The Dramatic Workshop began its first term at the New School for Social Research on January 15, 1940. And Stella began her first official teaching position. Her counterparts living on the Continent were not so lucky. That same month, Heinrich Himmler chose the town of Oswiecim (Auschwitz) as the location for a new concentration camp.

CHAPTER SIXTEEN

Stella and Harold had one of the greatest love relationships ever; I mean a deep care for each other's inner being.

—Jack Garfein

A T AGE THIRTY-NINE STELLA WAS FINDING IT MORE AND MORE difficult to accept the fact that life was not working out the way she had planned. Approaching middle age without having become an international star meant, in her mind, that she had not lived up to the Adler name, or even the American ideal of exceeding the achievements of one's parents. In spirit Jacob was alive and well, while Sara, who lived with Stella, served as a constant reminder of her parents' legend during the halcyon days of the Yiddish theater. Stella retained her childhood reverence for her parents without taking into account the singularity of the Yiddish theater compared to the evolving mediums of acting in the twentieth century. Jacob and Sara did not have to contend with radio, film, or the novelty of television, which would be showing up in more and more homes across the country.

Stella also judged herself a failure at creating a family and home, a concept she equated with a well-appointed hearth and all the outside trappings of stability and happiness, which is how she perceived her home during her formative years. The Adler clan had forged blood bonds through their work, heartache, grudges, reconciliations, failures, and successes. Stella could no more recreate the familial dynamic of her childhood than she could conjure back the Yiddish theater's golden age. The thought of marrying and building a home was laden with expectations of an unyielding desire for a man as regal and distinguished as her father. Stella knew Harold was not that man. Still, as Stella later wrote in an unpublished essay, "Harold was the man who created for me the most important opening of my talent, of my mind."[1] Besides, at least for now, Harold loved Stella unconditionally. She knew what a rare gift that was, even though she could not reciprocate his love, nor admit to Harold what it meant to her never having received such pure love from her parents. Harold's adoration of Stella and his deep attachment to Ellen were irreplaceable. When Stella could step back from her romanticized vision of her life, she sincerely appreciated, and in her own way, loved Harold.

In the new decade Stella mingled with New York's artistic elite and Washington's political elite. One could hardly assert that Stella had failed at becoming a celebrated figure. No less so than today, political leaders capitalized upon their association with celebrities. On March 4, 1940, Stella was invited to attend President Roosevelt's Cabinet dinner. The guests assembled on a Monday at Washington's Carlton Hotel to take a night off from the troubles of the world. The occasion marked the seventh year of the Roosevelt administration and the seventh month of Europe at war. The president's nearest and dearest surrounded him: the Secretaries of the Treasury, State, Labor, War, and the Interior, along with other members of the Cabinet. After dinner Stella would sing, with Andre Singer as her accompanist.

Stella felt nervous around people she esteemed. Like Jacob, Stanislavski, and the legendary director Max Reinhardt, Roosevelt was a man to be reckoned with. That evening she found herself in a line of people waiting to greet the president. When she approached him, she was so nervous she inadvertently shook the hand of the man standing next to him.

Dinner commenced at eight o'clock with caviar, sherry, and introductions. Stella would have removed her honey-smooth fur dinner jacket, which, as the times dictated, glittered with rhinestones on the ends of the lapels and cuffs. Perfumes such as Houbigant's Chantilly and D'Orsay's Le Dandy would have wafted through the spring air. Color was the rage and Stella never missed a chance to show off her eyes, so perhaps she chose a floor-length teal-colored gown with her signature plunging neckline. She would have pulled her hair back in a soft wave with a jeweled barrette and matching bracelet or pin—or both, as Stella was never one to skimp on accessories.

Dinner included the president's favorite dish of terrapin and pheasant. Later the guests enjoyed champagne and retired "into another room for informal entertainment—night club style,"[2] where Stella shone. Afterward she was invited to a late-night supper at the White House. According to the usher's diary during Roosevelt's presidency, the evening marked the only time Stella visited the president at his presidential home—an interesting fact, as Stella alluded several times to having had relations with "at least one president." It seems she was not referring to Roosevelt.

Stella's acting engagements were few and far between, so much so that Stella had to take up radio work to supplement her income, as she had in the Group days. In September New York's WEAF station hired Stella for a radio drama called *Johnny Bear* where she found herself working alongside two of her most contentious colleagues: Kazan and Carnovsky. A little water under the bridge, especially in the theatrical world, was par for the course. After leaving the Group during *The Three Sisters* of "you [Carnovsky] should be killed" fame, Stella ran into Carnovsky and his wife, Phoebe Brand, in Hollywood at a Russian war relief gathering. Brand recalled: "Everybody that was anybody was there from Hollywood. And Stella . . . said, 'Where's Morris?' And he came forward and we said, 'Russian vodka is the secret weapon for friendship!' . . . We forgave each other everything."[3]

Radio provided a poor outlet for Stella's ambition. She held on to her ties in Hollywood, hoping to make her break. The following year the producer Hunt Stromberg offered her a minor role in the most recent of the popular *Thin Man* films with Dick Powell and Myrna Loy: *The Shadow of a Thin Man*. During filming Stella felt compelled to explain to the press her reasons for returning to Hollywood: "I discovered . . . that I couldn't ignore the screen any longer. . . . People don't talk any more about going to the theater, as they used to and as they do about going to the movies. Now they say, 'Let's go see so and so in such and such.' Which indicates that the theater itself has ceased to be the principal attraction and it's the star of a certain play or a certain musical which is the determining influence."[4] Having transitioned from the Yiddish stage to Broadway, from Strasberg to Stanislavski, Stella displayed a forward-thinking approach toward the evolution of acting.

While in Hollywood Stella met with the studio magnate Louis B. Mayer, who asked her to work with the producer Arthur Freed on his roster of musical productions.[5] Without any forthcoming acting work, Stella was eager to learn about the business side of Hollywood—an alarming change from the familiar playground of the stage. During her interview, Mayer told Stella that she would not succeed as an executive: "You'll cry when you are insulted. I won't. You'll be indisposed at least two days a month. I won't."[6] Despite the discriminatory atmosphere, Stella became one of only a few women producing in Hollywood, developing such films as the Academy Award–winning *Madame Curie*, with Greer Garson and Walter

Pidgeon, and the star-studded musical *Du Barry Was a Lady*, with Gene Kelly, Lucille Ball, Zero Mostel, Ava Gardner, and Lana Turner.

From her suite at the Gotham Hotel while being fitted for a new fur jacket, Stella pontificated about her ideas for putting realism into the musical to a reporter from the *World Telegram*, who wrote: "Miss Adler's assignment as associate producer with Arthur Freed raises women to a perch the sex has never before enjoyed in pictures."[7] Predictably, the first item on Stella's agenda was to give every last character "something so real he'd be remembered all through the picture. And that goes double for the pretty girls in a musical." Stella had narrowed in on Judy Garland, which led to her coproducing the film *For Me and My Gal* with Garland and Gene Kelly. "Just because they are 5 feet 4 of pulchritude," Stella asserted, "is no reason for them to be used as scenery. . . . Don't start worrying right away. I'm not going to fill the line with flat-chested bookworms wearing glasses. As far as the eye goes the girls in the singing and dancing roles will be as alluring as ever, but, with their oomph, they'll also have brains."[8]

Stella turned the interview into an opportunity to politicize: "Suppose this Congressional investigation stopped Hollywood from making out and out anti-Nazi pictures. They'd get around it. Hollywood will say what it wants to about modern affairs. Who knows, maybe the musical will be a way of sugar-coating such ideas for fuddy-duddy Senators." Stella concluded the interview by acknowledging how Hollywood had been doing a fine job making musicals and how "one new arrival from the East is not going to revolutionize an industry." Stella had voiced her socialist beliefs, carefully couching her criticism within the context of putting a "fresh approach" into the musical, but little progress was going to be made in Hollywood when it came to expressing antifascist feelings. Jewish leaders and studio heads were unwilling to publicly support films that might ignite anti-Semitism. Capitalism would prevail, preferring financial profit to social reform.

EVEN BEFORE STELLA HAD OFFICIALLY LEFT THE GROUP THEATRE, IT BARELY resembled the idealistic, socially conscious ensemble Clurman, Strasberg, and Crawford had willed into existence. Original Group members who were not in the current play were left by the wayside, while film stars took their place in a blatant betrayal of the Group's democratic ideals. Members' personal dramas had always played out in the Group, but the infighting and tension wore at the delicate fabric with which the Group held itself together. The perennial lack of money and plays corroded the morale of the players and especially Clurman, who, after more than a decade of being the Group's ringleader, had lost his own inspiration. In March of 1941 Clurman allowed the Group Theatre to disband and boarded a train west to be near Stella.

Harold followed Stella's lead at MGM, becoming a producer for Columbia Pictures. He and Stella cultivated a life as Hollywood executives. On Saturday nights they would dine with Clifford Odets, who was now married to Bette Grayson. Charlie Chaplin frequently visited the Odetses' home. Clurman recalled that Chaplin was the life of the party wherever he went, always happy to recreate his films scene by scene. He had just finished shooting *Monsieur Verdoux* when Stella and Harold met him, and he reenacted his movie for them. Clurman thanked the screen idol. Now, he informed Chaplin, he wouldn't have to spring for the cost of a ticket.[9]

If not at the Odetses', Stella and Harold would spend Saturday evenings at Berthold and Salka Viertel's home. An Austrian poet, critic, stage, and film director who had fled Europe just as Nazism took hold, the noble and cultured Viertel was emblematic of the company Stella enjoyed. His wife had acted in Europe but now enjoyed life as an elite Hollywood hostess, orchestrating Saturday-night gatherings with actors, writers, directors, painters, and composers. Their home became a refuge for illustrious European artists who, escaping the encroachment of fascism, found themselves together in the unlikely town of Hollywood. Here Stella met Heinrich and Thomas Mann and the playwright Bertolt Brecht.

Sundays were less intellectual than leisurely at the home of their former Group colleague Franchot Tone and his wife, Joan Crawford. The day consisted of a late brunch, followed by badminton, sunbathing, swimming, drinks, and "nostalgic theater talk."[10] In the evenings the guests would gather in the screening room to view a recent film. One evening, speaking about the standard studio call-in time, Stella complained to Crawford about how arduous it was to get up at six in the morning to act. Stella was a theater actress; whether in rehearsals or during the run of a play, an actor's clock was oriented to late afternoon and evening. Rising at six in the morning seemed an absurd hour. Crawford, a Hollywood veteran, responded, "For what they pay us, it's more than worth it." Whereupon Stella quipped, "For what they pay *you*."[11]

The world-renowned director Max Reinhardt lived in an opulent house in Santa Monica, where he would host gatherings. At one dinner Stella was seated beside the exiled German writer Franz Werfel, whose work she was familiar with from the Yiddish stage. That evening Werfel began prattling about a Berlin critic, which led him into a discussion of other concerns until Stella finally broke into his soliloquy: "Please, Mr. Werfel. I am a woman sitting by your side. If you can't speak to me in recognition of that fact and are going to continue as you have been doing, I must tell you, I can go out to the bookstore and buy your ideas for five dollars!"[12]

Max Reinhardt had been as revered in the Adler household as Goldfaden, the father of the Yiddish theater. Every year, when Jacob and Sara traveled abroad, their itinerary included attending a production directed by Reinhardt. Stella recalled: "At our dining table, my father once looked at me over his glasses and said with the gravity of an important decision: 'You will go to Reinhardt when you are a little older; you will study with him.'"[13] Reinhardt's company crossed the Atlantic when Stella was still a teenager, and she was first in line to see his plays. "I still remember Sokolov standing high up on a staircase playing Robespierre; I remember Hartmann and Danton; Helen Thimig in *The Living Corpse*. . . . I loved what I saw: I sensed his towering size."[14]

When Stella met the director she found him every bit as prodigious as the reputation that preceded him. Reinhardt enjoyed the best of everything, from cigars to clothes, and he loved to laugh. Stella noted how when he laughed, his head tilted back and his eyes gleamed. She thought his entire demeanor, from his gait to his "very silhouette," was noble in nature. "He had the presence of a star."[15] One night while dining out Stella was sitting with Reinhardt and two friends when an acquaintance of hers appeared at the table requiring Stella to introduce him to her party. She was able to recall the names of the other two people at the table, but "went blank" when she had to introduce Reinhardt. She looked at the great director, flustered, embarrassed, and helpless when he came to the rescue, whispering in her ear, "Reinhardt is my name!'"[16]

Soon after meeting Reinhardt Stella was eager to return to the stage. She approached the director with an idea for working together in New York: "I gave him a proposal of coming back and doing repertoire in New York . . . and Harold disagreed with that. That was another big fight with Harold and me."[17] Stella had not given up her dreams of having a permanent theatrical home and, despite having disbanded the Group, Clurman maintained the ideal of a national theater, but they had different visions of how the venture with Reinhardt should play out.

Reinhardt was equally eager to produce plays of substance. He wrote to his son, Gottfried, that he had met Stella and Harold and described their plan for a repertory theater: they were to have a season of forty weeks doing five plays which would each run eight weeks, charging less for tickets than Broadway. The three decided they would have to raise $100,000 dollars, which, according to Clurman, would allow them to "work in peace."[18] Reinhardt included his impression of Stella in his letter to his son: "I have never seen her act. Though that never made much difference to me when I was casting. What is important is that she looks good, is of theater blood, has a strong temperament, pronounced humor and a sharply critical brain; above all, she is a personality, which, in the theater, is always the most important thing."[19]

Stella returned to New York to find backers to raise money. Harold remained in Hollywood where he could continue earning a steady paycheck, which offered Stella some sense of security, as she faced an uncertain future: the United States had entered the war in December of the previous year, and it was looking as if it would not be long before Harold was called up.

Stella enjoyed a long and quiet train ride back to the East Coast, only to find there was no one to meet her at the train station. She had sublet her apartment to some friends and could not return home. The gray day threatened rain as Stella wrangled twelve bags and her temper into a cab, cursing Harold under her breath, who seemed the most convenient person to blame for her predicament. She directed the cab up Seventh Avenue to the Savoy Plaza Hotel, where she hoped to get a room. The sea of crowds, buildings, and signs washed over her and softened her anger. Even the weather felt cozy and familiar. It was good to be home. There were no rooms at the hotel, but the concierge kindly offered to store her luggage, and from there, "I was in a whirl," as she later wrote to Harold.[21]

New York City. Stella had witnessed its relentless stretch upward, city block after city block of high-rises from the Lower East Side north past Central Park and into Harlem. She witnessed the conversion from gas streetlamps to electricity, the construction of the subway, and the transition from horse-drawn carriages to automobiles as Manhattan became the world's most modern metropolis. Stella had traveled across the globe with her father's troupe, but New York was her city. Even without a place to stay for the night, she walked the familiar avenues, taking in the heady scents of New York's cafés and street vendors, and without further ado, plunged into the "whirl" of it all. At the Savoy, Stella ran into a friend who said she knew a woman who might find a room for Stella. The two caught up over breakfast at Reuben's and arranged to meet the woman at noon at the Biltmore. But as soon as Stella arrived, she was escorted to the dais of the National Democratic Committee for Finances and put on the stage with Eleanor Roosevelt to raise money. While listening to the speeches and collecting donations, Stella looked out for the woman she was supposed to meet, but she never turned up. The luncheon ended, the room emptied, and Stella collected all her nickels to start making calls herself, but no amount of charm or cajoling brought her closer to her goal. It was three thirty in the afternoon, and it seemed every room in the entire city had been booked. She decided to go back to her apartment.[22]

Just as it began to rain Stella arrived to find sixteen-year-old Ellen home from Bard College. It was a lovely surprise to see her blossoming girl, whom Stella described as "a black flower with sequin eyes."[23] Stella and Ellen booked a box at Carnegie Hall. After the show, Stella went to the green room, which was filled with people she forgot she knew. Under a canopy of umbrellas, the group proceeded en masse to the Russian Tea Room. Stella dined and mingled until one-thirty in the morning, but the night was young. Afterward she went to the Café Royal, her family's old haunt on Second Avenue, until finally returning to the Savoy Plaza to retrieve her luggage. Apparently her charm had left an impression. The clerk had found her a room at the Sherry-Netherland Hotel. Stella tumbled into what she hoped would be the last cab of the day. A valet showed her to a student's room on the thirty-first floor overlooking Central Park. She entered the run-down but still charming quarters, grateful to have her own private bath. She walked over to the window to watch the rain fall, finally alone in a room for the first time after what seemed a long but happy day, "without much hope or direction, a little like a French farce. And I fell asleep and was not too unhappy."[24]

Her tenants told her they would take her in if she didn't put them out.[25] She moved into Ellen's room until their contract expired. Stella plunged into a social life, which consisted of a variety of circles—the majority of which were of a political nature—a speaking engagement for the Democratic Committee, "seeing the president," and being photographed with Senator Harry Truman on his way to Madison Square Garden. Her notoriety was being used on all sides of the political spectrum. The liberal party asked her to attend meetings. At one, David Dubinsky, labor leader and president of the International Ladies' Garment Workers' Union, winked at her, asking her why none of her "friends" were present. Stella flirted back, explaining that they were there, just well hidden. Among the friends Dubinsky alluded to were the panoply of Communist artists and intellectuals with whom Stella associated. Her allusion to being a "red" is tongue-in-cheek, however. Like Jacob, she never wholly committed herself to any cause except the theater. In less than a year the FBI would open a file on Stella when an unidentified informant who was in contact with the Communist party stated that "the Adler family has been connected with the movement for a long time."[27]

Stella was home, but neither the Yiddish theater nor the Group Theatre was around to engage her. She and Reinhardt struggled to find plays and raise funds to found a company, but backing was hard to come by. Unable to land a role as either a director or an actress, Stella felt discouraged. In a letter to Harold, she confided that she felt cheapened by doing theater and radio work as an underling. She stated that she had no interest in teaching. She confessed that the uncertainty of the future of her career and the distance between the two of them had its penalties, which she delineated as loneliness, defeat, lack of money, and what she called "enforced leisure." Stella was not one to be idle—her measure of self-worth was directly proportional to performing. Still, Stella was no pessimist. She reconciled her disappointment with life by also enumerating the things for which she was grateful—namely, her talent, her health, and Ellen. She concluded, "Work means so much to a man. Love means that to a woman and work is a substitution, but she can take it or leave it.[28]

We are each a product of our time, and Stella, as fiercely independent as they come, was no exception. Harold represented a safe harbor, according to the era's perception of the role of women. Yet, Stella no more believed her work in the theater could be substituted by romantic love than she believed in Strasberg's directing. More and more, however, she sensed her options dwindling. It was great to have been a star of the Yiddish stage, on Broadway, and even in Hollywood, but she knew an actress's career did not weather well. In her fourth decade, she was willing to consider marriage as the light upon the dimming horizon of her life as a solitary woman.

Several gnawing uncertainties plagued Stella. How long could she devote herself to establishing this theater with Reinhardt when no one seemed interested? Should she continue to take offers unworthy of her talent just to earn a paycheck? Was it possible to carve a career out of the brutal business of Broadway? At this time teaching held no attraction for her. As the United States' involvement in the war increased, even Harold could not be counted on to rescue her. "It seems altogether inevitable that I will be called into the Army," he wrote to Stella. "They are taking all healthy men regardless of secondary dependents."[29] The draft was a reality, even for men over forty. Already overwhelmed with feelings of failure and confused about how to proceed with her life, the thought of losing Harold exacerbated Stella's anxiety. She urged him not to join the army. "What would you suggest?" he responded sardonically. "That I declare myself a homo, induce a cardiac condition, or contract a venereal disease?"[30]

Struggling for money with an uncertain future was a life Stella tolerated in her youth, while she was finding her way, but hardly one she could accept when approaching middle age. Her political work fed a moral and intellectual fount, but without a full-time artistic endeavor, her creative mind turned in and against her. "I'm worried about you being drafted or enlisting" she wrote to Harold. "I should like to build something and we have nothing and I thought in the next few years you could provide us with some small place—a farm—and you would support me."[31]

To all intents and purposes, Stella believed—at least while writing this letter—that she could satisfy herself as a wife to Harold. Yet she would have never been content as a hausfrau. There was too much living and learning in her blood. The fear of losing Harold to the army supplanted the more rational and dynamic woman who lunched with luminaries and was photographed with senators. With her life of "enforced leisure," Stella spent her evenings at the theater or nightclubs, returning home to her loyal companions, her books and plays. She studied and jotted down notes until four o'clock in the morning, as much to maintain a feeling of productivity as to stave off sleep. She began having panic attacks that would wake her, "and then comes a tussle in the dark—which I will not speak about."[32]

Harold understood Stella's needs, but he also understood his inability to meet the standard of living to which she was accustomed. He sent money to assist her and Ellen, but it was a frustrating responsibility given Stella's obliviousness to expenses. He tried to explain his position to Stella and also to convince her to be more frugal: "I insist that given your tastes—which are always, despite yourself, on the idealistic side—toward Reinhardt . . . not toward Hunt Stromberg. That you have to make sacrifices as to your other tastes and preferences, namely toward Fifth Ave and 55th Street rather than Central Park West or W. 75th Street. I insist that unless you see this and act on this—despite the difficulty—you will be strangled in your inner creativity and freedom—by worry, by fear, by hopelessness."[33] In this twelve-page letter, Harold spelled out both his and Stella's core problem, revealing the ultimate dynamic that kept them at odds:

You have not been able to say to yourself, "Despite the fact that I love the lavishness of my father, despite the fact that I love outside form so much, despite the fact that an external ease, graciousness, luxury, tone and first-classness in all the outside attributes of living are so important to me, I can sacrifice some of these things at least as they manifest themselves in things that cost money, apartment, meals, drinks, parties, etc[.] I can sacrifice these things, I want to sacrifice these things for another kind of first-classness that this man has, this man who is a product of another time than that of Jacob Adler, Stanislavski, Reinhardt."[34]

It seemed a tall order, and Harold knew it. Just as much as Stella, he needed to know where they stood. He was looking at marriage with a woman whom he knew to be incapable of compromising her privileged lifestyle. Stella saw matrimony with Harold in terms of a respectable social status and a means of financial security. Neither of them was being realistic.

During their correspondence that spring and summer, Stella came to the decision to marry Harold. A consummate man of the theater, he stimulated Stella artistically and intellectually. She could talk to him about everything, from her bouts of depression to play analysis. Her companion, confidant, and devoted fan, she would not have taken the likelihood of his enlistment lightly. It also didn't hurt that they were three thousand miles apart. For a romantic like Stella, absence truly did make the heart grow fonder. Stella's concern with her financial future also played a part, but it did not deter her artistic temperament and gusto for living: "Darling . . . I feel our big problem is definitely *not money*, but living happily and really," Stella wrote to Harold. "Living has its own secrets—like all arts as we are just beginning to find out about them—maybe we started late, but that's over—we must go on living beautifully and fully."[36]

Bored with the film industry and Hollywood society, Harold couldn't wait to get back to "his girl." He replied to Stella's letter: "I wish I had a magic carpet and I could sail off to N.Y. on it. . . . (What a pity and folly that we were not married long ago."[37] Four days later he wrote Stella in response to a letter she had sent him: "I ought to point out that orgasms in bed aren't so very important (tho probably lots of fun) if one doesn't share them with a truly beloved."[38] While Stella's letters are intimate, the affectionate ones are few and far between. Harold's however, invariably maintain a steady current of affection, never failing to tell Stella: "I miss you very very much,

I miss your company, I miss you spiritually. I miss you physically[.]"[39] Finally, in early September, Harold completed his obligations at Columbia and was free to return to New York. He wrote to Stella: "How and where do you want to get married? . . . I am writing home that we are to be married. My mama will be overwhelmingly happy I'm sure. Oceans of love as my daughter Ellen says."[40]

Harold returned to New York, and he and Stella were married on the afternoon of September 28, 1942 at his parents' house in Brooklyn. Aaron Copland stood as his best man. The Rabbi Roland B. Gittlelsohn officiated at the ceremony. Afterward Stella asked the rabbi whether he would be around for the divorce. No one found her flippancy particularly funny, nor did she feel proud of herself for the remark afterward, though it was characteristic of the frivolous posturing Stella was guilty of in an effort to make light of a marriage she desperately wanted to succeed, but one that in her heart of hearts she knew would not.[41]

CHAPTER SEVENTEEN

All of us, Stella said, have a role in improving the world.

—Marlon Brando

B
Y THE SPRING OF 1943 SEVERAL MONTHS HAD PASSED AND THE money for starting a repertory theater still hadn't been raised. Reinhardt decided to produce a play by Irwin Shaw. Shaw's *Sons and Soldiers* was thought to be a war play, but was actually about a woman's imaginings of an unborn child. When Reinhardt cast the production, Shaw had just one problem: "Professor, I have nothing against this—what's his name—Peck, Gregory Peck? He's terrific-looking. Maybe he can play the part. Okay. But where does that get us? Hollywood will grab him up and my play will be a flop."[1] They went ahead with Peck, staking the name value of the well-known actors in the cast: Geraldine Fitzgerald, Karl Malden, and Stella Adler.

April of 1943 was unusually warm in New York. Although elegant and grand, the Morosco Theatre lacked air conditioning. The cast had to work in stifling humidity. The name players' dressing rooms were on the first floor backstage, but the heat was oppressive for the minor players on the third and fourth floors. Stella had a minor role (though she would have been given a dressing room on the first floor). The long-awaited opportunity to work with Reinhardt had finally arrived. There were only four weeks of rehearsals, but each was productive and everyone got on well.[2] At one point Stella had an idea for her character and took Reinhardt aside: "Professor, the characterization you have suggested to me is first-rate. I shall be glad to fulfill it. But I have something else in mind." Reinhardt was no Strasberg. He had enough confidence in himself and in his actors to put the play before his ego. After Stella illustrated her idea, Reinhardt responded, "Much better, you should play the part your way."[3]

Stella later wrote about what it was like to work with Reinhardt: "Sometimes he would ask you to come and confer on a part. In his suite, surrounded by his books, one felt that Reinhardt had absorbed all the literature, thought, philosophies, and religions of the world in order to understand plays. . . . He was without the hardness that one had got used to in the American theater. He brought love; and he brought an inner quiet that was the special gift he had—it gave him a quality beyond time."[4]

On opening night, Reinhardt gave each actor a bag of candy. "This took the tension off," Stella remembered. "It made you feel somebody loved you. Candy is something you give—a kind of giving that has no suffering in it: you were a better person around Reinhardt."[5] After the play audience members and colleagues flooded backstage to congratulate the cast. The play was generally well received. The *Christian Science Monitor* called it a "freshly imagined theatrical novelty" in which "Stella Adler gives a fluent performance that won her a burst of applause."[6] Although Stella's role as Peck's lady friend was minor, the *New York Daily News* lauded it as having been performed "intelligently."[7] Other critics were less appreciative of the play. Lewis Nichols of the *New York Times* wrote, "Mr. Reinhardt . . . has tried to bring out the minor characters, succeeding in the latter point to the extent that the play offers a number of fine vignettes, but he has not succeeded in disguising the fact the play is not there to begin with."[8] Although the criticism spoke to the playwriting rather than the directing, Reinhardt was determined to get it right. For the first time in his career he called a rehearsal immediately following opening night. Stella and the entire crew were waiting for him onstage an hour before curtain: "The actors listened to [Reinhardt] raptly and, as though it meant the show's chance for survival, each, in turn, toiled painstakingly over the slightest nuance in word, movement or breath he suggested."[9]

Throughout the remainder of the run the critics reflected favorably upon the production. As Shaw predicted, Peck did get picked up by Hollywood before the play closed on May 22, 1943, after only twenty-two performances.

THE WAR IN EUROPE AND ITS TRAGIC CONSEQUENCES FOR STELLA'S FELLOW Jews seemed hopeless. Stella wanted to lend her support but was not sure exactly where to start. The answer came to her from the Irgun Zvai Leumi

(National Military Organization), which requires an introduction to the group's beginnings. The Irgun began operating in Palestine in 1931 under the command of Vladimir Jabotinsky, a powerful speaker and influential Zionist leader whose career began during the Kishinev pogrom in 1903, the same event that had tapped into Stella's budding political voice when she was just two years old. During World War I Jabotinsky led the establishment of a Jewish army to fight beside the British against the Turks.

At the war's end the English were left with the collateral damage of Jews disenfranchised by the Turks who had fought with England against the Palestinians. As a concession to the Jews, the British issued the Balfour Declaration, which promised to help bring about a Jewish homeland in Palestine. Jewish immigration into Palestine increased after the British mandate, but consequent Arab rioting against the Jewish presence aggravated a population wary of Europeans.

Again during the 1930s, despite the Balfour Declaration, the English limited Jewish immigration into Palestine, setting quotas, which it allowed the Zionist-led Jewish Agency to enforce. As the rights of Jews living in Germany were stripped away, Jabotinsky condemned the Jewish Agency for enforcing the quotas. Consequently, Jabotinsky left the Zionists to establish a revisionist rendition of Zionism: the Irgun Zvai Leumi. The Irgun was already orchestrating an underground movement of illegal immigration when the world entered into a second war.

Wishing neither to add the Arab population as an enemy in the looming war against Germany nor to compromise their position of power in the Middle East, the British issued white papers, entirely reneging on their promise to support a Jewish homeland. Jabotinsky made good use of his flair for oratory to preach that Jews had the right to enter Palestine. More important, Jabotinsky declared that it was only through active armed force that they could ensure a Jewish state.[10] Before long, the British and the Zionists viewed the Irgun as an illegal terrorist organization.

Prior to the outbreak of the war, a young student named Hillel Kook had joined Jabotinsky's revisionist movement and together with other students established a military division. By 1939 Kook was at work smuggling Jews out of an increasingly dangerous Poland when he received orders from Jabotinsky to go to the United States to gather support for the Jewish cause. Specifically, Kook needed to arouse American interest to help secure passage of Europe's persecuted Jews to Palestine.

In the United States, under the alias Peter Bergson, Kook created what became known as the "Bergson Group," which was charged with the mission of establishing a Jewish army. The Committee for a Jewish Army pursued politicians and celebrities to lend credibility and popularity to the cause. Stella, well aware of the refugee problem from her political education in 1938 in London, was easily conscripted. "It was a closed group," Stella remembered, "and we were all very much involved. It was not a popular movement because the Zionists were antagonistic to it, and so we had that fight on our hands."[11] Leading American Jewish figures distrusted the Bergson Group and their radical measures, fearing the repercussions their actions might create for American Jews. They worried that calling attention to the Jewish plight would add kindling to the fire of anti-Semitism in the United States. Rabbi Stephen Wise, president of the American Jewish Congress, was the most visible Jewish leader opposing the Irgun's mission.

By 1943 Hitler's mass genocide had been confirmed, prompting the Bergson Group to shift focus from the Committee for a Jewish Army to the Emergency Committee to Save the Jewish People of Europe by raising public consciousness about the Holocaust. Since Kristallnacht, the *New York Times* had covered Nazi-mandated pogroms only sparsely. At the time of the tragedy, in November of 1938, a survey revealed that more than 70 percent of Americans were against "allowing a larger number of Jewish exiles to come to the United States to live."[12] In early 1943, with the death toll of Jews at two million, the Irgun sponsored a pageant in Madison Square Garden, *We Will Never Die*, to commemorate the murdered. Adverse to any measures that might be construed as anathema to assimilated American Jewry, Rabbi Wise wanted to cancel the performance.

Needing media attention and public support, the pageant's producers asked President Roosevelt if he would send a few words to be read, but Roosevelt refrained for fear of political repercussions. The producers then went to Governor Thomas Dewey to convince him to announce an official day of mourning in New York state on the day of the production. In retaliation, Rabbi Wise took a delegation of Jews to the capital. Wise and his people met with Dewey to persuade him to cancel the day of mourning, claiming Dewey would be prone to lose the people's support if he did not steer away from the "dangerous and irresponsible racketeers who are bringing terrible disgrace on our already harassed people."[13] The governor was not dissuaded: he proclaimed the first day of the production an official day of mourning for the state of New York.

As a member of the production committee of *We Will Never Die*, Stella gathered her forces, including her brother Luther and his wife, Sylvia Sydney, among others to join a cast of hundreds: two hundred rabbis, two hundred cantors, four hundred actors, and one hundred musicians. No doubt she would have recruited more of her talented siblings, but both Celia and Frances were playing together on the Yiddish stage at the Parkway Theatre in Brooklyn in a play titled, ironically, *God, Man, and Devil*.

On March 9 and 10, 1943, *We Will Never Die* played before an audience of over 40,000. Two days later the show was staged at Constitution Hall for Eleanor Roosevelt, six justices of the Supreme Court, and over 200 members of Congress. Millions of people reading about the pageant in the press learned for the first time about Hitler's genocide. The production went to six cities in total, culminating at the Hollywood Bowl on July 21, and was witnessed by over 100,000 spectators in all. Catapulted into the public's awareness by the publicity and exposure created by the pageant, the Bergson Group urged the president to take immediate action. Roosevelt's answer was to form the War Refugee Board, which has been credited with saving 200,000 people in the last eighteen months of the war.[14]

More should have been done. After seeing the pageant, the First Lady was so moved that she wrote about it in her daily column: "No one who heard each group come forward and give the story of what happened to it at the hands of a ruthless military will ever forget the haunting words, 'Remember us!'"[15] But Mrs. Roosevelt did not incite any reaction other than pity. The worse insult came during the pageant's week in Philadelphia, when Roosevelt met with the British in Bermuda to discuss the Jewish refugee problem. Not one delegate broached the idea of opening Palestine for the Jews. Roosevelt held resolute on maintaining a closed-door policy in the United States. Even mainstream Jewish leaders condemned the conference in Bermuda. They were led by Rabbi Israel Goldstein of the American Jewish Congress, who said in a statement: "The job of the Bermuda Conference apparently was not to rescue victims of Nazi terror, but to rescue our State Department and the British Foreign Office from possible embarrassment . . . [it] has been not only a failure but a mockery."[16]

It is as much a reflection of the tumultuous political atmosphere of the era as it was of Stella's dedication to freedom fighting that she had gone from socialism to Marxism to revisionist Zionism in the course of two decades. She saw it as her duty not only to find a home for Jewish refugees, but also to make the United States conscious of its need to help the persecuted. She became cochairperson of the Irgun's Committee for a Jewish Army. The Irgun sponsored a number of political action committees, including the Emergency Committee to Save the Jewish People of Europe, for which Stella and Orson Welles narrated Ben Hecht's scripts "The Battle of the Warsaw Ghetto" and "Dry Bones of Israel" at Carnegie Hall. The show was touted as a tribute to Sweden and Denmark for saving the Danish Jews, but the point of it was to urge the United Nations to take similar action to save European Jewry. Thousands of latecomers found the hall packed to capacity while inside the audience was "stirred to its nethermost depths by Stella Adler and Ralph Bellamy, who was also in the production, as they brought to life the 'battle of the Warsaw Ghetto.'"[17] Stella must have felt especially emotional: the previous night she had learned that her beloved friend and mentor Max Reinhardt had died at age seventy.

Stella wrote that upon hearing the news of Reinhardt's death, she was "stricken . . . I could not go into a theater for many months afterwards. Reinhardt was the theater, in its biggest, most creative sense."[18] Stella never failed to honor the importance of a life lived. She described how "somewhere between you and heaven, there stood Reinhardt—relaxed and communicative, close to you, always available, and yet larger than life."[19] Stella gathered among theater's notables, from Arturo Toscanini to Sholem Asch, to pay her respects at the Free Synagogue. Ironically, Rabbi Stephen Wise officiated at the ceremony. In Wise's final prayer he offered thanks to God "for [Reinhardt's] daring creativeness, rare gift of interpretation, for his translation of the beauty of holiness into the holiness of beauty."[20] No doubt Rabbi Wise was unaware he had an Irgun rebel member among the congress of mourners. Stella, however, was more concerned with honoring Reinhardt than with educating the conservative rabbi.

In tandem with producing pageants alerting the public to the Jewish plight, Bergson's group took out full-page ads, at a time when such explicitly personalized advertisements were not the norm, with headlines such as "How Well Are You Sleeping? Is There Something You Could Have Done to Save Millions of Innocent People—Men, Women, and Children—from Torture and Death?" and "Time Races Death: What Are We Waiting For?" Rabbi Wise and other mainstream American Jews were appalled by what they perceived as incendiary sensationalism that distorted the public perception of Jews.

At this juncture Menachem Begin, who would later become the sixth prime minister of Israel, took over leadership of the Irgun, beginning an armed struggle against the British in Palestine. For their first attack, the Irgun symbolically targeted the British immigration offices in Jerusalem, Tel Aviv, and Haifa, which were successfully bombed without accruing casualties. As the struggle ensued, the Irgun became more aggressive. In 1946 it set its sights on the King David Hotel, which housed the military offices of the British government. The Irgun phoned in a warning to vacate the building, but action was not taken. Seven stories of the southern wing of the hotel were leveled, killing a total of ninety-one people. The Bergson Group arm of the Irgun was concerned with pageants and rallies, so Stella would not have felt personally connected to the organization's terrorist acts; but it was only a matter of time before she would be called on for riskier assignments.

THAT FALL OF 1943 STELLA DIRECTED ROY WALLING'S *MANHATTAN Nocturne*, starring Eddie Dowling. The play opened at the Forest Theatre on October 26. The action of the play takes place in a hotel room between a married couple about to divorce. Lewis Nichols, of the *New York Times*, criticized the drama as a "long composition turned in for English 12, a course open to juniors." As for the direction, he offered: "Stella Adler in her direction has tried to disguise the fact that there is not much action there, but not always has she succeeded."[21] The play closed less than a month later.

Stella wound up back in the place she dreaded most: unemployment. To make matters worse, Harold, also in need of work, returned to Columbia Pictures, once again leaving Stella alone. "I spoke at a memorial for Romain Rolland," Stella begins a letter to Harold, describing a life of renown and socially conscious activity. That same day Stella also spoke on behalf of Spain. The Spanish Loyalists, whom Stella and her colleagues in the Group Theatre had supported throughout the Spanish Civil War, lost the fight against the Nationalists in 1939. Spain fell under the dictatorship of Francisco Franco, who would run the country for the next thirty-six years until his death in 1975. Political activism provided a useful outlet to voice Stella's convictions and optimize her self-worth. The management at the hotels and restaurants she frequented gave her VIP treatment, ordering out for scotch, if that was her request, which she would enjoy mixed with soda. She led a life of renown and activity, but political speeches did not pay the bills.[22]

One source of steady income came from teaching at the New School for Social Research, where she was in her third year at Erwin Piscator's Dramatic Workshop. Stella had met Piscator in Europe prior to his arrival in the United States in 1939. In the early 1930s Piscator, along with Bertolt Brecht, was a leading proponent of a genre of theater founded upon sociopolitical principles rather than commercial fluff. Piscator had had his own theater in Berlin, but once Hitler came to power in 1933 Piscator moved to the Soviet Union in self-imposed exile, where he continued directing until the Communist state became as unbearable as the home he had fled.

Stella was an obvious choice to join Piscator's faculty. Her theatricality made her popular among the students. Her dress, speech, and fervor for the actor harked back to the Yiddish theater, where actors were considered royalty. She infused her lectures with the nobility of the craft, inspiring her students with that same reverence. She brought in leading luminaries of the theater such as Clurman and Odets. And she shared with Piscator empathy for the tragedy playing out in Europe.

In the tradition of *We Will Never Die* Piscator channeled his resources to put on a pageant in the fall of 1943 to bring attention to the ever-dimming reality of European Jewry. *Rally of Hope* was staged on a Sunday afternoon at Madison Square Garden with an impressive cast of six thousand children. From a booth at the side of the arena, Stella narrated the words behind the movements and emotions that thirty actors pantomimed onstage in "The Golden Doors," a sketch symbolizing those storied doors of the temple of Jerusalem through which Jews, excommunicated over the centuries, could enter and live. A declaration was presented at the rally with over 100,000 signatures of Jewish children stating: "We can enjoy no happiness, nor can we rest while those of our blood, Jewish children and their parents, are tortured and put to death by a barbarous enemy. Their sorrow is our sorrow, their misery cannot be forgotten nor can their tormentors be forgiven."[23] The myth of the Promised Land was not merely symbolic for Stella; she was determined to see the realization of a home for her people.

CHAPTER EIGHTEEN

Stella imparts a most valuable kind of information—how to discover the nature of our own emotional mechanics and therefore those of others.

—Karl Malden

S TELLA TREATED HER TEACHING JOB AT THE DRAMATIC WORKSHOP like an acting engagement: breezing in late with coiffed hair, matching outfit and hat, heavily accessorized. She made it out to be a privilege for the students who volunteered to go pay the taxi still waiting for the fare. One had to look closely to see the telltale signs of her profession in the form of an unglued corner of an eyelash or missing rhinestones in her costume jewelry. Stella's lack of self-consciousness kept her mind free for larger concerns, namely instilling in her students the proper reverence for the actor's profession. Svelte, blonde, and long-legged, she had the sophistication of a woman of forty-two, but her face was ageless and would remain so for decades.

By 1943 the basement of the seven-story building of the New School at 66 West Twelfth Street was Stella's domain—to the dismay of Piscator. Like Strasberg, the founder and chief of the Dramatic Workshop was first and foremost a theatrical director. According to his view, the actors were there to partake of his wisdom and experience. Stella, on the other hand, was more interested in cultivating the talent and intuition of her students. She didn't work on plays in her early classes. She emphasized focusing techniques and physical exercises. Piscator resented Stella running her "isolated acting classes,"[1] as he put it. Stella charmed most men, but her redoubtable confidence rubbed self-proclaimed elitists like Strasberg and Piscator the wrong way.

Stella's salary—$75.99 a week[2]—would have been plenty to meet the needs of a small family at a time when a haircut cost fifty cents and dinner for two at a good restaurant ran three dollars plus a quarter tip.[3] For Stella's lifestyle, however, her teaching checks were barely enough to make ends meet. Along with travel, domestic help, and wardrobe upkeep, entertaining was high on Stella's list of necessities, whether out at Sardi's, at the Plaza, or in her own home.

Stella's apartment at 161 West Fifty-fourth Street, where she lived with Harold, Ellen, and Sara, was a magnet for Jewish artists and intellectuals she and Harold had known for years, from Moss Hart to Leonard Bernstein. The Adler family was as busy as ever. Frances and Celia were still acting on the Yiddish stage, and Stella's nieces Lulla and Pearl—Frances's daughters— were also carrying on the family profession; Luther and Sylvia were starring at the Plymouth Theatre that year in *Jane Eyre*. Stella continued to search for her own acting engagements while remaining closely involved with the Irgun's political action committees, recruiting family, friends, and associates to aid the cause.

In her classes Stella was developing a reputation for favoring male over female students, but she was attracted primarily to any student with enough talent and chutzpah to do something with it. In the fall of 1943 a nineteen-year-old recently expelled military-school student named Marlon Brando enrolled at the Dramatic Workshop. Brando was among the first of many fledglings Stella brought into her life. He would later say, "[Stella] taught me all I know. She took me under her wing and is responsible for any acting ability I have."[4] Stella offered Brando, still wet behind the ears, a design for living. As he described it: "A great teacher can show you some safe places to visit, to linger, to pine for, to think about living in. I was given a great syllabus for living from Stella, and when I followed it, good things happened."[5]

Seventeen-year-old Ellen remembered "when he [Brando] first came into our life like an angel,"[6] immediately taking to the soft-spoken, handsome ladies' man. Her love and admiration for him would grow stronger throughout their lives, even years later, after she had married her husband, David Oppenheim. Ellen's cousin recalled dining with Ellen and Oppenheim one evening when, in the middle of dinner, Brando called to invite Ellen to his home in Tahiti, an occurrence that apparently happened often enough that there was no discussion. Ellen packed her bags and went to Brando.[7] They remained close confidants until Brando's death in 2004.

Like Stella, Brando loved to imitate people, no one more so than his teacher. The composer David Diamond was among the stream of guests that frequented Stella's apartment. Diamond remembered how Brando's "parrot routine," as they referred to it, went: "She's talking, and when Stella talks nobody else talks. So Marlon is imitating every gesture." After ten or fifteen minutes of ignoring Marlon's antics, Stella, dressed in her peignoir with nothing on underneath, crossed her legs, "which are rather full down around the calves but gorgeous, gorgeous thighs. The peignoir just simply opened and this leg was there. So what does Marlon do? He takes off his pants, and there he is in his boxer shorts crossing his leg over, showing his thigh."[8]

Upon Stella's recommendation, Brando agreed to audition for a part in what became his first Broadway show, *I Remember Mama*. The play's producers, Richard Rodgers and Oscar Hammerstein, were still riding the coattails of their highly successful *Oklahoma!*, and an unknown like Brando was lucky to be in such company. Rehearsals for *Mama* began just as Ellen finished her liberal arts study at Bard College. She invariably found herself spending much of her time at the Music Box Theatre. Fran Heflin, also in the cast of *Mama*, remembered sometimes hiding Ellen in her dressing room whenever Stella came storming into the theater looking for the *shvartze* (literally, someone dark-skinned, and the term Stella used derisively for Ellen) to send home.[9] "She wanted to break up the relationship," Heflin recalled. "It was the only time in my life I saw her strike a maternal pose, and remember I'd known Stella for years since Van, my brother, had been in the Group."[10]

Many viewed Stella's reprisals as a form of jealousy. Physically, Ellen and Stella were opposites. Ellen's dark features contrasted with Stella's fair skin and light eyes. Brando's biographer described Ellen as "striking . . . a dark gypsy type with coal black hair, quick eyes, and a sense and presence that many found disturbingly precocious."[11] Robert Ellenstein, one of Ellen's suitors at the time, remarked how Stella would dress Ellen down in little girls' dresses—implying that Stella wanted the dark, classically beautiful Ellen to remain subordinate to her.

According to one account, during the production of *Mama* a cast member walked into Brando's dressing room and saw Stella and Brando on the floor, the latter naked. Rumors about Brando and Stella abounded, which were fueled by the fact that Stella did not go to any lengths to hide her sexual exploits even though she was now married to Harold. Another boyfriend of Ellen's from Bard remembered that he and Ellen often went out with Stella and one of her male friends—usually "an older guy with a lot of money who would take us out for delicious dinners."[12]

I Remember Mama opened on October 19, 1944, and put Brando on the map as a new force in the theater. Stella became concerned about how much Ellen and Brando were seeing of one another. One day she called Brando to the Plaza. Her agitation increasing as the conversation came to a head, she finally bellowed: "You are not to see Ellen anymore until you marry her!"[13] Several waiters dropped their trays. The piercing demand startled them not merely because of its volume, but because it carried the tone of a royal decree. Barely in his twenties with an unremitting sexual appetite, Brando would have found the idea of marriage unnerving—as Stella knew. As for the rumors about Stella herself, Brando excised them when he wrote in his autobiography: "We had a lot of flirtatious exchanges, and I suppose that somewhere not far beyond the horizon there was the possibility of a real encounter, but it never materialized."[14]

In the spring of 1944 Stella returned to the stage in a new play called *Pretty Little Parlor*. Stella played the lead role as an attractive woman her own age, something the Group Theatre had never offered her. The day before opening night, Stella gave an analysis of the drama: "A play like 'Pretty Little Parlor' which strips woman of her masquerade costume and presents her 100 percent in the flesh could have been written only by a woman. A woman is aware of the tricks of the trade, so to speak, of other women."[15] Ironically, Stella herself was never entirely "stripped of her masquerade." Many people were put off by Stella's theatricality, affected speech, and ostentatious attire. Gottfried Reinhardt wrote that Stella's "flamboyance often makes people underestimate her realism."[16] Her larger-than-life persona and nineteenth-century vestments and comportment acted as armor, preserving the youth she idealized under her father's wing.

Of the play, one reviewer remarked, "Stella Adler stepped in to touch [the character] up, and she obviously is having a field day. The fact that she cannot make the part real no doubt lies in the writing, for no one can say Miss Adler does not try. She is all over the stage, harassed, moaning, vicious in turn. A great deal of energy is being put forth at the National."[17] In the play Stella's character, Clotilde, connives her way into the lives of her husband and daughters, getting one daughter to steal away the boyfriend of a stepdaughter and flirting with railroad executives to get her husband a better paycheck.

"When *Pretty Little Parlor* played in Boston," Stella told an interviewer, "I was flooded with fan mail, mostly from women who identified Clotilde as a member of their own social circles. It's true—part of Clotilde is in every woman. I, too, know my share of Clotilde's. Not one of the fan letters I read, however, failed to add the postscript that the writer, of course, was not a Clotilde. Let me assure you and them that neither am I."[18] Stella continued to explain that Clotilde "dominates her empire by dominating over all the members of it."[19] Stella's dissociation from Clotilde's domineering nature is ironic. She fails to acknowledge her domination over those around her, still identifying as a shy, unanchored girl among a theatrical world of giants.

The play closed a week after it opened on April 22, 1944. Stella knew as well as any seasoned actor the fickle nature of show business. And if she forgot, Harold was always there to assuage the pain with his sober, idealistic consolations. Still in Hollywood, now working for RKO Radio Pictures, Clurman was as bound by the shackles of show business as his wife. He wrote to his "Golden Girl," enclosing a rent check and updating her with news of their colleagues—Odets, Kazan, and Sylvia Sydney (now divorced from Luther)—all equally caught up in Tinseltown's rat race.

Clurman described Odets as being in a slumber from which the only indication of life was teeth grinding and rolling over in his sleep—and even in the state of somnolence, Clurman added, Odets made money. Kazan was described as a glutton, silently eating his work, his girlfriend, time, and space. Sylvia came across to Clurman as a "wreck," though he didn't attribute it to her divorce or her faltering career, but rather her very being, which he characterized as bitter.

Ever the critic, whether of art or society, Clurman sees past the veneer and into the soul. He assures Stella that her own battles of the heart are of a different caliber than those of her former sister-in-law: "There is consequently no beauty of soul, no nobility, no richness of texture in her gaiety . . . that is far far worse than the assorted demons that dance in your heart. . . . You are always (or almost always) in touch with some greatness— of aspiration, dream, sorrow, laughter or wonder. Even your confusions— descents into the murky—have . . . a degree of stature about them."[21]

Harold knew just what to say to Stella. He characterizes her bouts of depression as courageously noble. Not one to indulge in self-pity, Stella took immediate action, volunteering to become vice chairperson of the Irgun's newest committee in charge of establishing a Jewish homeland: the

American League for a Free Palestine. Stella offered her Manhattan home for meetings, but the political work did not compensate for her real work in the theater. When her cohorts went home and the embers of day grew faint, Stella faced the darkness of night without even a footlight to illuminate the empty stage. Nights grew into months, dissatisfaction turned to failure, and mounting financial stress led to exhaustion and depression. On May 2 she wrote to Harold explaining that her doctor described her symptoms as "long periods of falling down into somewhere." Money, or the lack thereof, plagued her. She considered gong on a USO tour, but her doctor advised against it. Along with feeling emotionally dispirited, she lacked her usual boundless energy. "A doctor once told me 'you must live with this intense inner pain and ignore it—Just go on as if it weren't there' and that's what I'm doing—I must only try to get back my legs, my body which is wracked with fatigue by forces which I can't control."[22]

Stella's description of "periods of falling down into somewhere" is a classic one of clinical depression, with which she would be diagnosed later in life in correlation with stress or loss. She did not suffer ongoing depression, but rather what is sometimes referred to as "circumstantial" depression. At a time before antidepressants and popular awareness of the disease, it would have been confusing for Stella, with her voracious appetite for life, to experience such unaccountable hopelessness. She instructed Harold not to tell anyone that she was ill, saying that only he and Ellen knew the extent of her debilitation, euphemistically characterizing it as a simple case of bad nerves. Her only defense was to keep busy.

Soon after writing this letter, Stella went on tour in the prolific writer Ben Hecht's *A Guide for the Bedeviled* to raise awareness and money for the American League for a Free Palestine. The project reunited her with the Yiddish player Jacob Ben-Ami, reminding her of the Yiddish theater, which she called the "most important period of [my] life because [I] was happy."[23] Yet the happiness Stella remembered from her childhood had more to do with having an assigned role in the world than with the ethereal emotion of joy. When her childhood's theatrical life fell away, Stella had to begin defining for herself the purpose of her life. As long as she chased a past that could no longer be resurrected, she would be unable to create a new definition of happiness for herself.

Back in 1939, when Stella made the decision to leave the Group and break out on her own in Hollywood, she began a five-year-long struggle to make good. By the end of 1944, the depression mounted into symptoms of alienation and obsessive worrying that baffled her. She could not express her personal struggle to anyone, and was even unable to write to the two people closest to her, Harold and Ellen. She referred to this "new symptom" in a missive she finally drummed up the courage to send to Harold in December of 1944, in which she described her frustration at not being able to write to anyone, especially him and Ellen. She acknowledged that she had taken on "psychologically the blame for not being active theatrically.... On the surface, of course, things seem to be going rather well with me. I look well, am quite gay and there is a permanent duality which bothers me."[24]

In early March of 1945 Stella gave a cocktail party at her apartment to benefit the American Committee for Yugoslav Relief. Stella acted as mistress of ceremonies for a program featuring entertainers from various hit Broadway shows. The committee successfully collected and shipped used clothing and other supplies to Yugoslavia's liberated areas. Then the news came.

The ailing president had died. "I was on the hill from Bankhead's office when I heard Roosevelt died," Stella recalled. "And when I went back to what was going to be the Israeli Embassy . . . there wasn't a man who didn't say 'that son of a bitch, Roosevelt, he didn't give us a boat. We're glad he's dead.' . . . At any rate there was a little store when I came back home, nothing but mourning, there was a little tailor shop that said, 'Closed for the week, we have lost a member of our family.' That was the love for Roosevelt, but not the Jews. He had it in his hands to save them and he didn't. You could say that was the biggest mistake Roosevelt made."[25]

The following month American and Soviet troops finally defeated Germany. That summer the war officially ended, and all the horrors of the Holocaust came to light in an unfathomable onslaught of images and reportage. An estimated ten million people had been murdered, over half of them Jews. For the prisoners who survived, now refugees, the fight was hardly over. The initial plan was to send survivors back to their country of origin. This became a complicated issue for Jews without a country that would claim them. Displaced-person (DP) camps were set up during the months and years following the war where many European Jews remained malnourished, ill, and stateless.

As the images of ovens used for extermination, corpses piled into stacks like scrap heaps, and the living skeletons who were the survivors reached the world, people were shocked at what they chose not to believe before the end of the war. For Stella and the Irgun, the war's end was merely the beginning of their fight. Most American Jews who had remained silent during the war felt an unshakable shame. Stella, even with the work she had done, could not feel that it had been enough. The helpless clarity of hindsight sent convulsions of sobs that continue to reverberate in memorials and testimonies across the world. For Stella, work, as always, was the antidote.

In the fall of 1945 Stella collaborated with Gottfried Reinhardt on a new musical: *Polonaise*. Stella directed the performance, about which the *New York Times* stated, "Marching in measured tread on the Alvin Saturday night, *Polonaise* turned out to be one of the year's largest musicals, but one with comparable faults."[26] The critic proceeded to point out flaws in every area except the music and costumes: "'Polonaise' is mumbling with book trouble, the direction being such as to make the words more than a little foolish. The acting is studied rather than spirited, the dancing is athletic rather than imaginative." Whatever problems the production may have had, Stella worked with her players, and *Polonaise* continued for a successful 113 performances. Apparently the public saw something of worth in it that the critics did not. Stella had gotten "her legs back," *Polonaise* enjoying the longest run of anything she had directed until then.

In early 1946 Tyrone Guthrie came to town to direct *He Who Gets Slapped*. He wanted Stella in the play. At first she passed up the offer. The play deals with a jilted man who, betrayed by his wife and best friend, joins the circus. Guthrie wanted Stella to play the character of Zinaida, the lion tamer, and he would not take no for an answer. Finally Stella agreed because, as she later admitted, she wanted to see Guthrie direct.[27] Upon first meeting Guthrie and his wife, Judith, who had adapted the script, Stella was shocked by the shabbiness of their attire. "He had just come from London and he was in tatters. You wouldn't believe that Tony Guthrie was an aristocrat who owned a major estate in Ireland."[28] Stella bought Judith a fur coat.

On opening night, March 20, 1946, the play was a success, but Stella received mixed reviews. As much as Stella said to the contrary, it is unlikely she would have been unaware of the reviews; she was born into the theater, and like it or not, reviews were inherent to stage life. When she was later asked whether reviews affected her decision to stop acting, Stella demurred. "I don't know, and I didn't know about the notices. I probably would have stopped acting for the rest of my life."[29] Feelings of failure heightened the depression that she had been battling over the previous two years. As much as she struggled to maintain the façade of being "fine," others were noticing a difference in Stella.

Odets first noticed a "change in Stella's nature" at a gathering at Luther Adler's ranch in 1940.[30] Odets nursed an ongoing resentment toward Stella for treating Harold cruelly, but his observation is singular: "Something is happening to one side of [Stella]. For the first time I noticed that she is growing hard and vulgar."[31] Brando wrote in his autobiography that he saw Stella as "a woman much disappointed by what life had dealt her. She was a marvelous actress who unfortunately never got a chance to become a great star, and I think this embittered her."[32]

Brando's observation when he was both physically and emotionally near Stella has merit. No doubt many people observed a woman unhappy with "what life had dealt her," especially as it manifested in a fury and impatience with life. Stella had become tired of waiting for life to hurry up and align with her vision of success.

Her feelings of being trapped in the shadow of her parents and separate from others fostered a paradoxical sense of superiority in the midst of deep insecurity. Stella could be generous yet purposely withholding, independent yet fearful of being alone, irreverent yet punctilious, encouraging yet belittling, devoted and yet devastatingly cruel. This last trait is what most baffled those around her. One might be in her graces one moment and then, for reasons only known to Stella—impatience with a situation, financial insecurity, a bad hair day (Stella dyed her own hair and it didn't always turn out to be a flattering color)—one would have to bear the brunt of her rancor. In his memoir the playwright Arthur Laurents wrote, "Meet Stella Adler and in two minutes you knew she was a formidable whatever she wanted to be, including your enemy."[33]

Why did those around her subject themselves to her ire? Those who were intimate with Stella, of which there were few at a time, could tolerate her wrathful moments when they were put into context. They understood the fear underlying her behavior and waited the mood out. It was worth it because when life went her way, Stella enabled them to feel the potential of their greatness. She knew how to push others toward it. Her passion could be justified when taking into account the life force she exuded. When you were with Stella, testimony after testimony relates, you felt as if you were the most important person in the world.

Stella's contradictions were pronounced due to her acute sensitivity. She spoke to this nature of hers, and that of humankind, while lecturing on Eugene O'Neill:

> I can say for myself, logically, that I'm very nice, but internally I'm aghast at what goes on inside—at the mix-up in me. That's our inheritance. Some people inherited God and the way to live and pray, but most of us in the twentieth century inherited internal confusion.

We hang on to something logical—work or studies or becoming something—but the rest is in turmoil. If you dig down too far inside, you might go insane; we can deal with the outside much more logically. If you go inside, there's a great deal of anger, depression, belligerence. All of O'Neill's characters have this. He was a pioneer of that new sense of confusion.[34]

Stella's classes inspired her students to grow creatively while invariably elucidating their humanity. She was one of a few people in the United States talking about spiritual matters in a secular context. Her students gained a greater understanding of themselves. It was worth risking a brutal outburst once in a while.

Discussing acting, then, meant spotlighting the human condition, because that is what the playwrights illuminate. When lecturing on Tennessee Williams's *Summer and Smoke*, Stella delves into spiritual matters in order to elucidate the characters: "Illness in modern man is not so much physical; it comes from his anxiety and spiritual stress. When he satisfies his material side, it kills his instinct for the spiritual side. He's in trouble, and he knows it. People with inner troubles used to be told to go read or paint or do carpentry, or go to a rabbi or priest and pray. . . . You also had to use your hands. You had to weave, sew, do or make something useful, because it's not in a human being to be God-directed all the time. You had to balance it. . . . Actors have to go to work, too."[35]

During a lecture on Williams's *The Glass Menagerie*, Stella instructs students about finding the humanity in their characters:

Tennessee feels we are drawn to people who play music or write poetry or go off to see the world out of a desire to solve The Problem. . . . Do you know people who are attracted to you because you're "offbeat"? . . . The tendency in the beginning is to think of yourself as superior to such people. But they exist in you and me, too. You have to be damn stupid to feel superior to anybody, because the seed of that other person is in you. Discover the seed! If you do, you will educate yourself about life and about yourself. You don't know yourself. Nobody does. I don't know my own self. You see me as very strong. You don't know that I have a daughter who says, "Oh, Mother, you're so foolish—won't you ever learn?" And I take it from her. That's a side of me you don't see. . . . Never put yourself above the character. Since there are no heroes or villains anymore, you must ask, "What about him is human? How am I like him?"[36]

In art Stella found humility, but it was not easy for her to do the same in life.

Brando's observation of Stella as an embittered woman reflected his perception of Stella at a specific time in her life, which does not negate the person more often associated with a voracious appetite for life. A woman so engrossed with nature and literature and history and life's pursuits could have her bitter moments, but it certainly wasn't her most salient personality trait.

As *I Remember Mama* approached the anniversary of its second year running, Brando was becoming restless. Stella came to the rescue. She wanted her protégé to play in the production Clurman and Kazan were collaborating on, *Truckline Café*. Brando jumped at the opportunity to shake up his life and take on a new project.

As casting commenced, Clurman approached Kazan about Stella's suggestion to use Brando. Kazan didn't like the idea. He remembered all too clearly how he felt whenever Stella pushed her agenda into Group productions. He didn't want her to have any connection with this latest enterprise with Clurman, but the latter had a gift for persuasion that the up-and-coming Kazan could not resist. Brando was allowed to audition, and though it wasn't the best reading they had sat through, Clurman had seen enough of Brando in *Mama* to know he was perfect for the small role of the tormented Sage in *Truckline Café*. Kazan obliged his colleague. The play ended up failing dismally, but it was the vehicle that showcased Brando's talent and launched his career.

Everyone from Jessica Tandy to Karl Malden was floored by the "honesty" of Brando's performance, the way his entrance, however brief, "lit up" the stage.[37] Malden remembered that Brando "came through like a bolt of lightning. It was a monologue, a good page of script, why he killed his wife. In fifty years in the business, I've never seen it happen before, and it's never happened since: He stopped the show. Nobody could continue for over a minute and half, two minutes."[38] After seeing him perform, Sara Adler, with whom Brando would sit for hours in Stella's apartment listening to stories about the Yiddish stage, told him: "If you want, you can change your name to Adler."[39]

The reviews of the play were another story. The *New York Daily News* critic announced that it was the worst play he had seen in his entire career. À la Group Theatre zealousness, Clurman and Kazan took out an ad in the *New York Times* asking the public not to let the critics decide for them which plays were good and bad. An editorial dialogue erupted with a slew of incoming letters to the editors of New York presses, creating buzz for the doomed play. The play's strongest point, everyone agreed, was Brando, the fresh talent with such magnetic presence that he wound up being touted as the new Montgomery Clift.

David Diamond remembered dining in Sardi's with Stella and the producer Kermit Bloomgarden during the height of the controversy over *Truckline*. "Stella saw him [Brando] and immediately beckoned him over: 'How's my beautiful, wonderful genius? Come here!' Everybody knew who he was and he took it as though it were the most natural thing in the world. No shifting around, no discomfort as you'd see with Monty . . . he embraced Stella. As usual, she had one of her goddamn hats on, and I can still see him getting caught in her veil."[40] Being summoned and coddled by Stella Adler in Sardi's was not something to be taken lightly. Stella tended not to notice anyone beyond the person sitting next to her, but Brando was now as much a part of her inner sanctum as her immediate family. It was definitely a sign of how far he had come.

Before long MGM offered Brando a seven-year contract, but he adopted Stella's air of contempt for Hollywood, choosing instead to follow her lead and lend his talent to the cause at hand. Hollywood would have to wait.

The Irgun recruited Brando and other students to deliver soapbox speeches on Manhattan's sidewalks. When a crowd drew close, a League member would infiltrate to answer questions and debate arguments.[41] Indeed, Brando's next role couldn't have been further from Hollywood. Ben Hecht had completed a new script for the Jewish cause, *A Flag Is Born*, in which Luther Adler made his directorial debut. Although everyone else in the cast was Jewish, Stella recommended Brando for a part in the production. "Do you think he can play this?" Luther asked Stella. "He can play anything," she replied.[42] Rehearsals began for *A Flag Is Born* in an empty studio above Al and Dick's Restaurant on West Fifty-fourth Street.[43] Ellen became Luther's assistant in order to be near Marlon.

A melodrama in the truest sense, *A Flag Is Born* moved audiences to tears. The story is set in a graveyard where three Holocaust survivors meet: an elderly couple and a young man, David, played by Brando. The indomitable Celia Adler played the older woman. The screen star Paul Muni, who had also been trained on the Yiddish stage, played Celia's character's husband. Brando's character symbolized the new Jew leaving the "graveyard of Europe" for Palestine,[44] admonishing the American Jews for their silence. Brando later wrote about his experience: "Everyone in *A Flag Is Born* was Jewish but me. Paul Muni, the star, gave an astonishing performance, the best acting I have ever seen. I was onstage with him and he gave *me* goose bumps. . . . At one [performance] when I asked, 'Where were *you* when six million Jews were being burned to death in the ovens of Auschwitz?' a woman was so overcome with anger and guilt that she rose and shouted back at me, 'Where were *you*?'"[45]

Critics hailed the play and audiences kept it in demand, prompting an extension of its four-week run to ten weeks. When Paul Muni had to get back to work in Hollywood, Luther took over the part opposite his half sister, Celia. Stella was meanwhile embroiled in more hands-on work. Before *A Flag Is Born* went into production, Stella had departed on the *Queen Mary* to travel to England and France for the "business of production of plays," according to her FBI file, which by now was tracking her every movement. Europe was unrecognizable to Stella. An unsettling cloud of decay hovered over the Continent. When the Paris peace conference adjourned, Soviet imperialism under Stalin injected itself up and down Eastern and Central Europe. There was the physical devastation of the infrastructure, leading to horrid, unsanitary living conditions, while a more insidious unseen aftermath awaited Europe's nations, now in the hands of the Soviet and American victors.

From Europe the Irgun sent Stella to Mexico to establish a Mexican League for a Free Palestine, a trip that caused an uproar in Washington. A letter to the War Department dated October 23, 1946, came from a former army intelligence officer who had been vacationing in Mexico when he met Stella. In the report, the officer claimed Stella

said she was a member of the Adler Family of New York theatrical fame. When questioned as to why she was in Mexico, she stated she was here on a political mission connected with the Zionist movement. She liked to talk and very bitterly attacked the British Government. She also severely criticized the U.S. Government but had only praise for the USSR. As a solution for the trouble in Palestine, she suggested that Russia be allowed to move in and take over. Although she stated she was connected with the Zionist movement, most of her statements were in criticism of Great Britain and the USA and in praising Russia. . . . While in Mexico City she stayed at the Hotel Reforma and entertained lavishly.[46]

Rabbi Baruch Rabinowitz, who had been chosen by Bergson as a full-time lobbyist on Capitol Hill, accompanied Stella to Mexico City. Their mission was to organize the Jews in Mexico—many of whom had escaped to Mexico during and after the war—in support of those fighting underground to establish a Jewish state. However, they were not addressing a sympathetic audience. Mexican Jewry, like American, was antagonistic to what the media described as "terrorist" activity. The Irgun financed the rental of a large hall to accommodate as many gatherers as possible. One Yiddish paper reported that terrorists were using Stella's beauty and sex appeal to lure the Jews of Mexico into supporting the group. Though Stella was insulted by the accusation, the publicity helped bring in approximately a thousand Jews to the gathering.

Stella paced backstage before going on to deliver "My Dark Prayer." Rabinowitz later wrote, "Stella Adler was a great actress, but it was no act she put on that night. Ben Hecht wrote the words, but they poured out of her soul like furious, hissing fire. She felt what she spoke. The great assembly was silent. Stella stood there, shoulders back, head held high, her blonde hair like a golden halo around her angelic face."[47] On cue Stella delivered the speech: "The Jews who have been murdered by the Germans—a whole continent of them—are vague people to me, not as vague as the Chinese or the Greeks, but sufficiently diluted by distance and separate cultures to seem almost strangers. They never quite lived in my mind, and then never quite died. What lived and died was the beating of hearts, the warmth of faces and the rights of man."[48]

Stella's perfect Yiddish and practiced voice soothed the audience, melting away their armor of dissent just as she was ready to introduce Rabinowitz. The rabbi began to address the audience when a man in the crowd yelled, "Fascist, fascist." The rabbi recognized him as a leader in the Mexican Zionist Organization. People in the audience told the man to be quiet and let the rabbi proceed, but the man kept spewing forth accusations until he was finally removed from the crowd. Stella knew the assembly had been won over. She had learned how to read a crowd early on while touring as a toddler with Jacob to raise funds for such causes. Her early education had taught her that people give from emotion, not reason. Once Rabinowitz finished and the crowd had stood and stamped and whistled, Stella addressed the audience: "You see, you see, there are thousands like him, fighting for us all. We had no intention of asking for contributions, but now as a show of confidence, I ask you for money. We need money, the boys and girls in Palestine cannot fight with bare hands."[49] They collected 50,000 pesos, the equivalent of $2,000.

As the news of the meeting spread, Stella traveled throughout Mexico to Cuernavaca, Acapulco, and Taxco making speeches to spread the word for the Jewish refugees. At this time another unnamed "reliable source" reported to the FBI, "Miss Adler might well be a Communist agent being used for infiltration into the Jewish organizations."[50] As Stella's FBI file grew fatter, so did the supposed evidence of her Communist involvement, ammunition for the powers in government looking for a scapegoat.

In January *A Flag Is Born* went on the road, opening in Chicago with a four-week run. By the time the show reached Philadelphia, Stella had returned from Mexico, and she now stood in for Quentin Reynolds as the narrator. Sidney Lumet took over Brando's role, and Jacob Ben-Ami replaced Paul Muni. Stella joined the tour just as local Zionist organizations joined together to boycott the show. Demonstrators picketed with placards warning "Do not attend this play!" and "Do not contribute as the money is being wasted!"[51]

The production planned to appear in Baltimore next but ran into trouble when they discovered segregation mandates that made it impossible for blacks and whites to sit together in Washington. The League pulled the play from the National Theatre, and proceeded to find a different venue in Baltimore that would offer desegregated seating—an unprecedented move twenty years before the civil rights movement. A special railroad car brought members of Congress and their guests to the performance. It was the first time in Maryland's history that blacks and whites had sat next to one another in the legitimate theater.

By the end of the tour *A Flag Is Born* had raised $400,000. A portion of the money went toward buying a four-hundred-ton yacht to convey six hundred refugees to Palestine. Twenty-one American volunteers manned the ship, named the SS *Ben Hecht*. En route to Palestine, however, only ten miles from the shoreline, the British captured the vessel and sent its passengers to a detention camp in Cyprus—the fate of many similar attempts of refugees making their way to Palestine. With Americans on board, the Brits were deemed as inhospitable, arousing an anti-British sentiment that was something of a consolation for a cause little understood and less supported by the general public. The tide was shifting. In a little over a year Stella and the Irgun would see their efforts pay off in the founding of the state of Israel. But first Stella's involvement would become more dangerous: to her résumé of actress, director, and film producer, she would be adding gunrunner.

CHAPTER NINETEEN

The greatest role Stella ever played in her life was Stella.

—Jayne Meadows

A TREMENDOUS SENSE OF ALIENATION AND LOSS FESTERED AMONG many Americans who still related culturally to Europe and had ties there. Stella remembered the Vienna State Opera came to Carnegie Hall after the war. The audience for the Austrian company was composed largely of Europeans and Russians who had been brought up on German opera. They reveled in the familiar language and melodies, but when the production ended, the performers held hands and began to sing a German national song. "All those actors they couldn't do it," Stella remembered. "They all lined up and this orchestra started and they broke and the audience broke to pieces. I never saw anything absolutely so understanding than that audience. . . . There was such a weeping, such a nostalgia, having lost the comradeship and the closeness and all that was in us and that was in them, and when they broke, I tell you the whole audience broke. I can't even talk about it."[1]

For Stella and the Irgun, the continued refugee problem remained the most alarming aftermath of the war. On May 18, 1947, Stella attended the annual luncheon of the women's division of HIAS (Hebrew Immigrant Aid Society), where she spoke to one thousand members of the organization in the ballroom at the Waldorf-Astoria. She shared the stage with a Dr. Ruth Gruber, who had recently toured Europe, the Middle East, and Palestine urging the audience to write to President Harry Truman to support displaced persons. HIAS chose to sponsor Stella on a similar tour scheduled for the following year.

As the cold war began, the conservative powers in government began capitalizing upon the fear of war with the Soviet Union. The House Un-American Activities Committee (HUAC)—which, from 1934 to 1937, investigated political propaganda, especially that coming out of Nazi Germany—was reinstated. Now, however, HUAC was being used to infiltrate and destroy "subversive" activity among American citizens. Communism became a convenient target as HUAC set its sights on individuals in the entertainment industry, long associated with left-wing politics. The attack centered on entertainers for two main reasons: one, film had tremendous influence and could send "subversive" messages to a mass population; and two, because of their fame, celebrities attracted publicity for the Communist cause. When HUAC went after Stella's friends and colleagues, she remained close to events to lend her support.

In October of 1947 HUAC called "friendly" witnesses, who were asked to reveal their own and others' ties with the Communist party. Of these only eleven actually went to the investigative hearing. The German playwright Bertolt Brecht was among those summoned. Stella insisted on traveling with Brecht and the others to Washington from New York, a decision she'd be asked to account for in the near future.

In the courtroom Stella sat near Brecht, the only witness who cooperated with the committee. Brecht would be seen by his colleagues as a traitor and treated as a pariah, and Stella surmised that he would leave the country. At one point during the hearing she whispered to him, "When will I see you, Brecht?"[2] She didn't get the chance. As soon as the hearing ended Brecht boarded the next boat to East Germany. The other witnesses went down in history as the "Hollywood Ten." For exercising their Fifth Amendment right against self-incrimination and refusing to testify, they were sentenced to jail. Afterward, the artists were blacklisted from working in Hollywood.

Unbeknownst to Stella, while she was living on West Fifty-fourth Street her superintendent, Valentine Spaniak, was spying on her and supplying the FBI with information. Spaniak reported the temporary use of the apartment by two men who he made the point of mentioning were of "dark complexion."[3] Spaniak added that he overheard these men talking about baseball and quoted them saying the country "would be bombed to ashes before the pennant race is decided."[4] Adding fuel to the fire, Spaniak described Harold and Stella as having "arrogant, undemocratic manners" and holding "noisy parties" at their apartment.

In preparation for her HIAS-sponsored tour of Europe, Stella had to file for a new passport, since she had lost the original. Stories vary as to whether the FBI confiscated her passport, it expired, or she simply misplaced it. From Los Angles both Stella and Harold had to write letters as part of the application: it was apparently protocol for husbands to give wives permission. Stella's letter stated: "I am going to Paris, France with my daughter to join my sister and her family who are residing there. I expect to visit with them for five or six months, possibly go South with my sister during that time and return home at the end of six months."[5]

While her passport was being processed, United States Pictures contracted Stella for the small role of Mrs. Faludi, a Hungarian matriarch, in the film *My Girl Tisa*, a little-known film set in 1905 in which all the characters have recently immigrated to the United States. The role captures Stella's talent for characterization. With a dark mole painted on her cheek, a Hungarian accent, and the hands-on-hips stance of a hardworking rural mother, Stella gives a portrait of a stout, self-possessed woman whose forefathers lived off the land.

The press awaited Stella's arrival in Paris on May 20, 1948. She made a statement regarding her scheduled tour of the DP camps, which included going to Germany and Italy and then on to Palestine. Stella said she would "make a first hand report to the American public and especially to the women of America on the fate of the hundred[s] of thousands of displaced persons still remaining in camps throughout Europe,"[6] setting down in print her reason for being there. Stella emphasized women in her statement since she was officially there for the women's division of HIAS. No doubt it was her way of directing attention away from her unofficial reason for going to Europe.

The Irgun had planned an undercover mission for Stella. From Paris she was assigned to travel to Munich, carrying illegal passports that would allow the DPs from the camps to travel through Europe on their way to Palestine. Guns—supplied, ironically, by the defeated German army—were bought to give to the underground militia in Palestine. Stella remembered traveling to Munich two times, the weapons fitted discreetly into her traveling trunks. Luggage inspection was not as strict as it had been before or during the war, but getting caught with the guns was still a dangerous possibility.

One of the most frightening situations Stella recalled was trying to find a train to transfer the DPs out of the camps. If she failed, the guns and the documents would be for naught. Stella went to the American consulate to ask for a train, but the official on duty refused her request. Knowing what was at stake, Stella stood her ground and did what came naturally to her: she performed. She smiled at the official and categorically bluffed: "Then we'll get them without you."[7] Her confidence impressed the official.

He intimated that if she could get a train and he didn't know about it, she should go ahead and do it.[8] Stella assured the officer that discretion was her middle name, and a train was "unofficially" granted.

Getting the train out of Germany was another matter. As Stella and the displaced persons approached the Italian frontier, the border patrol stopped the train. Halted at the Italian border with forged passports, smuggled arms, and a train of Holocaust survivors in her care, she didn't have much time to process her predicament. Before disembarking perhaps Stella applied a fresh coat of lipstick. She stood up from her seat, patting down the suit. Once on solid ground, she saw the border guards waiting. Taking a breath, Stella strode toward them and, wasting no time, asked that the train be allowed to pass. They looked her over, perhaps conferred among themselves, and, to Stella's relief, allowed the train to move forward. Years later Stella would be credited with saving the lives of seven hundred Jewish refugees. Little more is known about the conclusion of her journey after she passed through Italy, but one can surmise that the refugees did not reach Palestine. Because of the British embargo preventing Jews from entering Palestine, the last ship aided by the Irgun to successfully get through the British dragnet arrived in February of 1940. Subsequent vessels were deported elsewhere, with refugees detained in camps until they were either later admitted to what would become Israel or simply directed back to Europe, where their fate lay in the hands of the Nazis.

While Stella secured transportation, smuggled illegal documents, and dispensed armaments for the Irgun, Clurman was safe in New York doing what he did best: directing. Since the Group broke up he had gotten several productions under his belt, including Arthur Miller's *All My Sons*, which enjoyed a substantial run. He had also taken over rehearsals from Kazan for *A Streetcar Named Desire*, Tennessee Williams's stellar hit that had been dazzling audiences since it opened in December of the previous year. Marlon Brando's animal magnetism in the lead role of Stanley Kowalski riveted audiences. In the fall of 1948 Clurman accepted another directing offer: *The Young and Fair*. With this production, his financial compensation was finally beginning to match his talent: he earned $3,500 for his services, twice what he had been paid for *Truckline Café*. For the time being Stella and Harold's financial worries were alleviated, and they could concern themselves with the worthier causes of politics and art.

Stella rang in the new year at a Manhattan party where she met a young poet who would become her on-again, off-again lover for the next few decades. Tall, erudite, distinguished-looking, Stanley Moss was the perfect escort. Their love affair was marked by tempestuous arguments and equally ardent capitulations. According to Moss, Stella wanted to marry him, but unlike Harold or other lovers blinded by love, Moss maintained a realistic view of Stella. He knew her secrets, her upbringing, her restless artist's heart, and judged it best to remain free of marital ties.

When this author interviewed Moss, he seemed to be the only person still living (besides Stella's daughter, who was not forthcoming) who knew about aspects of Stella's life she would never talk about with anyone except a lover. Moss informed the author that Stella had told him Jacob had slept in her bed until she was eighteen, as previously mentioned. He also recalled Jacob as having been arrested for child molestation, but reports were never found to corroborate Moss's story. Jacob came from an era and a culture in which it was not abnormal for him to wed sixteen-year-old Dinah Shtettin, his second wife, when he was thirty-one. Russian mores differed from those in the New World, where his penchant for girls would have had more serious consequences. When this author mentioned to Stella's daughter what Moss had shared about Jacob and Stella's sleeping arrangements, querying whether she thought Stella had had sexual relations with Jacob, Ellen flippantly responded that if things had gone that far Stella would have "bragged about it,"[9] illuminating the extent to which the Old World mentality prevailed.

Discussing the Russian lechery with Allison Adler, the daughter of Jacob's grandson and Stella's great-niece, Allison explained, "that behavior was acceptable." Allison had grown up close to her uncle Luther, but even he made a sexual advance toward her. Allison had the moxie to push him away. She stopped speaking to him for a while and then received a note telling her that he forgave her. Livid, their estrangement continued until Allison decided to forgive him. She recalled visiting him in Florida when she was seventeen years old, where he was filming *Absence of Malice*, and being introduced to Paul Newman. Allison also remembered one of Stella's teachers at her school who made a pass at her. When she told her aunt, Stella responded, "He's Russian and he's a man. What do you want me to do?"[10]

IN THE SUMMER OF 1948, STELLA SET SAIL ON THE *QUEEN MARY* FOR A European pilgrimage even though airplanes had begun replacing travel by sea, leaving in its wake a timeless history of the interludes between continents. Stella preferred traveling by ship—an island unto itself where the rest of the world ceased to exist. The elegant architecture, decorum, and catered life on board appealed to Stella's sensibilities. Later she wrote about this excursion, displaying her talent for writing (although she never felt she was any good at it):

> Nobody could be accused of bad manners in reporting that the most elegant Queen I know, Mary, was either as drunk as a lord or as disorganized as a first rehearsal, when she sailed for Europe. The exquisite self-confident pilot boat slipped away leaving us stumbling over baggage, bumping into old friends, tumbling into staterooms finding unexpected gifts and telegrams, and looking vainly for expected ones, catching a last glimpse of a mist-enveloped skyline which might have been laughing ruthlessly at this romantic chaos, but she rose too high above us and we were already far away.[11]

Her fellow passengers included celebrities, intellectuals, and royalty: "'Did I know the Countess of Sandwich,' I was asked as a tray of them slid away from my extended hand." Strolling one afternoon tranquilly along the sundeck, Harpo Marx perused a manuscript, explaining to Stella that the book was the story of the Marx Brothers by Kyle Creighton, which was sent for his approval. He told her it was really about his mother, whom he claimed was responsible for their success. Stella could identify; she understood the extent of parental influence. Harpo invited himself to her company, seemingly eager to talk to another performer, someone who understood. Marx slumped into his chair, smoking a cigarette, while Stella noted how typically English he was with his comely face and "actor's mask." They discussed Charlie Chaplin and the French actor Jean-Louis Barrault. Marx commented that Chaplin should have never become political. The conversation moved on to Alfred Hitchcock and the challenge his directing proved for Marx, while across the deck Stella observed Suzy Solidor, the famous cabaret singer, whose ankle had been injured and yet, Stella noted, how a couple of nights later "[Solidor] was conveying in three or four lines, Verlaine, Baudelaire, to a night club audience."[12]

The liner docked in the fog of Southampton, where Stella caught a train into London: "From an over laden top heavy fashion English cab," Stella wrote referring to the abundance of her luggage borne by the taxi, "leaving Waterloo Station, one quickly sees strong Gothic spires climbing the sky: Westminster, Parliament, the Embankment, the sober beauty of London. Moving briskly against this background, crowding into busses and metros, are the English people, poorly dressed, prepared for the rain, correct, polite and enormously eccentric." Stella noticed the scarcity of common goods such as fruits, butter, and meat. Postwar London had still not recovered. Still, Stella had means, and could either pay a high price for decent meals at a club or, as she wrote, "settle for a powdered omelet" at the Lion's Corner House.[13]

If Stella tried to look up Macartney, she wouldn't have had much luck. In 1946 Macartney wrote about his anti-Hitler activities during the war in a story published by the French newspaper, *Étoile du Soir*. He outlined how he had worked undercover for the MI5, the British counterintelligence and security agency, sending false information to the Germans about London targets. The British arrested Macartney for disclosing classified information under the Official Secrets Act. (A similar charge had sentenced him to ten years in jail under the same Act in 1928 for allegedly sharing information with the Soviets.) Macartney had come from considerable wealth but had deep allegiance to social justice, which led him to Communism. It is likely that in 1948, while Stella was visiting London, Macartney was still serving time from his 1946 conviction.

In London Stella went to the theater, where she saw Christopher Fry's premiere of *The Lady Is Not for Burning* and her old friend John Gielgud in *Antigone*. She also attended the current art exhibits before going to Paris, where she mingled with her fellow Americans visiting the city at the height of tourist season: "Young John Garfield not quite believing that French acting is more decorative than profound, Franchot Tone growing still another shaped beard and talking about the Burag Theatre [*recte*: Burgtheater] in Vienna. . . . There is Aaron Copland wise about everything except leaving Paris; Richard Wright still dispossessed; Irwin Shaw back from Israel, bright and restless, and Paul Bowles just in from Tangiers, sun burnt and glowing."[14] After Paris it was on to Italy, where Stella could wind down both socially and mentally. Italy was where Stella found solace, reflected, and rehabilitated from her New York travails of trying not to disappoint herself in her quest to reach the heights of accomplishment. In Italy she could regain the energy she needed to return in the fall and begin a new season of teaching, acting, and directing.

For Clurman, business was booming on Broadway. At the end of 1949 he started rehearsals for *The Member of the Wedding*, which he was paid $4,000 to direct and a share of 2 percent net profits for a play that ran well into the spring of the following year. Clurman's next play, *The Bird Cage*, opened at the Coronet Theatre; he had cast Stella in the lead role. The playwright, Arthur Laurents, recalled the first day of rehearsals later that year after Stella had returned from Europe: "Stella swept into rehearsal for the first reading of the play all in beige: suit, shoes, gloves, little hat with little veil over her ash-blond hair. A little kiss for Melvyn Douglas, a little flirtatious smile and a little pat on his cheek to acknowledge he was not her leading man, she was his leading lady. . . . Seating herself center stage, she read like royalty visiting a hospital, accepted compliments, left for lunch and never came back."[15] Stella and Harold had had one of their altercations, and she refused to take part in the play.

The following summer Stella and Harold returned to Europe, accompanied by strays from the cast of *The Bird Cage*, including Laurents, who bought a Hillman Minx convertible. Stella and Harold invited Laurents to spend the weekend in Deauville. "When I picked them up at their hotel," Laurents later wrote, "I anticipated chauffeuring the Stella Adler who had studied privately with Stanislavski in Paris: Isadora Duncan scarves, hatboxes, scorn for the size of the car. What I got was the Stella Adler who had used Paris as headquarters for running guns to Israel. Tying an old scarf around her head, she piled into the backseat saying: "I'm going to sleep. You boys sit in front and talk."[16]

After Deauville, Stella and Harold returned to Paris to pick up Ellen, now twenty-one years old, where she was living with the composer René Liebowitz. The party traveled to Stella's destination in Venice. Meanwhile the American Fund for Palestinian Institutions hired Clurman to direct the Habimah Players in *Montserrat*. After a successful production that garnered critical acclaim, Harold and Stella reunited in New York. Gushing with pride, he told his wife, "Honestly, Stella, after the success of *Montserrat* I was accepted and hailed by the cultural circles. Why you would have thought that I was Stanislavski and Reinhardt rolled into one." Never one to be upstaged, Stella countered, "Relax, Harold, in Minsk I was Greta Garbo."[17]

CHAPTER TWENTY

Stella is an American Treasure.

—Antonio Banderas

IN 1950 LOUIS F. BUDENZ, THE FORMER MANAGING EDITOR OF THE Communist-run publication *Daily Worker*, was interviewed by the FBI and asked to disclose the names of people he thought were Communists. Budenz named Stella as a "concealed communist," defined as someone "who would deny membership in the Party."[1] He cited her work in the Group Theatre. The Group's leftist viewpoints were well-known. Luther Adler was accused of being a "sympathizer who fought for Loyalist Spain." When asked to disclose his whereabouts during the duration of the Spanish Civil War, Luther handed over his play reviews. Still, Luther's struggle to clear his name lasted a dozen years, culminating in 1962 when his manager sent him a letter with documents for him to sign, after which, his manager assured him, "certain doors will swing wide open for you."[2] Many, like Stella, her brother Luther, and her nephew the screenwriter Allen Adler, were already adversely affected professionally, but at least they were still free and able to fend for themselves through freelance work and teaching.

With Budenz's statement, Stella was listed in the FBI "security index," adding her sponsorship in various organizations or causes as proof of her allegiance to the Communist Party. Among the organizations listed were such subversive sounding-entities as the League of Women Shoppers and the American Committee for Protection of Foreign Born. Stella was also listed as having been a judge for a dance contest for the Communist-run publication *New Masses* and as a sponsor on the program for the Scientific and Cultural Conference for World Peace in the spring of 1949.

The playwright Lillian Hellman also drew attention for sponsoring the Scientific and Cultural Conference. The state department kept a close eye on the event because it decided which scholars and artists would be allowed to get visas to enter the United States. When Hellman was called to a hearing before HUAC in the spring of 1942, she resolutely took the Fifth, though in the eyes of the Committee that was tantamount to admitting guilt. After months of anxious deliberation about the ensuing hearing, Hellman wrote to the Committee: "I am advised by counsel that if I answer the Committee's questions about myself, I must also answer questions about other people and that if I refuse to do so, I can be cited for contempt. . . . To hurt innocent people whom I knew many years ago in order to save myself is, to me, inhuman and indecent and dishonorable. I cannot and will not cut my conscience to fit this year's fashions."[3] The letter was put on the record during Hellman's testimony and copies were given to the press, which did not please the Committee. Perhaps owing to the resulting publicity, Hellman was one of only a few individuals who were not prosecuted for refusing to name names.

Not everyone held to these politics. Elia Kazan, who cooperated with the Committee by naming those he knew who were Communist Party members, later explained in his autobiography: "If you're asking if I believed that the social programs of the 'progressives' in the arts were influenced by those of the Party, my answer is yes. If you're asking did I believe that everyone who defended himself by calling on the Fifth Amendment—constitutional right though it is—was a Communist, I must confess I did believe that."[4] Kazan claimed he believed the Committee "had a proper duty" and that it was also his responsibility to "break open the secrecy."[5] Cooperation ensured that he would continue working in Hollywood. A few years after his testimony he directed *On the Waterfront*, a film transparently justifying his decision to inform on his former comrades.

Although a Communist threat of revolution was as unlikely as an apocalypse, people are notoriously duped by fear. It was only a matter of time before Stella would be summoned to testify before HUAC.

SUMMERS IN ITALY HAD BECOME AN INDISPENSABLE COMPONENT OF Stella's life. In 1950 Stella traveled to Portofino. There she met Eleanor Sheldon, who would become a lifelong friend. (When Stella liked someone, the actor John Abbot affirmed, "She didn't let you go. It was a life sentence.")[6] Stella first saw Eleanor and her husband, the director James Sheldon, swimming in the ocean. Stella knew James because he had once dated Ellen. Eleanor recalled that when they swam to shore, Stella "ran up to James" to inquire about his companion. "When I arrived on the beach," Eleanor said,

> she just took over and we became close friends and we spent a lot of time in Portofino together and then we met again in Venice that summer. When we got back that fall she was on the phone a great deal inviting us to her dinner parties and things of that sort, taking Saturday afternoon walks with her. She had a few good friends who were not of the theater. I guess I was kind of a bridge. There was a lawyer and his wife and a psychiatrist or two. All of them not of the theater, but all very devoted and adoring of Stella. So, it was her fan club.[7]

On June 22, while Stella was courting her new friend Eleanor, the right-wing journal *Counterattack* published a pamphlet, entitled "Red Channels," that listed 151 writers, directors, and performers as Communist subversives. The list was then sent to those in Hollywood in charge of hiring. Anyone on the alphabetized list—and Stella's name was at the top under the A—had "no chance," as Stella put it, of working in the entertainment field.[8] She had officially been blacklisted.

Meanwhile Harold was waiting in Rome for Stella to arrive: "I decided that the most perfect Venus," he wrote to his wife, "and work of art is none other than my Bubu Stella Adler, and I'd give all the museums up without regret just to be the curator for life of the perfect Venus and beauty and love. So far this is the extent of my wisdom and reflection in Italy. Hurry, hurry, hurry. I'm all alone."[9] Stella was not one to hurry anywhere, especially into the arms of Harold. Instead, she went straight to the Italian coast. Harold came to meet her, but she was not available; she had met a young French actor to escort her. The Sheldons were staying at a hotel near Stella, and Eleanor recalled that Stella "would come up for cocktails with Roberto and stay—the two of them, mind you."[10] Sheldon did not mention Harold's reaction to Stella's French actor, though it was obvious that he and Stella were having an affair. It wasn't the first or the last time Harold's hopes for Stella would be upstaged by her sexual appetites. However, Stella made it up to Harold before he returned to New York, as he alluded to in an optimistic letter he wrote in August telling his wife that her letter was a *"mitzvah"* that added years to his life. He made sure to mention how he had seen Madame Adler, now a septuagenarian, who looked "amazingly fresh," expressing to Harold how glad she was that he and Stella had made peace with each other.[11]

The following May Stella and Harold set out on their traditional summer trip to Europe. In August he returned home to find the apartment closed up. He wrote to Stella asking that she put the house back in order. She replied from Lausanne with a point-by-point missive in which she analyzed Harold's complaints and their solutions. In a glimpse into Stella's perspective, we gain an understanding of the couple's dynamic beyond the simplistic portrayal of the cruel Stella and the cuckolded Harold. Despite Stella's disloyalty and public humiliation of Harold, she took care of him as much as he did of her. They grew with each other.

Stella responded to Harold's letter by using an appropriate metaphor to explain to Harold that if he went to the theater and it was cluttered and dirty, he would call in a stage manager to clear the mess up so he could move forward with the production. Stella made it clear to Harold that straightening out the house was not her responsibility, and was quick to add exactly what she thought he meant by calling her home. She took it as an irrational demand made upon her as if it were her wifely duty, condescending to explain to him what she would do, which was to call in three "servants," a furniture man, and a maid to clean.

Harold was as capable of putting the house in order as Stella, but he relied upon Stella's domestic sensibilities. It represented for him one of the ways in which she, however marginally, conformed to his view of a traditional wife. There was also the issue of finances, a concern from which neither one of them had the luxury of being free for very long. Stella was often depicted as oblivious to money. True, she knew little about the machinery of currency transactions. She had others write out checks and balance registers. Yet she retained a clear grasp on finances, as seen through her advice to Harold in the same letter: "Now about money, you say you are trapped and lost, you have not enough for a hotel, you have debts and now I have to come back and help you. I am sending you a check to pay the September rent. . . . I'm sure my accountant can arrange to postpone your taxes for a few months. I'm also sending a check to cover Vera for a few weeks—now Harold I am doing this because you sound so desperate."[13]

In his reply Harold tried to clarify why he had called her home. His response provided him with a forum to express in writing what he could not convey in person. He consoled Stella, telling her that she made enough money and he didn't expect her to make more. He began to try to convince her that they weren't always "anxious" about finances, before tiring of the "dreadful" topic and turning to the meat of the letter. Cautiously, as if it were a taboo subject, Harold confessed that even if he were to have affairs with women, he would still be "sex starved," as Stella was the only woman he found attractive. Still, it was only the first part of their "double tragedy," the worst of which was his neurosis caused by the continuous strain between the two of them. The logical conclusion one draws is that Stella either withheld sex or criticized Harold about his performance, which Harold called an "obstacle" that they must traverse. He mentioned her justification for having "beaux," claiming she needed such affairs because of her age, to which Harold seemed to think the answer was for him to fulfill this need, whether it be as a lecherous lover or flirtatious dalliance. The fact that he didn't straight-out give Stella an ultimatum implies that she would have left him, or simply that it was not an option at this point in their marriage. Like Jacob's, Stella's adultery seemed somehow sanctioned, or at least above questioning, as if it were a compulsion she could not control. Harold would only be able to turn a blind eye for so long. For now he seemed relieved to simply tell Stella how he felt, putting it down in "black and white and not statements made by inference."[14]

When Stella returned from Europe, she and Harold decided to find a larger apartment. She went to her lawyer's office to enlist his help. He began making phone calls, telling one apartment owner, "We have somebody here, you probably know her, she wants this apartment." Stella then overheard the apartment owner exclaim: "Stella Adler? That son of a bitch, she's first in Red Channels!"[15] Stella recalled that it was then that she discovered she had been blacklisted.

At the end of September Stella and Harold settled into a fifth-floor apartment at 1016 Fifth Avenue. Stella took out a bathroom in order to make a room for her mother. By the time she finished remodeling and decorating, the décor called to mind a Venetian palace. Stella's new home was located only ten blocks north of the childhood brownstone where she had spent her formative years. In an apartment on Fifth Avenue, where in another era millionaire manors lined the boulevard, Stella found the place she would call home for the rest of her life.

STELLA'S TEACHING CAREER BEGAN TO TAKE MORE OF HER TIME AND energy. On September 13, 1950, Stella ran an ad for teaching acting technique in the *New York Times* with the headline "Course in Acting Opened." The ad read that classes were for both "professionals and beginners."[16] She already had a following from teaching at the Dramatic Workshop; all she needed was a space to rent. She found one at Malin Studios, at 245 West Fifty-second Street, where she taught acting technique every day from four to six in the afternoon.[17]

Stella's opportunities to act had diminished greatly. She believed she would have continued working had she not been blacklisted, saying: "Blacklisted actually meant that people didn't want to go near you. They didn't care what contribution you could make. You were blacklisted. You were un-American. You were a foreigner. You were somebody disgusting. . . . It was not an easy word to pass around you know, blacklisted. It was serious."[18]

The public fear of Communism escalated in the early 1950s. HUAC and now a new committee under McCarthy were loaded with ammunition to cleanse the nation. The Korean War provided a stark example of Communism's threat, while Mao's China represented its consummate evils. McCarthy made sure to televise the hearings during mid-morning, when more viewers could tune in. While the inquisitors enjoyed the success of their widely publicized heroics, those called to testify suffered. A witness who used the protection of the Fifth Amendment was as good as guilty, his means of livelihood, and often those of his associates, stripped away. Jail time was inevitable. If one chose to cooperate during the hearings, he was called to inform on his colleagues and friends, destroying their careers and reputations. It was a no-win situation, but clearly witnesses had a choice: suffer punishment alone or sacrifice others' lives to escape it.

By the summer of 1952 Stella began to feel the extent to which her rights were being stripped away. While she was trying to renew her passport to return to Europe, she was asked to notarize an affidavit to the state department explaining what they perceived as questionable activity. Otherwise unable to renew her passport, Stella played along, writing: "Sometime in the autumn of 1937, while I was in Hollywood, California, I had attended certain meetings which I understood as 'progressive.' After attending two or three of these so-called meetings, I wasn't particularly impressed with what 'progressiveness' meant. In short, it seemed to me that it was a bit too radical for me to take, no less difficult for me to understand."[19] Stella did not mind appearing dim-witted. The statement continued: "Prior to World War II, I lent my name in some instances which I cannot immediately recall; it was literally taken without my consent, for appearance on some sort of theatrical or entertainment committee of various organizations. I did not knowingly give or lend my name to any organization which in any way would be subversive to or against the interests of the United States of America."[20] Her "confession" expedited the renewal of her passport.

In February of 1953 Stella leased a space at 50 Central Park West where she began operating the Stella Adler Theatre School.[21] There are usually no definitive reasons for a change in the course of a life. More often, a combination of circumstances contributes to the directions we take. For Stella, the blacklist and the decision to open her own school corresponded with the pedagogical search she had begun years before when she first enrolled at the Lab. Like all artists, she had to make a living. But she didn't have to confine herself to the traditional conduits of Broadway and Hollywood. Through teaching, Stella found a way to continue honing her craft without compromising her ideals.

On March 1, 1953, an era ended with the death of Joseph Stalin. The thirty-year span of his reign that began with World War I was now threatening a third, nuclear war. In the midst of a very real fear of world annihilation, Stella received her summons to testify before HUAC. The summons itself would have felt like a sentence, knowing the fate of so many who had testified before her. But just as her own future felt as uncertain and terrifying as ever, Stella lost the woman who had been living with her on and off for most of her adult life, the woman whose elusive love had long since been accepted while she became an integral part of Stella's family life. On April 28, 1953, Sara Adler died.

The *New York Morning Telegraph* wrote that Sara had died at ninety-five, but *Variety* was closer to the truth when it gave her age as eighty-eight. The *Morning Telegraph*'s exaggeration set the tone for its tribute: "She was an empress of a whole area of the island of Manhattan, the empress of a family dazzling in its individual talents and, most certainly, empress of the Yiddish theater in America."[22] The writer then encapsulates Sara's legend by relating a story heard from Stella:

She was 88 when it happened: a time when most women are dead or, if they still live, have no heart for such gallantry. She was to meet her daughter, Stella, at 6 o'clock. At 7 o'clock, the empress had not yet arrived and Stella was frantic. After all, Sarah was nearing 90. But at 7:05, she walked in, erect, her hair freshly curled, a look of dismay on her face. "What happened, Mama?" Stella cried. "Ah, the men. Terrible!" the empress replied. "A woman of charm is not safe in the streets any more. Oglers; flirts. They give her no peace. Terrible!"[23]

Two weeks before Sara's death, her health was so poor that she had to be hospitalized. The family visited, brought flowers, held one another, and sat with Sara; but it was her time to go. While Stella mourned and arranged her mother's burial, the HUAC hearing was looming before her. Sara was interred at Mount Carmel next to Jacob, twenty-seven years after his death. The family gathered, laughing and crying and telling stories into the night.

Less than two weeks later Stella boarded a train with her attorney, Max Rubin, to Washington. It was unusually hot weather, with a record high in the nineties. Rubin and Stella were intimate, which must have been comforting for Stella, who always found the arms of a man reassuring. The night before Stella's hearing they shared a hotel room where Rubin coached his client. He instructed her to choose her words carefully, to use the phrase "to the best of my recollection,"[24] but despite all of Stella's acting training, she could not manage these simple lines. She and Rubin lay in bed until the early hours trying to master the phrase, neither of them certain of Stella's fate at the hands of the HUAC subcommittee.

The following morning Stella and Rubin had time for breakfast before Stella's eleven o'clock hearing.[25] They must have looked like a couple vacationing in the nation's capital, not a lawyer and his actress-client under suspicion for being a Communist subversive. After arriving at Independence Avenue, Stella, dressed in a conservative tailored skirt suit, gloves, and a hat, walked up the stairs to the entrance of the Old House Office Building, the oldest congressional office building on Capitol Hill. Her heart began to race. She had never felt so afraid in her life. She had nothing to compare it with. It had been frightening to run guns and illegally transport Jewish refugees during her freedom fighting days, but she did not have to suffer the fear, nor, as it turned out, the consequences of those actions. Now her own government sat against her, threatening her freedom.

The fact that she would be testifying before a subcommittee of the United States House of Representatives was daunting enough without the austere setting. The neoclassical exterior, with its Doric columns, echoed the interior marble entrance of Corinthian columns, which supported a large domed ceiling. The sobering rotunda crowned two marble staircases and a warren of state offices. All she had to do was find her way to room 226 and remember her lines. Later Stella recalled this moment in class: "When I went to Washington to the Capital, I walked through those marble halls. It was so big, and I got so little. But I was all America walking."[26]

The subcommittee commenced by swearing Stella in, followed by introductions to her three interlocutors, all men, with Representative Bernard W. Kearney presiding. Kearney swore Stella in. Just as he asked her to provide a brief sketch of her life and career, the quorum bells began ringing, requiring a recess until the subcommittee members returned from their duties. For the next half hour Stella sat waiting for her hearing to resume. It had to have been nerve-racking.

Once the preliminary questions were answered, a Mr. Scherer began with the first line of questioning relating to testimony given by a Martin Berkeley. Scherer read Berkeley's testimony, in which Stella was accused of having attended a subversive meeting at his home. "I remember meeting Mr. Berkeley very casually," Stella began nervously, "so casually that it just—but I do not remember ever having been at his home or ever having been in anything at his home in any way. I don't remember having been entertained by Mr. Berkeley at any occasion. I don't remember even really more than being introduced casually to him at all." Stella's confidence faltered as she reworked her responses, forgetting the rehearsed "to the best of my recollection," and relying on her instinct to supply the least incriminating answers. As the subcommittee fired off its questions, what unfolded would have been a comedic Adlerian story if the circumstances had been less dire:

MR. SCHERER: Do you recall the circumstances of that introduction—when and where it took place?

MISS ADLER: I don't. I do not. I remember very little about Mr. Martin Berkeley.

MR. SCHERER: Who was Martin Berkeley?

MISS ADLER: Well, I am told he is a distant relative.

MR. SCHERER: Of yourself?

MISS ADLER: Yes; of the Adler family.

Perhaps Stella was too nervous to see the humor in the fact that the person in question was actually a relative of hers—Jacob's infamous liaisons having extended the Adler clan to who knew how far. At this juncture in the questioning, a Mr. Tavenner stepped in with a line of questioning that played more on semantics and intimidation than on getting to the truth.

MR. TAVENNER: Do you recall having been in his home on any occasion?

MISS ADLER: No, sir; I do not recall having been in his home.

MR. TAVENNER: You say you do not recall?

MISS ADLER: I do not recall, no.

MR. TAVENNER: Do you mean by that that you are uncertain in your own memory as to whether you may have been in his home or that you know that you never have been?

MISS ADLER: Well, Mr. Tavenner, it seems to me if I had been in his home, vaguely remembering, oh—knowing vaguely that he was related to me—[I] think I would have known it. I think that would have more or less made me know that I was in the home of a distant relative. That seems to be something that I may have—I would have remembered.

Though she stammered, Stella managed to conclude her statements with clarity. The prosecutors proceeded, submitting as evidence her involvement with what the subcommittee defined as Communist organizations. The first pertained to Stella's sponsorship of a banquet given for Mother Ella Reeve Bloor, a feminist and later Communist who worked primarily as a humanitarian activist. Stella did not recall attending the banquet, after which the document of her sponsorship was submitted and marked as "Adler Exhibit Number 1."

The inquisition moved on to the Citizens' Committee for Harry Bridges, which was also condemned as a "Communist front." The Committee submitted a page of letterhead from the organization, "Exhibit Number 2," where Stella's name appeared as a sponsor. Stella's old beau, the great labor leader, had been under investigation as being a Communist since 1934. He suffered twenty-one years of surveillance, trials, and deportation threats. The Committee for Harry Bridges fought to keep him in the country, and Stella fervently sponsored the cause. "Exhibit Number 3" displayed Stella's signature on a petition for the Artists' and Scientists' Division of the American Committee declaring that the United States should cease relations with fascist Spain.

When questioned about her signatures and sponsorship of these various organizations, Stella responded, "I was a signer of things, Sir. I was not very thorough in examining." Stella refrained from defending her involvement in these organizations as being fully within her rights. Nor did she mention that while supporting the Loyalists of Spain against the fascists she was well in accordance with the United States' antifascist policy.

The interrogator saved the most inflammatory questions for last: Stella's presence at HUAC's hearing with her colleague Brecht and the "Hollywood Ten" in 1947. They asked Stella why she was in Washington during this hearing, which they saw as a protest against the call-up. Stella claimed she did not have any politically motivated reason for accompanying her friends to Washington. Instead, she circumvented the accusation altogether by explaining that her motivation was to be a representative of the theater in the midst of all the movie stars that were called up. Given her devotion to the theater, her response was as close to the truth as she could get by lying: "I remember I was asked to come to Washington at that time because it didn't look nice for all the stars to come because the theater was so shabby, and . . . it was kind of a shabby kind of group compared to all that glamour."

The subcommittee pressed Stella further as to her presence at the hearings and to jog her memory showed her a photograph with others who came to Washington. Finally Stella conceded what she did remember about the hearing: "I'm not quite sure that I remember any discussion except a great deal of noise and fighting, Sir."

"In other words," Mr. Kearny assumed, "it was a demonstration against the Thomas Committee?"

MISS ADLER: No. I don't think it was a demonstration but there was a lot of banging and a lot of shouting.

MR. KEARNY: Well, in other words, if they had been in the room as ordinary spectators in a courtroom, there wouldn't be any shouting and fighting, would there?

MISS ADLER: I don't know whether the shouting was so much from the spectators. It was from Mr. Thomas and the other members who were up there as defendants.

The overall impression Stella gave her interlocutors is of a ditzy actress who was not aware of politics in any sense of the word whatsoever. The prosecutors proceeded to explain to Stella why those witnesses were called up, spelling out what Stella already knew: that if any of the Hollywood Ten chose to "seek refuge behind the Fifth Amendment" they would be considered members of the Communist Party. Stella maintained that she had only come along with the Hollywood Ten to represent the theater so it wouldn't look "shabby." The prosecutor concluded exactly what Stella had led him to conclude, telling her, as if she were a naive country girl who had just arrived in the big city, that she had been "sold a bill of goods." Stella remained in character, having pulled off the performance of her life. "That was the thought I had," she stated. Stella was excused, having miraculously avoided incriminating herself or anyone else.

CHAPTER TWENTY-ONE

She was especially tough on women because she wanted
them to be more. She wanted them to stand up and be
strong. Those women that came through Stella were always
really strong ladies and really standup people who went for
the work, who did the work, who understood the work.

—James Coburn

WITH THE FEAR OF IMPRISONMENT BEHIND HER, STELLA RETURNED to New York, her home, where neither mother nor father remained. Instead, she had the family she had created with Clurman and Ellen. Harold, as much in love with Stella as ever, was still trying to meld his private and professional life with hers. Although dissatisfied in the marriage, Stella and Harold were getting something out of it. They chose to stay together because they could rely on one another, take care of one another. And their union was, if nothing else, collegial. They may have not been suited romantically, but they fueled each other creatively. For her part, Stella found herself more dedicated than ever to elucidating the craft of acting. She had been teaching for over a decade and pedagogy was becoming all the more fulfilling the more she traveled, studied, and returned home to disseminate her revelations.

That summer, while Stella was traveling through Europe with Principe, the shih tzu given her by Peggy Guggenheim, Clurman sailed to London on assignment with a play by Jean Giraudoux. En route Ellen mailed him a package with correspondence from Stella in Switzerland and Rome. Upon receiving word from her, Harold wrote to his wife informing her of his immediate plans, in which he hoped she would take part: "*St. Joan* opens in Princeton in mid-September after which I have to find another play…I'd like to be as close as possible to you in all ways but will you let me? Will you not prefer to be angry, feel betrayed, outraged and impatient? That seems to be the easier way for you. But no matter, I am yours—and you, my darling, brilliant, foolish one—know it."[1]

Harold concludes the letter by asking Stella, "Would you like to meet in Paris and show me a good time?" Stella seemed incapable of showing her devoted husband anything approximating a good time. The fact that Clurman was now dean of the theater world and directing full-time did not make up for the inadequacies Stella perceived in Harold. He reminded Stella how easy it would be for them to be happy if only she "accepted the fact that you are married to me," and told her that "the way to your husband and his way to you must be the smiling road of sympathy, kindness, warmth and not a road of curses, recrimination, and venom."[2]

Norma Barzman's memoir, *The Red and the Blacklist*, reports that the director Ben Barzman witnessed this venom firsthand. Barzman had given Clurman a play to consider directing that Stella set her mind on directing herself. One night Clurman brought Barzman home to their apartment. Stella heard the key in the door and before anyone appeared bellowed: "Harold-you-dirty-lousy-no-good-son-of-a-bitch-fucking-god-damn-bastard!"[3] When she saw Barzman, without skipping a beat Stella welcomed him with all the aplomb and self-possession of royalty. The rant she had thought she was directing at Harold, however, illustrates the verbal abuse he had to tolerate.

THE 1950S WERE A PIVOTAL DECADE FOR ACTING. SINCE THE 1930S THE major studios—RKO, MGM, Twentieth Century–Fox, Warner Bros., Paramount, Columbia, and Universal—had controlled the making and distribution of American films. Each would vie for profit over their competitors, largely by recycling the same genres of films that already proved successful with the stable of stars they had under contract. A trove of classic films came out of the studio years. It was the golden age of Judy Garland, Jimmy Stewart, and Clark Gable. During the 1950s, though, a paradigm shift occurred when antitrust legislation prohibited the studios from monopolizing the industry.

As production companies outside the system sprouted up, the studios no longer controlled movie houses. Competition also came in the form of television; families could be entertained in the comfort of their own home and save money on going out. Targeting an educated and more affluent audience, film scenarios became more sophisticated, with antiheroes and class struggles and more sexually provocative content. In 1951 Kazan adapted his Broadway hit *A Streetcar Named Desire* to film, with Marlon Brando's character epitomizing the new direction acting was taking. Karl Malden also played in the production. One day Stella visited the set. Malden recalled that Brando pointed to Stella and said, "If it hadn't been for her, maybe I wouldn't have gotten where I am. . . . She taught me to read, she taught me to look at art, she taught me to listen to music."[4] A new golden age emerged, with stars such as Montgomery Clift, Shelley Winters, and James Dean.

Not only Stella but also her colleagues from the Group Theatre intuitively understood the importance of disseminating acting training as it had been given to them. As early as 1934, after Stella returned to the Group Theatre with her understanding of Stanislavski's theories and began teaching classes to her colleagues, Sanford Meisner—similarly disillusioned with Strasberg's interpretation of Stanislavski—took what he had gleaned from Stella along with his experience with the Group's work and joined the faculty of the Neighborhood Playhouse School of the Theatre. The school had evolved out of the Neighborhood Playhouse Theatre on the Lower East Side, one of the first off-Broadway theaters that were part of the early settlement house movement. Never losing touch with the roots he laid down there, he became head of the drama department at the Playhouse, where he would hone the "Meisner technique" for the next sixty years.

With a similar interest in training actors, Kazan and Bobby Lewis had attempted to create a Group Theatre school in 1937 but after one semester found the endeavor unrealistic, what with the instability of the Group's finances. The seed had been planted, however, and in 1946, during the rehearsals of *A Streetcar Named Desire*, Kazan rekindled the idea of creating a center where actors could study. Bobby Lewis and Cheryl Crawford joined this effort and began building what would become the Actors Studio. The Studio officially opened in the fall of 1947, with Kazan as its director. Although history has revised the story behind the creation of the Studio, originally Lee Strasberg was excluded from the enterprise. Neither Lewis nor Kazan wanted Strasberg involved, not even as a guest lecturer. The founders still had misgivings about Strasberg's teaching methods, especially his emphasis on affective memory.[5]

Strasberg had spent his post-Group days capitalizing on his reputation of being the authority on acting in the United States. In the early 1940s he published "Acting and the Training of the Actor," a thirty-four page essay which deconstructed an American interpretation of the Russian system. In 1947 he wrote the introduction to *A Handbook of the Stanislavski*

Method, identifying himself as an expert on Stanislavski's system. After the first year of the Actors Studio, Kazan struggled with an inconsistent and unstable staff. He needed committed instructors, and if he knew nothing else about Strasberg from his Group Theatre days, he knew that Lee was a dedicated teacher. Kazan invited Strasberg to join his "unit" of classes. Kazan began spending more and more time away from the Studio in order to concentrate on his directing career, and Strasberg picked up the slack. By the following year Strasberg was officially acknowledged as the Studio's "guiding directorate,"[6] positioned to establish his method as the definitive style of American acting.

By the mid-1950s, any actor worth his salt went to study at the Actors Studio. With its new acting style, now referred to by critics as "method acting," it became a hotbed for both celebrities and up-and-coming stars. The word "method" harked back to Strasberg's insistence in the early Group days that the actors "were not following Stanislavski's system, but Strasberg's method." Nowadays, when people think of a "method actor," they associate the term with someone who literally takes on the physical and emotional persona of his or her character. This simplistic understanding— the idea of becoming emotionally vested in a character—underlies the debate between Stella and Strasberg. In truth, both teachers believed acting should be approached through a method or technique that involved several aspects of Stanislavski's system, from the actor's imagination to the justification of the character's actions. But Strasberg's method, which Stella thought overemphasized affective memory, has been wrongly perceived by most as training the actor to develop a character from nothing more than his or her personal experiences. Stella's emphasis on working from the character's actions within the circumstances of the play (or screenplay) is lesser known, but it is how most actors today approach their work. Actors call this working from "the outside in," which this writer found, after talking to countless celebrities and struggling thespians alike, both in the United States and abroad, is more common than working from "the inside out." Dustin Hoffman illustrates an example of working from the inside out in the apocryphal anecdote from the set of the movie *Marathon Man*, in which he starred with Laurence Olivier. Hoffman supposedly stayed up all night to play a character who had been up all night. When Olivier saw his costar come into work disheveled and sleep deprived, he said something to the effect of, "Why not try acting? It's much easier."

After Strasberg took over the Studio and became artistic director in its fifth season, Kazan's directing career skyrocketed. Kazan's films made an indelible impact on the American perception of the evolving craft of acting. Beginning with *Death of a Salesman* in 1949, Kazan's productions of *A Streetcar Named Desire*, *Viva Zapata!*, *On the Waterfront*, and *East of Eden* confirmed his genius year after year. Strasberg capitalized on the celebrities who attended the Studio through generous publicity.

The quintessential method actor, James Dean, actually worked very little in the classes he took at the Studio.[7] He was inhibited, and few of his fellow classmates recall having seen his scene work. At the end of each season Strasberg would give oral progress reports, summarizing students' work by means of criticism in front of his or her fellow actors. Dean didn't like the public embarrassment. Brando—who attended the Studio like any other "serious" actor of the era—apparently read the day's newspaper the year Strasberg analyzed his work.[8]

Few actors limited themselves to the Studio. Most availed themselves of studying with all three acting giants of the time: Strasberg at the Actors Studio, Meisner at the Neighborhood Playhouse, and Stella at the Stella Adler Theatre School.

Some actors discovered an affinity with a specific teacher, pledging loyalty throughout their career, but most actors took what they could from each expert. Shelley Winters was one Studio actor who called on Stella's expertise when she needed to. In the fall of 1955 Frank Corsaro was having difficulty directing Winters in the play *A Hatful of Rain*. As a movie actress, Winters was not well versed in the stage, which created enough of an obstacle; but she was also emotionally affected by the failing health of her costar, Anthony Franciosa. Winters had taken the part in the first place because Franciosa had shown her the script and wanted to work opposite her. When Franciosa fell ill with kidney stones during their Philadelphia run, Winters decided she would not proceed without him.

The producer Jay Julien suggested Stella Adler be brought in to coach Winters, and Corsaro, who often ran into Stella at the opera, felt comfortable bringing her on board. Stella arrived on the scene with Franciosa himself, escorting him back to the show after his stint at Mount Sinai Hospital in New York. With the hope that his health would be restored in time for the New York run, Winters began working with Stella. Winters's main trouble was carrying the show to its fruition, as she was emotionally exhausted after her scenes.

Staying throughout rehearsals in Washington, Stella managed to get Winters into shape through a greater exploration and understanding of her character. One night Stella kept Winters after the show until two in the morning ironing a shirt, which her character had to do in the first act. Winters later wrote that she paid Stella five hundred dollars for coaching her, an amount she admitted was a pittance for what she had learned. Winters conjectured that Stella agreed to come to Washington as a favor to the play's producer: "As an authority on the chemistry of sexual attraction," Winters writes in her autobiography, she was sure Stella and Julien were having an affair.[9] During this time Winters remembered an evening when Stella captivated a New York City nightclub upon entering the establishment:

> In the middle 1950s Stella Adler was a knockout. A few years before this, I was sitting in the Copa at a table with Marilyn Monroe, and we were done up to the teeth. Lana Turner, at a nearby table, was at her most beautiful. Stella Adler made an entrance in a black satin gown with black egrets in her blonde hair. For the next hour no one in the Copa looked at us movie stars. Stella had such a dynamite stage presence.[10]

The following fall, in October of 1956, Stella directed a revival of *Johnny Johnson*, the Kurt Weill musical that had originally been produced by the Group Theatre twenty-one years earlier. The *New York Times* wrote, "Stella Adler's direction of a large and ingratiating cast is highly inventive in the comedy scenes and brave in the preachy ones."[11] Rehearsals and the production itself took place in the theater underneath Carnegie Hall, then an off-Broadway venue.

Betsy Parrish, Stella's former student and a lifelong friend, played the French nurse in the production. Parrish recalled Brando visiting during one rehearsal. His presence sparked excitement in the entire cast. The music stood out in Parrish's mind as exquisite, while Stella's directing was no different from what Parrish was used to in the classroom. Stella understood the play and her vision for it. She conveyed that to her actors in her own exacting, demanding, and theatrical way. Parrish remembered the play "dying before its time,"[12] for reasons she did not understand. They certainly did not include a lack of good notices, since reviews praised everything about the production from the set design to the makeup artist: "Off Broadway is still running several lengths ahead of Broadway this season."[13]

The director Peter Bogdanovich was another of Stella's students cast in the musical, but when his true age of sixteen was revealed, state laws and Actors Equity rules prohibited him from working. Bogdanovich later remembered: "I only had the privilege with Stella for a short time on her striking, profoundly moving off-Broadway production of the Kurt Weill–Paul Green pacifist World War I musical drama, 'Johnny Johnson.' . . . Stella was an extraordinary[il]y specific director with the artistic eye of a hawk, and a vivid imagination. She rehearsed for months . . . she was so inspiring, brought such size, depth, and resonance to everything. . . . Stella was one of the two most brilliant actors' directors I ever worked with, Orson Welles being the other."[14]

At home, Stella wasn't as inspiring. By early 1957 the only warmth in the Clurman home came in the form of Ellen's marriage to David Oppenheim, a composer who had previously been married to Judy Holliday. Harold sprang for the wedding of his beloved stepdaughter, a day that seemed to mark the beginning of a new home, and the end of another. In April Harold wrote Stella from Stockholm to tell her he couldn't bear any more neglect: "If it hadn't been for Ellen's wedding I wouldn't be able to remember an hour of even 'formal' affection on your part. Nothing I have done in all these years could have justified this winter's deep freeze."[15]

That fall Harold moved out of his and Stella's home on Fifth Avenue and into the Chatham Hotel at Vanderbilt Avenue and Forty-eighth Street. Clearly, yet with sensitivity, he drew his line in the sand: he could no longer abide sharing her with others.

On October 18, 1957, he wrote to Stella from his hotel room. Sadly, the letter began "I love you." Harold then proceeded to express how he never expected marriage to be easy, nor to leave a marriage because it was difficult. Yet finally he was able to tell her: "I can't tolerate infidelity." As if rinsing a soiled rag through clean water, Harold dispensed all the pent-up injuries he had had to endure throughout the years. Infidelity wasn't the only thing he would no longer accept. He wrote that he could not continue to bear separate living quarters, nor Stella's disregard for his financial and work problems. He raised Stella's chief argument as that of him working alone and not sharing his work with anyone else. To what extent this is true is suspect. Clurman collaborated throughout his life with others. His efforts at combining his work with Stella's predated the Group Theatre while being the nerve of tension within the Group throughout its career.

In his defense, Harold accused Stella of being unable to compromise on any work-related issues involving the people with whom he had to collaborate. He was quick to point out that he had continuously helped her in her creative endeavors, mentioning how he raised over half of the money for her production of *Johnny Johnson*, and how on closing night Stella went to a party with Stanley Moss, "who had no relation to the company, a company which respected me as a theater man, not to speak of my position as your husband." Harold closed the letter as bravely and lovingly as he began it: "I can no longer bear the burden of being scorned, flouted, subjected in all departments of my life, sexual, spiritual, financial. On the basis of your souls [sic] needs you have disregarded all responsibility to me. I shall love you, but love doesn't mean suicide."[16] And with that, Harold signed his name, closing a chapter on his life that had plagued, excited, fed, and beguiled him for twenty-eight years.

Their marriage had always been on Stella's terms, and Harold had withstood it for as long as he could. She had driven away the one person who had unconditionally stood beside her, and she would have felt the absence throughout the months ahead. In the new year of 1958, Stella took a three-week vacation to Acapulco. Upon her return home, she had to face the emptiness of the Fifth Avenue apartment without Ellen or Harold. But Stella had no more than a few days to contemplate her new single life: on February 7 Ellen gave birth to her first child, making Stella a grandmother three days before turning fifty-seven.

The child was named Sara, after Stella's mother. A second child, Tom, was born in June of the following year. As instructed, they referred to their grandmother as "Stella." In her late fifties, Stella still passed for a woman in her late thirties, and she certainly wasn't prepared to respond to the call of "grandma." With her reverence for family, Stella delighted in these newest members of the Adler clan. The fact that family would be carried on attributed to its permanence, even though the previous generations and old ties were gone.

To understand Stella's thoughts and feelings as they concerned her failed marriage to Harold, one need look no further than her analysis of *Hedda Gabler*. In the spring of 1959 Stella began a script breakdown class on her favorite play by Henrik Ibsen. Stella pointed out that Ibsen titled the play with Hedda's maiden name, not her married name, to indicate that Hedda is her father's daughter rather than her husband's wife.

Stella emphasized Ibsen's distinction between the idealist who marries fully believing in the institution versus the realist who chooses to marry knowing marriage is unnatural to human instinct. From the realist's perspective, one may leave the marriage in order to be true to herself. Stella seemed to subscribe to both philosophies simultaneously: she entered marriage as an idealist but never conformed to its social conventions.

In Ibsen's plays, as in Stella's estimation, marriage remains the barometer of civilization. Stella adhered to social mores when she married her first husband, Horace Eliascheff. Marriage, she believed, would render her socially acceptable, able to fit in. Later she admitted to Irene Gilbert, her friend the last thirty years of her life, that she had actually felt incredulous that a man would want to marry a "consumptive" but believed Horace was not given much of a choice, remembering how her mother "sent for Horace" when Stella fell ill with tuberculosis and believing that he "came out of sympathy." Stella went on to say, "He had an alternative, a lovely girl, a pianist. He just came and said America's interesting. I'll get married to Stella, why not?"[17]

Hedda is one of Ibsen's most complicated and misunderstood characters. She takes her life not to escape marriage, but to be daring enough to do something truthful. Hedda, like Stella, remains an idealist to the end. Stella discusses Hedda's predicament, delving into the psychological ramifications informed by Stella's own feeling that she had failed at marriage, and what she believed that failure does to one's sense of well-being and, more important, to one's sense of belonging in the world:

> This is an Ibsen character: a woman who lives without identification in the marriage is a ghost, she has no place, she is the worst pursued of all because she cannot rest. . . . She is looking for rest when she comes into the room. She runs away in order to rest from it. Do you know what it is to pretend to do something and to be alien in the act? What goes on, an inner struggle that makes you complain. She is outwitted here by the truth. She is choking all the time. If I had to play her everything would be too ugly, that way he wore his dressing gown would be ugly, the way the aunt is. She reflects, she reacts to it, she is not critical. If she were critical she would be in a position that isn't hopeless. She is stifled. You must understand her point of view . . . the social trap of the family is the worst trap of all because there is no way out. She cannot not be married and she can't be married. Hedda cannot win in this society. She needs another society. The society itself makes Hedda into a liar.[18]

One thing Stella found fascinating was how Ibsen's women—having fewer choices in their era than she had in hers—react to the problem of marriage. In *A Doll's House*, Nora cannot conform; she is the quintessential realist when she leaves Torvald and their children, as Stella explained in a lecture given in Toronto:

> Torvald says, "You can't do that [leave]. Your first duty is to your home, to your husband and to your children." And Nora says, "I don't believe that anymore. My first duty is to myself." Now that particular problem has never been resolved. That is, you in the audience will go home and say, "Of course her duty is to her children." And the girl that is with you will say, "Well, I don't know." How many people see that these problems are not easily resolved? I don't know if somebody said to me, "Your duty is to yourself and not to your child," whether I wouldn't say, "Well, I'm too intelligent to think that I was put on this earth to have a career." I think that I'm sort of a, maybe a sister-in-law of Eve and Adam and they were put here to have children. To have children seems to be one of those inevitable needs to have the race go on.[19]

Stella's modesty seems disingenuous in light of her mothering, but she is merely extemporizing on the necessity of procreation. She understands a mother's place is with her children from a societal perspective; she believes in the idea because she knows how detrimental it is for a child to be raised without a mother; but, like her own mother, she did not sacrifice her career to raise her daughter. At the same time, family remained the pillar of Stella's existence, holding her up in the present while she leaned on the past.

One day during her course on Ibsen, she was reminded of that past, one that went all the way back to Russia. Stella's student Betsy Parrish, who would later teach at Stella's New York school, gave her a recording of a Jewish folk song, inspiring Stella to pen a thank-you note in an attempt to convey the wonder of how the Russian peasant roots of her ancestry and her own life were connected through the recording, but not in real life. She explains that when she was put in public school she felt as if she were jailed with "average" people, while her home life, in all of its opulence, felt eons away from the folk themes she heard on the record. She felt her life in the theater was at "cross purposes." To Stella's ears, the communal quality of the music was foreign to her life experience. She lamented that she still felt alien to a sense of community, as if "I were opening a straw thatched roof house . . . into family life of which I am no part . . . I am still a stranger in the world."[20] At fifty-eight years old, Stella had yet to relinquish that girl scrambling in the dark, looking for a stage door in place of a home. To compensate for her feelings of alienation, as always, Stella concentrated on work.

Stella kept a running list of books to study that changed depending on which play she was analyzing. If it was Tennessee Williams, her favorite book was W. J. Cash's *The Mind of the South*. If she was teaching Shakespeare, she obtained almanacs, histories, and philosophical works from the country in which the play was set. It was the actor's responsibility to research the work and the character, and nothing short of total commitment would render the truth needed to interpret that character for the audience. Stella once said, "I would be ignorant if it weren't for the characters I've had to study."[21]

Stella's preternatural talent at script analysis is where she shone above all other acting coaches in the United States. Like a detective, Stella dissected every line of a play, each beat between the lines. She studied the playwright's biography, the central themes of his work, in order to, as the playwright Jerome Lawrence observed, "find things in plays that I don't think the playwrights themselves knew were there."[22] From her meticulous study, Stella uncovered the building blocks she used to understand the characters and their circumstances. Then, while lecturing, she led her students through her own revelations so that they would understand how they might go about creating anything from a character's gait to his vocal cadence. Simultaneously, Stella would build a character's background beyond that provided by the text to discover the motivations behind every word and action onstage.

The spiritual nature of Stella's classes has been pointed out by the way in which she exhorted her students to learn who they were as human beings by finding the humanity in their characters. Another element that added to the religious quality of Stella's classes came from the call-and-response nature of her teaching style. She did not lecture on a playwright or play without checking in with her students. Stella relied upon her class to let her know whether they understood what she was saying. This came in the form of direct questions such as "Who understands?" and "Do you agree?" Once she received affirmation, Stella would continue her discourse.

In class Stella focused so thoroughly on the material she could not be bothered with matters such as decorum. On more than one occasion she tore open her button-down, always to the astonishment of the class. Antics aside, Stella cared most about her effectiveness in delivering the message, the technique, to her students so they could utilize the knowledge in their own work. During a scene or play analysis Stella spoke in definitives, her hands in constant motion as if facilitating the extraction of words from her mind to her lips. She mussed her hair, pounded the table, clutched her breasts, seeking, exposing, and siphoning the meanings she had grasped and wanted to give away. Stella the egocentric actress transformed into the very spirit of pedagogy wherein honesty of self and the material were paramount. Stella extrapolated the themes not just for their significance in the play, but for their bearing upon universal truths. She marveled at the craftsmanship of the writer, had the class applaud his talent, and then challenged the class: "Script analysis means you understand your life, not just the play."[23]

Students and even auditors who witnessed her classes claimed they had been in the presence of genius. At times she would wistfully identify with a character as if she herself were experiencing the gravity of his or her circumstances—the tool of any great orator to move an audience into learning. Peter Bogdanovich recalled how Stella "acted constantly in class—with such intuitive brilliance, with a technique so well tuned, it was beyond second nature. I believe she could transform herself into any character, any animal, any style, any period. She was kinder, generally speaking, to men than to women, but she could be brutal to either sex."[24] Stella's consummate presence in the moment of the scene or the play left little room for diplomacy. If an actor came unprepared, it was left unsaid that he would be eaten up and spat out in front of the rest of the class. James Coburn commented on Stella's reputation for being "harder" on women: "She was especially tough on women because she wanted them to be more. She wanted them to stand up and be strong. Those women that came through Stella were always really strong ladies and really standup people who went for the work, who did the work, who understood the work."[25] A generation later Benicio Del Toro reiterated the sentiment: "Stella was tough. I mean, people cried in that class. People walked out. It wasn't like your were having fun. No, no, no. It was do or die. It was like gladiators. I would say 75 percent of what she said I didn't want to hear. But everything she said was right."[26]

Without a "proper" family life, without a husband, Stella would have to accept being alone. Although this filled her with dread, the work was all that really mattered.

CHAPTER TWENTY-TWO

*Wait till everyone sees this performance. The legend of
Stella Adler will finally coalesce with a reality on stage.*

—Frank Corsaro

NINETEEN-SIXTY-ONE BEGAN IN PARIS. STELLA INCORPORATED
her love of theater and travel by spearheading a tour abroad for
twenty students. On January 21 the group saw productions at the
Comédie Française and the Jean-Louise Barrault company. In England
they visited the Old Vic, with a side trip to Stratford-upon-Avon and then
to Berlin for opera. The seventeen-day tour culminated in East Berlin with
a visit to Berthold Brecht's company. The *New York Times* ran a spot on the
trip, highlighting a "baggage allowance . . . (of) forty-four pounds"—a lark
to anyone familiar with Stella's manner of travel. Even in the modern age
of the 1960s, she traveled with trunks like a betrothed heiress migrating
through the Continent, hauling along framed photographs of her family,
books, and her perennial shih tzus.

Later that year Frank Corsaro commenced directing the farce *Oh Dad,
Poor Dad, Mamma's Hung You in the Closet and I'm Feelin' So Sad*. He
thought Stella would be perfect for the lead role of Madame Rosepettle.
To everybody's surprise, Stella accepted the offer. It had been over fifteen
years since her last stage appearance, but she knew Corsaro's directing
from working with Shelley Winters on *A Hatful of Rain*. The London stage
was different, more refined, than Broadway. Perhaps, at sixty-one years old,
under those specific circumstances, Stella felt it was time for her comeback.
Sara Adler had also come out of retirement in a similar manner fifteen
years after being away from the stage.

In an interview with the author, Corsaro recalled rehearsals in London as "a combination of the most wonderful and the most hectic."[1] The director felt Stella "proved to be quite extraordinary . . . she was funny, she was beautiful, she was menacing but all with a great sense of humor. And I thought, 'Wait till everyone sees this performance. The legend of Stella Adler will finally coalesce with a reality on stage.'" Prior to leaving New York for rehearsals in London, Stella asked the director if she could excise a line from the play: "He was mine to love, mine to kill," explaining that she could show this physically without saying it. Corsaro spoke to the playwright, the twenty-four-year-old New Yorker Arthur Kopit, who agreed to withdraw the line. The show went to Cambridge for previews. "Stella was simply sterling," Corsaro remembered, "and the reviews reflected it." That made both Corsaro and the playwright eager to have the producers see the show when it opened in London.

In the interim, Kopit had decided he wanted to reinsert the line Stella had asked to remove from the script. Corsaro went backstage to discuss the change with Stella in her dressing room, where she was "remarkably immodest about herself." Stella had long since discarded any pretenses of covering up. Having grown up in the Yiddish theater, modesty was an unnecessary inconvenience, especially for character actors such as Stella who had to change costumes frequently. Corsaro inquired whether Stella had any problem with putting back the line she had taken out of the play. She appeared to agree, but Corsaro thought the lines' restoration was the genesis of what was to come in London.

Corsaro and Kopit left the province to replace a cast member. Upon returning, Corsaro heard, that in his absence, Stella had approached the cast to explain how "serious the play was, and that it must now be played with a sense of its tragic import." Corsaro looked in on the next performance to find "there was no laughter whereas on opening night there was uproarious response. And I realized that the play had become a tragedy. And the focal point of the entire evening was this line . . . that had been put back into the script where Stella had simply broken down emotionally on stage."

After the play, Corsaro knocked on the door of Stella's dressing room. He entered and asked her why her performance had changed. Stella contended that nothing had changed. Corsaro persisted "and suddenly she went to her dressing table which was loaded with cosmetics and with one gesture knocked all the bottles and powders and turned on me with a face that was absolutely virulent with hatred and said, 'It is exactly the way we've been playing it.'" Corsaro assumed that the meaning of the line "He was mine to love, mine to kill" was related to Stella's reliving of guilt over an abortion she was rumored to have had during the Group Theatre days, a conjecture for which there has never been any direct support. More likely Stella's breakdown had more do with something relevant to that particular time in her life.

The causes leading up to an emotional upset are varied and often inconclusive. Certainly Stella suffered from stage fright, starting with her performance in *A Doll's House* at age three. It may have been traumatizing to be back on the platform after such a long time away. Perhaps performing in the play was merely the breaking point of a variety of culminating factors. Stella's friend Eleanor Sheldon recalled this time as being very difficult for Stella, not the least of the reasons being her divorce from Harold.[2] Harold had met an actress, Juleen Compton, whom he was courting and wanted to marry. There is also something Stella confessed to her class once: "I'd like you to see me when I'm myself, acting, not all dressed up for you like now. When I act, nobody can be near me, talk to me, even say hello. People hated me. I hated people. The moment I work, I'm not nice at all, because what I work with is the demon in me."[3]

While working on *Oh Dad*, Stella rented an apartment in London. A psychiatrist friend and Stanley Moss, Stella's lover, were staying with her. According to Corsaro, the psychiatrist acted as a liaison between Stella and himself, telling the director that Stella was unable to proceed with the play and that she was suffering a "breakdown." Stella focused her animus upon Corsaro and the playwright, accusing them of "working against her" and declaring that she would continue with the part only if neither of them attended rehearsals. Corsaro remembered hiding in the theater so Stella would not see him, having to communicate with his actress by handing notes to the choreographer to be passed on to her.

Despite her seemingly fragile condition, Stella wanted to open the play in London. Corsaro remembered her coming to rehearsals "shaking like a leaf." The director's depiction of Stella as suffering a nervous breakdown may be tinted with his own disappointment over the play's reception. When Betsy Parrish went to London and stayed with Stella for the premiere of *Oh Dad*, she did not recall anything unusual in Stella's disposition. While internal despair can be hidden from the eyes of others, a total breakdown would not be easily masked, especially from a close friend. In a master class years later, Stella told her students, "If you have talent, the wearing down by life gets to you and hurts you. Guard against it. Fight it your whole life."[4] Life seemed to have been wearing away at Stella ever since Jacob's death. She bore it, fought through it, but perhaps it was time to surrender.

On opening night, July 5, 1961, Stella left early to the theater to fix her wig and prepare for her part. Her guests at home, Moss and Parrish, took a walk in a nearby park to pass the time before curtain. Moss was concerned about Stella; he knew how agitated she got before going onstage. Years later Parrish recalled admiring Stella's performance, not just on opening night but also the following night. She remembered the downcast moods of the actors due to the poor reviews and Stella being the one, as she was in the Group days, to keep morale high and the production moving.[5] Still, the opening-night notices reveal a performance more akin to Corsaro's recollection.

A report from London to the *New York Times* stated that the production "proved to be as baffling as its title."[6] At curtain call there were "some vocal noises of an uncertain nature." Another notice read, "Mr. Frank Corsaro's direction and Miss Stella Adler's playing of the leading part are so heavy handed that the audience has some difficulty in making up their minds whether to laugh at or with the author of the skit."[7] One London critic found Stella "preternaturally solemn."[8]

A couple days after the reviews came out, Corsaro returned to the theater to discover Stella playing her role the way it was originally rehearsed: "She was funny. She was brilliant." He referred to what Stella had gone through as a "spell." Upon asking her why she changed the tone back to its original flavor, Stella "implied that this is the way they had been playing it" all along. The show, however, could not recover from the poor reviews and the producers were not willing to risk its instability. The play closed.

Stella returned to Italy, her spiritual home, to recuperate and reflect. It seems acting had once again lost its joy. *Oh Dad* was her final performance on the professional stage. Teaching replaced the "soul satisfaction" Stella once drew from acting. It was only through teaching that Stella could honor her pledge to Stanislavski to disseminate his system in the United States.

IN THE FALL OF 1961 A FIVE-FOOT-NINE, THIN-FRAMED ACTOR NAMED Robert De Niro signed up at Stella's Conservatory in Murray Hill. Like Stella, De Niro was a native New Yorker and the son of two artists. But De Niro came from an entirely different milieu, growing up on the streets of Little Italy, where he was nicknamed "Bobby Milk" because of his milky complexion and small frame. De Niro was eighteen years old when he met Stella, the same age as Brando was two decades prior; but unlike Brando, he was not impressionable. He had already studied at the Dramatic Workshop at age sixteen and attended a public school of the arts. De Niro knew he wanted to be an actor, whereas Brando stumbled into the profession. Another major difference between the only two actors to win Academy Awards for the same character in a role (that of Vito Corleone in *The Godfather I* and *II* respectively) was that Stella instantly took Brando in and cultivated a lifelong relationship with him, whereas De Niro was not one of her "favorites." She didn't invite him to her house after class as she did her "darlings," and De Niro felt unacknowledged. "I wasn't anybody who made an impression on her when I studied there," he told the author in an interview.[9]

Why Stella gravitated toward certain people and not others is as mysterious as human chemistry itself. What is clear is that Stella didn't place any stock in celebrity: "The pregnancy of the artist is the desire to fulfill himself through his work," Stella lectured to her class, "not just his mind. 'I have a passion for this work!' When that dies, they may have all the money in the world, but they're dead. All of Hollywood is dead. The only effort that is valued is the moneymaking effort. But success is just an accidental aspect of a person's life. The man who works and tries and fails is to me just as much a success as someone on the marquee."[10] When asked by the *New York Times* who of her many famous students were her favorites, Stella responded: "I have a principle that fame is a matter of luck. The historical moment brings a great deal of this element of luck—you can be picked up because of television or movies. . . . So I can't say who my favorites are, because they won the prize by accident. There are as many talented people who are not known, because the accident didn't happen, as there are actors who are known, who are God's favorites."[11]

Although De Niro studied with Stella for the next four years until the conservatory found a semipermanent home in the recently built Lincoln Center, her "grandiosity," as De Niro termed it, rubbed him the wrong way. He felt her affectations went against her technique, which focused on authenticity. Still, he stayed because her approach to acting made sense to him, utilizing her emphasis on researching the character throughout his career. De Niro said, "I was also impressed with her keeping it [the role] about what it was about so it's not about you. . . . The character represents an attitude of the world, or a part of humanity, if you will, and she gave me that sense. That made an impression on me. . . . How she taught how it applies to a bigger vision."[12]

In January of 1963 Stella again boarded a plane to Moscow. She was going to attend the Stanislavski Centenary, the hundredth anniversary of the founder of the Moscow Art Theater. Thirty years had passed since Stella vowed to pay Stanislavski back for his contribution to the craft of acting. According to the journal she kept at the time, Stella arrived late one winter night in the mythic city named for the Moskva River. Her journal reports that after only a few hours of sleep, before daybreak, Stella awoke in her hotel room. Her gold compact alarm clock read six o'clock, an hour with which she was not well acquainted. She rose from bed wearing a new velvet negligee from Bonwit Teller and directly enveloped herself in the matching pink quilted robe. Pulling back the portieres and lace sheers from the French window, Stella peered onto the street. The Russian fog hovered over the scene. Lampposts, ledges, and streets were covered in the pristine brilliance of new snow. Stella felt she had been caught in history, in a mysterious scene from the Old World, the world of Tolstoy and Gorky. It was still dark an hour later when life began to appear upon the streets in the form of cars and human silhouettes. Stella fixed her gaze upon what seemed a measureless horizon of trees before going back to the warm refuge of her bed. Hours later she was up and eager to meet the day.

Stella dressed for the day in the mode of the majority of Muscovites. Her fur coat, thick gloves, hat, and solid waterproof boots were a necessary and yet cumbersome ensemble to protect her from temperatures that never quite managed to rise above freezing. She felt invigorated to be among the people, her kin, and noticed how everyone dressed against the winter, leveling them to the same status.[13] The boulevards were wide, some ten lanes long, and the sense of space arrested Stella. When she went indoors to eat or into a museum, removing her layers of accoutrements seemed a redundant chore, but the Russians had strict mores regarding indoor and outdoor attire.

Stella wasn't one to bother herself with societal expectations of conduct, not at home or abroad. She would be the woman to commit the gaffe of entering the Vatican without proper covering or assume that the candies and magazines at a checkout line were free for the taking. If reproached, she would react with a superiority that either intimidated or infuriated her interrogator. One day in Moscow Stella ventured into a museum cafeteria without removing her gloves, boots, or shawl. As soon as Stella sat down and plopped her bags on the table, an employee rushed over to reprimand her. "You are wearing your boots, your hat! Look at yourself!" It was such a scolding, Stella felt as if the woman were related to her.[14] No one but family would speak to another with such intimate scrutiny. It gave Stella a sense of belonging, and instead of taking a defensive stance, she peeled off the necessary items.

Stella had never seen so many theaters in her life as she did in Moscow.[15] There were seventy running theaters, and each one performed a different play each night. As during her first visit to the Soviet Union in 1934, she marveled at how the actors were permanently employed, the repertories tireless. Half an hour before curtain, people began gathering outside the theater, foraging for an extra ticket. They gathered in the snow and the sleet, even while knowing the house was full to capacity, on the off chance of gaining entrance.

The first meeting of the Stanislavski Centenary commenced on January 17. Stella arrived at the Moscow Art Theater at eleven o'clock among a group mostly made up of directors who had been influenced by Stanislavski. The lobby displayed photographs of Stanislavski's theatrical companies and stage productions. The most inspiring realization for Stella that day was that in all of the Soviet Union, not just Moscow, Stanislavski's theories were honored; there was no debate. Each school, director, and theater had Stanislavski's system at its foundation. In that moment she had the idea of taking representatives of the Moscow Art Theater to the United States to clarify his system once and for all.

During the month-long centenary celebration, Stella went to the theater every night, then to parties and informal gatherings. She didn't speak Russian, but acting transcended language. She attended *Bluebird* and *The Merry Wives of Windsor*, supper clubs, and embassy gatherings. Before leaving for Vienna at the end of January, Stella met with Ekaterina Furtseva, the Soviet minister of culture. She broached the idea of holding a seminar in New York with representatives of the Moscow Art Theater. Furtseva agreed to facilitate clearance for travel once the event was planned. For Stella the seminar would be a culmination of all things sacred: her heritage, her craft, and the promise she had made to Stanislavski.

THAT SUMMER OF 1963, STELLA CONDUCTED HER FIRST TEACHING COURSE in Los Angeles. A petite twenty-eight-year-old redhead with warm, liquid brown eyes named Irene Gilbert sat mesmerized. Gilbert had been born in Brandenburg, Germany, in 1934. Under the mounting persecution of the Nazi Party, the family moved to New York in 1938. She had four older stepbrothers from her father's previous marriage who also came to the United States just before the war. Irene's father continued his millinery business in Manhattan, her mother beside him selling ladies' hats. One day Gilbert's parents locked up the store and began walking home on Madison Avenue when they were struck and killed in a hit-and-run by a drunken cab driver. Now an orphan, four-year-old Irene was taken in temporarily by an uncle.

All four of Gilbert's brothers joined the war. In 1943 the eldest died in an army hospital. The others survived, but two died as young men, leaving only Gilbert's half brother John. John's mother, Ruth, adopted Irene, but by the time the girl was fifteen her aunt could no longer afford to take care of her. Ruth decided to uproot Irene and send her to an uncle in Israel. Early on Gilbert learned there were no promises in life; but instead of buckling under her losses, she marched on. She handled what life dealt her, and although on the outside it may have seemed she was not fazed, it took its toll. Through all the tragedy, through all the abandonment, she maintained a soft heart.

When Gilbert returned to the United States she had already decided to pursue a career in acting. She wound up in Hollywood, like so many displaced girls dreaming of stardom. Gilbert found it difficult to trust others. However, the day she met Stella Adler, she felt compelled to know and be close to her.[16] After class Gilbert spoke to the organizer who had arranged the Hollywood workshop and discovered there were no plans for Stella to hold future classes in Los Angeles. It became Gilbert's mission to bring Stella back to the West Coast, a commitment she pursued in various forms for the rest of her life. Today the Stella Adler Academy of Acting, cofounded by Gilbert, Stella, and the actress Joanne Linville, is located on Hollywood Boulevard. Stella's Walk of Fame star glimmers just outside the school's entrance.

In September of 1963 Stella returned to Moscow with a dual agenda: she needed to find the right people to invite to the United States to participate in the seminar, and she wanted to study. For the next month she worked at the Stanislavski Theater from nine o'clock in the morning till six o'clock at night. She had been studying and teaching acting for over thirty years with a mentality that aligned with that of the Russians. Acting was not something you mastered; it was a lifetime practice. Before leaving Moscow, Stella secured a date for the American seminar with the Moscow Art Theater's representatives for the following November.

Meanwhile Gilbert had arranged for Stella to return to teach a course on acting during the summer of 1964. Appropriately for Tinseltown, one of the classes was filmed. "Stella Adler and the Actor" aired on July 13, 1964. The host, Robert Crane, sat opposite Stella, interviewing her; outtakes from her acting workshop show Stella lecturing to a small audience of students. At the top of the show, Crane asks Stella to define method acting. Stella explains that there have always been different techniques of acting, but that when the modern play evolved, Constantin Stanislavski developed a system to accommodate the new play. She points out that what has been termed method acting in the United States is a "distortion" of Stanislavski's intentions. Interestingly, she does not blame Strasberg, but rather "some actors" who in their attempt to be "real" have become too relaxed, slouching, mumbling, and complains that the picture of the method actor is that of a "madman."[17] Stella had no proclivity for the term "method acting," but for economy's sake she uses it to discuss the style of acting engendered by the Group Theatre. In an interview given prior to the opening of *Oh Dad, Poor Dad* in 1961, Stella had summed up American acting in a remark that sardonically compared the "method" to Christianity: "It started with one idea and now there are how many denominations?"[18]

The most fascinating inquiry that Stella addresses is whether she considers herself a teacher. Crane asks, "You were an actress?"

"You have to constantly act. I worked with Stanislavski. I worked with Reinhardt . . . when they were watching you they were giving the better performance. They were the geniuses."

The host persisted: "Would you consider yourself a teacher?"

"I would say in a tradition of a teacher in any society where there is a theater the teacher is an actor and a director."[19]

Stella viewed the teacher not as the schoolmarms she knew at public school, but as the manager-actor in the Yiddish theater, like Jacob Adler, or the director-actor of the Moscow Art Theater, like Stanislavski.

Crane, best known as the character Colonel Hogan of television's *Hogan's Heroes*, was enrolled in Stella's class at the time "Stella Adler and the Actor" was filmed. In the *Florida Evening Independent*, Crane shared his experience:

"I read in the newspaper, Stella Adler, famous New York drama coach, is coming to town to give lessons for eight weeks," says Crane, "and I decided to enroll in the advanced workshop. In High School, my mind wandered all the time," says Crane. "But not here. I am alert." For his graduation monologue, Crane played a Jewish lawyer in the South. Crane the comic . . . lets all the stops out and afterwards he discovers Miss Adler kissing him. He is a hit. "I look over Stella's shoulder and who's behind her but Marlon Brando. Oh, am I glad I didn't see him before I did the bit," says Crane.[20]

The summer of 1964 marked the first time Irene Gilbert arranged for Stella to come to California to teach. She would continue to rent a space, advertise, register students, and rent a house for Stella every summer from then on.

CHAPTER TWENTY-THREE

Stella could be warm and she could be awful.

—Allison Adler

S TELLA FILLED HER LIFE WITH FRIENDS AND WORK, ADOPTING favorite students to take in to become a part of her menagerie of admirers. Those admirers included friends and colleagues who attached themselves to Stella because she was famous and ran in artistic circles. Stella attracted acolytes and kept them around for their willingness to serve and adore her.

Stella's friends and associates held her in such high esteem, and she maintained the stance of "holding court" to such a degree, that a mutual regard was rare. Anita Nye, wife of the comedian Louis Nye, is an example of a quintessential Stella "friendship." As a young woman of twenty, Nye met Stella when she was teaching at the New School in 1948. Nye accompanied Stella during her touring days to raise awareness and money for the League for a Free Palestine—entirely unaware the League was a political action committee for the Irgun. Nye gave Ellen piano lessons; once Stella brought Nye along with her to Italy. It was a forty-plus-year relationship, and yet when asked how Nye would characterize her ties to Stella, she was apprehensive about describing herself as a friend: "I guess I don't know what else to call me. I wasn't a colleague, certainly, but I was more than an acquaintance. I was somebody. I feel that she loved me and treasured me, not the way I treasured her. But she always liked me by her side and I accommodated her that way because I loved being around her."[1] A similar air of deference permeated most of Stella's "friendships."

The only requirement of Stella's favorites was that they be hers exclusively. Eleanor Sheldon, whom Stella befriended in Portofino in 1950, remembered Stella coming to her rescue when her marriage to James Sheldon ended. Stella insisted that Eleanor, a single mother on her own, live with her. "I moved back and I stayed with Stella until I found a place. . . . And she made sure I had something to do almost every night and afternoon and she was very attentive. She is also a very possessive person. Didn't want you to be with anyone else necessarily."[2] Stella's possessiveness stemmed from her upbringing. Having been reared in an unstable atmosphere, Stella created her own "family." She encouraged those she chose to be around her, expecting greatness, which uplifted them. Praise and a magnification of one's strengths seemed to cancel out Stella's possessive demands.

Sheldon began advising Stella financially. By the early 1960s, "everyone was stealing from her," Sheldon said. "So I went in to try to get that straightened out because the studio was largely a cash business and people were pocketing the cash. She wanted to hire me. I would not be hired. I took over her checkbook and I took over her jewelry and things of that sort for her protection and I paid off her bills."[3] Sheldon continued advising Stella as her school grew.

Still, the Adler family remained the cornerstone of Stella's identity, and so, appropriately, she appointed her nieces Lulla and Pearl to the staff at her studio. Days prior to her sixty-third birthday, Stella's nephew Allen Adler died at age forty during surgery for a narrowing of his esophagus. Allen was the son of Abe, Jacob's first and only son from his first wife. Allen left behind a wife, Mary Adler, and baby daughter, Allison. Seeing her nephew's family without an income, Stella invited Mary to run the office at her school, where Mary eventually took over the day-to-day operations.

Unlike most of the people who surrounded Stella, Mary did not back down in the face of Stella's moods. They were often found yelling at one another in the office, neither willing to acquiesce to the other. One day Allison fell sick, and Mary called the school to let them know she was not coming in to work. Incredulous, Stella telephoned Mary wondering what exactly she had to be at home to do. "I'm making her soup. She's in bed." Mary explained. "Oh, I didn't realize,"[4] Stella responded, now that she could picture the reality. Needless to say, Stella was oblivious to the needs of a child sick at home.

Allison remembered her Aunt Stella's cruelty toward her mother: "She would feel free to say things to my mother, which would hurt my feelings. The way she would talk to my mother. But they did love each other even though they had a difficult relationship."[5] Allison's earliest memory of Stella was running amok through her Fifth Avenue apartment:

> It was so fascinating to be there as a kid because you could have this big imaginary life because the whole apartment was like a salon in Venice or Paris, and there were cherubs everywhere. She had this one little room off her bedroom, which she may have used as a dressing room. It was all mirrors, all these Venetian cut mirrors, with built-in glass drawers with jewelry and a small stool that was upholstered, and I remember as a kid just sitting there and looking at myself from different angles. And sometimes she would watch me, and sometimes she would let me take something and try it on.[6]

Milton Justice, the Oscar-winning producer turned acting teacher, remembered Stella calling on Mary Adler one evening after inviting him over for dinner. Notoriously inept in the kitchen and at the time at odds with her housekeeper, Mary (not to be confused with Mary Adler), Stella was left to her own devices this night. Recalled Justice:

> Stella had a maid named Mary for years. I don't know how many times she fired Mary and how many times Mary quit, but at any rate, Stella invited me to dinner and she had discovered frozen quiche. And I'm sure that the man at the store told her exactly what to do with it and what the temperature was in the oven. And so we went to her kitchen, and she started to light the oven, and I swear I thought the house was going to blow. . . . I mean, what on earth made this woman think she could light an oven? So, she ended up calling Mary Adler [to come help].[7]

Justice had first met Stella in Los Angeles, where he had been working as a television producer. He had begun hating his career and wanted something more out of life. After six weeks studying with Stella, he found what was missing:

> With Stella I always felt that she brought us up to the level of the play. And I think that's what everyone responded to. The first note I have from the first class I took with her was, "I'm only interested in teaching actors who are willing to take on their shoulders four thousand years of the actors who have gone before them." And

that was it. In her mind you didn't walk onstage. When you walked onstage there were four thousand years of actors behind you, walking on stage with you. So some of us, especially any of us who had been working commercially, really felt like we were pissing in church or something. . . . Stella [told us], "What we're doing is noble. What we're doing is lifting people." And she was quoted in the book Lulla put together, "We're making it better for them (the audience)." And I think that's really what she carried with her. She was making it better for the audience; she was making it better for the students. She was trying to lift everyone up to this ideal.[8]

Justice packed his bags and moved to New York to study full-time with Stella. He knew he didn't want to be an actor, but he stayed because, as he explained, "I said to somebody once that a lot of people when they're depressed and lose their way go to church. Most of us that I know go to Stella's class, and then we reconnect."[9]

Justice recalled once seeing Stella and her niece Pearl in a supermarket in the Hamptons: "Pearl and Stella were walking down the aisles at Wilco, examining products. And they'd pick up this product, and the two of them would discuss it. 'It's like a mop. This is a mop cleaner. Of course one should clean a mop,' as if they knew the etiquette especially for mops. And then they'd put that down, and they'd go to something else, and then there'd be 'attention shoppers' over the PA system, and on aisle 3 there was something on special. The two of them would go trotting off to aisle 3, and they had to see what was on special."[10]

Although Justice's stories depict Stella as the neophyte she was when it came to such things as grocery shopping and cooking dinner, Stella's observations in the supermarket were no different from her lessons walking on the Lower East Side with her father. She spent her life studying the world around her. Like a scientist, she collected data, assembling it to experiment with in the laboratory of her classroom.

Stella's longtime student Betsy Parrish remembered studying at the conservatory during the 1950s and 1960s, when the students "still thought of acting as a religion, a calling."[11] Toward the end of one semester her class was doing scene work. Stella stayed with them through the night, "no extra money," Parrish added, "and one night, it's two, three in the morning and someone said, 'Stella, Stella, it's time to go home!' And I happened to be looking at her and I saw her haul herself out of the concentration. . . . I think we were working on Spanish Catholic imagery, and she hauled herself out of it and said, 'What's so great about home?'" Stella had in fact made a new home for herself. With performance, study, and family ties, her studio was as good a substitute as any for home.

When Parrish's class graduated they concocted a plan to continue working with Stella:

> We gathered together and we rented a cold-water flat. . . . We had a plan for ourselves and we wrote it all out and we took Stella out [to] an Italian place with Italian wine and we thought it was all genuine and wonderful and glamorous. And she took our pages, turned them upside down, and said, "What do you want?" And we said, we don't want anything. We got this group and we wondered if once in a while you'd come, just to see our work. And she said, "All right, when?" Saturday. Fine. Saturday she came, looked at the peeling wallpaper with grapes, the water-stained walls, smelled the gas, and said, "You'd better come to me."[12]

The group began meeting every Saturday morning in Stella's living room on Fifth Avenue. Because Stella was accustomed to rising late, someone would have to wake her with a fresh cup of coffee. She wouldn't bother to change, simply stepping out in a negligee and smeared mascara and looking "ravishing," Parrish recalled.

One weekend in 1964 Stella was called to Washington for an interview with a writer named Mitchell Wilson. Trained as a physicist, Wilson assisted Enrico Fermi when the Nobel laureate worked on atomic fusion at Columbia University. Wilson wrote ten novels and three nonfiction books, which were known best in the Soviet Union. Although most of his books, even the novels, had scientific themes, he had a profound knowledge of and interest in the theater. Stella was "struck" by the tall and debonair Wilson. Due back in New York for rehearsals, Stella called Parrish from Washington: "Betsy, I've been hit in the head like a rock. I was minding my own business walking along. I've been hit. I won't be there."[13]

Their romance flourished. The following summer Stella planned a vacation in Palm Springs with Wilson prior to the workshop Gilbert had arranged for her in Hollywood. Stella telephoned Gilbert. "Irene, you know how to get to Palm Springs? I want you to come this weekend."[14] Gilbert drove two hours to the desert, found the address to which Stella had directed her, knocked on the door, and was promptly introduced to Wilson. Later Stella asked Gilbert what she thought of the new man in her life. "He was marvelous, quiet, charming," Gilbert remembered. "He knew as much about the theater practically as she did. He was very involved in all of that and he knew it and I think that's one of the reasons they got along so well. . . . He had a problem. He limped. I don't know whether it was from polio earlier on. He always dressed exquisitely."[15] As the story goes, before they married Wilson gave Stella an ultimatum: "no more playing around."[16]

Who knows how long Stella's promise lasted. When asked whether Stella could be faithful, Stanley Moss responded, "No. Nor a child,"[17] meaning that Stella's loyalty was capricious by nature, like that of a child who follows her appetite, easily led astray by the need for instant gratification. "When Mitchell would go out of town," Moss said, "it was kind of a knee-jerk reaction. She would call me."[18] Out of everyone this writer spoke to, from Stella's daughter to her close friends, Moss was the only person who denied that Wilson was the love of Stella's life.

The following year Wilson and Stella were married. Stella's new husband was the sole object of her adoration, so much so that others, such as Eleanor Sheldon, receded into the background. "I knew what was happening and she loved me until it became inconvenient," Sheldon recalled. "I gave her her checkbook back and I gave her her jewelry back."[19] Sheldon would not remain estranged for long. Stella never let those she loved stay away for too long. Like Prokofiev, her first husband, Horace, and Clurman, Eleanor would remain Stella's lifelong friend.

In late November of 1964 the Stanislavski seminar finally came to fruition. The Institute of International Education hosted the three-day seminar. Stella had personally addressed thirty invitations to her colleagues, all representatives in their own right of the American theater. The old gang from the Group Theatre reunited, including Clurman, Robert Lewis, and Cheryl Crawford. Lee Strasberg didn't attend, but his wife, Paula, was present. Uta Hagen, Shelley Winters, and Lincoln Center Repertory's Hal Holbrook and Paul Mann were also in attendance among others. Guests wore headphones to translate the Russian into English.

The previous August Clifford Odets, who was living in Los Angeles, went to the hospital for stomach ulcers. The doctors discovered he had stomach cancer. Less than a month later Odets died at the age of fifty-seven. With his death still fresh in the mind of his friends, he would have been sorely missed at this reunion.

Offstage candid with Harold Clurman, ca. 1938. (PHOTO BY ROMAN BOHNEN, USED BY PERMISSION)

Stella in London with Clifford Odets (*left*) and Luther Adler, 1938. (©BETTMANN/CORBIS)

Stella, ca. 1944. (PHOTO BY MARCUS BLECHMAN, THE MUSEUM OF THE CITY OF NEW YORK / ART RESOURCE, NY)

Stella (*center*) serving as vice chairman for the American League for a Free Palestine, 1943. (HARRY RANSOM CENTER, THE UNIVERSITY OF TEXAS AT AUSTIN)

Stella in the film *Shadow of the Thin Man*, 1941. (IRENE GILBERT ARCHIVAL COLLECTION, STELLA ADLER ACADEMY AND THEATRES LOS ANGELES)

Stella in *He Who Gets Slapped*, 1946. (FROM THE AUTHOR'S COLLECTION)

Stella in the film *My Girl Tisa*, 1948. (FROM THE AUTHOR'S COLLECTION)

Stella holding her granddaughter, Sara, 1958. (COURTESY OF SARA OPPENHEIM)

Storytelling with a passive Lee Strasberg looking on, 1963. (HARRY RANSOM CENTER, THE UNIVERSITY OF TEXAS AT AUSTIN)

Stella with her daughter, Ellen, ca. 1950s. (HARRY RANSOM CENTER, THE UNIVERSITY OF TEXAS AT AUSTIN)

Stella with her
third husband,
Mitchell Wilson,
ca. late 1960s.
(COURTESY OF IRENE GILBERT)

Stella and Harold, late 1970s. (IRENE GILBERT ARCHIVAL COLLECTION, STELLA ADLER
ACADEMY AND THEATRES LOS ANGELES)

Stella still in grief over the loss of Mitchell Wilson, 1974. (PHOTO BY BRIAN SYRON, USED BY PERMISSION)

Stella with her daughter and grandchildren, 1988. *From left*: Tom Oppenheim, Ellen Adler, Stella, and Sara Oppenheim. (IRENE GILBERT ARCHIVAL COLLECTION, STELLA ADLER ACADEMY AND THEATRES LOS ANGELES)

Stella in a scene study class with Irene Gilbert, 1989. (IRENE GILBERT ARCHIVAL COLLECTION, STELLA ADLER ACADEMY AND THEATRES LOS ANGELES)

Stella arranged for the appearance of four representatives of the Moscow Art Theater, including its director, two actors who studied under Stanislavski, and a historian of Soviet theater. Finally she would be able to clarify the Stanislavski System and rid American theater of Strasberg's emphasis on affective memory.

The first day of the seminar commenced with the Russian actor referencing the gripe that had existed for the last three decades in the United States: "We have been told that the Method here has given rise to tendencies that are opposed to his [Stanislavski's] ideas."[20] The Americans acknowledged the accusation with nervous laughter. After the speeches and demonstrations by the Russian actors, a question-and-answer session followed in which Shelley Winters "launched into a bit of autobiography." This irritated Stella, who reprimanded Winters, saying, "We are here to learn from them, not from you," and exited the room before the Russians said that they "would like to hear about the Americans' experiences too." Toward the end of the seminar the director of the Moscow Art Theater still couldn't "understand the confusion that existed" in the United States regarding Stanislavski's system. Exasperated, Stella declared: "If it isn't clear now, it never will be."[21]

If a room of her closest colleagues could not clarify the confusion, it would be impossible to expect the theater community at large to understand Stanislavski's system. Stella felt her efforts were futile. What she neglected to acknowledge was that individuals learn through experience. Theirs were not the same as hers. She forged her view of Stanislavski from her own perspective and life experiences. Not everyone saw the system from her point of view, nor did they perceive other interpretations as especially hazardous to the craft. It was the frustration of a mother who has not yet instilled in the child the need to stop and look both ways before crossing the street. The mother sees the entire picture, the oncoming traffic, the need for precaution, and a systematic approach to taking an action. The child sees the goal, not the pitfalls. It was clear to Stella, but she seemed incapable of conceding more than one way to cross the street.

Lee Strasberg's son, John Strasberg, views the system less definitively, placing its effectiveness upon the individual and not a specific technique:

> My father is credited with turning Marlon Brando, Robert De Niro, James Dean, Montgomery Clift, and anyone else who was a member of the Actors Studio into what and who they are. . . . However, the myth has led us to think that it is the system one studied, rather than the way in which the artist develops himself from that study that

is important. . . . My father's "Method" is based on an organized, workable technique of creating and expressing sensation and emotion; Stella's work is based on one's ability to become involved as the result of an analysis of the play. He lacked imagination and spontaneity; she lacked the organization to consciously impart to others what she was really doing.[22]

John Strasberg's description reduces Lee's and Stella's teachings to their own myth: Strasberg only taught affective memory and Stella only focused on the given circumstances of the play. This was an oversimplification. Strasberg and Stella both taught their interpretations of Stanislavski's other precepts, such as the through-line action, the imagination, and the given circumstances, but John Strasberg's point is well taken. In their quest to lay claim to a definitive approach, Stella and Strasberg contradicted what they both knew to be true: acting, like any art—writing, dancing, composing—is ever expanding, malleable, and evolves with the human being. This, not prioritizing one aspect of the system over another, is what Stanislavski theorized. However frustrated Stella may have felt over her and her fellow actors' and teachers' failure to reach a common understanding of the system, she would not be deterred from upholding her promise to Stanislavski to generations of actors through teaching.

NINETEEN-SIXTY-FOUR ENDED WITH THE DEATH OF STELLA'S OLDEST sister, Frances Adler, mother of Stella's beloved nieces, Lulla and Pearl. An acclaimed star of the Yiddish stage, Frances Adler's passing was a brutal reminder of Stella's idealized youth, an era that withdrew into the unredeemable past as each Yiddish actor took leave of the world. For reasons that are unclear but may have had to do with her relationship with Jacob Adler, Stella's sister Julia had married and left New York and acting. Now, with Frances's death, Stella became the family matriarch, a role she took on with the dutiful air of a sovereign born to her position.

Her stately residence on Fifth Avenue became the center of family gatherings, and with such a large family, there were always new Adlers to be brought into the fold. Lulla's daughter, Josie Oppenheim, recalled her first memory of Stella outside her apartment: "I was four years old and my mother took me to 1016 where Stella was living, and what I remember was that there was this radiator on the side of the lobby and I remember I put my head down on the radiator so I was seeing her [Stella] upside-down. This is the extraordinary thing about the experience. She was so beautiful. She was so beautiful that it literally, not figuratively, but literally took my breath away."[23]

At ease with the comfort of a new marriage, acclaimed as theater's authority on script interpretation, and with an ever growing roster of students, Stella had finally found a modicum of satisfaction with life. She continued to compare herself with her parents and grieve the golden age of the Yiddish theater, but nostalgia quit vying for so much of her heart. Self-acceptance began to take its place.

CHAPTER TWENTY-FOUR

It was said that if you could get through Stella's training,
nothing would ever frighten you again.

—Robert Brustein

O N A SPRING DAY IN 1966 ROBERT BRUSTEIN, THE NEW DEAN OF the Yale School of Drama, called on Stella at her Fifth Avenue apartment to ask her to join his faculty. Her and Brustein's acquaintance went back several years. Over tea they discussed Brustein's proposal. Stella felt reluctant. She held traditional institutions such as Yale in high regard, but the commute was something to which she was entirely unaccustomed. And then there was the matter of classroom size. She was used to the large studio space at her school. She expressed that she might be able to help him out if she could compress her classes into two days a week. Still, she was unwilling to consider the offer unless Brustein agreed to a certain contingency.

Brustein recalled that "Stella was convinced that performance was earned only after strenuous training; otherwise, the actor only calcified bad habits."[1] She insisted that the Yale students not give public performances until they had finished two years of training. Brustein knew his students. Consisting of mostly privileged WASPs in an era of a countercultural revolution, the majority of the undergraduates had an attitude of entitlement, viewing authority with skepticism. They would rebel against the notion of not being able to perform publicly. When prodded, Stella agreed to reduce her terms to one year of training before a performance. "I'll do it," she said fluttering her eyelashes and pursing her lips, "I'll do it . . . *for you*"—a coda she attached to most of her duties as a servant to the theater.[2]

Brustein held auditions for new candidates at the Establishment Theatre in New York, where he marveled at Stella's boundless energy. Throughout the 250 auditions, Stella's concentration never wavered. Together they chose an incoming class of thirty students, and the remaining faculty was hired, including the legendary Joseph Papp to teach directing.

At her studio Stella held court while both the faculty and the student body deferred to her. Yale was a different animal. She hadn't anticipated the students' overall louche comportment—slouching in their chairs, doodling, and chewing gum. She referred to them as *pischers*, kids who didn't know the first thing about the acting tradition. She was lucky to get a student who tucked in his shirt.

By the end of her first year, Brustein made Stella head of the drama department. He then began creating ensemble groups led by student directors, playwrights, and actors. Dismayed, Stella held her condition of not allowing students to perform before a year of training—an ironic demand from someone who learned to act through stage experience. Yet acting was no longer made up of stock gestures and bellowed oaths. A craft had been developed. An actor had to be prepared with a solid technique.

The next fall Stella wearily commenced her commute to New Haven two days a week. Sometimes she found her classes half empty. She would urge the students, "You must present yourself—show who you are. Do you understand that? You must expose yourself to the world!"[3] Stella became restless with her class; she decided to shake them up by tearing open her blouse. Everyone froze as Stella stared down the class defiantly: "Now you have to learn how to be present. How to be present in life and how to be present on stage. I have performed a symbolic gesture. You must be able to do this without this gesture. But you must know what that gesture *feels* like—what it is like to be exposed."[4]

One student reported that he felt she expected too much from them, especially when they were lacking the life experience she had. Another student recalled encountering a classmate crying in the parking lot after class. He asked her what was wrong, and she explained that nothing was wrong. Rather, she had never been so moved in her life before meeting Ms. Adler.[5] This was an exception, however; the majority viewed Stella as an archaic authority figure. When the academic year came to a close, Stella handed in her resignation. She didn't belong at Yale and had never done well within a conventional environment. She went back home to her own studio.

In 1967 Stella publicly conceded, in a rare disclosure to the press about her personal life, that she and Ellen were estranged: "She [Ellen] was the center of my life," Stella confided in an interview. "Now, for better or for worse, she has removed herself from this strong tie . . . she has broken it off."[6] Having lived in the shadow of a figure such as Stella Adler and abandoned by her mother while growing up, there is no doubt Ellen held deep-rooted resentments. For this reason, Ellen could not bear to watch Stella teach. This particular estrangement was not the first time Ellen had distanced herself from Stella, and would not be the last. Stella seemed unable to acknowledge her own contribution to the troubled mother-daughter dynamic. It is also likely that Stella's marriage to Mitchell Wilson, now in its second year, consumed what little attention Stella had left for personal relationships.

Wilson had two daughters of his own who Stella viewed as a threat. She didn't like to have to share her husband. The situation worsened when Wilson went to Stella's friend Eleanor Sheldon for advice. "Stella was upset with me," Sheldon recalled, "because he came to me, and upset with him because I told her to ease up, he wants his children close."[7] Stella was spared the part about Wilson's advances toward Sheldon. Similar advances toward Irene Gilbert were also kept from Stella. Wilson underestimated the loyalty of Stella's friends. It worked in his favor, as neither woman would dare dispel Stella's vision of her devoted husband.

With time, Stella did "ease up," and even began developing her own relationships with his daughters. According to Sheldon, the older of the two, Victoria Wilson, became "extremely attached" to Stella.[8] "She sat in on all of Stella's classes,"[9] remembered Irene Gilbert. Later, as an editor at Knopf, Victoria stewarded the publication of two volumes of Stella's master classes on the great playwrights.

In the spring of 1967 Mitchell Wilson fell ill. Ever since Jacob's death and the vacuum left by that loss, Stella had feared the death of a loved one. She wrote to Irene Gilbert: "Mitch has been very ill and just came out of a crisis as I'm writing and so I can only say I have to learn to live with a deep love for him and a fear I must overcome."[10] Stella spent endless hours at the hospital with her husband, staying the summer with him in her country house in East Hampton instead of teaching in California. Mitchell recovered, but the fear of losing him clawed at Stella's heart.

Although Stella had spent a lifetime criticizing the sterility of Los Angeles, the film capital actually became an uplifting destination for her, thanks to her summer teaching courses. Once summer hit southern

California, everyone knew Stella would be coming to teach. She arrived like an empress and was received as one. Irene Gilbert could be counted on to procure a summer rental, always with a pool so that Stella and Wilson could comfortably transition into California living. Before long Stella assembled a coterie made up of celebrities in the television and film industry.

Stella's arrival in Los Angeles would spark a series of parties given in her honor. It might begin with the producer Stanley Ruben and his wife, the actress Kathleen Hughes, hosting a welcome-back party for Stella; the following weekend Jayne Meadows and Steve Allen might organize a dinner; Anita and Louis Nye would offer up their house the subsequent weekend. And so it went throughout the summer: always the same supporting cast, just a different house. Stella once told her class, "When I go to California, I am a great celebrity—big star. Why? Because Stella is the only one who talks about Chekhov. The others talk about movies. They talk about *Star Wars* and I talk about Ibsen. . . . I get to be a star in a different way."[11]

Stella came to expect the parties, preparing for them as she would a performance. It was a consistent gig each summer, and Stella felt comforted knowing that she would be in demand. Los Angeles was waiting for her to arrive, to come onstage and be Stella. "She made herself," Jayne Meadows commented. "She gave classes where she would say, 'Ruth Gordon was born with bowlegs so she went to the hospital and had her legs broken and straightened. . . . You don't like your name, change it. You don't like your nose, change your nose. You become whatever you want to become.'"[12]

Meadows's relationship with Stella had come a long way since Jayne was a naive newlywed in New York starting out as an actress. Meadows married the Hollywood writer Milton Krims, who was the grandson of the great Yiddish comedian Boris Thomashefsky. Thomashefsky had lived in opulence at his estate in the Catskills, with automobiles, horses, gardens, even an eight-hundred-seat open-air theater. Three years Stella's junior, Krims had come up with her in the Yiddish theater.

By contrast, Meadows had been born in China, where her parents worked as missionaries. When she was eight years old the family returned to the United States and settled down in a small town in Connecticut, where her father became an Episcopal minister. At eighteen she moved to New York to pursue a career in acting. She soon met and married Krims. Having led a relatively sheltered life, Meadows had never encountered anyone like Stella Adler.

Meadows first met Stella as her dinner guest in the late 1940s when Stella and Harold were still married. Meadows recalled, "We were sitting and we were all talking and she was big busted. She went right into her bosom, right in to her bra, took out one of her bosoms and sat there the whole time she was talking to me just stroking her bare bosom and Milton said, 'Stella!' And Harold never said a word. It was just like 'Oh my God, not again.' And my husband was furious because he knew me and he knew that I had never seen anything like that."[13] Later in the evening, Meadows said, Stella took her aside and told her: "Now you know my husband can make you a star. Of course to be a star, you should have an affair with my husband." The accuracy of Meadows's story is anyone's guess, but it wouldn't be out of character for Stella to resort to such mischief, say, if Krims and Clurman were giving all their attention to the young actress at dinner. Perhaps Stella was trying to get even with Harold for a pre-dinner argument by exposing herself to Krims. Maybe she was simply trying to shock the innocence out of the girl, as she did to so many of her students wanting to be actors. Whatever her reasons, Stella's goal of getting attention had certainly been successful.

The next time Stella and Meadows crossed paths was as teacher and student. Meadows enrolled in Stella's class in the 1950s, during which time Meadows suffered a miscarriage. She remembered Stella's deep concern for her. "Stella was the sweetest; I think one of the first bouquets I got in the hospital was from Stella. She knew. I cry easily and I was devastated. When I came back to class, I remember crying when she was just being sympathetic."[14] Meadows describes her relationship with Stella as one in which they "became friends." When they met again in the late 1960s, that first strange dinner party now twenty years in the past, Meadows had enjoyed tremendous success as a Broadway and television actor. She was now married to the legendary Steve Allen, whom Stella adored and who she was adored by. Meadows vividly remembered one party she and Steve threw for Stella at which she had deliberately seated Stella at a table surrounded by men. Stella made her entrance, took her seat, and smiled meekly at those around her until she realized all the other tables had mixed seating. She burst out in laughter. "When she laughed," Meadows remembered, "that mouth would come open, the tongue would be in mid-air and you could see her epiglottis laughing. So you can imagine when she cried."[15]

Stella's former student Betsy Parrish recalled: "There was a time, there was a night in fact when she burst into tears at a party, and looked at me and we were talking about something, and she said, 'Who can inspire me, Betsy? Where can I go to be lifted?'"[16] Stella mastered the art of impassioning people with intellect, rage, and affection. She watched and listened to those who came to her and enabled them to feel the universal size of life and its pursuits. But it was the rare individual who could get past his awe of Stella to mutually invigorate her. Art itself was the most divine power that could "lift" Stella, a secular Jew. Her comment expressed a soul in need of spiritual inspiration.

In 1971 Elizabeth Parrish wrote to Stella in Los Angeles. The letter reveals the complex way in which Stella's relationships operated. From the hospital where she is about to have a mastectomy, Parrish writes: "Well, my friend, light of my life—this letter is almost impossible to write—and—I imagine—will be very difficult to read. Please read it in a moment when you are quiet—with Mitchell close by." The pains Parrish takes to ensure that Stella's response to the news of a friend fallen ill with cancer are more than an attempt to soften the blow; it borders on a reluctance to burden Stella. Parrish continues, "I would not for the world have the winds of heaven visit your cheek too roughly (Shakespeare!)[.] But as you are so much of my life—I have to tell you what's happening to me. . . ."[17] The kid gloves are not used out of fear, as a superficial reading may provide, but rather from a keen understanding of Stella's magnified sensitivity to the pain of others. Stella's heightened sense of emotion, both joyous and sorrowful, made for a richly lived yet at times unbearably burdened life.

CHAPTER TWENTY-FIVE

It was too overpowering to have any relationship with her and watch her teach.

—Ellen Adler

OWING PERHAPS TO THE INCONSISTENT, EVEN UNRELIABLE NATURE of her parents' love, Stella kept herself from being vulnerable to romantic love. She loved her first two husbands in her own way, but she had never lost her heart to them, had never let her love for them run "too deep," as her mother had warned her. However, Stella did not heed her mother's advice when it came to Mitchell Wilson. He became the world to her. They went everywhere together: summers teaching in Los Angeles, returning home to New York or her country house in the Hamptons the remainder of the year, interim sojourns to Europe as necessary. "I think he fulfilled some sort of vision she had," observed Ellen Adler. "He was very distinguished looking and he dressed very beautifully and she was more and more obsessed with that kind of thing. And then he was a scientist, which had nothing to do with the theater. She was intrigued by that. She felt that he was a giant. And he was just at the right [time]; she was ready to admire and love. She did love him. No question."[1]

"I resigned myself to the fact that my destiny was to be total loneliness," Stella recalled feeling after her divorce from Harold. "My love went to all the people I worked with—my students, and to my friends. And the most rewarding present I got in return was their amazing response. I considered it a miracle when I fell in love with Mitch Wilson. When this happened I knew I could live my life with him without the pain and agitation that comes when one works and gives of oneself to others."[2]

Stella recalled watching the day of the first lunar landing with Mitchell: "I watched it on TV. I saw Armstrong stepping down and going on to the moon. My husband, Mitchell Wilson, was a physicist and understood the inner workings. How he cried because of the complexity of it! I didn't cry, but he cried because he understood what that performance was. I cry when there is a good Hamlet."[3]

Mitchell and Stella's personal dynamic was quite different from what she had had with Harold. Allison Adler remembered Stella's "histrionics out in the country" house, where Stella would say, "I want a divorce," and Wilson would say, "Okay, fine we'll get a divorce," and walk away. Unlike Harold, Wilson was quiet. He wasn't going to be lured into an argument. Mostly, Allison remembered Stella "always with her hand on" Wilson, wanting to be physically connected to him.

In September of 1971 Stella wrote to Irene Gilbert from Europe expressing a wistful attitude toward the past and simultaneous sorrow and appreciation for the present.

> One day . . . Mitch got lost and we drove for hours over the longest and worst mountain range in Italy with cozy towns tucked in between but we pulled thru. . . . Drove up to Venice and all my old memories. Tears flowed, my heart ached all . . . lovers, husbands, friends—shop keepers—each filled my heart with pain. And then sitting in the Piazza which Napoleon called the greatest ballroom in Europe. . . . People came up and said, "Bonjourno Signora Stella"—Shop keepers, hotel people, how extraordinary the beauty stays but the heart of man suffers [when] it looks up at the sky which stays. Mitch caught a cold and so now we are in Paris.[4]

Wilson fit perfectly into Stella's lifestyle, which she supported financially. They returned that fall in time for Stella to resume teaching, but Wilson became so ill he had to be hospitalized.

Stella spent days in the hospital waiting for her husband to recover from his current medical crisis. One morning, two weeks after her seventy-first birthday, Stella and Mitchell awoke at home. Allison Adler recalled being told that Wilson simply announced that he didn't feel well, "and he sat down on the chair and had a heart attack."[5] Stella called to him, and when he didn't answer she remembered there was a doctor in her building, but it was already too late to save her husband. The funeral was held two days later at the Park West Memorial Chapel.

Stella was inconsolable. She later told Bobby Lewis that she and Wilson had had an argument the night before he died and she felt his death was her fault.[6] The family came to the apartment to see her, but she remained in bed. Ellen slept over on the couch to take care of her mother. Stella's niece Pamela Adler Golden recalled the "impression left by Mitchell Wilson's body on the ice blue satin sheets with instructions that it is not to be touched."[7] From Hollywood Jay Adler wrote: "Dearest Stella, Please forgive me for not being near you in your hour of need. It's not easy for me to travel to NY. I am not well enough to do so. I haven't many more words to say except hold on darling. I love you very much and dearly. Your brother, Jay."[8]

Wilson's death came in the middle of the semester of Stella's renowned script interpretation class. At seventy-one, Stella still passed for a woman in her late fifties. Her body was not as svelte, but she could pull off the popular slim-legged pantsuits of the era flatteringly with her hallmark décolletage. After a week, she went back to work, leaving her apartment to find a city undisturbed by her personal loss. The crisp wintry air stung her as an affirmation of nature's sovereignty over life. Similar to the surreal state one feels after emerging from days of sickness into the world, Stella entered the Central Synagogue, where she gave her classes (her studio was not large enough for the hundred-plus students), to find that life carried on. For those few hours she channeled her grief into her work.

A new student, the photojournalist Rue Drew, remembered, "She was magnificent because all of this pain just came out in pure brilliance."[9] Drew became Stella's chauffeur, accompanying her in taxis around the city and driving her to the country on weekends.

> She didn't pay people to do things. She would even ask students to come in and paint her apartment and she'd say, "You don't want to get paid do you, darling? Look who you're working for!" She manipulated people and seduced the men . . . she was brilliant in class and she was a hellion out of class. You'd go out to the country and the tension was such. . . . Ron kept saying she's Miss Nuts-and-Bolts at the country. Everything had to be fixed. She didn't know what to do with herself. "Ron, call the furniture man to fix that chair." [She was] absolutely lost so she had to take control of the house.[10]

Ron Burrus was an aspiring young actor studying at Stella's studio at the time he was hired to help out at the house in the Hamptons. "She stayed in her room and cried for months," Burrus remembered. "The family stayed away because there was no consoling her. So I stayed there that summer. Psychologically, she wanted me closer all the time."[11] Stella felt more comfortable grieving with a doting young student than with a close friend or family member; with Burrus there was no need to keep up pretenses, not even on a physical level since he was gay.

Stella wrote to Irene Gilbert in June: "I wanted so much for you to come. I wanted to give you what I had when I had everything. But now it's sad. I couldn't bear it. I had to go from great happiness and now my heart hurts and I couldn't let you see that."[12] Never one to be deterred, especially when it came to Stella, Gilbert went to the country house anyway. There were many visitors that summer, but their stays were brief. Burrus and the housekeeper, Mary, were Stella's only constant companions.

That fall back at work Stella invited Burrus to assist her in class. She wanted him near, even if it was just sitting next to her while she taught. Once class was over, "she would go home and grieve."[13] Betsy Parrish visited often. "I would go and try to take her for a walk. 'Let's get out, Stella.' So sometimes that would work, but sometimes she would say, 'No, Betsy, I'm clinically depressed. You can't help me.'"[14] Alone again, Stella had to find a way of negotiating the dark demons that visited upon her.

That summer Stella returned to Los Angeles, accompanied this time by her new protégé, Burrus. Her late husband was still foremost in her thoughts, his pictures arranged around the rental house to maintain the presence lost and ached for. Keeping busy eased the sorrow. "I could get by in the daytime," she wrote to Gilbert, "but at night I shook with pain."[15] Burrus became overwhelmed with all the activity: "There would be a lot of parties, a little too many for me. And I would tell Stella, 'No, not another party. And she would say, 'Yes, Ron, we're almost done.' You would have a lunch and then [a party] every night of the weekend. And I said, if we were running for politics, we would be elected."[16]

One evening Jayne Meadows planned a dinner for Stella. "I had a very small group," Meadows recalled. "I took a private room in a Chinese restaurant because she loved Chinese food."[17] Burrus and Stella ascended the stairs to the dinner party. "[After] I saw who was in the room," Burrus said, "I went and threw water on my face. I thought, this is never going to happen again, and it never did. At this gathering were me and Stella; Jayne and Steve Allen, and now Steve's gone; Milton Berle, he's gone; George Burns, he's gone; Lucille Ball, she's gone; James Coburn; Marge and Gower Champion, they were a dance team in the movies in the fifties."[18] George Burns and Milton Berle entertained with stories about their vaudeville days.

Returning to New York was upsetting, and Stella staved off the sorrow by keeping busy. One of her students, Joanna Rotte, who later taught Stella's technique, recalled a humbling lesson during this time:

While rehearsing Wilder's *Happy Journey*, we actors inadvertently made a mess of the backstage area. The room was way too small for our cast of five, with costumes and makeup, books and gear, but still, we hadn't helped the situation by strewing coffee cups, cigarette butts, used tissues, and garbage in general. On the weekend of dress rehearsal, Stella came backstage to greet us. . . . To say that she was appalled would not be overstating [it]. She called for a broom, a bucket of suds, a scrub brush, and a trash bin. As soon as we had gathered up the garbage, Stella got down on her seventy-three-year-old hands and knees to scrub the floor. . . . When the floor was clean, she said, "The actor is the sanity of the theatre. It's up to you to keep the theatre healthy."[19]

The summer of 1974 Stella was asked to teach in Sydney. She invited Burrus to accompany her to Australia and then travel around the world. Betsy Parrish saw them off at the airport: "I'll never forget her in a mink coat as she turned from the doorway [as] you enter the plane. And the tears came up and she turned with tears in her eyes."[20]

Stella invited her nephew Jody, Luther's son, to stay at her apartment while she was away. Jody's health was languishing and he needed to see doctors in the city. Soon he would learn he had amyotrophic lateral sclerosis (ALS), for which there was no treatment. His letters to Stella, which she saved, draw a portrait of two souls commiserating through their respective tragedies:

Dear Aunt Stella,
I received your postcard from Fiji, and by now you would be in Australia. . . . I have been living in your apartment for about ten days. . . . You have watched my condition deteriorate, as have others. I imagine it must be rather sad. But all I can do is cope the best I can, and not worry about how others may feel. I have no place in my life for those who are weak, and no use for those who cannot speak to me openly and directly. . . . This evening I shall leave for the National Institute of Health in Bethesda, Md. . . . Also, Aunt Stella, I want you to know that I know too much to expect miracles. I rather expect that

my fight against this disease will take years. So I am preparing myself for a protracted battle.[21]

Jody's letters put Mitchell's death into perspective. They undoubtedly reminded Stella of the strength of her family and its spirited fight for life.

Stella found an apartment in a section of Sydney called Darling Point, a cliffside complex overlooking the harbor. "The entire country is surrounded with thousands of miles of sea and boats keep passing by all the time," she wrote to Gilbert. As Stella explained in her letter, "It was easier here than in California because there were no memories and that seemed to settle me more."[22]

After a month in Sydney, Burrus and Stella began a trek around the world, first to Hong Kong, then Tel Aviv, making various stops on the way to Lisbon, from where they flew back to New York. She arrived home to find a letter from Jody, most likely still in treatment at the National Institute of Health:

Dear Aunt Stella,
I received your letters, yet really don't know how to answer them. Both of us are trapped. I by my disease. In some ways I am more fortunate than you, yet I envy anyone who can get on a bus. . . . I think of you often. The trip around the world was very good for you. It may have been an escape but an escape from a reality unpleasant and unproductive can't be all that bad. And you said that in Israel you learned that you were just a plain Jewish girl. This I got to see! An uncomplicated Adler![23]

At home again Stella painstakingly came to terms with the loss of Wilson. She gradually stopped secluding herself, and by autumn of 1974, the day-to-day grieving had ended.

In late September, after a month in the Hamptons, Stella sat down and wrote a letter to Irene Gilbert in longhand, which was rare for Stella as she thought her handwriting atrocious. The sincerity of the letter indicates that suffering had opened her heart in a way that led her to begin cultivating her relationships differently, allowing others to comfort her, allowing herself to be vulnerable:

Well, Irene. It's still terribly lonely and I am alone. A lot of people are alone, only I don't want a life apart from Mitchell. I depended so deeply on him that it is like trying to walk without legs. The season has started—there is maximum registration—all the classes are over-sized—so that I have assistants to help out—while I work I am fully involved and afterwards I fall back on my half-hearted appetites. I want you to know me as I live and therefore I am making myself known to you. I think of you dear friend and although we are parted so much it is with all my heart that I care for you and love you.[24]

Work remained Stella's priority, but it was no longer her sole sustenance. With time and loss, she was becoming more appreciative, intimate, and reliant on others. Roles in life are difficult to break, however, and when it came to family, Stella was still the Adler matriarch. Just as Stella was a favorite of Jacob's, Ellen's daughter Sara was a favorite of Stella's. She felt a special affection for her granddaughter who had been named after her mother and whose blonde hair and blue eyes resembled Stella's. Stella's efforts at forging a more intimate relationship with Sara are demonstrated in letters she wrote while Sara was studying at college. A psychology major, Sara would hand this author letters from her grandmother explaining that they expressed a closeness that she herself could not fully comprehend, Stella being as far from the stereotypical grandmother crocheting afghans and making hot cocoa as one could get.

Sara explained that she could not sit and chat with Stella as she did with her own mother. Indeed, Stella did not chat with anyone. The letters, however, reveal a closeness that appears to have been reciprocated despite what Sara remembers. "These letters were very poignant to me," Sara said, "and I just happened to be looking at them the other day, but I probably underestimated her affection to me. They seem like love letters; they seem like the kind of thing that you write to a lover, not to a grandchild."[25] In many of her letters to people Stella cared about, her expression of language could border on rhapsodic. Stella's place in life—growing older, the inevitable loss of friends and colleagues—would also attribute to their sentimentality:

Sara, my love, my darling, I've been thinking of you and I hope you'll come into town. I'm worried you haven't the proper clothes for winter. So, I stick my nose into magazines to see what you possibly could use. But, I will probably see you during Thanksgiving. That's the pedestrian side of me, maternal and boring. The other side is that I'm working hard trying to penetrate the lives of characters in Strindberg. . . . I called Tommy. You're quite right. "Reach out. Just keep reaching out." It's a good way to live in a world with people. A lot has happened; the loss of a friend and getting used to truly living alone, the loss of my puppy, the change of seasons and the turmoil around turmoil. It's like a band of drums playing, just drums.[26]

During our meeting Sara shared a photograph of Stella holding her as a newborn baby. With both hands, Stella raises her swaddled granddaughter against her cheek. Sara confided that Ellen had never held Sara's children, for which she offered an explanation: "My mother was sent to boarding school when I think she was two and half, three, and I think didn't see her mother for years. . . . I think that Stella had a life to live . . . she wasn't a mother, and she had my mother more or less continuously in boarding schools and foster homes until she was about sixteen or seventeen when she came home finally. So, my mother just had this one dazzling human being as a mother, but if you ever saw the letters my mother wrote [to Stella], it's really heartbreaking."[27]

According to Sara, in these letters Ellen "begs" Stella to call her; the letters themselves were too private for Ellen to share with the author. In interview after interview, Ellen Adler refused to discuss her personal relationship with her mother. Rather, her own daughter's words illuminate the complexity of Stella and Ellen's relationship: "My mother was also the most beautiful woman. I mean, I don't know if you've heard that, but literally the most dazzling. Way beyond Stella. I mean Stella had stature and presence; she was beautiful in a very different way. My mother was just to-kill-you-like-Vivien-Leigh kind of beautiful and I think Stella was very competitive and mean with her. But I think on the other hand it was also a very loving, passionate relationship. It wasn't just one thing. So, I think my mother was just seized, and her whole identity has been about her somehow."[28] As recently as 2012 Ellen sat on a panel for the release of a book of Stella's master classes on American playwrights. Discussing how harsh Stella could be, Ellen said, "She was not hard with me. She was afraid of me."[29] It is not surprising that Ellen was aware of Stella's fear of her, which undoubtedly arose from the guilt Stella felt for having chosen her career over her child.

Stella intimated her remorse to Sara but never addressed the facts specifically. "When I visited her in L.A. last," Sara recalled, "she said that when my mother was born . . . everybody was visiting, and she sort of realized now that it wasn't about the baby for her. So, I think at the end of her life she had some understanding."[30] The story calls to mind how, hours after giving birth, Stella was so caught up in the attention given to her that she completely forgot there was a new baby in the picture. In the past Stella would tell the story as an amusing anecdote; now it was a tragic one.

Throughout her life Stella compensated for her failures at intimacy with financial support. During the Depression, as a single mother, she provided for her daughter and her mother, who lived with her even after Stella and Harold were married. When she began her teaching career, she continued to sustain Ellen and other members of the family, including, later in life, her last husband, Wilson. As Stella aged and her income depended on the success of her school, her major concern continued to be how she would financially support her loved ones. Although Stella was known for being magnanimous with money—buying Tyrone Guthrie's wife a fur coat or paying for her granddaughter's education—she could also be parsimonious. She did not want to die poverty-stricken like her parents.

Once, after a concert at Lincoln Center, Stella invited the family to dinner at the Gingerman Restaurant. Her niece Allison Adler remembered, "We went out and Sara ordered a cognac and that turned into World War III. [Stella attacked her granddaughter:] 'Who are you to order a cognac? Can you pay for that?' It just turned into this whole thing where finally Sara asked if they'd take it back."[31] In an effort to explain her aunt's behavior, Allison added, "Your ego becomes so large and Stella was also very intelligent, and I think she was allowed to act out in the family. She'd make a scene and it would be so strong you wouldn't necessarily go back at her because it was a little bit too much."[32]

Time and again financial insecurity manifested as depression, as Stella confessed to her granddaughter:

Sara, my dearest and sweetest and smartest girl, I'm suffering from depression, while Life and work are looking after me. I'm able to work but the responsibilities apparently are too threatening to my health and so I know you'll understand—Sweetheart—that you must try for the first time but really try your best [to reduce the] enormous amount of money I am sending to you. . . . Should there be an ungodly, bad streak of fate and if I should become ill, it would not necessarily take away from your schooling income for about three years, but the other expense . . . is becoming a threat to my health. The expense of supporting your mother and you has suddenly revealed itself. It's the main source [of] threat to my health.[33]

Every clan needs a leader, and in an effort to uphold the Adler name, Stella appointed herself to that role, even as she often resented the financial responsibility. Between her brash, mercurial nature and her bottomless, giving heart she could just as well easily humiliate her granddaughter over a glass of cognac as she could champion and finance the girl's choice of career. Meanwhile, Stella's fear of an "ungodly bad streak of fate" would never materialize. When her time came, she would prepare herself methodically as if it were another role she were to play.

CHAPTER TWENTY-SIX

*I watched Stella be vulnerable without being intimate. I
watched her open her soul and yet keep herself to herself.*

—Janis Ian

ESPITE STELLA'S SINGLE-MINDED FOCUS ON ART, HER SCHOOL WAS
in fact a business, which relied on a certain amount of income in
order to pay her, the faculty, and the overhead. Ellen's husband,
David Oppenheim, the dean of New York University's Tisch School of the
Arts, began sending his students to Stella's school in the early 1970s. The
alliance was as profitable in terms of lending prestige to NYU as it was
for the Stella Adler Conservatory, as it was renamed. Yet by the middle of
the decade the school was in financial straits aggravated by the closing of
City Center, which left not only the Conservatory homeless, but also the
National Orchestra Society and the Joffrey Ballet.

Rue Drew, whose husband, Robert Drew, a former *Life* magazine editor,
was now making documentaries, had the idea of doing an article for *Life*
on Stella. "She would not let anyone take her picture," Rue recalled, "and
she had all these pictures up in her office looking like the movie stars of
the 1920s. And I thought, God if I could get her teaching!"[1] But Rue knew
Stella viewed publicity as vulgar. Stella didn't want anyone depicting who
she was.

Rue decided to take matters into her own hands. One day she set up
a tripod in the back of the classroom while Stella was teaching. At any
moment she expected Stella to stop and berate her for interrupting her
work. Rue fastened her camera atop the tripod, set up the shot, and, with
the trepidation of a child reaching into the cookie jar, snapped the shutter.
She waited. Stella continued teaching as if nothing had happened. "And

that's how I have all these wonderful pictures of her. I think they're the only ones that are spontaneous."[2]

The black-and-white stills are the only professional candids of Stella teaching. *Life* was prepared to do a spread on Stella when a debate arose regarding whether Marlon Brando had studied with Stella or at the Actors Studio—such was the stock attributed to Strasberg as king of the "method." *Life* pulled the story, but Rue wasn't ready to give up. She pitched the article to the *New York Times* and contacted Brando. "I kept calling and finally he talked to me and I said, 'I want you to come out and say who taught you acting because no one knows it and I'm doing a story in the *New York Times* and I want to use it in there and can I use it?' . . . So, he finally came out with it."[3]

Rue waited anxiously for the next Thursday, when she would have confirmation from the *Times* that the story would run. It did. That Sunday she called Stella, who was staying in the Hamptons for the weekend. "She just blew up at me," Drew recalled: "'How dare you! How dare you! You can't even write. Who are you? You're nothing!'"[4] But when the calls started coming in to congratulate Stella for the story, as reported by the housekeeper, Mary, Stella's tone changed: "Oh did you like that? I didn't even know they were going to do this." Call after call came in. "You shoulda seen her," Mary said. "She would hang up the phone and she would say 'How dare she?' and then the phone would ring again and she would play coy."[5]

Mary Adler, still running the Conservatory, called Rue after the article came out: "My God, Rue, what have you done? They're six across and all the way to the corner waiting to sign up [for class]." Six months later Rue received a call from Stella: "Rue, darling, my public relations man said I should double your salary for what you did. Come back, darling. Come back."[6]

THROUGHOUT THE 1970S, WHEN STELLA WENT TO HOLLYWOOD TO TEACH her summer classes, Jay Adler would show up and hang around the studio. Sometimes he would sit in on a class. Jayne Meadows recalled that Stella referred to Jay as "the heart of the family."[7] Stella saw in her older brother a vulnerability that made him more sensitive than her other siblings. Jay's career had consisted mostly of a steady string of roles in 1950s television series such as *The Twilight Zone* and *The Untouchables* in which he was typecast as a thug. His niece Allison Adler remembered her Uncle Jay as "the real kind of nut in the family. He stayed with us when I was a kid with my mother and I. If I could tell you how many young girls he brought into the house that my mother had to sneak out the back door you wouldn't believe it. 'I'm a big producer, I'm so and so, I'm from the Adler family,' and this twenty-year-old girl would come in with this sixty-, seventy-year-old man and my mother would take one look at the girl, wait until he would go into the bathroom, and tell her to get out. 'He's old, he's nuts.'"[8] As he grew older, Jay spent more and more time on the West Coast; he ended up moving there for the easier California lifestyle.

By the time Jay hit his mid-seventies, his health was steadily declining. It wasn't as easy to turn a trick, charm a young girl. In September of 1978 he died. "Mary called me," Irene Gilbert remembered, "and said we have nobody out there who can make these arrangements. Will you do it for Stella? And I said of course I would. So I went and got him a coffin and made the arrangements to have him sent back to New York because Stella wanted him buried with the family."[9]

Lulla, the family historian, described Jay's place in the family as she read his eulogy:

> He was a hedonist, a man who lived frankly for life's pleasures. He had his masks, but we who were close to him were never really deceived by them. We remember too well the boy who went his own way, asking so little of us—hiding whatever life had given him of loneliness and hurt. . . . Jay had no great pretensions to any very lofty virtue. Truth to tell, he had no interest in anything so dull as that. Like Nunia Adler—like Allen and Abe Adler—he belongs with the rebels of our family. The world does not always approve of such people—but oh, how badly they are missed when they go![10]

Stella's grandniece commented on the "pack" mentality of the Adlers, perceiving the family as a band of gypsies: "You always really felt as if you were in a sordid family of gypsies because you could feel this Russian peasant thing underneath all the kind of grandeur . . . this band of people that hung around together and had odd people around them, some intellectuals, some artists, some very big celebrity-types, but mostly there was a very gypsy quality to everyone. If you go out to the cemetery where everyone's buried, there's this weird feeling of this clannish pack of people with the eagle looking over."[11]

It seemed death lived on Stella's doorstep. True, everyone was getting older, including Stella. Ever since Jacob's death, Stella's aversion to loss had been sealed. Since Wilson's death she had been given a reprieve, but time's inevitable thrust was putting an end to that. On September 9, 1980, the United States' most influential theatrical luminary and Stella's greatest admirer, Harold Clurman, died of cancer.

Only a few years earlier, in the late 1970s, the director and acting teacher Jack Garfein had invited Clurman to his school in Los Angeles to lecture on acting. Before the event Stella made a point of telephoning Garfein to ask him to reserve a seat in the third row center. Although there was no prearranged seating, Garfein obliged her.

Movie stars and directors crammed into the one-hundred-seat theater awaiting the man who was famous for his high-volume, evangelical lectures that ignited the actor's soul. "Suddenly Harold comes out," Garfein recalled. "It's a Harold none of us ever knew: quiet, whispering. Sometimes you couldn't even hear him, walking back and forth. And there was a break and Dustin Hoffman came up to me and said, 'Hey, Jack this is a disaster; you better do something about it. Listen, that's what you're there for, whether it's Olivier or Harold Clurman you guys are supposed to give us comfort, so you better do something.' So I go backstage and Harold is walking around with his head down, and I say, 'Harold, what's the matter? What happened?'"[12]

Clurman managed to stop pacing for a moment, focused on Garfein, and said, "Listen, I know exactly what's she thinking: 'Okay, Harold, you know about directing, you know about playwriting, you know about dramatic criticism, but what the hell do you know about acting?'" Garfein intuited that "she" referred to Stella. Like a good director, he told Harold to "use it," use the energy he was experiencing in the form of resentment. "And he sort of nodded and said, 'Okay, okay, okay.' . . . And now he came out for the second half, walked right up to the third row, where she was sitting, looked at her and said, 'Some people think I know nothing about acting. Okay. So, I don't know, but I'm going to talk about it anyway!'"[13]

The codependent dynamic between Stella and Harold well after their divorce encapsulates their relationship. More than ever Stella symbolized for Harold all that he admired about life, with its intrinsic theatrical currents, while Stella simultaneously belittled Harold and held him in great esteem as a man of the theater. The foundation of their relationship, beyond the mutual respect of theatrical abstractions, remained tied to their loyalty to one another as a man and woman who had shared their prime years, with all of their faults, fears, and triumphs. Harold remained until his death hopelessly devoted to Stella.

In early May of 1979 the *New York Times* had commemorated Clurman's fifty-five-year career in the theater. In the article Stella's description of Harold borders on self-portrait: "He relates very emotionally to art, but in life, he cools it, so that he won't be hurt. Maybe he overprotected himself. He walks on the esplanade alone. The sea doesn't threaten him at all. If he allowed himself vulnerability, he might have been destroyed."[14] Stella describes her life with Harold as "a struggle to free myself from the oppressive, dominant, biblical quality that he had. He was completely unsuited to sharing a relationship with another person. He was very willing to accept married life. He was very much the father of my daughter . . . and when my mother moved in with us, he accepted her as the head of the table. But he was not interested in painting or in furnishing a home, in plants or fish or birds."[15] Stella's enumerations bring to mind Jacob and his passion for a beautiful home, to the extent of the details of how Jacob would populate the home with pets and plants. Harold's total acceptance of Stella's daughter and mother are, in Stella's mind, overshadowed by his lack of interest in "furnishing a home." Stella's priorities seem to be forever dictated by her father; Harold remains destined to "compete with a dead man."

"Harold submitted to the luxurious life without altering anything in himself," Stella continued in the interview. "His own life was Spartan. He hung around with men of the theater, which I found adolescent." Stella's own tendency to surround herself with theater people was presumably a professional endeavor. It isn't difficult to sense the Adlerian possessiveness in her accusation of Harold's being "adolescent." His theatrical relationships took attention away from Stella. In the same breath, Stella pays homage to him professionally: "He became a very, very profound director with the mind, the vision and the size to make a mature contribution. . . . Harold's mind dominates his total body. He is all mind, which accelerates into passion. There's nobody like him around!"[16]

Between 1945 and 1980 Clurman directed over forty plays, wrote seven books, and became the country's most respected drama critic. He had done more than live life; he had enjoyed it. "One mustn't be afraid of death," Clurman said in the same *New York Times* commemoration, sixteen months before he died. "That doesn't mean you should seek death or pain. Certain things that are painful must be gone through. If you can't accept that, you will never be mature."[17] Though they no longer shared a life together, Stella and Harold maintained the same parlance for their standards. They emphasized maturity as being the pinnacle of a human being's pursuit: to humble oneself before nature's course. Growing old, dealing with the loss of loved ones, realizing past mistakes—these were all challenges one was expected to face like a grown-up.

Clurman had touched so many lives that there was no lack of friends and supporters around when it was his time to go. Jack Garfein kept a constant vigil at his hospital bedside. He recalled an altercation with Clurman's second wife, Juleen Compton, because Clurman had "left everything" to Stella. "I was in the hospital every day with Harold," Garfein told this author in an interview:

> And one day Juleen Compton showed up with a paper. And Harold was already with all the things in his nose and arteries. And she came and wanted Harold to sign over some parts of his will to her. And I said, "What are you going to do, go in and ask him to sign over right now?" And she said to me, "I'm not sentimental about death." She said she had given him some money, not that he owed her the money, but something that he did with that money that had a return . . . whereas Stella never dealt with any aspect like that, his money or will. . . . Stella seemed very stoic when she arrived. She didn't say anything. It was like she wanted you to sense things through her eyes and through her being, but she didn't say anything.[18]

During the last decade of his life Harold admired a young woman, Joan Ungaro, whom he would escort to parties and theater events. According to Ungaro, who was some fifty years his junior, the relationship remained platonic. She remembered sitting in the waiting room at the hospital during Harold's final days. Stella was also visiting. Though she was struggling with the impending loss of a loved one, Stella's sense of justice prompted her to speak to Ungaro: "Joan, I understand that woman has been dreadful to everyone and especially to you and I won't hear of it. I'll let you know that I plan to write her a letter and inform her that Harold loves you and she must treat you better."[19] Stella was referring to Juleen, who after supposedly divorcing Clurman had never filed the papers and consequently inherited certain rights to his writings. Ungaro "found that extraordinary that Stella would call me over to her and say, look, in effect I want to defend you of this horror. . . . I think that says a lot about Stella."[20] Although Ungaro let Stella know she didn't think it was worth her time to write a letter, she felt honored to be considered so important to Stella.

"I assume every day that I'm going to die," Clurman said at the end of the 1979 *Times* feature. "The greatest achievement is being here this very minute. I want to live a thousand years—out of curiosity. If I found out that the world was going to end, do you know what I would do? I would take a girl to dinner."[21] In the hospital, with little strength left to speak, Harold looked up at Stella's face. His last words were: "Isn't she beautiful?"[22]

Stella arranged for Harold to be buried in the Adler plot at Mount Carmel.

The brilliant colors of fall dramatized the all-too-familiar trek to the burial ground. The loss of Mitchell, Jay, and now Harold converged upon Stella's heart with intolerable weight. When she arrived at the cemetery there was nothing left to do but run to her father's grave, to the larger-than-life sculpture of an eagle, and wrap her arms around the cold stone. "I don't think she did that deliberately," Jack Garfein recollected. "That's her. That was her life. And I think when she saw her father's tombstone, to her, I guess she wanted everybody in a sense to know that that was going on within her."[23]

With Harold's passing, the man who had filled in for the absence of Jacob—however inadequately, from Stella's point of view—was now gone as well. Clurman's very life evoked an era that for most people had ended before the Depression. His death rekindled Stella's grief for her father as well as for the passing of a time when a man could love, with his entire being, both the theater and the actress. Stella's demeanor, her dress, speech, and worldview, carried the lost era through to the present, but it was becoming more difficult to pull off.

Times were rapidly changing. The new decade drifted toward the casual, even unseemly dress and deportment of MTV consumer culture. The mentality of the modern actor forfeited history and tradition for television and stardom. Stella had gotten a taste of the apathy at Yale in the late 1960s: slouching students who chewed gum and thought they knew as much about the theater as she did. It was truly deplorable. Americans were devolving. Stella told her class, "Mitchell Wilson wrote in the *New York Times* that ten years have been added to man in the last decade, that men live longer. But in America, it was added to the childhood, not to the maturity."[24]

CHAPTER TWENTY-SEVEN

In Stella's eyes, service to the great ideas of a play or film was the actor's greatest responsibility.

—Mark Ruffalo

At the entrance to Stella's New York school students were forewarned with a sign that read: "Stella would like all the actors to know that CRITICISM in the Conservatory is not Personal. Nothing in the Theater is Personal. THEATER IS FOR THE WORLD." Similarly, Stella maintained that her debate with Strasberg was not personal, yet nothing could be more personal to Stella than following through on her self-appointed quest to "correct" the craft of acting.

Half a century after the demise of the Group Theatre, Stella and Strasberg were still debating the supremacy of their acting techniques. In 1979 the *New York Times* featured an expose highlighting their rivalry:

"Lee Strasberg?" Stella Adler says. "I think what he does is sick. Too many of his students have come to me ready for an institution."

"Stella Adler?" Lee Strasberg says. "What about her? There's no comparison between the people who have come out of my school and the people who have come out of her school."[1]

When Strasberg's biographer Cindy Adams asked Stella about Strasberg, her response was that "Lee's teaching was a jolt into the world that opened up a great many of our talents, therefore one of the most important theatrical experiences of our lives in spite of the misery. But he was not a pleasant man. It's insanity that this personally ugly little man should become the leader of the American theater."[2] Asked about Stella, Strasberg told his biographer: "I don't like to call names. I haven't wanted to call attention to reviews she got after she left me. She once was a leading lady and she thought, well, sure, on her own she could go places. So, where did Miss Adler go? Is she still working as an actress?"[3] Neither acting coach limited their insults to the work; they attacked specific individual qualities. The "ugly little man" and the actress who didn't "go places" would take their acrimony to the grave. Even after Strasberg's death in 1982, Stella continued to feel an obligation to "correct the harm" she felt he had done to the art of acting.

While Strasberg was acknowledged as a genius at publicity, Stella neglected to spend time or money advocating for herself; but when the opportunity arose, she spoke her mind. As she aged she drew more and more attention as one of American theater's icons. Once she attended an event held at B. Altman's sportswear department for the Theater Collection at the Museum of the City of New York. On exhibit were photographs of theatrical luminaries. Stella appeared superbly coiffed, sporting purple leather gloves and large sunglasses. Upon entering she began searching for her photograph among those displayed on the wall. Finally, she found her portrait in one of the sale bins. She immediately seized the photographer and exclaimed, "You don't know my value."[4]

It was one thing to be captured by the press or paparazzi at a social venue and quite another to purposefully seek publicity. Stella disdained Strasberg's self-advertisement:

Strasberg is a very well advertised product, like cigarettes. This doesn't mean it isn't dangerous. . . . As for his reputation; it's rather an American thing—a public relations thing. It's not about how big you are but how big you want to be. It's about stardom. It's against my ethic to talk about stardom, because I think that when you are a teacher you don't emphasize the people who have hit it big in Hollywood. You emphasize the people who haven't hit it big in Hollywood, and who often are the better actors—the more important actors. As for making one's name as a teacher, I suppose I could have had a much bigger name than Strasberg if, for example, I were to have announced that I'm only interested in the sexual aspect of acting. Had I done that, I could have had anything I wanted.[5]

Strasberg's son John wrote: "The competitive jealousy between my father and Stella spawned the notion that there exists an ultimate technique for becoming an artist. . . . It has made teachers lay claim to being responsible for creating artist[s]."[6] Unquestionably, each school takes credit for the students of note who attended, displaying their names and pictures on the walls, in the literature, and so on, but while Strasberg took responsibility for Stella's acting being at its best under his direction, Stella never acknowledged herself as responsible for an individual actor's work.

THOUGH THERE WAS STILL WORK TO BE DONE IN THE THEATER, AT EIGHTY years old Stella finally seemed to settle into a place where she felt she belonged: "I can honestly say that I'm the only person I know who lives through love," she said in an interview. "People throw their love at me. These days, I can't go anywhere without being showered with affection and embraces. I'm almost tempted to say that I get too much out of life. I suppose that if you give people what they need, their minds and hearts open up. So my life is full of joy—full of a kind of ecstasy that continually nourishes me."[7] In a time as unlikely as the 1980s, under a conservative president and a culturally anemic nation, Stella had created for herself a lifestyle comparable to that of her parents. Jacob and Sara Adler had opened the hearts and minds of the Lower East Siders and in turn were treated as royalty. Stella was known and respected around the world, befriended by heads of state, artists, and intellectuals, and deferred to by a court of players who loved and admired her and followed her every whim. Stella managed to create a kingdom that, if it could not compare, at least could compete with the one in which she was a princess so long ago.

In the early winter of 1980 Stella received a phone call notifying her that she would be receiving the Jabotinsky Centennial Citation. "I don't like gossipy things in the papers," Stella later remarked, "like Miss Adler was seen here and there, but this is important."[8] Forty years after running guns and smuggling documents for the Irgun Zvai Leumi, the Israeli prime minister, Menachem Begin, wanted to recognize her work. The award marked the hundredth anniversary of the birth of Ze'ev Vladimir Jabotinsky. Stella booked a room at the Waldorf-Astoria. Betsy Parrish remembered arriving at Stella's hotel room, where her current clique of chosen students had gathered. Stella ordered up a continental spread of coffee and cakes. "She was very full of respect." Parrish reflected. "She was always aware if there was a historical moment. Lulla wrote *Bright Star of Exile*; Stella gave a party at the studio for Lulla to mark it. When Tennessee Williams died, nobody paid attention, everybody laughed because he choked on a bottle top or something. Stella gave an evening at the studio to say something about this happening."[9] When an event called for ceremony, Stella fulfilled the protocol.

After seeing Ingrid Berman in the television film *A Woman Called Golda* on the life of the Israeli prime minister Golda Meir, Stella felt compelled to write to Bergman to tell her that in Paris she had once seen her crossing the Avenue Georges V and how she had been stopped dead in her tracks by simply watching Bergman traverse the street. Stella wrote that again she was stopped after seeing *A Woman Called Golda*. She felt as if Golda had to tear off "mercilessly layer after layer her raw flesh, trying to reach further through this raw flesh an essence," which is what Stella thought was required in order for Golda to serve the people of Israel. Stella conveyed how such a performance could change a person's life. Ending the letter, she applauded Bergman for adding another piece of art to the world, writing that she was a member of the Irgun, "a militant, political movement for the creation of Israel, and very militant it was."[10]

Stella's letter to Bergman is dated three months before the latter's death at sixty-seven. In it Stella exposes a deep humility with respect not to Bergman as a world-renowned actress, but to her art. Stella's inspiration came from the universal truths of the human condition. She identified with Golda Meir as a servant of a cause not only through her own service to Israel, but also through her service to the craft of acting. She understood that it was through sharing ideas, passions, and craft that people make a difference in the world. Though Stella was undeniably a woman who demanded to be served, to be revered and admired, she was not above humbling herself before others—Jacob, Sara, Maurice Schwartz, Max Reinhardt, Stanislavski, Jabotinsky, Ingrid Bergman—all emblems of this universal truth which Stella personified throughout her life, altering rooms and people with her own "raw essence."

Stella attributed her robust health to this essence, this life force inherent in her craft: "The instinct to act is a healthy instinct because nobody can fulfill himself on a realistic level of life. Everybody has many sides that are unfulfilled—the killer, the opposite of the killer, the lover, the citizen, the wanting to be beautiful, the wanting to be Quasimodo-ugly. . . . Acting is a very healthy profession. . . . Jesus Christ, I've never had a headache."[11]

Still, the inevitable limitations of age began to appear. While in Los Angeles at yet another party thrown in Stella's honor, Stella slipped on a rug and broke her hip, resulting in a convalescence that changed her life. For a woman used to coming and going as she pleased, suddenly being dependent upon others was startling. When she returned to New York her assistant put in a ramp that led up to the stage, where there was a curtain. Betsy Parrish remembered, "When the curtains opened she was there. Nobody knew she couldn't walk."[12]

Stella always had helpers around, no less so when she was recuperating. She did not like to discuss the injury. Like her age, it was a taboo topic. One anecdote clarifies the source of Stella's vanity. Arthur Miller recalled being at Stella's fiftieth birthday party, where her mother was also in attendance. He overheard someone ask Sara her age, to which Madame Adler replied that she was sixty-two. When questioned about the age discrepancy, that Stella was just turning fifty, Sara responded, "That's her problem."[13]

Within a few months Stella was up walking and carrying on with the performance of life, but the injury never entirely healed. As she had feared so long ago, Stella was "losing her legs," the vehicle she needed to walk in character, imitate, perform. There was always someone by her side to grasp her hand and steady her. She did not like this. Often she would swat the helping hand away, feeling the claustrophobic panic of someone who has known physical incapacity and dare not return.

Confronting the impediments of age was doubly challenging for a person often referred to as a "force of nature," "larger than life," and beautiful to boot. Stella had maintained a royal stateliness, fallible but immortalized, outliving the other immortals of her time. The theatrical world was seeing the vulnerability of its queen, like a young adult realizing for the first time that a parent is less than perfect, no longer invincible.

The injury also seemed to trigger Stella's own fears that she would pass without having put things in their proper order. At eighty-one Stella began preparing for her death. She outlined exactly what she wanted, beginning with logistics:

1. I wish to be buried next to Mitchell in the East Hampton cemetery, which belongs to me. It has space for six people.
2. To have services in New York where Mitchell had his.
3. To decide whether the funeral services should be private or public.
4. If public, to have some pictures for the students.

She followed these wishes with fourteen instructions for the funeral itself, directing her burial as she would a performance.

1. I want the family to be in a separate room without visitors.
2. People to be asked to be seated upon arrival.

3. When services start, the family should come in after all are seated.
4. If Lulla will speak, ask her to be dressed in black and she will know what to say.
5. Music to be selected by the family.
6. A short speech in Hebrew at the end.
7. A limousine for the casket should be ready and should be outside.
8. The family will follow the casket from the funeral parlor into their cars.
9. When this is done the people should be allowed to rise and go out after the family and casket.
10. No meeting in the street before cars depart.
11. Flowers allowed?
12. Don't want anyone from Equity or any trade union to speak.
13. I want Sara to wear black.
14. If a poem is used use a translation for a Jewish poet.[14]

Tradition, above all else, was crucial, and tradition held that the Adler family would adhere to the proper and customary practices. Lulla, who traditionally wrote the family eulogies, would speak, not some representative from the acting profession. There would be no congregation of mourners to break the solemnity of conveying Stella from the funeral parlor to the cemetery, no dramatic scenes to deter from her ceremony, no empathizing I-can't-believe-she's-gone well-wishers.

Stella's dress rehearsal was premature. She still had a generation of actors to instruct. She went back to work.

Irene Gilbert and Stella had been informally operating a summer school in Los Angeles for two decades. It was time to build a studio on the West Coast. "When we were first opening the school we played this game," Gilbert recalled, "I'd say to Stella, 'I think you should have a school in Los Angeles.' And she'd say, 'No, I think you should have a school in Los Angeles.' And I said, 'Stella, I'm doing this for you.' And she said, 'No, darling, I'm doing this for you.' I wanted her to have something out here, not just in New York and she insisted that it was for me, that she wanted me to have something for the future. . . . I really think she wanted me to carry it on and she wanted to give something to me that I could go on with.[15] At first named the Stella Adler Conservatory West, after the Conservatory in New York, the school was officially opened in 1986, later becoming the Stella Adler Academy of Acting.

Whether in Los Angeles or New York, the students responded the same when Stella entered the room: applause. It hadn't always been that way. Robert Ellenstein, who studied with Stella at the New School in the 1940s, audited a class in Los Angeles in the 1980s. "She became a star. She had a chair onstage. She never did that when I studied with her. It became a lot about Stella."[16] The change, one imagines, came when Stella had decided her role was as a teacher. She was no less important than the actors she was coaching, and thus they all shared the platform together.

One thing that didn't change was Stella's rancor toward Strasberg. In 1982 the *Sunday Los Angeles Times Calendar* ran an article on Stella's class in West Hollywood. "If I was to play Marie Antoinette, and I was on the way to the gallows, I need only to look into the crowd, I might imagine seeing my scullery maid kneeling and crying. That would do it. I don't have to see my uncle in Brooklyn. Mr. Strasberg would want me to dredge up my uncle in Brooklyn. This was the big fight between myself and Mr. Strasberg. He knew it. I knew it. I guess you even knew it. It was a fight to the blood."[17] Strasberg had died six months earlier, but that didn't change Stella's mission, which she summed up when she told her class, "A great disservice was done to American actors when they were persuaded that they had to experience themselves on the stage instead of experiencing the play."[18]

One way to clarify Stella's theories of acting was to begin writing her own book on the subject, something Stella had had in the back of her mind for years but feared to proceed with lest she fail. Once she resigned herself to the endeavor, the project proved to be fraught with more complications and challenges than she could have imagined. She began working with an editor named Henry Rossen but switched over in mid-project to another editor named Stuart Little to lend an apparently missing "personal touch" to the tone of the book.[19] By the time Little came on board, Bantam Books had offered Stella a $40,000 advance. The materials to be drawn upon included dozens of binders of teaching notes that Stella had spent a lifetime assembling. There were lessons from week 1 to week 12 of Technique I and Technique II; exercises for Scene Study; Script Interpretation analyses of plays from Shakespeare to Shaw; and innumerable video and audio recordings of Stella's master classes. It would have been difficult enough to cull the trove if it had been organized. It was not. Stella wrote to Irene Gilbert regarding the sorry state of her teaching materials, which she had left in the hands of others, never one to be bothered with secretarial duties herself, complaining that the majority of the work was misplaced, while half of it had been stolen. Stella's sense of entitlement emphasized her utter lack of personal accountability. She stated how she would never submit the work in its present condition. "It took years of developing lack of respect, lack of order, no self-discipline on the part of my colleagues, to get to this chaos."[20]

Stella's fickleness created a recipe for disaster. As Eleanor Sheldon, her financial adviser, knew, one day you could be trusted to handle her affairs and the next you could be banished. The following fall Little submitted his version of the edited book, which Stella promptly rejected. At this juncture yet another editor, Mel Gordon, was called in to take over the project. Gordon inherited a project that had been through two previous editors and at least three others who had been editing alongside Stella. Stella rejected his draft of her book as well. Gordon agreed to rework his edits, now with Gilbert simultaneously working on the sidelines correcting and revising the manuscript. In the late summer of 1986 Gordon sent another completed version of the manuscript to Stella in California. There was a celebration for the book's completion in February, at which point Stella finally read Gordon's latest version. Again she found it inadequate. Despite two rejections, Gordon persevered with the project, advising Stella to work with a secretary daily to write new text in the necessary places. The plan was to have Gordon edit the newest manuscript and prepare it for Bantam.

Either Stella withdrew the project from Gordon or he withdrew from her. She wrote to her lawyer, Jerry Lurie, who oversaw all of her legal affairs, including those with Bantam. She explained the state of affairs with the book, blaming Mel Gordon for "convincing" Lurie that there were only one or two chapters left to edit, which she admonished as a deliberate lie on the part of Gordon. Stella informed her lawyer that Irene Gilbert would be coming to accompany her to see the editor at Bantam, but ultimately the book was "in trouble," and "I don't know who is most at fault in putting it together."[21]

In its final, published form, the book offers step-by-step instructions. It outlines the major tenets of her technique, which the book claims "is based not only on Stanislavski's ideas, but also on a natural system available to anyone."[22] Like any artistic pursuit, acting requires experience. You cannot learn it from a book. Perhaps that is what made Stella reluctant to write *The Technique of Acting*. It is full of philosophical gems about humanity and society, but the nuts and bolts of Stella's acting technique, the exercises themselves, translate prosaically to paper.

"It's just too thin a book," she lamented to Gilbert. "I should have done more and then everyone would've taken it seriously."[23] Irene reassured her that the book was taken seriously, explaining, "Your other fella, whose name we don't mention, wrote a book that nobody understands at all. Uta Hagen wrote a book that a lot of people read, but I never got through it. . . . Yours they don't get lost in because it's specific and it's doable."[24] Gilbert could always be counted on to assuage Stella's insecurities.

In his foreword to the book, Marlon Brando alludes to the "fella whose name we don't mention": "It is troubling to me that because she has not lent herself to vulgar exploitations, as some other well-known so-called 'methods' of acting have done, her contributions to the theatrical culture have remained largely unknown, unrecognized, and unappreciated."[25] It seems Stella and Strasberg had, in fact, something in common, as his son John Strasberg reveals: "My father only spoke of Stella to the extent that, 'There are some teachers who I won't mention.'"[26]

Brando was not the only one to acknowledge Stella's contributions. In 1985 the first of four honorary degrees was given to Stella in recognition of her work. The New School of Social Research honored Stella with the degree of Doctor of Humane Letters. In 1987 Stella received an honorary Doctorate of Fine Arts from Smith College. That same year Stella was visiting a friend one afternoon when her hip gave out. It had been five years since her last injury, but she was now eighty-six. Whereas she had begun walking a few months after the first accident, Stella never fully recovered from the second injury. She would need to rely on wheelchairs, canes, and strong grips from people who always seemed to be scuttling behind her like a mother after a toddler. Stella began a rigorous course of physical therapy four times a week from July through September before returning to New York to begin the school year, where she taught a Character class twice a week and Script Analysis once a week.

The following year, in the spring of 1988, the Museum of Jewish History in Philadelphia opened an exhibition in honor of Jacob Adler's life and work. Stella was thrilled. Stella had always said her father was a legendary theatrical man, but now an esteemed institution confirmed it. She attended the event in a wheelchair because of her injury, but she was as magnetic as ever. As spokeswoman Stella set the tone of the day with a quintessential Adlerian anecdote with the proper amount of family lore and storytelling humor: "A great actor once told me, 'I will always remember the first time I was applauded.' I heard that and I thought about it. It didn't occur to me that I would remember; but I do remember . . . I was quite little and in the opulent drawing room of my family, there were some guests. I was brought in by a nurse and I was introduced. They said, 'This is the youngest daughter of Jacob and Sara Adler and her name is Stella and she never wets the bed.' Talent grows early."[27]

No sooner had these honors sunk in than Stella was on her way to Paris to attend a conference for the fiftieth anniversary of Stanislavski's death. The *New York Times* caught her before her flight to ask if she was planning on slowing down any time soon. Stella answered, "I have obligations. One of them is paying the rent. So, I think that would postpone any idea of retiring."[28] Always preoccupied with money, Stella would not consider retiring. As for the conference, Stanislavski's system had taken on different incarnations and hybrid interpretations; the best Stella could hope to achieve in Paris was to teach her own technique based on her understanding of Stanislavski's intentions.

CHAPTER TWENTY-EIGHT

Virtually all acting in motion pictures today stems from her,
and she had an extraordinary effect on the culture of her time.

—Marlon Brando

Stella, Stella for Star!

—Tennessee Williams, *A Streetcar Named Desire*

OR STELLA, 1989 BEGAN IN LOS ANGELES WITH MORE PHYSICAL therapy. Despite the pain and incapacity caused by her injury, Stella continued her work. Irene Gilbert, who had for years now stretched her services beyond colleague to caretaker, made sure Stella kept her doctors' visits and took her medication. After the injury Irene began interviewing professional live-in caretakers. It wasn't an easy task finding someone to deal with the tempestuous moods of a physically frustrated actress, but the minute Samuella Harris walked into Gilbert's office she had a hunch Harris was up for the job.

At six feet tall, Harris was a stalwart, soulful woman who would quickly learn how to deal with Stella's temperament. Harris had cared for several elderly clients at the end of life, and she had experienced the specific emotions they faced in the process of dying. The deciding moment in the interview came when Gilbert asked Harris, "Do you know who Stella Adler is?" Harris, as far away from the theater as Stella was from nursing, shook her head. Harris was hired to help Stella "recuperate from her hip," as she recalled, but she stayed till the end.[1]

Stella returned to New York in late February. She began teaching four times a week: a Script and Character class at her studio and a Scene class at NYU. It was an exhausting spring, and time, though she was loath to admit it, to slow down. Gilbert and everyone else in California had been asking Stella to stay there ever since she began venturing to the West Coast in the 1960s. Compared to the flurry of New York, life was simply easier in Los

Angeles. Stella began spending more and more of the year in California until by 1990 she was living there permanently.

During this time Gilbert began recording her conversations with Stella at night when Stella's mind quieted down and she wanted to reminisce about her family and the Yiddish theater. Together they would look at pictures or read passages about the family or Stella's own career. A stream-of-conscious narrative wove in and out of the present and past wherein Stella would sometimes confess personal and oftentimes contradictory feelings. She grappled with the idea of continuing to teach. One minute she would say she was through, and the next she would want to be left alone to prepare for class.

One recording reveals the dynamic between the two old friends. Gilbert's agenda is to keep Stella active, while Stella, undecided, laments having lost reign over her classes because of her depleted energy and health. "I don't want to see scenes that I don't direct," Stella says in a quiet, gravelly voice.

GILBERT: How are you going to direct then?

STELLA: I can't.

GILBERT: So you're saying you don't want to do a class?

STELLA: No.

GILBERT: Okay, because I'm going to have to tell all the people that are calling.

[*Long pause*]

STELLA: You don't know the actors?

GILBERT: Well, like always we'd have to audition them. And see if anything excites you; otherwise forget it.

STELLA: No, no, no.

GILBERT: What are you going to do with yourself?

STELLA: What do you care?

GILBERT: I care.

STELLA: I have a lot to do.

GILBERT: But will you get up and do it?

STELLA: No.

GILBERT: "I have a lot to do. But will you get up and do it? No." So you don't have anything to do.

STELLA: *You* don't have anything to do. I've got a million plays to do.

GILBERT: Okay, what are you going to do with them?

STELLA: Analyze them, work on them, and understand them. [*Pause*] I'd like to have money, but it doesn't work that way. I have to have complete control of anything that's public.

GILBERT: What kind of control do you want? Would you like to direct a few good actors in something? Would you like to work with a few good actors even if you did it right here in the living room?

STELLA: I've done my job.

GILBERT: Yes, you have.

STELLA: Finished.[2]

In class, Stella would have to be wheeled next to a desk offstage where she would watch the students perform scenes. Stella would be informed beforehand which scenes were being presented. Gilbert had Stella's notes typed, which Stella would refer to before introducing a scene. This caused endless frustration, as she would forget where she left off reading on the page after she began extemporaneously lecturing. Gilbert would sit next to Stella to guide her through the notes, which she would then take away as Stella reviewed them in an effort to keep Stella on track. Sometimes Stella would confuse the characters in the play. Often she would swat at Irene's invading hands as they adjusted Stella's microphone, turned a page of the lectures, or moved her glass of soda. She wanted Irene sitting next to her, but she hated being distracted.

However difficult it was to remember names of characters or follow lecture notes, Stella didn't lose her ability to assess the quality of a student's acting. She watched the scene work like a scholar reading a book, her long, slender fingers tapping the desk as she concentrated on the actors. She was still in demand. Students continued registering for her class, leaving Gilbert in the position of needing to know whether Stella intended to go on teaching. She had an ulterior motive: she was afraid that without her work Stella would languish.

Stella had her own agenda: if she stopped teaching, she would stop making money. Economic insecurity continued to plague her, although, by all accounts, she had nothing to worry about. Her assets included the

Fifth Avenue apartment, valued at $1,000,000; the house in the country, at $500,000; and stocks with an estimated value of over $100,000. Her monthly income from the New York school, Social Security, annuities, and dividends came to $10,000.[3] Gilbert, on the other hand, was struggling to keep the West Coast school afloat. Eleanor Sheldon received a letter from Gilbert in 1991: "At the moment I am trying desperately to keep the Conservatory and myself going short of bankruptcy. Unfortunately we do not have what the New York Conservatory has which is support from NYU. First, so you understand where I am, I have had to put $38,000 on my personal credit cards; I have not been paid anything for the past seven months; and I have had to re-finance my house to pay my bills as well as some of the Conservatory's bills."[4] (Fifteen years later Gilbert continued to support the school on her personal credit cards to the tune of more than $300,000 until 2006, when, for health reasons, she had to relinquish ownership of the school.)

In 1990 Stella made the decision to stop teaching. She began to spend much of her time in bed surrounded by books, plays, and lists of things she wanted to study, from Socrates to existentialism. She continued dictating letters to her admirers and loved ones; more often than not her missives were post-holiday, post-birthday, post-party thank-you notes. People sent flowers, perfume, candies, and accessories year round. And even if there were no occasion, she would dictate a letter because it was necessary:

Dear Irene,
Somewhere, a long time ago, a wandering child was holding a rose and she did not know where to put it. She found a place and stayed with the rose and the place, and I was there by accident; and so you, the rose and I are still together. Do you see what an accident does?[5]

Irene continued to record their late-night conversations. At times Stella felt that creating her technique was the "most important thing" she had accomplished.[6] "Isn't it interesting the best actors came from Stella?" she said to Irene, following that with where she believed the true credit lay: "It has something to do with the [family] line. How do I know the plays as well as I know them? I got something special in the history of America, and I survived enough to save some of it and create some good, and a kind of standard of what acting is."[7] At other times she disdained her past in the theater, telling Gilbert the last thing she remembered telling a student was, "'I don't care if you die, but don't kill O'Neill.' Terrible temper. Terrible editing, terrible demands. I don't want that anymore."[8]

In one of her later lectures on Eugene O'Neill Stella underscored the playwright's message, which paralleled her own end-of-life preoccupations:

> O'Neill says every man has to struggle to keep up with being a man. It's hard; most of us fail. In *Long Day's Journey*, he is trying to come to grips with his own failures as a man and as an artist, trying to make peace with his past, trying to forgive his family as well as himself. We are all trying to do that, or should be. In doing so, we go to the sources that can nurture us—to the people who struggled before us—and we find there is an eternal yearning in man to keep himself high through his work, through his thought, through his inheritance. Man has inherited property in art, in literature, in science, in philosophy. It is there for you. Unless you take and use that, you are not just a failure; you are truly lost."[9]

Stella could pontificate upon the healing, transcendent nature of art, but when it came to her personal ambitions, she held on to an unattainable ideal she set for herself.

One night while recording Stella, Gilbert asked her if she finally felt she had matched the talent of her parents. Exasperated, Stella said:

> Touch their talent? Are you out of your mind? There's no one in the whole world that I have seen that could touch them. It was indescribable in as far as what they did, what they played, and what they did with what they played. Nobody ever forgot it. If you said, "Do you remember Adler in the *Merchant of Venice*?" Yes, I remember him sitting with his feet crossed, sharpening the knife. And the way he sharpened, nobody ever forgot that moment. It had nothing to do with what you're seeing, living through. It was on another level. You can understand the level it's on because I'm telling you everything else is childish.[10]

But it came at a price, which Stella called a "horrible life." When Irene asked what would have made it better, Stella responded: "A home. A proper mother. A sense of belonging to something steady, steadier than the theater. A miserable life for children who have parents in the theater."[11]

At times Stella seemed to reconcile herself with the life she lived, only to berate herself again. In another recording she said: "I told you what I realized that everything has its nature. Once you know that there is nothing to keep out of your life. I realized I was judgmental and stupid. Everything has its life. . . . I'm very tired and I'm glad that I can have the leisure. I don't feel guilty if I sleep all day, or I rest. I don't want to keep up. The only thing I regret is that three times I tried to make a home . . . and I lost. I'm a failure."[12]

Stella continued to talk about her failed attempts at marriage, but her greatest remorse concerned a topic she rarely discussed: her daughter. "She felt she could've done more," Samuella Harris remembered Stella saying during her last years, "but at the time she did the best that she could to provide for her family. She worked and she provided. She knew that the relationship she had with her daughter was not what she wanted."[13] Above all else, Harris remembered, Stella had an overwhelming desire for Ellen to know that her mother loved her.

Ellen recalled on her last visit with her mother that Stella said to her, "You're very beautiful, Ellen. You always were and you always will be."[14] Stella didn't take this opportunity, however, to share her regret over having neglected Ellen or to proclaim her love to her only child. A life had been lived. Either Stella wanted to spare Ellen her own remorse or she lacked the courage to make amends. Instead, Stella fell back on humor to lighten the mood. Her last words to Ellen were: "I don't know why you never married again." Then, quietly playing the role of the quintessential Jewish mother fussing over her child's appearance, she quipped: "Maybe if you had done something better with your hair."[15]

The summer of 1990 Gilbert rented another house off Sunset Boulevard on Thrasher Street. Visitors came and went, but the primary occupants were Stella, Gilbert, and Harris. Harris recalled that Stella

made preparations two years prior because she was separating herself from different people who she knew could not handle her death. It would be too hard on them. It was just a process that people do . . . and toward the end I would get up every two hours and check on her, and every hour and check on her, and the last time I checked on her I just got up and went in and gave her some water, and we laughed and talked a few minutes like we always do in the middle of the night. Sometimes we'd go skinny-dipping in the swimming pool in the middle of the night because that was the way it was if she couldn't sleep or she was having a restless night. I would either massage her or we'd go swimming. . . . She wasn't suffering, she was never on all kind of medication.[16]

Never one for modesty, the first time Stella decided to go swimming without a bathing suit, Harris was caught unawares. Stella explained to Harris that if she were willing to go nude, Harris would have to as well. Unlike Stella, Harris had not led the bohemian, half-dressed life of an actress, but she obliged Stella anyway.

On the night of December 20, 1992, Gilbert was in Stella's room at bedtime. Sometimes Gilbert sat on the bed next to Stella while she fell asleep. Other times Stella asked Gilbert to climb into bed next to her. Lying alongside one another, like girls at a slumber party, Gilbert could tell there was something on Stella's mind. Finally, Stella took Gilbert's hand and broke the silence in the form of a question: "Are you going to be okay if I go?" Gilbert knew she was speaking of her death, responding, "It has nothing to do with me. It has to do with you, darling."[17]

Harris woke up near dawn the next morning with a feeling that she should check on Stella: "I relive it all the time because it was a moment that was so beautiful and I deal with death all the time. . . . I walked into her room and there was just this aura, beautiful aura. I mean it gives me chills, it was so beautiful. At first I had nothing to compare it with, and then I was watching TV one night and I saw the northern lights that they were talking about. And this is how this aura was in her room."[18] Like everything else in her life, Stella decided when it was time to go. Appropriately, it was the third night into the Jewish Festival of Lights. The smile on Stella's lips seemed to say coquettishly, "Stella means star. Everybody thinks I don't know that."

Irene arranged everything: embalming the body and buying a coffin to take Stella back to New York. Not wanting to leave Stella alone, she booked a ticket on the flight for herself and arranged for the body to be delivered into the hands of a funeral home chosen by Ellen. The plot waiting for Stella lay next to Harold's at Mount Carmel cemetery, a few feet away from Jacob's eagle.

Ellen selected a passage from Euripides' *The Bacchae* to inscribe on Stella's footstone. The passage from which the line is taken occurs just as the god Dionysus has tricked the king of Thebes, Pentheus, into changing into his mother's clothes and spying on the women possessed by Dionysus, which results in Pentheus's being ripped apart limb from limb by his mother and other female relatives who, like him, refuse to acknowledge that Dionysus is a god.

Given Stella's respect for the circumstances of the play, she would have understood how Dionysus's actions sanction the role of the gods in Greek society. If Ellen were aware of the context of the line it would most likely have been from Stella's perspective, that of upholding a tradition. Most likely Ellen's choice was simply a tribute to Stella's beauty—not just the physical, but also that inner loveliness that lifted art, like Dionysus, to the godly station of the immortals. Through her gesture, Ellen celebrated her mother's choice to dedicate her life to the theater and the transcendental power of art—an act of forgiveness that would have given Stella great peace. The inscription on her footstone reads: "And shall not loveliness be lovely forever?"

EPILOGUE

Although Stella had instructed that she be buried next to Mitchell Wilson in the Hamptons, no one could dispute that she belonged at Mount Carmel, with Jacob Adler's eagle watching over the family. The self-described "Jewish broad from Odessa" had carried her family's spirit to stages and screens around the world and then, appropriately, returned it to its place of rest.

Stella could be as imperial as a queen, but she never overcame her childhood insecurities. This lack of self-esteem carried over into her work both as an actress and as a teacher. One of her mentees, the producer Milton Justice, recalled: "At one point we were at the school when it was on Fifty-sixth Street, and she said, 'You know the only reason they let me have this school is because they knew my father.' And I said, 'Stella! What are you talking about? You're Stella Adler. Of course you can rent this space.' But in her mind it was just Adler."[739] Yet, even though she struggled to live up to her image of her parents, Stella succeeded in fulfilling her promise to Stanislavski to promulgate a technique of acting based on his system, one that empowered the actor and refined the craft.

In the foreword to Stella's book on acting, Marlon Brando wrote: "Little did she know that through her teachings she would impact theatrical culture worldwide. Almost all filmmakers anywhere in the world have felt the effects of American films, which have been in turn influenced by Stella Adler's teachings."[740]

Stella knew exactly what she was doing; she understood the transformative potential of art and its capacity to edify humanity. Without a craft to interpret, modern-day acting would be unable to portray realism and its successors. Ibsen, Shaw, Ionesco, Miller, Williams would all be left rudderless through exaggerated, demonstrative acting. Like her fellow members of the Group Theatre who promulgated Stanislavski's teachings, Stella used the technique to turn the actor from a caricature into a three-dimensional human being, a transformation from which we all—the writer, the actor, the audience— benefit. As Peter Bogdanovich observed, although it was Stella's undying ambition to be an international movie star, "how she taught acting led ultimately to the fall of the personality-star hierarchy to which she had once aspired."[741] Like Brando, Bogdanovich acknowledged that Stella's lifelong devotion to the craft of acting ended up "essentially altering the process the way that America, and therefore the world, thought about actors and acting, in the theater and in pictures."[742]

Stella honored the playwright's intention, raising it to the level worthy of the characters we carry in our collective consciousness, whether they be Lady Macbeth or Stanley Kowalski. The job of today's actor is the feat of the historian, the literary scholar, the vocalist, and the artist's creative imagination. Stella's talent in imparting the soul-bearing truth of the art of acting was her gift to the world.

In lecture after lecture Stella urged that only through knowing himself could the actor authentically bring a character to life and create a human being. It had to start with the actor. So, although Stella taught acting exercises and analyzed plays, her classes led the actor to discover who he was and how he operated in society. The two were interdependent. When lecturing on a scene, play, or playwright, Stella inevitably drew out the universal issues of modern society. Just like the plays themselves, her lectures offer timeless truths on the plight of modern humanity:

> Everybody feels threatened. Either there'll be in a fire in the subway or a power blackout or you'll have your driver's license taken away. . . . Miller makes you see they are living under all sorts of conscious and unconscious tension. The play comes out of an atmosphere of where people aren't sure how to live anymore. "Will I get a job interview? . . . If I get the interview, will I get the job? Will they like me? . . . There's no relaxation. "There's no rest for the wicked," my mother used to say. There's no space or blade of grass for Willy to come back to and sit down, open up the paper, smoke a cigarette, watch the sun go down. . . . This alienation, this anxiety that you see in *Death of a Salesman* planted itself and took root so strongly that by the time it got to your generation, the whole fabric of American family and social life was eaten away by it. There's nothing left to do but turn on the television.[743]

It is telling that Stella left her legacy divided between two unaffiliated schools and a handful of apprentices. The New York Studio stayed in the family, bestowed on her daughter, Ellen, and today Ellen's son, Tom Oppenheim, is its artistic director. Stella bequeathed the West Coast school to Irene Gilbert. Six years younger than Ellen, Irene looked up to Stella as a mother figure. Acrimony between Ellen and Stella's friend of thirty years played out like sibling rivalry, exacerbated by Stella's leaving the Hollywood school to Gilbert. The schools remain unaffiliated to this day, even after the death of Irene Gilbert on May 21, 2011.

Throughout the years after Stella's death, each school has claimed to be the one to pass on Stella's legacy "authentically." While interviewing Tom Oppenheim, this author asked him why he had taken the job of running the studio. He said, "It's too complicated and it doesn't really have to do with Stella. That would be my biography."[744] Oppenheim explained that when he took over, he wanted to "navigate" the school in a way that seemed true to Stella's spirit, but also Clurman's: "I felt like I had to let go of the idea that we had to be a dogmatic, one-technique type of institution because Stella didn't train teachers."[745]

A handful of teachers currently giving credit to Stella's technique as they instruct scores of acting students may beg to differ. Ron Burrus, with whom Stella worked closely and upon whom she relied after Mitchell Wilson's death, is one example. "I was with her for ten years," Burrus spoke of his tutelage under Stella; "We did technique three times a week and then she would monitor me." Burrus explained that at times Stella would just simply tell him to "take over."[746] Today he heads the Art of Acting Studio, the New York Studio's arm in Los Angeles, which cannot use Stella's name on the West Coast.

One of Stella's most ardent apprentices, Arthur Mendoza, built his own school, the Actors Circle Theatre, in West Los Angeles. The school's brochure explains its history: "Arthur Mendoza opened the Actors Circle Theatre in 1991 in order to preserve the exact teachings of the late Stella Adler. Mr. Mendoza worked closely and meticulously with Ms. Adler to build a curriculum that would synthesize her most essential teachings into separate eleven-week semesters. Ms. Adler then instructed Mr. Mendoza to build his theater in such a way that the Adler technique and love of the craft would be the constant center of the theater's existence, letting word of mouth bring students whose thirst for knowledge would make this their home."[747] Mendoza, who has been on an indefinite hiatus since 2012, teaches an anthropological, one might even say Adlerian, way of viewing Stella and her work. Along with the collaborators on *The Technique of Acting*, Mendoza also helped organize the exercises in the book. Speaking to the author, he said, "People thought she had to let you get in, but at the basic foundation of it, she was a woman. A woman. Who was looking for someone to treat her like that. She didn't even realize it. She wasn't manipulative; there wasn't a game to it. Her whole technique was action/reaction. She would react to what you do. Her life was a living metaphor for the work. Her action was to clear out the work of Strasberg."[748]

Charles Waxberg began working at Stella's New York Studio in 1985. Committed to "planting apple-seeds from her orchard everywhere I go,"[749] he would sit at Stella's side while she taught classes at both the Studio and NYU. Waxberg explained his training with Stella:

> During class, when a script question came up, she would partly direct the answer at me, and occasionally add a comment to me personally. She spoke in few words and you had to catch them because each was a diamond in the air. Those mini-directions for five years trained me to teach in my script class what she wanted them to know. She allowed me to sit in on any class I wanted and she knew I was studying her. It wasn't the same formal training for students who had been through her program. She knew I was already an established teacher. Her training was subtle, perhaps manipulative (in a way I wished to be manipulated) and made sure I understood exactly what she was thinking and why. This is how I remember those five years. I feel it as a cross between an observer and an apprentice.[750]

Waxberg echoed Oppenheim's remark that the Studio teaches in the "spirit" of Stella. However, he claims that the New York Studio actually veers away from what Stella herself taught. He points out that few of the teachers who teach at the Studio actually studied with Stella, while up until a few years ago everyone on staff at the Los Angeles Academy had studied directly with her. As time passes and people age, there are fewer of those teachers left.

Today Waxberg teaches Stella's technique in Seattle. In recent correspondence with Waxberg the author mentioned that Stella's technique, as Brando wrote, is ubiquitous. But Waxberg disagreed:

> Because Stella's techniques were stolen by so many others and credit never given, she was extremely guarded about spreading her technique around everywhere (like Meisner) where it could be distorted and plagiarized. Also, Strasberg was such a consummate self-promoter that Stella found that extremely distasteful for anyone. What you are seeing in the country today is . . . abandoning the indulgent methods of Strasberg and what is left is the LATE teaching of Stanislavsky. Stella was the first and only American to study with him and brought his THEORIES here. Her genius contributed practical TECHNIQUE to teaching his theories. But even she would tell you this is not her, this is Stanislavsky.[751]

Tom Oppenheim's explanation for straying from Stella's technique, a word he seemed to recoil from during our interview, stems from a genuine intention of increasing the actor's humanity:

> Her training was very much about one's humanity and depth of one's humanity. Stella carried the whole history of Western art in her being. She used slides of paintings and sculptures in her character class. A lot of the stuff I worry about is preservation actually. It's a tricky business, as I say, because you don't want a wax museum devoted to the preservation of her. . . . Most imitations of her are bad imitations of her. But there was a spirit that will never die because it was never really hers. It comes from [the] prehistoric past and through the Greeks and Elizabethans, but she tapped into it. It came roaring up through her, and that's available. That's what I'm trying to facilitate and keep alive, that part of her voice.[752]

The common denominator, from Brando to Stella's grandson, is that Stella's teachings were not about Stella, but something larger. The focus of her technique is on art and its indispensable value to society, not on the teacher who dispenses her wisdom.

In 2006 Stella was given a star on Hollywood Boulevard, just steps from the door of the Los Angeles Academy. Ellen Adler and Tom Oppenheim were present to take part in the occasion. It was the last time Ellen and Irene Gilbert saw one another.

Those who knew Stella—her imperious temperance coupled with her deference to art, her inexhaustible study and service to acting, her ability to ignite the imagination of the actor—realize the irony of a star for Stella on Hollywood Boulevard. The honor was undoubtedly for her teaching, not her acting; stardom eluding her even posthumously. And not the least of ironies is the Walk of Fame's earthly provinciality compared to the celestial heights to which Stella raised the craft of acting. Like very few actors in history, Stella represented her profession the way a queen represents her country—ostentatiously, reverentially, and ruthlessly.

Stella's unremitting idealism—idolizing a father she admitted was a "degenerate"[753]; lamenting the failure of never becoming an internationally acclaimed actress while still devoting her life to acting; living with the frustration of her perception of Strasberg's misuse of Stanislavski's system; committing herself to clarifying the theories of the Russian master—that idealism wrestled with what Stella believed was the most significant obstacle to the artist (and to the human being): his ego.

Milton Justice, who was asked to teach Stella's technique at Yale although he was not formally trained by her, explained: "It was never about her. She dressed for every class as if she was going to opening night. She was very aware of how she looked. She would check her makeup before she went into class. And one would think that someone was going in for a performance. If I were doing text analysis on her preparation for class I could very easily come up with this is a person who is much more worried about her appearance than what she is teaching. But the fact is it was all really in service of what she was teaching."[754]

Each class, for Stella, was a performance, one undertaken with the express objective of instructing the students: "You serve the playwright, who serves God, who serves the universe."[755] She dressed as she expected her actors to dress, by owning a costume as one would own his or her character's action. She dressed the way her parents dressed. They were expected to look like royalty as they led a homesick mass of immigrants. Like them, she considered it her duty to lead her students, her acolytes, her audiences, toward the universal themes of art that guided their lives as human beings. She dressed even when she had to drape a scarf over a torn sleeve or safety pin a broken button. It was her costume.

Stella was an actress, and there's no doubt she also dressed to feel attractive and be noticed. That was the Stella Adler people could easily cast off as disingenuous. It didn't matter. She did not care what people thought of her so much as what they thought, period: "I do not give a goddamn about *me*, only what I can give you. That is what's important. That is why my life has been important."[756] Once the master is gone, the spirit is still alive, but it must be preserved in order to survive. This book was written in service to that survival.

NOTES ON SOURCES

Materials from the Irene Gilbert Collection are cited according to how they were labeled when I began working from the collection in 2001. In 2007 I inventoried the collection and donated it to the Billy Rose Theatre Division at the New York Public Library for the Performing Arts. In some cases I had to label certain materials such as audiocassette tapes in order to create a working inventory. My notes reflect these and Gilbert's attributions, not the way in which the Billy Rose Theatre Division has archived the collection. Some materials are still in my possession, as I had not finished working with them for the biography.

The Group Theatre scholar Robert Ellerman lent me invaluable unpublished materials, including Stella Adler's copies of Richard Boleslavski's lectures at the American Laboratory Theatre (1925–26); Group member Tony Kraber's class notebook, including notes on classes he took with Stella (1936); Stella's entry in the Brookfield Diary; and unpublished interviews that included Ron Willis's 1963 interview with Stella Adler and a former student of the Lab, Blanch Tancock, and Jerry Roberts's 1975 interview with Stella.

NOTES

Prologue

1 Jack Garfein, in discussion with the author, October 25, 2005.
2 Jack Garfein, "Jack Garfein on Life and Acting," interview by Leonard Lopate, *The Leonard Lopate Show*, WNYC, March 18, 2011, hosted by Leonard Lopate, accessed September 5, 2013, http://www.wnyc.org /shows/lopate/2011/mar/18/jack-garfein-life-and-acting/.
3 Ibid.
4 Mel Gussow, "Lee Strasberg of Actors Studio Dead," the *New York Times*, February 18, 1983.
5 Jack Garfein, in discussion with the author, October 25, 2005.
6 Stella Adler, *Stella Adler on America's Master Playwrights*, ed. Barry Paris (New York: Knopf, 2012), 74.
7 Stella Adler, entry in Brookfield Diary, 1931, provided to author by Robert Ellerman.
8 John Strasberg, *Accidentally on Purpose: Reflections on Life, Acting, and the Nine Natural Laws of Creativity* (New York: Applause, 1996), 77.
9 Peter Hay, *Broadway Anecdotes* (New York: Oxford University Press, 1990), 359.

Chapter One

1 PBS American Masters Series, "Stella Adler: Awake and Dream!," season 4, episode 2, aired July 10, 1989 (hereafter cited as "Stella Adler: Awake and Dream!").
2 Lulla Rosenfeld, *Bright Star of Exile: Jacob Adler and the Yiddish Theater* (New York: Thomas Y. Crowell, 1977), 282.
3 Interview with Lulla Rosenfeld, October 26, 1987, American Jewish Committee Oral History Collection, Dorot Jewish Division, New York Public Library, Astor, Lenox and Tilden Foundations.
4 Ibid.
5 Stella Adler, in discussion with Irene Gilbert, Los Angeles, CA, May 24, 1991, audiocassette.
6 "She Wasn't Reared In a Trunk, Though Born in the Theater," *New York Herald Tribune*, April 9, 1939, Julia Adler Papers, Billy Rose Theatre Division, New York Public Library for the Performing Arts (hereafter cited as Billy Rose Theatre Division).

7 Allison Adler, in discussion with the author, December 29, 2003.

8 Lulla Rosenfeld, "The Yiddish Idol," *The New York Times Magazine*, June 12, 1977, 45.

9 "Stella Adler: Awake and Dream!"

10 Ibid.

11 "The Yiddish *Broken Hearts*," the *New York Times*, September 23, 1903.

12 Stella Adler, introduction to Jacob Adler, *Jacob Adler: A Life on the Stage; A Memoir*, trans. Lulla Rosenfeld (New York: Applause, 2001), viii.

13 Ruth Limmer and Andrew S. Dolkart, "The Tenement as History and Housing," Tenement Museum, last modified 2012, accessed September 5, 2013, http://www.thirteen.org/tenement/eagle.html#lower.

14 Rosenfeld, *Bright Star of Exile*, 345.

15 Interview with Lulla Rosenfeld, October 26, 1987, Dorot Jewish Division, New York Public Library.

Chapter Two

1 Jacob Adler, *A Life on the Stage*, 23.

2 Ibid., 286.

3 Ibid.

Chapter Three

1 Maralyn Lois Polak, "Stella Adler: Granting an Audience," *Inquirer*, 1985, 9.

2 Rosenfeld, *Bright Star of Exile*, 222.

3 Diane Cypkin, "Second Avenue: The Yiddish Broadway" (Ph.D. diss., New York University, 1986), 4.

4 Jacob Adler, *A Life on the Stage*, 310.

5 Selwyn Freed, in discussion with the author, November 17, 2003.

6 Rosenfeld, *Bright Star of Exile*, 246.

7 Jacob Adler, *A Life on the Stage*, 314.

8 Nahma Sandrow, *Vagabond Stars: A World History of the Yiddish Theater* (New York: Harper & Row, 1977), 72.

9 Ibid., 94.

10 Jacob Adler, *A Life on the Stage*, 324.

11 Joel Berkowitz, *Shakespeare on the American Yiddish Stage* (Iowa City: University of Iowa Press, 2002), 38.

12 Rosenfeld, "The Yiddish Idol," 41–42.

13 Frederick Goldman, "When Lear Spoke Yiddish: 100 Years of Jewish Theater," the *New York Times*, September 19, 1982.

14 Berkowitz, *Shakespeare on the American Yiddish Stage*, 50.

15 Jacob Adler, *A Life on the Stage*, 344.

16 Rosenfeld, "The Yiddish Idol," 42.

Chapter Four

1 Lawrence Christon, "Stella Adler Sums Up a Life in the Theater," *Los Angeles Times*, Calendar Section, September 6, 1988, 8.

2 Tenement Encyclopedia, "The Lower East Side," 64, accessed August 30, 2013, http://www.tenement.org/encyclopedia/lower_landscape.htm.

3 Cypkin, "Second Avenue," 41.

4 "She Wasn't Reared in a Trunk," *New York Herald Tribune*, April 9, 1939.

5 Stella Adler, in discussion with Irene Gilbert, circa 1991, audiocassette, Irene Gilbert Collection.

6 Joseph Schildkraut, *My Father and I* (New York: Viking Press, 1959), 117.

7 Ibid., 117.

8 Polak, "Stella Adler," 10.

9 Cypkin, "Second Avenue," 34.

10 Christon, "Stella Adler Sums Up a Life," 8.

11 Rosenfeld, *Bright Star of Exile*, 282.

12 Joanna Rotte, *Acting with Adler* (New York: Limelight Editions, 2000), 72.

13 Ibid.

14 "Stella Adler Upholds a Tradition," *New York Herald Tribune*, January 22, 1933, Jacob Adler Papers, Billy Rose Theatre Division.

15 "Actor Adler Hurt in a Theater Fight," the *New York Times*, April 27, 1909, Jacob Adler Papers, Billy Rose Theatre Division.

16 Ibid.

17 "Love Making Scene Causes $20,000 Suit," *St. Louis Star*, October 28, 1910, Sara Adler Papers, Billy Rose Theatre Division.

18 "Stella Adler: Awake and Dream!"

19 Ibid.

20 "Reminiscences of Harold Edgar Clurman," interview by Louis Sheaffer, 1979, transcript, Columbia University Center for Oral History Collection, Butler Library, 52.

21 Stella Adler, discussion with Mel Gordon, 1985, videocassette, transcribed by the author; interview funded by PBS.

22 Harold Clurman, *All People Are Famous* (New York: Harcourt, Brace, Jovanovich, 1974), 112.

23 Rosenfeld, *Bright Star of Exile*, 313.

24 Ibid.

25 Ibid., 312.

Chapter Five

1 *Vanity Fair*, February 11, 1911, Frances Adler Papers, Billy Rose Theatre Divison.

2 Ibid.

3 Stella Adler, in discussion with Irene Gilbert, circa 1991, audiocassette, Irene Gilbert Collection.

4 Stella Adler, *On America's Master Playwrights*, 77–78.

5 Stanley Moss, in discussion with the author, October 27, 2002.

6 Ibid.

7 Stella Adler, in discussion with friends, n.d., audiocassette, titled "SA 2," Irene Gilbert Collection.

8 Ibid.

9 Stella Adler, in discussion with Irene Gilbert, circa 1990, audiocassette, titled "SA," Irene Gilbert Collection.

10 Stella Adler's Permanent Record Card, 1919, Wadleigh High School Archives, New York.

11 Ibid.

12 Serge Prokofiev, *Diary, 1919–1933*, trans. Diana Farafanova (Paris: Serge Prokofiev Foundation, 2002), 24.

13 Ibid.

14 Ibid., 27.

15 Ibid., 28.

16 Stella Adler, in discussion with guests in her home, circa 1987, audiocassette, titled "SA B," Irene Gilbert Collection.

17 "Stella Adler Upholds a Tradition."

18 Prokofiev, *Diary, 1919–1933*, 30.

19 Ibid., 43.

20 John Gruen, "Stella at Yale," *World Journal Tribune*, 1967.

21 Ellen Adler, in discussion with the author, April 12, 2004.

22 Prokofiev, *Diary, 1919–1933*, 25.

23 John Gruen, *Close Up* (New York: Viking Press, 1968), 113.

24 Stella Adler, in discussion with John Gruen, March 10, 1981, videocassette, Billy Rose Theatre Division.

25 "Heredity Asserts Itself," n.d., unattributed essay from the offices of Oliver M. Sayler, Jacob Adler Papers, Billy Rose Theatre Division.

26 Ibid.

27 Ibid.

28 "Adler Daughter to Star in English," *Evening Wisconsin,* June 20, 1915, Frances Adler Papers, Billy Rose Theatre Division.

29 Rosenfeld, "The Yiddish Idol," 47.

30 Interview with Lulla Rosenfeld, October 26, 1987, Dorot Jewish Division, New York Public Library.

31 John Corbin, "Moscow Players Open to a Throng," the *New York Times*, January 9, 1923.

32 Jacob Adler, *A Life on the Stage*, 376.

33 Ellen Adler, in discussion with the author, April 12, 2004.

34 Stella Adler, "Question and Answer" session, recorded at the Stella Adler Studio of Acting, New York, November 1979, Stella Adler and Harold Clurman Papers, Harry Ransom Center, University of Texas, Austin (hereafter cited as HRC).

35 "Tuberculosis: Curing in the Adirondacks," Adirondack History Network, last modified 2000, accessed August 30, 2013, http://www.adirondackhistory.org/newtb/four.html.

Chapter Six

1 Irene Gilbert, in discussion with the author, September 15, 2002.

2 Stanley Moss, in discussion with the author, October 27, 2002.

3 "Stella Adler 1989," YouTube, video file, 03:24, posted by PacificAct, January 29, 2009, accessed September 13, 2013, http://www.youtube.com/watch?v=LVTo5kPTlgg.

4 Robert Rusie, "Broadway 101: The History of the Great White Way," Talkin' Broadway, last modified 1999, http://www.talkinbroadway.com/bway101/1.html.

5 Ibid.

6 Ibid.

7 Cypkin, "Second Avenue," 43.

8 Ibid., 458.

9 Ibid., 464.

10 Ibid., 466.

11 Jacob Adler, *A Life on the Stage*, 376.

12 Rosenfeld, "The Yiddish Idol," 47.

13 Tom Oppenheim, in discussion with the author, September 19, 2002.

14 Ibid.

15 Stella Adler, in discussion with Ron Willis, December 1963, transcript, 1.

16 Ibid.

17 Stella Adler, in discussion with Jerry Roberts, October 21, 1975, transcript, 1.

18 Blanch Tancock, "Shirley White Letters," in discussion with Ron Willis, March 1964, ed. and transcribed J. W. Roberts, July 1978, 27.

19 Ibid., 28.

20 Ibid., 30.

21 Stella Adler, in discussion with Jerry Roberts, October 21, 1975, transcript, 2.

22 Blanch Tancock, in discussion with Ron Willis, March 1964, transcript, 33.

23 Stella Adler, in discussion with Irene Gilbert, May 24, 1991, audiocassette.

24 Stella Adler, "Stella Stories," August 7, 1988, audiocassette, Irene Gilbert Collection.

Chapter Seven

1 Allison Adler, in discussion with the author, April 12, 2004.

2 Stella Adler, in discussion with Irene Gilbert, May 24, 1991, audiocassette.

3 Ellen Adler, in discussion with the author, April 12, 2004.

4 "'Midway' a Drama in Four Acts," *The Telegraph*, October 3, 1927, Yiddish Art Theater Clippings, Billy Rose Theatre Division.

5 Rosenfeld, "The Yiddish Idol," 41–42.

6 David Freeland, "The Jews of Second Avenue," NYPress.com, last modified February 1, 2006, accessed September 14, 2013, http://nypress.com/the-jews-of-second-ave/.

7 Celia Adler, *Celia Adler Dertseylt (The Celia Adler Story)*, trans. Sarah Traister Moskovitz (New York: Celia Adler Foundation, 1959), 616.

8 Ibid.

9 Selwyn Freed, in discussion with the author, April 13, 2004.

10 Rosenfeld, *Bright Star of Exile*, 354.

11 Celia Adler, *The Celia Adler Story*, 94.

12 Selwyn Freed, "Second Avenue," 2003, unpublished essay.

13 Ibid.

14 "The Witch of Castile," the *New York Times*, October 25, 1930, in *New York Times Theater Reviews, 1920–1970* (New York: New York Times & Arno Press, 1971).

15 Freeland, "The Jews of Second Avenue," NYPress.com.

Chapter Eight

1 Harold Clurman, *The Fervent Years: The Group Theatre and the Thirties* (New York: Da Capo Press, 1975), 6.

2 T. H. Watkins, *The Great Depression: America in the 1930s* (Boston: Little, Brown, 1993), 56.

3 Clurman, *All People Are Famous*, 65.

4 Cindy Adams, *Lee Strasberg: The Imperfect Genius of the Actors Studio* (New York: Doubleday, 1980), 81.

5 Ibid.

6 Ibid., 10.

7 Clurman, *All People Are Famous*, 74.

8 Adams, *Lee Strasberg*, 96.

9 Clurman, *The Fervent Years*, 28.

10 Stella Adler, "Stella Stories."

11 Stella Adler, in discussion with Mel Gordon, 1985.

12 Clurman, *The Fervent Years*, 26.

13 Wendy Smith, *Real Life Drama: The Group Theatre and America, 1931–1940* (New York: Knopf, 1990), 5.

14 Stella Adler, in discussion with Mel Gordon, 1986, videocassette, transcribed by the author; interview funded by PBS.

15 "Timeline of the Great Depression," American Experience, last modified 2010, accessed August 30, 2013, http://www.pbs.org/wgbh/americanexperience/features/timeline/rails-timeline/.

16 "Adler Family Seen at Monument National," *Montreal Daily Star*, May 20, 1930, Frances Adler Papers, Billy Rose Theatre Division.

17 Philip A. Adler, "Adler Family in Melodrama," unidentified Detroit periodical, May 30, 1930, Frances Adler Papers, Billy Rose Theatre Division.

18 "Jewish Cast Seen in Gripping Play," n.d., Frances Adler Papers, Billy Rose Theatre Division.

19 Stella Adler, "Stella Stories."

20 Clurman, *All People Are Famous*, 110.

21 Harold Clurman, "Group Theater Daily Journal, 1941," Harold Clurman Papers, Billy Rose Theatre Division.

22 Clurman, *The Fervent Years*, 29.
23 "Adler Family Acts 'Millions' in Yiddish," the *New York Times*, October 3, 1930.
24 Ellen Adler, in panel discussion with Foster Hirsh, "Dramatist Guild: Stella Adler on America's Master Playwrights," Livestream, streaming video, posted by #NEWPLAY TV, January 22, 2013, http://new .livestream.com/.
25 Clurman, "Group Theater Daily Journal, 1941."
26 Ibid.

Chapter Nine

1 Smith, *Real Life Drama*, 35.
2 Robert H. Hethmon, ed., *Strasberg at the Actors Studio: Tape-Recorded Sessions* (New York: Theater Communications Group, 1965), 96.
3 S. Loraine Hull, *Strasberg's Method as Taught by Lorrie Hull* (Woodbridge, CT: Ox Bow Press, 1985), 82.
4 Hethmon, *Strasberg at the Actors Studio*, 110.
5 Helen Krich Chinoy, "Reunion: A Self-Portrait of the Group Theatre," *Educational Theatre Journal* 28, no. 4 (December 1976): 522.
6 Hethmon, *Strasberg at the Actors Studio*, 112.
7 Stella Adler, in discussion with Jerry Roberts, October 21, 1975, 7.
8 Blanch Tancock, in discussion with Ron Willis, March 1964, transcript, 26.
9 Richard Boleslavsky, "Lectures at the American Laboratory Theatre," circa 1925–26, ed. Jerry Roberts (unpublished collection).
10 Jack Garfein, *Life and Acting: Techniques for the Actor* (Evanston, IL: Northwestern University Press, 2010), 67.
11 Jack Garfein, in discussion with the author, October 25, 2002.
12 Chinoy, "Reunion: A Self-Portrait of the Group," 508.
13 Hethmon, *Strasberg at the Actors Studio*, 111.
14 Paul Gray, "The Reality of Doing: Interviews with Vera Soloviova, Stella Adler, and Sanford Meisner," in *Stanislavski and America*, ed. Erika Munk (New York: Hill & Wang, 1966), 217.
15 Stella Adler, *On America's Master Playwrights*, 230.
16 Ibid.
17 Chinoy, "Reunion: A Self-Portrait of the Group," 508.
18 Adams, *Lee Strasberg*, 123.
19 Ibid., 124.
20 Smith, *Real Life Drama*, 45.

21 Ibid.

22 Robert Lewis, *Slings and Arrows: Theatre in My Live* (New York: Stein & Day, 1984), 44.

23 Watkins, *The Great Depression*, 56.

24 Ibid., 55.

25 Clurman, "Group Theater Daily Journal, 1941."

26 Ibid.

27 Brooks Atkinson, "The Play: Epic of the South," the *New York Times*, September 29, 1931.

28 Brooks Atkinson, "The Play: Creatures That Once Were Men," the *New York Times*, December 11, 1931.

29 Payroll ledger for "Night over Taos," labeled "weekend ending March 12, 1932," Luther Adler Papers, Billy Rose Theatre Division.

30 Clurman, *The Fervent Years*, 85.

31 Elia Kazan, *Elia Kazan: A Life* (New York: Doubleday, 1988), 57.

Chapter Ten

1 Chinoy, "Reunion: A Self-Portrait of the Group," 550.

2 Adams, *Lee Strasberg*, 148.

3 Lewis, *Slings and Arrows*, 78.

4 Brooks Atkinson, "The Play: The Group Theater Commences Its Second Season," the *New York Times*, September 27, 1932.

5 Smith, *Real Life Drama*, 110.

6 Ibid., 111.

7 "Agitating the Sabbath Calm," the *New York Times*, October 23, 1932.

8 Dawn Powell, *The Diaries of Dawn Powell, 1931–1965*, ed. Tim Page (South Royalton, VT: Steerforth Press, 1995), 278.

9 Robert Ellerman, in discussion with the author, March 24, 1999.

10 Smith, *Real Life Drama*, 107.

11 Kazan, *A Life*, 85.

12 Ibid., 60.

13 Smith, *Real Life Drama*, 121.

14 Frederick Lewis Allen, *Since Yesterday: The 1930s in America* (New York: Harper & Row, 1939), 84.

15 Kazan, *A Life*, 100.

16 Smith, *Real Life Drama*, 141.

17 Ibid., 144.

18 Ibid., 143.

19 Ibid., 166.

20 Ibid., 167.

21 Clurman, *The Fervent Years*, 136.

22 Ibid.

23 Ellen Adler, in discussion with the author, September 19, 2002.

Chapter Eleven

1 Stella Adler, *On America's Master Playwrights*, 256.

2 Erik Larson, *In the Garden of Beasts: Love, Terror, and an American Family in Hitler's Berlin* (New York: Crown, 2011), 128.

3 Janet Thorne, "It Makes You Weep: An Interview with Stella Adler on Soviet Actors," *New Theatre*, 1935, 8.

4 Ibid.

5 Ibid.

6 Ibid.

7 Adams, *Lee Strasberg*, 168.

8 Margaret Brenman-Gibson, *Clifford Odets: American Playwright; The Years from 1906 to 1940* (New York: Atheneum, 1981), 289.

9 Clurman, *All People Are Famous*, 82.

10 Stella Adler, "How I Met Stanislavski," n.d., typescript, HRC, 5.

11 Ibid.

12 Clurman, *All People Are Famous*, 82.

13 Stella Adler, "How I Met Stanislavski," 6.

14 Clurman, *All People Are Famous*, 83.

15 Sharon Marie Carnicke, "Stanislavski's System: Pathways for the Actor," in *Twentieth Century Actor Training*, ed. Alison Hodge (New York: Routledge, 2000), 33.

16 Ibid.

17 Rotte, *Acting with Adler*, 87.

18 Boris Filippov, *Actors without Make-Up*, trans. Kathelene Cook (Moscow: Progress Publishers, 1977), 59.

19 Ibid.

20 Clurman, "Group Theater Daily Journal, 1941."

21 Tom Oppenheim, "Stella Adler Technique," in *Training of the American Actor*, ed. Arthur Bartow (New York: Theater Communications Group, 2006), 46.

22 Stella Adler, *The Art of Acting*, ed. Howard Kissel (New York: Bantam Books, 1988), 139.

23 Ibid.
24 Sharon Marie Carnicke, *Stanislavski in Focus: An Acting Master for the Twenty-first Century*, 2nd ed. (New York: Routledge, 2009), 153.
25 David Krasner, "Strasberg, Adler, and Meisner," in Hodge, *Twentieth Century Actor Training*, 147.
26 Stella Adler, in discussion with Mel Gordon, 1985.
27 Clurman, *The Fervent Years*, 139.
28 Ibid., 175.
29 Adams, *Lee Strasberg*, 179.
30 Clurman, *The Fervent Years*, 139.
31 Tony Kraber, "Tony Kraber's Group Theater Notebooks (1936–1938)," unpublished transcript, 36.
32 Smith, *Real Life Drama*, 181.
33 Phoebe Brand, in discussion with the author, March 24, 1999.
34 Smith, *Real Life Drama*, 181.
35 Clurman, *The Fervent Years*, 139.
36 Kraber, "Tony Kraber's Group Theater Notebooks," 34.
37 Ibid.
38 Brenman-Gibson, *Clifford Odets*, 298.
39 Ibid.
40 Clurman, *The Fervent Years*, 139.
41 Brenman-Gibson, *Clifford Odets*, 301.
42 Ibid., 293.
43 Clurman, *The Fervent Years*, 144.
44 Smith, *Real Life Drama*, 187.
45 "All's Fair in Love and Costuming with the Group," *Boston Herald*, n.d., Group Theater Scrapbooks, Billy Rose Theatre Division (hereafter cited as Scrapbooks).
46 "Stella Adler Is from Well Known Theatrical Family," *Boston Globe*, n.d., Scrapbooks.
47 "$346,660 for Jewish Charities," *Boston Post*, November 3, 1934, Scrapbooks.
48 Clurman, *The Fervent Years*, 142.
49 Brooks Atkinson, "Gold Eagle Guy with the Group Theater," the *New York Times*, November 29, 1934.
50 Ibid.
51 Clurman, *The Fervent Years*, 142.
52 Ibid., 144.

53 Brenman-Gibson, *Clifford Odets*, 311.

54 Ibid., 312.

55 Ibid.

Chapter Twelve

1 Stella Adler, in discussion with friends, August 29, 1987, audiocassette, Irene Gilbert Collection.

2 Clurman, *The Fervent Years*, 147–48.

3 Watkins, *The Great Depression*, 168.

4 Ibid., 170.

5 Smith, *Real Life Drama*, 198.

6 Ibid., 199.

7 Brenman-Gibson, *Clifford Odets*, 316.

8 Ibid., 317.

9 Ibid.

10 Ibid., 316.

11 Ibid., 254.

12 Ibid.

13 Peter Bogdanovich, *Who the Hell's In It: Portraits and Conversations* (New York: Knopf, 2004), 77.

14 Lewis, *Slings and Arrows*, 83.

15 Kazan, *A Life*, 121.

16 Brenman-Gibson, *Clifford Odets*, 322.

17 Kazan, *A Life*, 122.

18 Brenman-Gibson, *Clifford Odets*, 324.

19 Gilbert W. Gabriel, "Ten Best Performances: Brilliant Acting Is Reviewed," *New York American*, March 10, 1935, Scrapbooks.

20 "Awake and Sing," *Women's Wear*, February 20, 1935, Scrapbooks.

21 "The Play's the Thing," *Brooklyn College Beacon*, March 18, 1935, Scrapbooks.

22 Mary Virginia Farmer, "Awake and Sing," *New Theatre*, March 1935, Scrapbooks.

23 Untitled, syndicated, n.d. (circa 1935), Scrapbooks.

24 Brenman-Gibson, *Clifford Odets*, 324.

25 Kazan, *A Life*, 132.

26 Allen, *Since Yesterday*, 274.

27 Brenman-Gibson, *Clifford Odets*, 325.

28 Clurman, "Group Theater Daily Journal, 1941."

29 Meyer F. Steinglass, "The Adlers Carry On," *B'nai B'rith Magazine*, October 1936, Scrapbooks.

30 Brenman-Gibson, *Clifford Odets*, 328.

31 Ibid., 352.

32 Ibid.

33 Peter Stirling, "Two Odets Dramas on Broad St. Stage Real and Gripping," *Philadelphia Record*, October 1, 1935, Scrapbooks.

34 Steinglass, "The Adlers Carry On."

Chapter Thirteen

1 Allen, *Since Yesterday*, 177.

2 Chinoy, "Reunion: A Self-Portrait of the Group," 511.

3 Brenman-Gibson, *Clifford Odets*, 383.

4 Ibid., 385.

5 Ibid., 388.

6 Ibid., 386.

7 Lewis, *Slings and Arrows*, 84.

8 Arthur Miller, *Timebends: A Life* (New York: Penguin Books, 1995), 230.

9 Clurman, *The Fervent Years*, 178.

10 Ibid., 182.

11 "Actors Take Their Hair Down," *New York Midweek Pictorial*, October 17, 1936, Scrapbooks.

12 Robert Ellerman, in discussion with the author, March 24, 1999.

13 Elizabeth Parrish, in discussion with the author, September 21, 2002.

14 Ellen Adler, in discussion with the author, April 12, 2004.

15 Kazan, *A Life*, 154.

16 Sanford Meisner to Luther Adler, n.d., Luther Adler Papers, Billy Rose Theatre Division.

17 Kazan, *A Life*, 153.

18 Christina Duarte, "Stella Adler and the Group Theatre: Conflicts and Contributions" (Ph.D. diss., Hunter College, 2003), 36.

19 Smith, *Real Life Drama*, 276.

20 Steinglass, "The Adlers Carry On."

21 Smith, *Real Life Drama*, 288–93.

22 Clurman, *The Fervent Years*, 188.

23 Ibid., 188–89.

24 Ibid., 189.

25 Clurman, "Group Theater Daily Journal, 1941."

26 The *New York Times*, December 21, 1936, Scrapbooks.

27 Robert Claiborne, *Loose Cannons and Red Herrings: A Book of Lost Metaphors* (New York: Norton, 1988), 193.

Chapter Fourteen

1 Clurman, *The Fervent Years*, 197.
2 Chinoy, "Reunion: A Self-Portrait of the Group," 511.
3 Brenman-Gibson, *Clifford Odets*, 456.
4 Stella Adler, in discussion with Mel Gordon, 1985.
5 Ibid.
6 Ibid.
7 Brenman-Gibson, *Clifford Odets*, 457.
8 Smith, *Real Life Drama*, 302.
9 Ibid., 307.
10 Ibid.
11 Clurman, *The Fervent Years*, 206.
12 Duarte, "Stella Adler and the Group Theatre," 43–44.
13 Diggory Venn, "From Ibsen's Glaciers to Love on Toast," unidentified San Francisco newspaper, n.d. (circa October 1937), Scrapbooks.
14 Smith, *Real Life Drama*, 322.
15 Stella Adler, in discussion with Mel Gordon, 1986.
16 Review of "Love on Toast," *Variety*, n.d. (circa December 1937), Scrapbooks.
17 *New York Evening Journal*, March 2, 1935, Scrapbooks.
18 Florence Lawrence, "Directing Offers New Careers for Women," *Los Angeles Examiner*, March 6, 1935, Scrapbooks.
19 Harry Mines, "Raves and Raps," *Los Angeles Evening News*, March 5, 1938, Scrapbooks.
20 Ellen Adler, Western Union telegram to Stella Adler, April 1, 1938, HRC.
21 "Stella Adler Reveals Plans for Hollywood Branch of Group Theater," *Hollywood Citizen News*, May 6, 1938, Scrapbooks.
22 Mines, "Raves & Raps."
23 Ibid.
24 Ellen Adler, "A Different Kind of Success: A Conversation with Ellen Adler," *Lincoln Center Theater Review*, no. 42 (Spring 2006): 19.

Chapter Fifteen

1 Clurman, *All People Are Famous*, 172–73.
2 Stella Adler to Ellen Adler, London, n.d. (circa 1938), HRC.
3 Ellen Adler, "A Different Kind of Success," 21.
4 Stella Adler, *Stella Adler on Ibsen, Strindberg, and Chekhov*, ed. Barry Paris (New York: Knopf, 1999), 209.

5 Ibid., 212.

6 Ibid.

7 Ibid., 211.

8 Clurman, *The Fervent Years*, 226.

9 Brenman-Gibson, *Clifford Odets*, 510.

10 Clurman, *The Fervent Years*, 227–28.

11 Stella Adler to Ellen Adler, London, n.d. (circa 1938), HRC.

12 Gulie Ne'eman Arad, *America, Its Jews, and the Rise of Nazism* (Indianapolis: Indiana University Press, 2000), 127.

13 Stella Adler, in discussion with Mel Gordon, 1986.

14 Stella Adler, in discussion with Mel Gordon, 1985.

15 Stella Adler, in discussion with Mel Gordon, 1986.

16 Larson, *In the Garden of Beasts*, 131.

17 Wilfred Macartney to Stella Adler, February 4, 1939, HRC.

18 Wilfred Macartney to Stella Adler, n.d. (circa March 1939), HRC.

19 Ibid.

20 Ibid.

21 Irene Gilbert, in discussion with the author, September 15, 2002.

22 Allen, *Since Yesterday*, 274.

23 Wilfred Macartney to Stella Adler, n.d. (circa 1939), HRC.

24 Smith, *Real Life Drama*, 374.

25 Arnold Sundgaard, "The Group Remembered," *Journal of American Drama and Theatre* 8, no. 2 (Spring 1996): 10.

26 The last extant letter from Macartney is dated October 12, 1939. We don't know if he and Stella ever met again. There is nothing on record about his postwar life, although he lived to be seventy.

27 Smith, *Real Life Drama*, 388.

28 Duarte, "Stella Adler and the Group Theatre," 75.

29 "School to Teach Work of the Stage," the *New York Times*, December 10, 1939.

Chapter Sixteen

1 Stella Adler, "How I Met Stanislavski," 4.

2 "Roosevelts Dine at Cabinet Fete," the *New York Times*, March 5, 1940.

3 Duarte, "Stella Adler and the Group Theatre," 75.

4 Carl Combs, "Well, Well—A Pretty Producer!," *Citizen-News*, November 25, 1941, Scrapbooks.

5 Ibid.

6 Stella Adler, "Bon Voyage Party," 1989, videocassette, Irene Gilbert Collection.

7 Allan Keller, "Stella Adler, in Hollywood, Plans to Put Realism in Musicals, Bans 'Dumb' Type," *World Telegram,* September 22, 1941, Stella Adler Papers, Billy Rose Theatre Division.

8 Ibid.

9 Clurman, *All People Are Famous,* 124.

10 Ibid.

11 Ibid., 122.

12 Ibid., 151.

13 Stella Adler, "Sketch of Reinhardt," HRC, 1.

14 Ibid.

15 Ibid., 2.

16 Ibid., 3.

17 Stella Adler, in discussion with Mel Gordon, 1986.

18 Gottfried Reinhardt, *The Genius: A Memoir of Max Reinhardt* (New York: Knopf, 1979), 114.

19 Ibid., 115.

20 "Harold and Stella: Love Letters," typescript, ed. Helen Krich Chinoy and Mira Felner, 1–2 (hereafter cited as "Love Letters"; these letters were first made public when they were read at the Sylvia and Danny Kaye Playhouse at Hunter College for a Harold Clurman celebration, November 21, 1993).

21 Ibid., 2.

22 Ibid., 3–4.

23 Ibid., 4.

24 Ibid., 4–5.

25 Ibid.

26 Ibid., 6–7.

27 FBI report, SAC (Special Agent in Charge), Los Angeles, 7/22/43, LOLA ADLER; PEARL ADLER; STELLA ADLER, with aliases, Stella Ardler, Mrs. Harold Clurman, Bureau File 100-18558, 2.

28 "Love Letters," 42.

29 Ibid., 55.

30 Harold Clurman to Stella Adler, August 29, 1942, HRC.

31 "Love Letters," 34–35.

32 Ibid., 38–39.

33 Ibid., 16–21.

34 Ibid.

35 Ibid.

36 Ibid., 45.

37 Harold Clurman to Stella Adler, July 13, 1942, HRC.

38 Ibid., July 18, 1942.

39 Ibid., August 14, 1942.

40 Ibid., September 2, 1942.

41 Stella Adler, in discussion with Irene Gilbert, May 24, 1991, audiocassette.

Chapter Seventeen

1 Reinhardt, *The Genius*, 120.

2 Mel Gordon, in discussion with the author, January 8, 2005.

3 Clurman, *All People Are Famous*, 144.

4 Stella Adler, "Sketch of Reinhardt," 3.

5 Ibid., 4.

6 E. C. Sherburne, "Sons and Soldiers," *Christian Science Monitor*, May 5, 1943, Scrapbooks.

7 Burns Mantle, "'Sons and Soldiers' a Well Acted Drama, Handsomely Staged," *New York Daily News*, May 5, 1943, Scrapbooks.

8 Ibid.

9 Reinhardt, *The Genius*, 121.

10 Few people realize that as a movement Palestinian nationalism is as old as Zionism, as Rashid Khalidi's *Palestinian Identity: The Construction of Modern National Consciousness* (New York: Columbia University Press, 1997), elucidates.

11 Stella Adler, in discussion with Mel Gordon, 1986.

12 *New York Times* clipping from "Exhibit 12" of *The Holocaust*, teaching materials for *The Diary of Anne Frank*, Scholastic.

13 Ben Hecht, *A Child of the Century* (New York: Simon & Schuster, 1954), 576.

14 "'We Will Never Die': Shattering the Silence Surrounding the Holocaust," Holocaust Encyclopedia, last modified March 29, 2005, accessed August 16, 2013, http://www.ushmm.org/wlc/en/article .php?ModuleId=10007036.

15 Louise Rapoport, *Shake Heaven and Earth: Peter Bergson and the Struggle to Rescue the Jews of Europe* (Jerusalem: Gefen, 1999), 74.

16 "Refugee Conference Ends; Rabbi Calls Talks 'Mocker[y]," *Christian Science Monitor*, April 29, 1943, Irene Gilbert Collection.

17 *The Answer*, December 5, 1943, publication of the Emergency Committee to Save the Jewish People of Europe, 15.

18 Stella Adler, "Sketch of Reinhardt," 5.

19 Ibid.

20 "Associates Attend Rites for Reinhardt," the *New York Times*, November 4, 1943.

21 Lewis Nichols, "The Broadway Theatre Serves Up a Double Fault," the *New York Times*, October 27, 1943.

22 "Love Letters," 12–13.

23 "Children to Ask Jews Be Rescued," *Brooklyn New York Citizen*, May 24, 1943, Irene Gilbert Collection.

Chapter Eighteen

1 Peter Manso, *Brando: The Biography* (New York: Hyperion, 1994), 108.

2 FBI report, SAC, Los Angeles, 5/11/44, STELLA ADLER (MRS. HAROLD CLURMAN), with alias, Stella Ardler, Bureau File 100-18558, 3.

3 Cabell Phillips, *Decade of Triumph and Trouble* (New York: Macmillan, 1975), 10.

4 "Kup's Sunday Column," *Chicago Sun Times*, December 19, 1976.

5 James Grissom, "Brando on Stella Adler: Believing in Majesty," *Follies of God by James Grissom* (blog), entry posted August 25, 2012, accessed August 30, 2013, http://jamesgrissom.blogspot.com/2012/08/brando-on-stella-adler-believing-in.html?q=stella+adler.

6 Manso, *Brando*, 105.

7 Allison Adler, in discussion with the author, April 14, 2004.

8 Manso, *Brando*, 112.

9 Ibid., 153.

10 Ibid.

11 Ibid., 151.

12 Ibid., 152.

13 Elaine Stritch, in discussion with the author, November 8, 2004.

14 Marlon Brando, *Songs My Mother Taught Me*, with Robert Lindsey (New York: Random House, 1994), 99.

15 "It Takes a Woman to Know a Woman, Says Stella Adler," 1944, unidentified clipping, Stella Adler Papers, Billy Rose Theatre Division.

16 Reinhardt, *The Genius*, 200.

17 Lewis Nichols, "The Play: The Wayward on Stage," the *New York Times*, April 18, 1944.

18 "Stella Adler in 'Little Parlor' Stops Being 'Other Woman,'" April 16, 1944, Stella Adler Papers, Billy Rose Theatre Division.

19 Ibid.

20 Harold Clurman to Stella Adler, June 3, 1944, HRC.
21 Ibid.
22 Stella Adler to Harold Clurman, May 2, 1942, HRC.
23 Stella Adler, in discussion with Mel Gordon, 1985.
24 Stella Adler to Harold Clurman, December 7, 1944, HRC.
25 Stella Adler, in discussion with Irene Gilbert, June 18, 1991, audiocassette, Irene Gilbert Collection.
26 Lewis Nichols, "The Play," the *New York Times*, October 8, 1945.
27 Stella Adler, in discussion with Mel Gordon, 1985.
28 Ibid.
29 Stella Adler, in discussion with Mel Gordon, 1986.
30 Clifford Odets, *The Time Is Ripe: The 1940 Journal of Clifford Odets* (New York: Grove Press, 1988), 204.
31 Ibid.
32 Brando, *Songs My Mother Taught Me*, 78.
33 Arthur Laurents, *Original Story By* (New York: Applause Books, 2000), 175.
34 Stella Adler, *On America's Master Playwrights*, 70–71.
35 Ibid., 289.
36 Ibid., 239.
37 Manso, *Brando*, 174.
38 Ibid.
39 Ibid.
40 Ibid.
41 Atay Citron, "Pageantry and Theater in the Service of Jewish Nationalism" (Ph.D. diss., New York University, 1989), 364.
42 Manso, *Brando*, 182.
43 Ibid., 183.
44 "Chapter 78: A Flag Is Born," American Jewish Historical Society, last modified August 12, 2002, accessed August 16, 2002, http://www.ajhs. org/publications/chapters/chapter.cfm?documentID=268.
45 Brando, *Songs My Mother Taught Me*, 108.
46 FBI letter, Director, FBI, to Civil Attache, Mexico, D.F., 11/7/46, STELLA ADLER SECURITY MATTER—C, Bureau File 100-221724-10.
47 Rabbi Baruch Rabinowitz, unpublished memoir, HRC, 153.
48 Ibid., 152.
49 Ibid., 155.
50 FBI report, SAC, Mexico City, 2/7/47, Mrs. HAROLD CLURMAN, with aliases Stella Adler, Stella Ardler, Bureau File 100-533, 2.
51 Citron, "Pageantry and Theater," 417.

Chapter Nineteen

1 Stella Adler, in discussion with friends, audiocassette, n.d., titled "SA 2."
2 Stella Adler, in discussion with friends, April 7, 1991, audiocassette, Irene Gilbert Collection.
3 FBI report, SAC, New York, 3/24/44, LOLA ADLER, With Aliases: Pearl Adler, Stella A. Adler, Bureau File 100-55874.
4 Ibid.
5 Ibid.
6 "Stella Adler in Paris," May 20, 1948, Stella Adler Papers, Billy Rose Theatre Division.
7 Stella Adler, in discussion with Mel Gordon, 1985.
8 Ibid.
9 Ellen Adler, in discussion with the author, September 19, 2002.
10 Allison Adler, in discussion with the author, November 16, 2003.
11 Stella Adler, Untitled Works, HRC.
12 Ibid.
13 Ibid.
14 Ibid.
15 Laurents, *Original Story By*, 156.
16 Ibid., 173.
17 "Domestic Interlude," the *New York Times*, November 23, 1949, Stella Adler Papers, Billy Rose Theatre Division.

Chapter Twenty

1 FBI memo, SAC, New York, to Director, FBI, 8/18/50, RE: STELLA ADLER SECURITY MATTER—C, Bureau File 100-99082, 1.
2 Luther Adler's manager to Luther Adler, May 21, 1964, Luther Adler Papers, Billy Rose Theatre Division.
3 Lillian Hellman, *Scoundrel Time* (Boston: Little, Brown, 1976), 93.
4 Kazan, *A Life*, 458.
5 Ibid., 464.
6 "Stella Adler: Awake and Dream!"
7 Eleanor Sheldon, in discussion with the author, September 29, 2003.
8 Stella Adler, in discussion with Mel Gordon, 1986.
9 Harold Clurman to Stella Adler, Rome, May 11, 1950, Stella Adler Papers, HRC.
10 Eleanor Sheldon, in discussion with the author, September 29, 2003.
11 Harold Clurman to Stella Adler, New York, August 16, 1950, Stella Adler Papers, HRC.

12 Stella Adler to Harold Clurman, Lausanne, August 22, 1951, Stella Adler Papers, HRC.

13 Ibid.

14 Harold Clurman to Stella Adler, New York, September 7, 1951, HRC.

15 Stella Adler, "Stella Stories."

16 "Course in Acting Opened," the *New York Times*, September 13, 1950.

17 Although Stella's school has been dated as having been founded in 1949, it is clear she officially began offering classes in 1950. She did not own and operate her own school until 1953.

18 Stella Adler, in discussion with Mel Gordon, 1986.

19 FBI memo, SAC, New York, to Director, FBI, 12/14/54, STELLA ADLER CLURMAN, was.—SM—C, Bureau File 100-55874 Stella Adler File.

20 Ibid.

21 FBI memo, Director, FBI, to Mr. William P. Rogers, Deputy Attorney General, 3/13/56, STELLA ADLER, aka. STELLA ADLER CLURMAN, MRS. HAROLD CLURMAN, STELLA ADLER, Bureau File 100-221724.

22 Whitney Bolton, "Sara Adler Was Truly an Empress," *New York Morning Telegraph*, May 2, 1953, Sara Adler Clippings, Billy Rose Theatre Division.

23 Ibid.

24 Stella Adler, in discussion with friends, audiocassette, April 7, 1991.

25 *Hearings before the Committee on Un-American Activities*, 83d Cong., 1st Sess. (1953) (statement of Stella Adler). (All subsequent references to the hearings in the chapter come from this same source.)

26 Stella Adler, *On America's Master Playwrights*, 51.

Chapter Twenty-one

1 Harold Clurman to Stella Adler, July 1954, HRC.

2 Harold Clurman to Stella Adler, March 18, 1955, HRC.

3 Norma Barzman, *The Red and Blacklist: The Intimate Memoir of a Hollywood Expatriate* (New York: Thunder's Mouth Press/Nation Books, 2003), 33.

4 Manso, *Brando*, 106.

5 David Garfield, *A Player's Place: The Story of the Actors Studio* (New York: Macmillan, 1980), 80.

6 Ibid., 83.

7 Ibid., 94.

8 Ibid., 83.

9 Shelley Winters, *Shelley II* (New York: Simon & Schuster, 1989), 147.

10 Ibid.

11 Arthur Gleb, "The Theater: Revival: 'Johnny Johnson' Opens at Carnegie Playhouse," the *New York Times*, October 22, 1956.

12 Elizabeth Parrish, in discussion with the author, July 16, 2005.

13 Ibid.

14 Bogdanovich, *Who The Hell's In It*, 80.

15 Harold Clurman to Stella Adler, April 28, 1957, HRC.

16 Harold Clurman to Stella Adler, October 18, 1957, HRC.

17 Stella Adler, in discussion with Irene Gilbert, May 20, 1991, audiocassette, Irene Gilbert Collection.

18 Stella Adler, Stella Adler's Teaching Materials, April 13, 1959, Irene Gilbert Collection.

19 Stella Adler, "Stella Adler in Toronto," April 10, 1983, audiocassette, Irene Gilbert Collection.

20 Stella Adler to Elizabeth Parrish, March 23, 1959, Suzanne Miller Collection, University of Toledo.

21 Stella Adler, masterclass on Ibsen, September 29, 1980, videocassette, HRC.

22 Christon, "Stella Adler Sums Up a Life," 7.

23 Stella Adler, Masterclass at City Center, October 22, 1979, videocassette, HRC.

24 Bogdanovich, *Who the Hell's In It*, 84.

25 Jamie Painter, "Grit and Glory," *Back Stage West*, January 7, 1999.

26 Benicio Del Toro, interview in *Talk*, April 2001, 180.

Chapter Twenty-two

1 Frank Corsaro, in discussion with the author, September 28, 2003. Unless otherwise stated all quotes regarding *Oh Dad, Poor Dad* come from this discussion.

2 Eleanor Sheldon, in discussion with the author, September 29, 2003.

3 Stella Adler, *On Ibsen, Strindberg, and Chekhov*, 271.

4 Irene Gilbert, collection of Stella Adler quotes, Irene Gilbert Collection.

5 Elizabeth Parrish, in discussion with the author, July 16, 2005.

6 "U.S. Play in London," the *New York Times*, July 6, 1961.

7 Untitled, n.d. (circa July 1961), Irene Gilbert Collection.

8 "A Skit on the Ionesco Playwrights' School," Raymond Mander and Joe Mitchenson Theatre Collection, Trinity College of Music.

9 Robert De Niro, in discussion with the author, April 25, 2011.

10 Stella Adler, *On America's Master Playwrights*, 71.

11 Mervyn Rothstein, "Stella Adler In Her Latest Role: Author," the *New York Times*, September 4, 1988, Arts & Leisure, 9.

12 Ibid.

13 Stella Adler, "Russian Data," 1963, HRC.

14 Ibid.

15 Stella Adler, transcription of class on Stella's Moscow Visit, circa 1963, HRC.

16 Irene Gilbert, in discussion with the author, September 15, 2002.

17 Stella Adler, *Stella Adler and the Actor*, KTLA, first broadcast July 13, 1964.

18 Laurence Kitchin, *Mid-Century Drama* (London: Faber & Faber, 1962), 227.

19 Ibid.

20 "Donna's Doctor's Head and Image Trimmed," *Evening Independent*, August 26, 1964.

Chapter Twenty-three

1 Anita Leonard Nye, in discussion with the author, June 8, 2002.

2 Eleanor Sheldon, in discussion with the author, September 29, 2003.

3 Ibid.

4 Allison Adler, in discussion with the author, December 29, 2003.

5 Allison Adler, in discussion with the author, November 16, 2003.

6 Ibid.

7 Milton Justice, in discussion with the author, June 8, 2011.

8 Ibid.

9 Ibid.

10 Ibid.

11 Elizabeth Parrish, in discussion with the author, September 21, 2002.

12 Ibid.

13 Ibid.

14 Irene Gilbert, in discussion with the author, September 21, 2004.

15 Ibid.

16 Ibid.

17 Stanley Moss, in discussion with the author, October 27, 2002.

18 Ibid.

19 Eleanor Sheldon, in discussion with the author, September 29, 2003.

20 Irving Drutman, "Russian Method-ists Meet the American," the *New York Times*, December 13, 1964.

21 Ibid.
22 John Strasberg, introduction to *Accidentally on Purpose*, x.
23 Josie Oppenheim, in discussion with the author, September 30, 2003.

Chapter Twenty-four

1 Robert Brustein, *Making Sense: A Personal History of the Turbulent Years at Yale* (New York: Random, 1981), 16.
2 Ibid.
3 Gruen, *Close Up*, 111.
4 Ibid., 112.
5 Ibid.
6 Ibid., 117.
7 Eleanor Sheldon, in discussion with the author, September 29, 2003.
8 Ibid.
9 Irene Gilbert, in discussion with the author, September 15, 2002.
10 Stella Adler to Irene Gilbert, March 15, 1967, Irene Gilbert Collection.
11 Stella Adler, *On Ibsen, Strindberg, and Chekhov*, 81.
12 Jayne Meadows, in discussion with the author, May 30, 2004.
13 Jayne Meadows, in discussion with the author, May 22, 2004.
14 Ibid.
15 Charles Waxberg, in discussion with the author, September 22, 2003.
16 Elizabeth Parrish, in discussion with the author, September 21, 2002.
17 Elizabeth Parrish to Stella Adler, July 19, 1971, HRC.

Chapter Twenty-five

1 Ellen Adler, in discussion with the author, September 19, 2002.
2 John Gruen, "The Arts," *Avenue*, March 1981.
3 Stella Adler, *On America's Master Playwrights*, 99.
4 Stella Adler to Irene Gilbert, September 28, 1971, Irene Gilbert Collection.
5 Allison Adler, in discussion with the author, November 16, 2003.
6 Robert Ellerman, in discussion with the author, March 24, 1999.
7 Pamela Adler Golden, email interview with author, September 29, 2005.
8 Jay Adler to Stella Adler, Los Angeles, March 1, 1973, HRC.
9 Rue Drew, in discussion with the author, April 11, 2004.
10 Ibid.
11 Ron Burrus, in discussion with the author, September 21, 2002.
12 Stella Adler to Irene Gilbert, June 29, 1973, Irene Gilbert Collection.
13 Ron Burrus, in discussion with the author, September 21, 2002.

14 Elizabeth Parrish, in discussion with the author, September 21, 2002.

15 Stella Adler to Irene Gilbert, Sydney, June 29, 1974, Irene Gilbert Collection.

16 Ron Burrus, in discussion with the author, September 21, 2002.

17 Jayne Meadows, in discussion with the author, May 22, 2004.

18 Ron Burrus, in discussion with the author, September 21, 2002.

19 Rotte, *Acting with Adler*, 23.

20 Elizabeth Parrish, in discussion with the author, September 21, 2002.

21 Jody Adler to Stella Adler, June 16, 1974, HRC.

22 Stella Adler to Irene Gilbert, Sydney, June 28, 1974, Irene Gilbert Collection.

23 Jody Adler to Stella Adler, September 3, 1974, HRC.

24 Stella Adler to Irene Gilbert, September 28, 1974, Irene Gilbert Collection.

25 Sara Oppenheim, in discussion with the author, September 20, 2002.

26 Stella Adler to Sara Oppenheim, November 4, 1983, Sara Oppenheim Collection.

27 Sara Oppenheim, in discussion with the author, September 20, 2002.

28 Ibid.

29 Ellen Adler, "Dramatist Guild: Stella Adler on America's Master Playwrights."

30 Sara Oppenheim, in discussion with the author, September 20, 2002.

31 Allison Adler, in discussion with the author, December 3, 2004.

32 Allison Adler, in discussion with the author, November 16, 2003.

33 Stella Adler to Sara Oppenheim, July 14, 1984, Sara Oppenheim Collection.

Chapter Twenty-six

1 Rue Drew, in discussion with the author, April 11, 2004.

2 Ibid.

3 Ibid.

4 Ibid.

5 Ibid.

6 Ibid.

7 Jayne Meadows, in discussion with the author, May 22, 2004.

8 Allison Adler, in discussion with the author, December 29, 2003.

9 Irene Gilbert, in discussion with the author, April 9, 2005.

10 Lulla Rosenfeld, eulogy for Jay Adler, provided by Allison Adler.

11 Allison Adler, in discussion with the author, November 16, 2003.

12 Jack Garfein, in discussion with the author, October 25, 2005.

13 Ibid.

14 Mel Gussow, "A Long Life in the Theater," the *New York Times*, May 6, 1979.

15 Ibid.

16 Ibid.

17 Ibid.

18 Jack Garfein, in discussion with the author, October 25, 2005.

19 Joan Ungaro, in discussion with the author, October 20, 2002.

20 Ibid.

21 Gussow, "A Long Life."

22 David Margulies, in discussion with the author, November 8, 2004.

23 Jack Garfein, in discussion with the author, October 25, 2005.

24 Stella Adler, *On America's Master Playwrights*, 313.

25 Suzanne O'Malley, "Can the Method Survive the Madness," the *New York Times Magazine*, October 7, 1979, 32.

Chapter Twenty-seven

1 Cindy Adams, *New York Post*, December 23, 1992, Stella Adler Papers, Billy Rose Theatre Division.

2 Ibid.

3 *New York Daily News*, October 30, 1980, Scrapbooks.

4 Gruen, "The Arts."

5 John Strasberg, introduction to *Accidentally on Purpose*, x.

6 Gruen, "The Arts."

7 The *New York Times*, November 4, 1980, Irene Gilbert Collection.

8 Elizabeth Parrish, in discussion with the author, September 21, 2002.

9 Stella Adler to Ingrid Bergman, May 23, 1982, HRC.

10 Howard Kissel, "Taking a Lesson from Stella Adler," *Women's Wear Daily*, September 23–30, 1983, 14.

11 Elizabeth Parrish, in discussion with the author, September 21, 2002.

12 Arthur Miller, in discussion with the author, October 25, 1999.

13 Stella Adler, funeral instructions, Irene Gilbert Collection.

14 Irene Gilbert, in discussion with the author, April 9, 2005.

15 Robert Ellenstein, in discussion with the author, December 3, 2005.

16 Paul Rosenfield, "Stella Adler: Teaching Actors How to Imagine," *Los Angeles Times*, Calendar Section, August 15, 1982.

17 Stella Adler, *The Art of Acting*, 65.

18 Stella Adler to Irene Gilbert, November 17, 1984, HRC.

19 Ibid.

20 Stella Adler to Jerry Lurie, May 7, 1987, HRC.

21 Stella Adler, *The Technique of Acting* (New York: Bantam Books, 1990), 6.

22 Stella Adler, in discussion with Irene Gilbert, May 24, 1991, audiocassette.

23 Ibid.

24 Marlon Brando, foreword to Stella Adler, *The Technique of Acting*, 1.

25 John Strasberg, introduction to *Accidentally on Purpose*, x.

26 Stella Adler, speech, National Museum of American Jewish History, Spring 1988, videocassette, HRC.

27 Mervyn Rothstein, "Stella Adler in Her Latest Role: Author," the *New York Times*, September 4, 1988, Arts & Leisure.

Chapter Twenty-eight

1 Samuella Harris, in discussion with the author, April 27, 2005.

2 Stella Adler, in discussion with Irene Gilbert, circa 1990, audiocassette, titled "SA," Irene Gilbert Collection.

3 Irene Gilbert, ledger for Stella Adler's assets, Irene Gilbert Collection.

4 Irene Gilbert to Eleanor Sheldon, October 24, 1991, Irene Gilbert Collection.

5 Stella Adler to Irene Gilbert, October 20, 1990, Irene Gilbert Collection.

6 Stella Adler, in discussion with Irene Gilbert, May 24, 1991, audiocassette.

7 Ibid.

8 Ibid.

9 Stella Adler, *Stella Adler on America's Master Playwrights*, 79–80.

10 Stella Adler, in discussion with Irene Gilbert, May 24, 1991, audiocassette.

11 Ibid.

12 Stella Adler, in discussion with Irene Gilbert, circa 1990, audiocassette, titled "SA."

13 Samuella Harris, in discussion with the author, April 27, 2005.

14 Ellen Adler, "Dramatist Guild: Stella Adler on America's Master Playwrights."

15 Ibid.

16 Samuella Harris, in discussion with the author, April 27, 2005.

17 Irene Gilbert, in discussion with the author, April 9, 2005.

18 Samuella Harris, in discussion with the author, April 27, 2005.

19 Milton Justice, in discussion with the author, June 8, 2011.

Epilogue

1 Brando, foreword to Stella Adler, *The Technique of Acting*, 1.
2 Bogdanovich, *Who the Hell's In It*, 77.
3 Ibid.
4 Stella Adler, *On America's Master Playwrights*, 337.
5 Tom Oppenheim, in discussion with the author, September 19, 2002.
6 Ibid.
7 Ron Burrus, in discussion with the author, September 21, 2002.
8 Arthur Mendoza, "Act," *Actors Circle Theater*, http://www.actorscircle. net/.
9 Arthur Mendoza, in discussion with the author, August 26, 2006.
10 Charles Waxberg, email message to the author, August 2, 2011.
11 Ibid.
12 Ibid.
13 Tom Oppenheim, in discussion with the author, September 19, 2002.
14 Stanley Moss, in discussion with the author, October 27, 2002.
15 Milton Justice, in discussion with the author, June 8, 2011.
16 Irene Gilbert, collection of Stella Adler quotes, Irene Gilbert Collection.
17 Stella Adler, *On Ibsen, Strindberg, and Chekhov*, 90.

SELECTED BIBLIOGRAPHY

Adams, Cindy. *Lee Strasberg: The Imperfect Genius of the Actors Studio.* New York: Doubleday, 1980.

Adler, Celia. *Celia Adler Dertseylt (The Celia Adler Story).* Translated by Sarah Traister Moskovitz. New York: Celia Adler Foundation, 1959.

Adler, Ellen. "A Different Kind of Success: A Conversation with Ellen Adler." *Lincoln Center Theater Review* 42 (Spring 2006).

Adler, Jacob. *Jacob Adler: A Life on the Stage.* Translated by Lulla Rosenfeld. New York: Applause Books, 2001.

Adler, Stella. *The Art of Acting.* Edited by Howard Kissel. New York: Applause, 2000.

Adler, Stella. *Stella Adler on America's Master Playwrights.* Edited by Barry Paris. New York: Knopf, 2012.

Adler, Stella. *Stella Adler on Ibsen, Strindberg, and Chekhov.* Edited by Barry Paris. New York: Knopf, 1999.

Adler, Stella. *The Technique of Acting.* New York: Bantam Books, 1988.

Allen, Frederick Lewis. *Since Yesterday: The 1930s in America.* New York: Harper & Row, 1939.

Arad, Gulie Ne'eman. *America, Its Jews, and the Rise of Nazism.* Indianapolis: Indiana University Press, 2000.

Berkowitz, Joel. *Shakespeare on the American Yiddish Stage.* Iowa City: University of Iowa Press, 2002.

Bogdanovich, Peter. *Who the Hell's In It: Portraits and Conversations.* New York: Knopf, 2004.

Brando, Marlon. *Songs My Mother Taught Me.* With Robert Lindsey. New York: Random House, 1994.

Brenman-Gibson, Margaret. *Clifford Odets: American Playwright; The Years from 1906 to 1940.* New York: Atheneum, 1981.

Brustein, Robert. *Making Sense: A Personal History of the Turbulent Years at Yale.* New York: Random House, 1981.

Carnicke, Sharon Marie. "Stanislavski's System: Pathways for the Actor." In *Twentieth Century Actor Training,* edited by Alison Hodge, 11–36. New York: Routledge, 2000.

Carnicke, Sharon Marie. *Stanislavski in Focus: An Acting Master for the Twenty-first Century.* 2nd ed. New York: Routledge, 2009.

Citron, Atay. "Pageantry and Theater in the Service of Jewish Nationalism." Ph.D. diss., New York University, 1989.

Chinoy, Helen Krich. "Reunion: A Self-Portrait of the Group Theatre." *Educational Theatre Journal* 28, no. 4 (December 1976).

Clurman, Harold. *All People Are Famous*. New York: Harcourt, Brace, Jovanovich, 1974.

Clurman, Harold. *The Fervent Years: The Group Theatre and the Thirties*. New York: Da Capo Press, 1975.

Cypkin, Diane. "Second Avenue: The Yiddish Broadway." Ph.D. diss., New York University, 1986.

Duarte, Christina. "Stella Adler and the Group Theatre: Conflicts and Contributions." Ph.D. diss., Hunter College, 2003.

Filippov, Boris. *Actors without Make-Up. Translated by Kathelene Cook*. Moscow: Progress Publishers, 1977.

Garfein, Jack. *Life and Acting: Techniques for the Actor*. Evanston, IL: Northwestern University Press, 2010.

Gray, Paul. "The Reality of Doing: Interviews with Vera Soloviova, Stella Adler, and Sanford Meisner." In *Stanislavski and America*, edited by Erika Munk, 210–227. New York: Hill & Wang, 1966.

Hecht, Ben. *A Child of the Century*. New York: Simon & Schuster, 1954.

Gruen, John. "The Arts." *Avenue*, March 1981.

Gruen, John. *Close Up*. New York: Viking Press, 1968.

Hellman, Lillian. *Scoundrel Time*. Boston: Little, Brown, 1975.

Hethmon, Robert H., ed. *Strasberg at the Actors Studio: Tape-Recorded Sessions*. New York: Theater Communications Group, 1965.

Hull, S. Loraine. *Strasberg's Method as Taught by Lorrie Hull: A Practical Guide for Actors, Teachers and Directors*. Woodbridge, CT: Ox Bow Press, 1985.

Kazan, Elia. *Elia Kazan: A Life*. New York: Knopf, 1988.

Khalidis, Rashid. *Palestinian Identity: The Construction of Modern National Consciousness*. New York: Columbia University Press, 1997.

Kitchin, Laurence. *Mid-Century Drama*. London: Faber & Faber, 1962.

Laurents, Arthur. *Original Story By*. New York: Applause Books, 2000.

Larson, Erik. *In the Garden of Beasts: Love, Terror, and an American Family in Hitler's Berlin*. New York: Crown, 2011.

Lewis, Robert. *Slings and Arrows: Theatre in My Life*. New York: Stein & Day, 1984.

Manso, Peter. *Brando: The Biography*. New York: Hyperion, 1994.

Miller, Arthur. *Timebends: A Life*. New York: Penguin Books, 1995.

Odets, Clifford. *The Time Is Ripe: The 1940 Journal of Clifford Odets*. New York: Grove Press, 1988.

Oppenheim, Tom. "Stella Adler Technique." In *Training of the American Actor*, edited by Arthur Bartow, 29–46. New York: Theater Communications Group, 2006.

Painter, Jaimie. "Grit and Glory." *Backstage West Magazine.* January 7, 1999.

Phillips, Cabell. *Decade of Triumph and Trouble.* New York: Macmillan, 1975.

Powell, Dawn. *The Diaries of Dawn Powell, 1931–1965.* Edited by Tim Page. South Royalton, VT: Steerforth Press, 1995.

Prokofiev, Serge. *Diary, 1919–1933.* Translated by Diana Farafanova. Paris: Serge Prokofiev Foundation, 2002.

Rapoport, Louise. *Shake Heaven and Earth: Peter Bergson and the Struggle to Rescue the Jews of Europe.* Jerusalem: Gefen, 1999.

Reinhardt, Gottfried. *The Genius: A Memoir of Max Reinhardt.* New York: Knopf, 1979.

Rosenfeld, Lulla. *Bright Star of Exile: Jacob Adler and the Yiddish Theatre.* New York: Thomas Y. Crowell, 1977.

Rotte, Joanna. *Acting with Adler.* New York: Limelight Editions, 2000.

Sandrow, Nahma. *Vagabond Stars: A World History of the Yiddish Theatre.* New York: Harper & Row, 1977.

Schildkraut, Joseph. *My Father and I.* New York: Viking Press, 1959.

Smith, Wendy. *Real Life Drama: The Group Theatre and America, 1931–1940.* New York: Knopf, 1990.

Strasberg, John. *Accidentally on Purpose: Reflections on Life, Acting, and the Nine Natural Laws of Creativity.* New York: Applause, 1996.

Sundgaard, Arnold. "The Group Remembered." *Journal of American Drama and Theatre* 8, no. 2 (Spring 1996).

Watkins, T. H. *The Great Depression: America in the 1930s.* Boston: Little, Brown, 1993.

Winters, Shelley. *Shelley II.* New York: Simon & Schuster, 1989.

INDEX